RENEWING
AMERICA'S PURPOSE

Policy Addresses of George W. Bush
July 1999 – July 2000

Published by the Republican National Committee and
Bush for President, Inc.

Printed in the United States of America.

Photography on pages 10, 108, 208, 210, 241, 244, 326, 388, 452
by Charles Ommaney
Photography on page 106 by Bill Records
Photography on page 390 by Steve Oleson
Biography Photo by Gray Hawn

Design by RSD Advertising, Austin, Texas

TABLE OF CONTENTS

TABLE OF CONTENTS

PART III: Strengthening Social Security and Medicare

PART IV: Economy, Environment and Entrepreneurship

PART V: Reforming Our Government

TABLE OF CONTENTS

PART VI: National Strength and Purpose

INTRODUCTION

In the following pages, you will find a remarkable series of speeches and policy statements from Texas Governor George W. Bush. Thoughtful and specific, these speeches provide a glimpse into the heart and soul of Governor Bush, as well as the kind of leadership he offers America.

Governor Bush's vision for the future is grounded in a few simple yet profound values. Family. Faith. Freedom. These principles constitute Governor Bush's guiding light in how he deals with serious issues ranging from reforming our public schools to lowering our taxes to saving and strengthening Social Security and Medicare to rebuilding our military's might and morale.

After years of partisan politics as usual, I think you will agree with me that Governor Bush's approach on these issues is as refreshing as it is revealing. He attacks problems, not people. And in each speech, he proposes solutions rather than pinning the blame.

Governor Bush is a different kind of leader. Hopeful. Optimistic. Positive. He sets a different tone. He believes in the power of great ideas and in the importance of "Renewing America's Purpose."

> Jim Nicholson
> Chairman,
> Republican National Committee

PREFACE

The story of a campaign is much larger than the written record it leaves behind. But what applies in life applies even more in presidential politics: a man's word must truly be his bond.

The materials in this book cover the written record of my campaign so far, from July 1999 to July 2000. They are the record of my pledge to the American people to raise our government's standards, to reclaim our society's values, and to renew our nation's purpose.

A candidate is called upon to address a wide array of matters, and in coming months, I will address other important issues. This book gathers dozens of speeches and detailed position papers under six broad categories: education, social policy, Social Security and Medicare; economic and environmental policy; government reform; and defense and foreign policy. These statements will give you a sense of my priorities, and the fundamental principles behind them. Taken together, these principles offer a new approach to the leadership of my party and our country.

Government should do a few things and do them well. Its powers should be carefully limited, and its goals clear and direct. Whether the problem is failing schools or the challenge of expanding opportunity, as argued in Parts I and II, government has the responsibility to act. I am a conservative. I am an activist. And I see no conflict between the two.

Government is defined not just by the commitments it makes, but by the commitments it keeps. Part III addresses the challenge of preserving Social Security and Medicare for generations to come. It's time to end the needless delays and partisanship that have prevented sound reforms of those vital programs.

Government must always be the people's servant, not their master. In its power to tax the people and regulate the economy, it has overstepped its boundaries. Parts IV and V address the pressing need for tax relief, common-sense stewardship of the environment, and a variety of reforms in government itself.

Above all, government must defend the American people and their vital interests abroad. Part VI brings together my major addresses on national security, foreign policy, and trade. In the end, all of the other goals outlined in this book depend on rebuilding our nation's military strength – on extending a peace favorable to freedom.

Very soon, the American people will choose their next president. I have done my best to define not just an agenda for this campaign, but an agenda worthy of our nation. I hope you will consider these words, and join me in this great cause.

George W. Bush
July 2000

PART I
Educating Every Child

Education has been the constant focus of my service as governor and of my campaign for President. If our country fails in its responsibility to educate every child, we're likely to fail in many other areas. But if we succeed there, many other successes will follow – throughout our country, and in the lives of our citizens.

I came to the governor's office with three goals to guide public education: We must set high standards for our schools – not just to build knowledge, but to shape character. We must demand accountability from our schools. And we must align authority and responsibility at the local level, leaving control to school boards, teachers, and parents.

With these goals firmly in mind, we've achieved major reforms – and serious, substantial improvements – in Texas schools. Test scores are on the rise, especially among disadvantaged students. Texas has been recognized as one of the two states that have made the most progress in education. And in each of the last six years, all ethnic groups in all grades have improved in reading and math.

In the speeches and position papers that follow, I lay out my agenda for nationwide education reform. It's a set of specific proposals aimed at closing the achievement gap between rich and poor students, returning high standards and discipline to our schools, supporting teachers, returning authority to states and communities, and empowering parents with more choices.

Taken together, the reforms I've offered express my deep belief in our public schools and their mission – to build the mind and character of every child, of every background, in every part of America.

Education:
No Child Left Behind

Latin Business Association Luncheon
Los Angeles, California

September 2, 1999

It is good to be with you – with men and women who are building the new economy of California.

We are witnessing a Latino economic miracle – *un milagro económico*. There are now 440,000 Latino businesses in Southern California. They generate $47 billion in sales each year. Latino businesses are the largest and fastest growing part of the small business community in this region. When half of the new businesses in Los Angeles are Latino-owned, this is no longer a niche market. It is the mainstream of our economic hopes.

This marks a new era – a permanent revolution - in California, and in many other places, including my state of Texas. An era in which the Latino market will demand the attention of our whole economy. An era in which our prosperity is as broad and diverse as our nation. This community has saved and worked and struggled. And now it has arrived.

The health of the Latino business community is reflected in the health and growth of this organization – the largest association of Latino entrepreneurs in the state. The Latin Business Association is doing well, and it is also doing good work by helping other entrepreneurs realize their dreams.

I am here with you today because you are leaders and because you embody the permanent hope, the durable dream, of this nation:

to build a better life for ourselves and our children.

I am an optimist. I believe that the next century will be a time of incredible prosperity - if we create an environment where entrepreneurs like you can dream and flourish. A prosperity sustained by low taxes, unleashed by lighter regulation, energized by new technologies, expanded by free trade. A prosperity beyond all our expectations, but within our grasp.

Yet all around this country, I have argued that prosperity must have a higher purpose. The purpose of prosperity is to make sure the American dream touches every willing heart. The purpose of prosperity is to leave no one out - to leave no one behind.

This noble goal will remain a distant goal until our nation fulfills a solemn pledge: to educate every child. In coming weeks, I plan to talk about the safety of our schools, the character of our children, the education standards we should set, and the accountability we should expect.

But I want to start where educational failure has its highest price. I want to begin with disadvantaged children in struggling schools, and the federal role in helping them. Their voices are not the loudest in our education debates. But we owe them the pride and promise of learning. Our New Economy - requiring higher and higher skills - demands it. And so does our conscience. No child in America should be segregated by low expectations...imprisoned by illiteracy...abandoned to frustration and the darkness of self-doubt.

National wealth is a worthy goal. But what would it profit our nation to gain the whole world and lose our own children?

In response to this challenge, the last several years have been a time of bold change in education. A drizzle of innovation has become a flood of reform - a great movement of conscience and hope. A movement of parents and political leaders, voters and educators, hungry for high standards, tough accountability and real choices. Five years ago, only eight states had charter school laws. Today there are 35. A few years ago, no state had school-by-school report cards. Now there are at least three dozen.

Unlike past fads and fashions, these reforms are proving that public education can be improved – swiftly and dramatically.

I have seen it with my own eyes. The skeptics of education reform should visit KIPP Academy in Houston – a charter school that mainly serves the children of Latino immigrants. KIPP refuses to accept the "high-risk" label, demanding high standards and hard work. Children have nine-and-a-half-hour days, class on Saturday and two hours of homework a night. The director promises, "If you're off the bus, you're working." And it is an incredibly cheerful and hopeful place. When you go there, you can see the light of ambition and discovery in young eyes. You can sense the self-esteem that comes from real accomplishment. After one year at KIPP, nearly 100 percent of students pass our state skills test in math and reading, making it the number one public middle school in all of Houston.

Or look at the Bennett-Kew Elementary School near here in Inglewood. A school I recently visited. A haven of hope. Nearly 8 in 10 students are disadvantaged, but it posts some of the strongest test scores in Los Angeles County. It teaches mastery of reading in kindergarten, and promotion in every grade level is tied to achievement. The principal explains: "We believe all children can learn. And they do."

Why do some schools work in places where so many schools fail? We can see the emerging outlines of an answer. In places all around our country, like Texas and North Carolina and California and Virginia and Massachusetts, governors and parents and teachers – Republican and Democrat and none-of-the-above – are embracing reforms and calling for excellence.

- First, schools must have a few clear, measurable goals, focused on basic skills and essential knowledge. Education is about results, not theories; about knowledge, not intentions. "If you

15

don't know where you are going," said Yogi Berra, "chances are, you'll end up someplace else." When I became Governor of Texas, we had 48 separate educational goals – which meant that a school might achieve 40 goals, and still not teach children to read. We reduced that number to four goals: excellence in reading, math, science and social studies.

- Second, we must measure to make sure standards are met. In Texas, we measure. We test because parents must know if education is taking place. We test because informed parents become more involved. We test because children must get the help they need before they are lost in the system. We test because hard data allows teachers and principals to examine their methods and change their direction. Measurement makes some people nervous. But without tests, there is no pressure for progress.

- Third, effective reform requires accountability. Someone should be praised when schools succeed, and someone must be responsible when schools fail. As much as 37 percent of school principals in low-performing Texas schools have been replaced or retired each year, because citizens and parents have refused to accept failure.

- Fourth, accountability is empty without local control of schools. It is essential to align responsibility and accountability at the local level; to separate them provides a convenient excuse for failure – just blame the central office. Higher standards demand broader flexibility.

- Finally, we must recognize the essential role of competition in achieving our goals – competition from charters and parental choice and home schooling. All monopolies are slow to reform when consumers have no power to express their frustration. In education, parents who have options have influence. When the Children's Scholarship Fund recently offered 40,000, privately funded, partial scholarships to poor children, it received a million applications. One million – even though parents had to match this help with money of their own. This was a direct challenge to failing public schools – and should be a motive for change. Charter schools are another good example. When they passed in Texas, critics charged they'd be a haven for fleeing Anglo students. In reality, 78 percent of students enrolled in Texas charters are minorities. These diverse, creative schools are proof that parents from all walks of life are willing to challenge the status quo if it means a better education for their children.

These reforms are proving their worth, but the movement I am talking about requires more than sound goals.

It requires a mindset that all children can learn, and no child should be left behind. It does not matter where they live, or how much their parents earn. It does not matter if they grow up in foster care or a two-parent family. These circumstances are challenges, but they are not excuses. I believe that every child can learn the basic skills on which the rest of their life depends.

Some say it is unfair to hold disadvantaged children to rigorous standards. I say it is discrimination to require anything less – the soft bigotry of low expectations. Some say that schools can't be expected to teach, because there are too many broken families, too many immigrants, too much diversity. I say that pigment and poverty need not determine performance. That myth is disproved by good schools every day. Excuse-making must end before learning can begin.

This reform movement also requires a different mindset in politics. Education is too important to have a strategy of divide and conquer. Unless parents and principals, teachers and academics, Republicans and Democrats can find common purposes, reform will fail. I have worked closely with both parties in my state, because I know that if we set out to score partisan points, we will never solve problems. If we do not share credit for progress, all of us deserve the blame for failure.

In Texas, we are proud of our results. We have more than 7,000 public schools, as diverse as any in America. Since 1994, the number of minority children passing our state skills test jumped from 38 percent to 72 percent. Between 1994 and 1999, Hispanic eighth graders posted a 40 point gain on our math exam. African-American fourth graders have better math skills in Texas than in any state in the country.

A lot of people deserve credit – students and parents and teachers and principals and legislators – and I am proud of my part. Education has been and will be a priority for me. I will carry a passion for high standards and high hopes to the highest office in the land.

For all the advances some states have made, too many children are being left behind. We are a nation where a majority of fourth graders in our cities can't read or understand a simple children's book. Where ninth-graders too often have fourth-grade reading skills. Where the achievement gap between rich and poor, Anglo and minority, is wide – and, in some cases, growing wider still.

It is a scandal of the first order when the average test scores of African-American and Latino students at age 17 are roughly the same as white 13-year-olds. Whatever the cause, the effect is discrimination. Children who never master reading will never master learning. They face a life of frustration on the fringes of society. Large numbers turn to crime and end up in prison. This is a personal tragedy. More and more, we are divided into two nations, separate and unequal. One that reads and one that can't. One that dreams and one that doesn't.

For many years the federal government has tried to close this gap of hope – armed with good intentions and billions of dollars. But sacks of money and the best of motives have made little difference in the performance of disadvantaged children.

At last count, the federal government had 760 different education programs operating within 39 different agencies, boards and commissions. Each was launched as a step toward reform. But the actual results are usually a mystery, because no one measures them. The only thing we know for sure is that federal money comes with a lot of regulations and paperwork. By one estimate, this consumes about 50 million hours each year – the equivalent of 25,000 full-time employees just to process forms.

The problem here is that failure never turns to wisdom. New layers of federal mandates and procedures have been added to the old, until their original purpose is long forgotten. It is a sad story. High hopes, low achievement. Grand plans, unmet goals.

My Administration will do things differently.

We do not have a national school board, and do not need one. A president is not a federal principal, and I will not be one.

The federal government must be humble enough to stay out of the day-to-day operation of local schools, wise enough to give states and school districts more authority and freedom, and strong enough to require proven performance in return. When we spend federal money, we want results – especially when it comes to disadvantaged children.

Today, I want to outline three reforms to help ensure that no child is left behind:

We will start by funding only what works in education – only those methods and ideas that prove their power to close the achievement gap. We need good, reliable, scientific information on the best methods of teaching. What the federal government sponsors, however, is often sloppy and trendy, focusing on self-esteem over basic skills. My Administration will require every federal program – in teacher training, curriculum research, school safety – to prove results. If it can't, we will shift that money into a program that is using it wisely. No federal education program will be reauthorized merely because it has existed for years. It is more important to do good than to feel good.

Take, for example, teaching children to read and comprehend English. If a good immersion program works, I say fine. If a good bilingual program works to teach children English, we should applaud it. What matters is not the varying methods, but the common standards and goals. The standard is English literacy. The goal is equal opportunity. All in an atmosphere where every heritage is respected and celebrated.

Esta propuesta la he llamado "Inglés y Más," porque yo me opongo al "Inglés solamente." "Inglés solamente" significa "solo yo," sin tomar en cuenta a otros. "Inglés y Más" significa "todos nosotros, pero juntos." Children – of any background – should not be used as pawns in bitter debates on education and immigration, or punished to make a broader political point.

There is one area where the teaching research is definitive: The best way to teach children to read is phonics. No new theory or method has ever improved on it, as Californians know better than anyone. The National Institutes of Health – in the kind of rigorous research we need – has proven that phonics works, and that children can learn to read much earlier than we assumed.

But we must take this a step further. We now have compelling evidence that children ages three and four can begin to read. We also have a massive Head Start program, serving 840,000 disadvantaged children at just those ages. This is a perfect fit. My Administration will reform Head Start programs and aggressively emphasize early reading skills.

Head Start was originally intended as a literacy program, designed to close the achievement gap between rich and poor. It evolved into a day-care, health and nutrition program. And it has done good work, not only helping poor children, but also employing some of their parents as teachers and aides. Yet at $4.4 billion a year, it could be accomplishing so much more. Last year, Washington set some new goals for this program. Now we need a president to strongly implement them. My Administration will move Head Start out of the Department of Health and Human Services and over to the Department of Education. Head Start will be an education program. It will fund only those local centers that emphasize the first steps toward reading and school-readiness. We will provide them with the basic research and material on early childhood education. And each time a Head Start contract is up for renewal, we will subject that site to an independent evaluation – to make sure they are successfully putting our children on the track to learning and literacy. If not, the operation of a Head Start site will be put up for competitive bidding – allowing someone, including churches and synagogues and community groups, to serve our children better. These children deserve the opportunities found in many private preschools, with trained teachers and high expectations. And all this will be done without sacrificing Head Start's important social and medical services.

The third reform concerns Title I – at $7.7 billion, the federal government's largest educational commitment to poor children. I respect that commitment, and will honor it. But I do not respect poor results with public money. In my Administration, federal money will no longer flow to failure. Public funds must be spent on things that work.

My plan will make sure that every school getting Title I funds tests its disadvantaged students on the academic basics every year. The state, not the federal government, will choose and administer those tests. If the scores are improving – making progress toward the state standard – a school will be rewarded with a grant and special recognition. If the disadvantaged children in a school are not making progress, the school will be warned that it is failing. It will be given time to adjust, to reform, to change. But if, at the end of three years, there is still no progress, its Title I funds will be divided up, matched by other federal education money given to the state, and made directly available to parents – coming to about $1,500 per year. This money can then be used by students for tutoring, for a charter school, for a working public school in a different district, for a private school – for whatever parents choose. For whatever offers hope.

States that want to pursue this kind of reform immediately will be free to do so. But eventually, in every case where a school does not teach and will not change, the status quo must be challenged.

The goal here is to strengthen public schools by expecting performance – to increase the number of schools where children are likely to learn. But if a school, with ample time to change, continues to fail, there must be some final point of accountability. Some moment of truth. In the best case, these schools will rise to the challenge and regain the confidence of parents. In the worst case, we will offer scholarships to America's neediest children, allowing them to get the emergency help they should have. In any case, the federal government will no longer pay schools to cheat poor children.

The enormous frustration with public education in America leads to two temptations. One is to dictate local policies from Washington. But this is an approach that has been discredited by 30 years of failure. Our schools do not need more bureaucratic oversight, they need the pressure to perform and the freedom to change. Education, it's been said, is not the filling of a pail, it is the lighting of a fire. We need that spirit today, and no master plan of government can light it.

But there is another temptation – to give up on public education entirely. To talk only of ending agencies or slashing programs. But this approach is too limited. One-sixth of the American population is in public schools. The content of their education will determine the character of our country. Will America be prepared for the new economy? Will we have the informed citizens that self-government requires?

At their best, America's public schools have been a source of shared ideals. They gave millions of immigrants a start in life and a dream to follow. They were united by a golden thread of principle: that everyone, if given a chance, could rise in the world and contribute to their country. In all its simplicity, that is still the mission and mandate of public education in America.

A president does not bear responsibility for every policy in every school in every district. But every president must be the keeper of our common ideals. A president speaks for everyone. Not just for schools and those who run them. Not for one interest or ethnic group over another. Not for one class above the rest. A president – and sometimes only a president – can speak for the common good.

Our common good is found in our common schools. And we must make those schools worthy of all our children. Whatever their background, their cause is our cause, and it must not be lost.

Position Paper
Education: No Child Left Behind

September 2, 1999

"More and more, we are divided into two nations, separate and unequal. One that reads and one that can't. One that dreams and one that doesn't...All children can learn, and no child should be left behind."

Governor George W. Bush

EXECUTIVE SUMMARY

Governor Bush believes all children can learn, and no child should be left behind. That is why he considers it a scandal that the educational achievement gap between rich and poor, Anglo and minority, is not only wide, but in key areas such as reading, is wider than it was in 1992.

As President, Governor Bush will commit his administration to closing the achievement gap, as he is doing in Texas. During each of his years as Governor, all ethnic groups in Texas – in all grades – have advanced in reading and math. Indeed, according to the National Education Goals Panel, Texas is one of two states that has made the greatest progress in education in recent years.

While our children's education remains the primary concern of states, communities, and parents, Governor Bush believes the federal government can – and must – help close the achievement gap through three key reforms:

To Ensure that Federal Education Programs Produce Results, Governor Bush will:

- Require federally funded programs to boost student achievement, or be replaced by programs that succeed in reducing the achievement gap.

- Reform the Office of Education Research and Improvement so that it operates independently and scientifically, and empowers states with research on how to teach children most effectively.

To Make Education the Top Priority of Head Start, Governor Bush will:

- Move Head Start to the Education Department and make school readiness – instruction of pre-reading and numeracy skills – its top priority.

- Require Head Start programs to adopt a proven core curriculum.

- Award Head Start contracts on a competitive basis to spur improvements.

To Ensure that Federal Funds Underwrite Success Not Failure, Governor Bush will:

- Require states to improve academic performance for federally benefited students in return for federal funding and unprecedented flexibility.

- Award "Achievement in Education" bonus funds to states and schools that are closing the achievement gap.

- Require states to offer parents of Title I students stuck in persistently failing schools the option of using their federal education dollars to participate in another school or program of their choice.

The National Achievement Gap Has Grown During the 1990s

Governor Bush is concerned that the educational achievement gap is not only wide, but in some cases, growing wider still:

- Disparity between ethnic group performance on the National Assessment of Education Progress (NAEP) has grown or remained substantial. The NAEP is the only nationally representative continuing assessment of what America's students know in key subject areas.

- The achievement gap on NAEP math and reading exams has widened since 1990. The reading gap between Hispanic and white students is larger today than it was in 1992.

- The Administration concedes 68 percent of fourth graders in the highest poverty schools could not read in 1998 at NAEP's "basic" level. In low-poverty schools, by contrast, more than three-quarters of the children read at or above the basic level.

- In a 1998 report, the Citizens' Commission on Civil Rights criticized "the widespread propensity of school officials to maintain and tolerate a permanent underclass of low-achieving students who are disproportionately poor and minority."

Governor Bush believes that it is precisely among these disadvantaged children in struggling schools that educational failure exacts its highest price. He believes we owe these children the pride and promise of learning – and that the new "knowledge-based" economy demands it.

A Philosophy of Reform

In the last several years, a movement of parents and legislators, voters and educators, has resulted in an explosion of innovation in education. This movement is proving public education can be improved dramatically. Governor Bush believes that out of these efforts a philosophy of reform aimed at a culture of excellence is emerging, based upon these principles:

- First, schools must have clear, measurable goals. These goals should be focused on the acquisition of basic skills and essential knowledge.

- Second, there must be regular testing and measurement to ensure that the goals are met. Education is about results, and testing helps educators and parents judge whether the desired results are being achieved.

- Third, effective reform requires accountability. The only sure way to create a culture of excellence is to have incentives for success and consequences for failure.

- Fourth, accountability must be accompanied by local control. If schools are to be held to high standards, they must have the freedom to meet those standards as they think best.

- Finally, competition is an essential ingredient in raising standards and creating accountability. Only the pressure of competition – and the power of parental choice – can change the status quo.

The Federal Role in Education – Making Sure No Child is Left Behind

Governor Bush believes the federal government can – and must – play a key role in closing the achievement gap. In return for increased federal funds and unprecedented flexibility in using those funds, the states must be held accountable for improving the academic achievement of students who benefit from federal assistance. The federal government should offer incentives for success in narrowing the achievement gap, impose consequences for failure, and encourage competition to spur improvement. As President, Governor Bush will champion three key reforms designed to ensure no child is left behind.

Reform 1: Ensure that Federal Education Programs Produce Results

The federal government funds more than 760 different education programs. These programs produce a lot of paperwork: it is estimated that processing forms alone requires 25,000 full-time employees. What is not known is whether these programs produce results. Unfortunately, federal money too often funds faddish, rather than rigorous research, and too few federal programs are scientifically evaluated.

The Department of Education's Office of Educational Research and Improvement (OERI) is supposed to sponsor reliable research. But despite receiving $510 million annually, it has generally failed to fulfill its task of developing and disseminating successful teaching techniques.

OERI's largest sponsored research program is the ten regional education laboratories, funded at $50 million a year. Established in 1965, the labs were intended to help states discover and implement what works in education. Instead, they have undertaken research that is fragmented, faddish, and vulnerable to politicization. Two former Assistant Secretaries of OERI have written that the regional labs "undertake a mishmash of research, dissemination, and technical assistance activities, aimed mostly at state and local education agencies...the program as a whole has outlived whatever justification it once had."

Governor Bush believes solid research in education can identify the most effective means of teaching children and closing the achievement gap. For example, recent National Institutes of Health research has shown that phonics-based instruction is a necessary component of teaching children to read. Research on early learning must also be a priority so solid curricula and teaching strategies for use in Head Start and other pre-school settings can be developed.

Therefore, to ensure improved student achievement, as President, Governor Bush will:

<u>Require that the Federal Investment in Education Demonstrate Results:</u> The federal government will insist that every program it funds will boost student

achievement, or else it will be replaced by other education programs that succeed in reducing the achievement gap.

Reform the Office of Education Research and Improvement: In order to generate valid research that will empower the states, districts and educators with research-based programs that most effectively teach children, OERI will be overhauled to ensure that it operates independently and consistently with the standards of a science-based research center. The regional education laboratories, which have failed to meet their purpose of providing helpful research to states and educators, will be sunset and opened to competitive bid.

Reform 2: Return Head Start to its Original Purpose – Education

Effective early childhood education programs can have a tremendous bearing on the future academic success of our children. That is why Governor Bush believes that Head Start should be reformed, not scrapped.

Established in 1965, Head Start was intended to narrow the achievement gap. Today, it is the largest federal early childhood development program, funded at $4.4 billion a year. It serves more than 840,000 low-income children, most of whom are three- and four-year-olds. It is administered through the Department of Health and Human Services (HHS), which contracts with local providers to run the programs.

However, while some local Head Start programs have produced cognitive gains for participating youngsters, there is no pervasive evidence of the educational effectiveness of Head Start as a whole. The largest evaluation of Head Start to date, an April 1997 GAO report summarizing the findings of nearly 600 Head Start studies, shows that after three decades, Head Start lacks consistent results in preparing children academically for school.

Thus, to reform Head Start, Governor Bush will:

Move Head Start to the Department of Education: To ensure that Head Start makes education a priority and focuses on building skills for school readiness, especially pre-reading and numeracy, the Department of Education, not HHS, will oversee the administration and evaluation of local Head Start programs.

Require Head Start Programs to Adopt a Proven Core Curriculum: The federal government will identify model curricula and effective methods of teaching pre-reading and school readiness. These research-based best practices will be made available to local Head Start programs so they can better prepare youngsters to enter school ready to learn.

Award Head Start Contracts on a Competitive Basis: New Head Start grants will be open to competition and awarded on a selective basis. Upon renewal of each existing Head Start contract, the program will be evaluated based on its effectiveness. If a program is found ineffective in teaching pre-reading and school readiness, its contract will be opened up for competitive bid.

Reform 3: Restructure Title I to Close the Achievement Gap

Title I was created in 1965 as the federal government's principal means of closing the achievement gap between the children of low-income families and their counterparts. It provides $7.7 billion annually to local school districts to supplement the education of 11 million low-income students. Nearly half of all public schools and 94 percent of all school districts now receive Title I money.

Little evidence exists that Title I has made any appreciable progress in closing the achievement gap. Two long-term studies mandated by Congress, "Sustaining Effects" in the late 1970's and "Prospects" in the early 1990's, concluded that after billions of dollars, Title I had achieved virtually no lasting gains in academic improvement. Even the most recent study, the "Longitudinal Evaluation of School Change and Performance," begun after the 1994 reform of Title I, reports disappointing results. The interim report, released to Congress in July of 1999, seems to suggest Title I students are growing academically at less than a year's progress for each year in school.

Governor Bush believes we must stop using federal money to fund failure by imposing quick and rigorous consequences for performance. Schools that produce results should be rewarded. But when a school fails – after being given an opportunity to change – its Title I funds should be given directly to parents to use for the educational program or school of their choice.

As President, Governor Bush will administer Title I to ensure that schools have both the pressure to perform and the freedom to succeed. Specifically, he will:

Focus Title I Funds on Earlier Grades: Students in K-12 will still be eligible for Title I, but Title I funds will focus on students in the elementary grades, where the achievement gap in reading and math skills begins.

Hold Schools Accountable for Performance of Title I Students: All states must annually assess Title I students in grades 3-8 in reading and math and report the results on a disaggregated basis. Each state that has not already done so must adopt its own standards of acceptable student performance and institute reforms that will move Title I students toward that standard through

29

improved academic results, thus closing the achievement gap.

Establish an "Achievement in Education" Fund to Reward Success: States that make the greatest progress in closing the gap for economically disadvantaged students, and schools within each state that make the greatest gains in moving Title I students toward the state-set standards, will be rewarded significantly through an "Achievement in Education" bonus fund.

Give Low-Performing Schools Three Years to Reform: States will have three years to reform failing schools by restructuring management, changing personnel, reallocating resources, taking over persistently low-performing schools or districts, transferring education dollars to the parents, and/or implementing a school choice system. If a state enacts private or public school choice, it should be able to offer parents of Title I students in failing schools a *pro rata* share of Title I funds to help pay for these choice options.

Make Funds Portable After Three Years: If, after three years, state reforms have not worked and the combined academic results of Title I students enrolled in a school still do not demonstrate progress toward the state-set standard of acceptable performance, the state will be required to:

- Give Title I students in these schools the option (fully paid for) of transferring to a school that is closing the gap for such students; or

- Offer parents of these students portable funds, which can be used to obtain for their child an education at a school of their choice or supplemental education services. These funds (worth an average $1,500 per child) will consist of the student's *pro rata* share of Title I funds, provided by the Local Education Agency, and an equal amount provided by the state from its federal or state funds. Portability would be in effect for the period of time the child would have been enrolled in the failing school.

Education:
A Culture of Achievement

Manhattan Institute Luncheon
New York, New York

October 5, 1999

Last month in California, I talked about disadvantaged children in troubled schools. I argued that the diminished hopes of our current system are sad and serious – the soft bigotry of low expectations.

And I set out a simple principle: Federal funds will no longer flow to failure. Schools that do not teach and will not change must have some final point of accountability. A moment of truth, when their Title I funds are divided up and given to parents, for tutoring or a charter school or some other hopeful option. In the best case, schools that are failing will rise to the challenge and regain the confidence of parents. In the worst case, we will offer scholarships to America's neediest children.

In any case, the federal government will no longer pay schools to cheat poor children.

But this is the beginning of our challenge, not its end. The final object of education reform is not just to shun mediocrity; it is to seek excellence. It is not just to avoid failure; it is to encourage achievement.

Our nation has a moral duty to ensure that no child is left behind.

And we also, at this moment, have a great national opportunity – to ensure that every child, in every public school, is challenged by high standards that meet the high hopes of parents. To build a culture of achievement that matches the optimism and aspirations of our country.

Not long ago, this would have seemed incredible. Our education debates were captured by a deep pessimism.

For decades, waves of reform were quickly revealed as passing fads, with little lasting result. For decades, funding rose while performance stagnated. Most parents, except in some urban districts, have not seen the collapse of education. They have seen a slow slide of expectations and standards. Schools where poor spelling is called "creative." Where math is "fuzzy" and grammar is optional. Where grade inflation is the norm.

Schools where spelling bees are canceled for being too competitive and selecting a single valedictorian is considered too exclusive. Where advancing from one grade to the next is unconnected to advancing skills. Schools where, as in *Alice in Wonderland*, "Everyone has won, and all must have prizes."

We are left with a nagging sense of lost potential. A sense of what could be, but is not.

It led the late Albert Shanker, of the American Federation of Teachers, to conclude: "Very few American pupils are performing anywhere near where they could be performing."

This cuts against the grain of American character. Most parents know that the self-esteem of children is not built by low standards, it is built by real accomplishments. Most parents know that good character is tied to an ethic of study and hard work and merit – and that setbacks are as much a part of learning as awards.

Most Americans know that a healthy democracy must be committed both to equality and to excellence.

Until a few years ago, the debates of politics seemed irrelevant to these concerns. Democrats and Republicans argued mainly about funding and procedures – about dollars and devolution. Few talked of standards or accountability or of excellence for all our children.

But all this is beginning to change. In state after state, we are seeing a profound shift of priorities. An "age of accountability" is starting to replace an era of low expectations. And there is a growing conviction and confidence that the problems of public education are not an endless road or a hopeless maze.

The principles of this movement are similar from New York to Florida, from Massachusetts to Michigan. Raise the bar of standards.

Give schools the flexibility to meet them. Measure progress. Insist on results. Blow the whistle on failure. Provide parents with options to increase their influence. And don't give up on anyone.

There are now countless examples of public schools transformed by great expectations. Places like Earhart Elementary in Chicago, where students are expected to compose essays by the second grade.

Where these young children participate in a Junior Great Books program, and sixth graders are reading *To Kill a Mockingbird*. The principal explains, "All our children are expected to work above grade level and learn for the sake of learning... We instill a desire to overachieve. Give us an average child and we'll make him an overachiever."

This is a public school, and not a wealthy one. And it proves what is possible.

No one in Texas now doubts that public schools can improve. We are witnessing the promise of high standards and accountability. We require that every child read by the third grade, without exception or excuse. Every year, we test students on the academic basics. We disclose those results by school. We encourage the diversity and creativity of charters. We give local schools and districts the freedom to chart their own path to excellence.

I certainly don't claim credit for all these changes. But my state is proud of what we have accomplished together. Last week, the federal Department of Education announced that Texas eighth graders have some of the best writing skills in the country. In 1994, there were 67 schools in Texas rated "exemplary" according to our tests. This year, there are 1,120. We are proud, but we are not content. Now that we are meeting our current standards, I am insisting that we elevate those standards.

Now that we are clearing the bar, we are going to raise the bar – because we have set our sights on excellence.

At the beginning of the 1990s, so many of our nation's problems, from education to crime to welfare, seemed intractable – beyond our control. But something unexpected happened on the way to cultural decline. Problems that seemed inevitable proved to be reversible. They gave way to an optimistic, governing conservatism.

Here in New York, Mayor Giuliani brought order and civility back to the streets – cutting crime rates by 50 percent. In Wisconsin, Governor Tommy Thompson proved that welfare dependence could be reversed – reducing his rolls by 91 percent. Innovative mayors and governors followed their lead – cutting national welfare rolls by nearly half since 1994, and reducing the murder rate to the lowest point since 1967.

Now education reform is gaining a critical mass of results.

In the process, conservatism has become the creed of hope. The creed of aggressive, persistent reform. The creed of social progress.

Too often, on social issues, my party has painted an image of America slouching toward Gomorrah. Of course there are challenges to the character and compassion of our nation – too many broken homes and broken lives.

But many of our problems – particularly education, crime and welfare dependence – are yielding to good sense and strength and idealism. In states and cities around the country, we are making, not just points and pledges, but progress. We are demonstrating the genius for self-renewal at the heart of the American experiment.

34

Too often, my party has focused on the national economy, to the exclusion of all else – speaking a sterile language of rates and numbers, of CBO this and GNP that.

Of course we want growth and vigor in our economy. But there are human problems that persist in the shadow of affluence. And the strongest argument for conservative ideals – for responsibility and accountability and the virtues of our tradition – is that they lead to greater justice, less suffering, more opportunity.

Too often, my party has confused the need for limited government with a disdain for government itself.

But this is not an option for conservatives. At the constitutional convention in 1787, Benjamin Franklin argued that the strength of our nation depends "on the general opinion of the goodness of government." Our Founders rejected cynicism, and cultivated a noble love of country. That love is undermined by sprawling, arrogant, aimless government. It is restored by focused and effective and energetic government.

And that should be our goal: A limited government, respected for doing a few things and doing them well.

This is an approach with echoes in our history. Echoes of Lincoln and emancipation and the Homestead Act and land-grant colleges. Echoes of Theodore Roosevelt and national parks and the Panama Canal. Echoes of Reagan and a confrontation with communism that sought victory, not stalemate.

What are the issues that challenge us, that summon us, in our time? Surely one of them must be excellence in education. Surely one of them must be to rekindle the spirit of learning and ambition in our common schools. And one of our great opportunities and urgent duties is to remake the federal role.

Even as many states embrace education reform, the federal government is mired in bureaucracy and mediocrity.

It is an obstacle, not an ally. Education bills are often rituals of symbolic spending without real accountability – like pumping gas into a flooded engine. For decades, fashionable ideas have been turned into programs, with little knowledge of their benefits for students and teachers. And even the obvious failures seldom disappear.

This is a perfect example of government that is big – and weak. Of government that is grasping – and impotent.

Let me share an example. The Department of Education recently streamlined the grant application process for states. The old procedure involved 487 different steps, taking an average of 26 weeks. So, a few years ago, the best minds of the administration got together and "reinvented" the grant process. Now it takes a mere 216 steps, and the wait is 20 weeks.

If this is reinventing government, it makes you wonder how this administration was ever skilled enough and efficient enough to create the Internet. I don't want to tinker with the machinery of the federal role in education. I want to redefine that role entirely.

I strongly believe in local control of schools and curriculum. I have consistently placed my faith in states and schools and parents and teachers – and that faith, in Texas, has been rewarded.

I also believe a president should define and defend the unifying ideals of our nation – including the quality of our common schools. He must lead, without controlling. He must set high goals – without being high-handed. The inertia of our education bureaucracy is a national problem, requiring a national response. Sometimes inaction is not restraint – it is complicity. Sometimes it takes the use of executive power to empower others.

Effective education reform requires both pressure from above and competition from below – a demand for high standards and measurement at the top, given momentum and urgency by expanded options for parents and students. So, as President, here is what I'll do. First, I will fundamentally change the relationship of the states and federal government in education. Now we have a system of excessive regulation and no standards. In my administration, we will have minimal regulation and high standards.

Second, I will promote more choices for parents in the education of their children. In the end, it is parents, armed with information and options, who turn the theory of reform into the reality of excellence.

All reform begins with freedom and local control. It unleashes creativity. It permits those closest to children to exercise their judgment. And it also removes the excuse for failure. Only those with the ability to change can be held to account.

But local control has seldom been a priority in Washington. In 1965, when President Johnson signed the very first Elementary and Secondary Education Act, not one school board trustee, from anywhere in the country, was invited to the ceremony. Local officials were viewed as the enemy. And that attitude has lingered too long.

As President, I will begin by taking most of the 60 different categories of federal education grants and paring them down to five: improving achievement among disadvantaged children; promoting fluency in English; training and recruiting teachers; encouraging character and school safety; and promoting innovation and parental choice. Within these divisions, states will have maximum flexibility to determine their priorities.

They will only be asked to certify that their funds are being used for the specific purposes intended – and the federal red tape ends there.

This will spread authority to levels of government that people can touch. And it will reduce paperwork – allowing schools to spend less on filing forms and more on what matters: teachers' salaries and children themselves.

In return, we will ask that every state have a real accountability system – meaning that they test every child, every year, in grades three through eight, on the basics of reading and math; broadly disclose those results by school, including on the Internet; and have clear consequences for success and failure. States will pick their own tests, and the federal government will share the costs of administering them.

States can choose tests off-the-shelf, like Arizona; adapt tests like California; or contract for new tests like Texas. Over time, if a state's results are improving, it will be rewarded with extra money – a total of $500 million in awards over five years. If scores are stagnant or dropping, the administrative portion of their federal funding – about 5 percent – will be diverted to a fund for charter schools.

We will praise and reward success – and shine a spotlight of shame on failure.

What I am proposing today is a fresh start for the federal role in education. A pact of principle. Freedom in exchange for achievement. Latitude in return for results. Local control with one national goal: excellence for every child.

I am opposed to national tests, written by the federal government.

If Washington can control the content of tests, it can dictate the content of state curricula – a role our central government should not play.

But measurement at the state level is essential. Without testing, reform is a journey without a compass. Without testing, teachers and administrators cannot adjust their methods to meet high goals. Without testing, standards are little more than scraps of paper.

Without testing, true competition is impossible. Without testing, parents are left in the dark.

In fact, the greatest benefit of testing – with the power to transform a school or a system – is the information it gives to parents. They will know – not just by rumor or reputation, but by hard numbers – which schools are succeeding and which are not.

Given that information, more parents will be pulled into activism – becoming participants, not spectators, in the education of their children. Armed with that information, parents will have the leverage to force reform.

Information is essential. But reform also requires options. Monopolies seldom change on their own – no matter how good the intentions of those who lead them. Competition is required to jolt a bureaucracy out of its lethargy.

So my second goal for the federal role of education is to increase the options and influence of parents.

The reform of Title I I've proposed would begin this process. We will give parents with children in failing schools – schools where the test scores of Title I children show no improvement over three years – the resources to seek more hopeful options. This will amount to a scholarship of about $1,500 a year.

And parents can use those funds for tutoring or tuition – for anything that gives their children a fighting chance at learning. The theory is simple. Public funds must be spent on things that work – on helping children, not sustaining failed schools that refuse to change.

The response to this plan has been deeply encouraging. Yet some politicians have gone to low performing schools and claimed my plan would undermine them.

Think a moment about what that means. It means visiting a school and saying, in essence, "You are hopeless. Not only can't you achieve, you can't even improve." That is not a defense of public education, it is a surrender to despair. That is not liberalism, it is pessimism. It is accepting and excusing an educational apartheid in our country – segregating poor children into a world without the hope of change.

Everyone, in both parties, seems to agree with accountability in theory. But what could accountability possibly mean if children attend schools for 12 years without learning to read or write? Accountability without consequences is empty – the hollow shell of reform. And all our children deserve better.

In our education reform plan, we will give states more flexibility to use federal funds, at their option, for choice programs – including private school choice.

In some neighborhoods, these new options are the first sign of hope, of real change, that parents have seen for a generation.

But not everyone wants or needs private school choice. Many parents in America want more choices, higher standards and more influence *within* their public schools. This is the great promise of charter schools – the path that New York is now beginning. And this, in great part, is a tribute to the Manhattan Institute.

If charters are properly done – free to hire their own teachers, adopt their own curriculum, set their own operating rules and high standards – they will change the face of American education. Public schools – without bureaucracy. Public schools – controlled by parents. Public schools – held to the highest goals. Public schools – as we imagined they could be.

For parents, they are schools on a human scale, where their voice is heard and heeded. For students, they are more like a family than a factory – a place where it is harder to get lost. For teachers, who often help found charter schools, they are a chance to teach as they've always wanted. Says one charter school teacher in Boston: "We don't have to wait to make changes. We don't have to wait for the district to decide that what we are doing is within the rules...So we can really put the interests of the kids first."

This morning I visited the new Sisulu Children's Academy in Harlem – New York's first charter school. In an area where only a quarter of children can read at or above grade level, Sisulu Academy offers a core curriculum of reading, math, science and history. There will be an extended school day, and the kids will also learn computer skills, art, music and dance. And there is a waiting list of 100 children.

This is a new approach – even a new definition of public education. These schools are public because they are publicly funded and publicly accountable for results. The vision of parents and teachers and principals determines the rest. Money follows the child. The units of delivery get smaller and more personal. Some charters go back to basics...some attract the gifted...some emphasize the arts.

It is a reform movement that welcomes diversity, but demands excellence. And this is the essence of real reform.

Charter schools benefit the children within them – as well as the public school students beyond them. The evidence shows that competition often strengthens all the schools in a district. In Arizona, in places where charters have arrived – teaching phonics and extending hours and involving parents – suddenly many traditional public schools are following suit.

The greatest problem facing charter schools is practical – the cost of building them. Unlike regular public schools, they receive no capital funds. And the typical charter costs about $1.5 million to construct. Some are forced to start in vacant hotel rooms or strip malls.

As President, I want to fan the spark of charter schools into a flame. My Administration will establish a Charter School Homestead Fund, to help finance these start-up costs.

We will provide capital to education entrepreneurs – planting new schools on the frontiers of reform. This fund will support $3 billion in loan guarantees in my first two years in office – enough to seed 2,000 schools. Enough to double the existing number.

This will be a direct challenge to the status quo in public education – in a way that both changes it and strengthens it. With charters, someone cares enough to say, "I'm dissatisfied."

Someone is bold enough to say, "I can do better." And all our schools will aim higher if we reward that kind of courage and vision.

And we will do one thing more for parents. We will expand Education Savings Accounts to cover education expenses in grades K through 12, allowing parents or grandparents to contribute up to

$5,000 dollars per year, per student. Those funds can be withdrawn tax-free for tuition payments, or books, or tutoring or transportation – whatever students need most.

Often this nation sets out to reform education for all the wrong reasons – or at least for incomplete ones. Because the Soviets launch Sputnik. Or because children in Singapore have high test scores. Or because our new economy demands computer operators.

But when parents hope for their children, they hope with nobler goals. Yes, we want them to have the basic skills of life. But life is more than a race for riches.

A good education leads to intellectual self-confidence, and ambition and a quickened imagination. It helps us, not just to live, but to live well.

And this private good has public consequences. In his first address to Congress, President Washington called education "the surest basis of public happiness." America's founders believed that self-government requires a certain kind of citizen.

Schooled to think clearly and critically, and to know America's civic ideals. Freed, by learning, to rise, by merit. Education is the way a democratic culture reproduces itself through time.

This is the reason a conservative should be passionate about education reform – the reason a conservative should fight strongly and care deeply. Our common schools carry a great burden for the common good. And they must be more than schools of last resort.

Every child must have a quality education – not just in islands of excellence. Because we are a single nation with a shared future. Because, as Lincoln said, we are "brothers of a common country."

Position Paper
Education: A Culture of Achievement
October 5, 1999

"The final object of education reform is not just to shun mediocrity; it is to seek excellence. It is not just to avoid failure; it is to reward achievement. Our nation has a moral duty to ensure no child is left behind. And we also, at this moment, have a great national opportunity – to ensure that every child, in every public school, is challenged by high standards that meet the high hopes of parents. To build a culture of achievement that matches the optimism and aspirations of our country."

Governor George W. Bush

EXECUTIVE SUMMARY

Governor Bush believes America must be committed to both equality and excellence in education. In addition to closing the achievement gap between rich and poor students, we must raise standards of excellence for <u>all</u> students. This requires pressure from above for high standards, and competition from below to provide parents and students with information and options.

To Redefine the Relationship Between the States and the Federal Government, Granting Freedom from Regulation in Exchange for Results, Governor Bush will:

- Free states from regulation by consolidating most of the 60 elementary and secondary education programs into five flexible categories: improving achievement of disadvantaged children, promoting fluency in English, training and recruiting teachers, encouraging character and school safety, and promoting innovation and informed parental choice.

- Offer states the option to become "charter" states, providing them with even more flexibility in return for meeting rigorous performance standards.

- Require all states to establish an accountability system in which they test every child, every year, in grades 3-8 on reading and math. States will be free to choose their own tests, and the federal government will equally share the cost.

- Pay for states to administer an annual National Assessment of Educational Progress (NAEP) sample exam, or its equivalent, in reading and math.

- Establish a $500 million fund to reward states that improve student performance, and commit to withdraw the administrative portion of federal funding – about 5 percent – from states that permit student performance to stagnate or decline.

To Promote Competition to Increase the Options and Influence of Parents, Governor Bush will:

- Require school-by-school report cards to be published on the Internet and elsewhere.

- Establish a Charter School Homestead Fund to provide $3 billion of loan guarantees to help establish or improve 2,000 charter schools in two years.

- Expand Education Savings Accounts by allowing parents to increase their annual contributions from $500 per student to $5,000, and withdraw funds tax-free to pay for education expenses from kindergarten to college.

Redefining the Federal Role in Education

Determined parents, educators and legislators across America have embraced education reform. Too often, however, these reformers are finding that the heavy hand of federal bureaucracy is hindering their efforts.

Federal education dollars are spread over too many programs – and cost too much to administer. The paperwork involved in tracking and accounting for federal dollars drains resources from schools that would be better spent on teachers' salaries and students. In some states, an estimated 50 percent of paperwork done by local schools is spent administering federal education programs, even though federal funds account for only 7 percent of total spending. According to a 1998 study by the U.S. Department of Education, only 85 cents out of every federal education dollar actually reaches the school district, and even less reaches the classroom.

But federal red tape is not the only problem reformers face. Not only does the federal system currently fail to provide states with the flexibility they need to improve their schools, the system also fails to demand academic results:

- A 1997 GAO report on federal education funding stated that "federally funded programs have historically placed a low priority on results and accountability."

- A 1998 report by the U.S. House Subcommittee on Education found that "it has been years since many [federal education] programs have been evaluated, and often those reviews are more concerned with process – accounting for numbers of participants and educators, not whether the children are actually better off."

Governor Bush believes that the "era of low expectations" must now be replaced with an "age of accountability." Effective school reform requires pressure from above to establish high standards, and competition from below to expand information and options for parents and students. Thus, as President, to promote a culture of excellence in the nation's schools, Governor Bush will:

- Redefine the relationship between the states and the federal government, offering states unprecedented freedom from regulation in exchange for measurable achievement; and

- Increase the options and influence of parents by providing information on school performance and promoting competition.

Goal 1: A New Federal-State Education Pact – Freedom in Exchange for Results

Governor Bush believes that to reform education it is necessary to redefine the relationship between the states and the federal government. Therefore, he is proposing a new federal-state pact offering freedom from regulation and bureaucratic red tape, in exchange for achievement.

Providing Freedom from Regulation

The Elementary and Secondary Education Act (ESEA), established in 1965, is the largest source of federal funding for K-12 education. It provides nearly $14 billion annually through more than 60 different programs designated under 13 different Titles. The largest portion of these funds is contained in Title I, an $8 billion program aimed at assisting disadvantaged children. Other ESEA programs address issues ranging from teacher training to teen drug use to funding for arts in education.

The proliferation of ESEA programs has generated a corresponding increase in regulation and red tape. As a result, hearings held by the House Education and Workforce Committee in 1997 revealed that the U.S. government spends almost twice as much on administering education programs as other industrialized countries.

The complexity of the ESEA system also imposes higher costs on the states. In the state of Georgia, for example, it takes 4.5 times as many people to administer a federal education dollar as it does to administer a state education dollar.

As President, Governor Bush will free the states from the regulation, red tape, and high costs of administering ESEA funds. Specifically, Governor Bush will:

Consolidate and Simplify ESEA Funding: The current categorical system of 60 separate programs will be replaced with five flexible categories, representing broad education goals:

- Improving the Academic Performance of Disadvantaged Students.

- Moving Limited English Proficient (LEP) Students to English Fluency.

- Preparing, Training and Recruiting Qualified Teachers.

- Creating a Safe Culture for Learning.

- Promoting Informed Parental Choice and Research-based Innovative Practices.

A few specific programs, such as Impact Aid, which is granted to districts affected by military bases and other federal activities, will remain unchanged. Administrative funds will be separated and provided in one lump sum.

Eliminate Restrictions and Red Tape: Within the five broad categories, states will have freedom to determine priorities and to assign responsibility for administering the funds within state government, so long as they certify that the funds are being spent for the intended purposes.

Offer States the Option to Become "Charter" States: States will have the option of entering into a charter agreement with the federal government, whereby they would commit to meet especially high levels of academic achievement for all students, particularly disadvantaged ones, in exchange for further consolidation of their federal education funding – and further flexibility in spending. The same contract option will also be made available to individual districts.

Ensuring Accountability

In return for this increased freedom from regulation, Governor Bush will ask that every state implement an accountability system, involving high standards and regular performance measurement.

Many states have set education standards, but often they are too low to ensure excellence. In 1998, the Fordham Foundation appraised state standards in English, history, geography, mathematics, and science. Independent reviewers assigned a letter grade – A, B, C, D, or F – to each state, based on the clarity, rigor and effectiveness of the state standards. The results showed most state standards must be improved before they will guarantee excellence. When assigned composite grades based on the average grades of all its standards, no state earned an "A" average; only three earned "B" averages; and nine flunked. The national cumulative GPA was a "D +."

Governor Bush believes that not only should high standards be set, they must be accompanied by performance measurement. Testing makes standards meaningful, promotes competition, and empowers parents and teachers to seek change. Unfortunately, while many states test some students, fewer than 12 states test all students in consecutive grades, every year.

Therefore, as President, in exchange for giving states unprecedented freedom in spending federal funds, Governor Bush will:

Require States to Set Up Their Own Accountability Systems: All states receiving federal education assistance will be required to establish within three years an accountability system with the goal of achieving and demonstrating academic improvement. Each state will be free to set its own standards and craft its own system free of federal control, so long as those systems contain certain minimum elements:

- High standards in core subjects: English, math, science and history.

- Annual assessment of all students in at least grades 3-8 in reading and math. States will be free to choose their own tests, and the federal government will share equally in the cost of administering them. Any student exemptions from testing should be based upon a limited and consistently applied standard.

- A commitment to reward school success and impose consequences for failure. States' responses to school results could include an array of actions, including honors and/or rewards; restructured management; personnel changes; takeover of persistently low-performing schools and districts; and even the transfer of education dollars to the parent and implementation of a choice system.

Ask States to Participate in Annual NAEP Exams: As part of the new federal-state education pact, the federal government will pay for states to participate in an annual National Assessment of Educational Progress (NAEP) sample exam, or its equivalent, for students in grades 4 and 8 in reading and math. All states receiving federal education assistance must participate in the sample exam, which can be done reliably with sample sizes of no more than 1,700 to 2,600 students per state. If a state would prefer to use another test in lieu of the NAEP and can show that its results can be equated with those of NAEP, the state can, at its own expense, use or continue using such a test.

Ensure an Independent NAEP: To insulate NAEP from political influence, the office that administers NAEP and the bipartisan board that sets policy for it, will be made independent of the Department of Education.

Establishing Consequences for Success and Failure

Governor Bush believes that accountability must be accompanied by consequences. As President, to ensure that success in achieving high standards is rewarded, while stagnating or declining performance is not tolerated, Governor Bush will:

Reward States that Demonstrate Academic Improvement: An "Achievement in Education" fund will be created to reward states that demonstrate substantial and valid progress on the state assessments, as verified by NAEP. A total of $500 million will be made available to be awarded over five years. Rewards will be based upon achievement of one or more of the following goals, with the size of the reward increasing with the number of goals achieved:

- Closing the achievement gap, by raising the achievement of disadvantaged students.

- Increasing overall student performance, by raising the achievement of all students.

- Increasing opportunities for advanced academic achievement, by increasing, for example, the percentage of students who are deemed proficient on NAEP, raising SAT/ACT scores, and increasing the number of students who take and pass Advanced Placement and International Baccalaureate exams.

Impose Consequences on States that Fail to Demonstrate Results: States that fail to demonstrate results in academic achievement over the course of five years will have the administrative portion of their federal funding – roughly 5 percent of the total – withdrawn and re-directed into the charter school grant fund.

Goal 2: Empower Parents by Promoting Competition

Governor Bush believes that increased competition is an essential factor in raising education standards. Ultimately, only the pressure of accountability and competition – combined with the power of parental choice – can change the status quo. Promoting effective competition will require parents to have information, options, and resources.

Arming Parents with Information

Governor Bush believes that parents are the most important enforcers of accountability in education. But parents must be armed with more information to determine whether quality education is taking place. Unfortunately, too few parents have access to adequate information about their schools. A 1999 *Education Week* survey found that 76 percent of parents thought widely publicized ratings on such measures as test scores and graduation rates motivate public school teachers to work harder to improve schools' performance. Yet, only 39 percent of parents in the survey said that they had ever seen a school-by-school report card in their community. Indeed, currently, only 36 states provide parents with school-by-school report cards.

Governor Bush believes that information empowers parents, providing them with the leverage to press for change and a reason to become participants in the education of their children. Thus, to arm parents with information, as President, Governor Bush will:

Require School-by-School Report Cards: States will be asked to provide school-by-school report cards, publicizing assessment and testing results, particularly in reading and math. The results should be disaggregated by race, gender, poverty, and English proficiency, and should be published widely, including on the Internet.

Expanding Charter Schools and Parental Choice

Information alone, however, is not enough to empower parents and spur competition. There must be viable options, as well. While vouchers for private schools represent one such option, most parents want more choices, higher standards and more influence within their public schools. That is the promise of the charter school movement. In charter schools, freedom and accountability combine with parental choice to create a culture of achievement.

Charter schools are independent public schools that are formed by teachers, community leaders, parents or others with a desire to break free of the bureaucracy and regulatory red tape that characterize too many of today's public school systems. Attendance at charter schools is free: funds that would otherwise be allocated to a child at his or her regular public school follow the child to the charter school.

Unlike traditional public schools, charter schools are held to the highest level of accountability – consumer demand. If charter schools fail to meet the expectations of parents and teachers, they will be unable to attract students and, as a result, their charters will be revoked.

The demand for charter schools is great. According to the Department of Education, the number of charter schools grew by more than 50 percent in 1998. Just seven years ago, there was only one charter school in existence. Today, 36 states and the District of Columbia have charter school laws, and there are over 350,000 students attending nearly 1,700 charter schools. Seven out of every ten charter schools have a waiting list of students.

According to the Pioneer Institute and the Department of Education, a lack of readily available start-up funding is the most significant barrier faced by charter school organizers. While the typical charter school receives 50 to 100 percent of the average funding per student allocated by the local school district to school *operations*, most receive no *capital* funds. The Department of Education offered $100 million in grants to charter schools in 1999, but those grants may be used only for equipment and teacher training, not to acquire, lease, or renovate a facility.

To encourage the growth of charter schools and spur competition, Governor Bush will:

Create a "Charter School Homestead Fund:" The fund will support $3 billion in loan guarantees to private lenders. The goal of the fund will be to upgrade or establish 2,000 charter schools – potentially doubling the number now in existence – within the first two years of Governor Bush's administration:

- The loan guarantees will be made available to lenders who agree to finance charter school start-up or improvement costs, including the acquisition, lease and/or renovation of a facility, teacher training, and the purchase of equipment and instructional material.

- To leverage private equity, the fund will provide guarantees ranging from 75 to 100 percent, depending upon the amount of private equity the organizers raise (the greater the equity, the higher the guarantee).

- Priority will be given to schools in states with charter laws that promote high standards and accountability, allow parental involvement, permit principals to select and terminate teachers, and reward teachers on performance.

- The existing grant program will be maintained and administered in coordination with the loan guarantees.

Allow Federal Funds to Be Used for Choice in Education: The consolidation of federal ESEA funds into a handful of flexible categories will allow states and districts to use these funds to expand educational options for parents, including private school choice programs.

Expanding Education Savings Accounts

Information on school performance, and options such as charter schools, will stimulate competition. Yet, many parents still need additional resources to deal with the specific needs of their children. Whether their children attend pub-lic, private, religious, charter, or home schools, parents need funds to pay fees buy books and supplies, cover transportation costs, support after-school pro-grams, and pay for tutoring and special needs.

In principle, education savings accounts could empower parents, allowing parent-directed dollars to be applied to specific problems. However, the current education savings accounts – which permit parents to contribute $500 annual-ly and to withdraw those dollars tax free – can only be used to pay for college and other higher education expenses.

Unfortunately, President Clinton vetoed the Taxpayer Refund and Relief Act of 1999, which would have expanded the existing savings accounts by increas-ing the maximum annual contribution from $500 to $2,000, and by allowing the accounts to be used for expenses associated with K-12 education.

Therefore, to empower parents with additional education resources, as President, Governor Bush will:

Expand Education Savings Accounts: Allow families or individuals with incomes up to $150,000 (or single earners with annual incomes up to $95,000) to contribute up to $5,000 annually per child into Education Savings Accounts. Parents will be permitted to withdraw funds tax free (i.e., without being taxed on any gain or interest earned) to use for education-related purposes – from kindergarten to college and beyond – in public, private, religious, or home schools.

Education:
The True Goal of Education

Northern White Mountain Chamber of Commerce
Gorham, New Hampshire

November 2, 1999

It is a pleasure to be here, and to join in marking the chamber's Business Appreciation Month. New Hampshire is a state of small businesses. Many of them here in the North Country are prospering, and this organization has played an important part. I am honored by your invitation.

I am an optimist. I believe that the next century will be a time of incredible prosperity – if we can create an environment where entrepreneurs like you can dream and flourish. A prosperity sustained by low taxes, unleashed by lighter regulation, energized by new technologies, expanded by free trade. A prosperity beyond all our expectations, but within our grasp.

But this hope, in the long-run, depends directly on the education of our children – on young men and women with the skills and character to succeed. So, for the past few months, I have focused on the problems and promise of our public schools.

In September, I talked about disadvantaged children left behind by failed schools. The diminished hopes of our current system are sad and serious – the soft bigotry of low expectations. Schools that do not teach and will not change must have some final point of accountability. A moment of truth, when their federal funds, intended to help the poorest children, are divided up and given to parents – for tutoring or a charter school or some other hopeful option.

Last month, I talked about raising the academic ambitions of every public school in America – creating a culture of achievement. My plan lifts the burden of bureaucracy, and gives states unprecedented freedom in spending federal education dollars. In return for this flexibility, each state must adopt a system of real accountability and high standards. Students must be tested on the basics of reading and math each year – and those results posted, by school, on the Internet. This will give parents the information to know if education is actually taking place – and the leverage to demand reform.

My education proposals are bound by a thread of principle. The federal government must be humble enough to stay out of the day-to-day operation of local schools. It must be wise enough to give states and school districts more authority and freedom. And it must be strong enough to require proven performance in return. The federal role in education is to foster excellence and challenge failure with charters and choice. The federal role in education is not to serve the system. It is to serve the children.

Yet this is only part of an agenda. Yes, we want our children to be smart and successful. But even more, we want them to be good and kind and decent. Yes, our children must learn how to make a living. But even more, they must learn how to live, and what to love. "Intelligence is not enough," said Martin Luther King, Jr. "Intelligence plus character – that is the true goal of education."

So today, here in New Hampshire, I want to make the case for moral education. Teaching is more than training, and learning is more than literacy. Our children must be educated in reading and writing – but also in right and wrong.

Of course, every generation worries about the next. "Children today are tyrants," said one educator. "They contradict their parents, gobble their food, and tyrannize their teachers." And that teacher's name was...Socrates.

Some things don't change. The real problem comes, not when children challenge the rules, but when adults won't defend the rules. And for about three decades, many American schools surrendered this role. Values were "clarified," not taught. Students were given moral puzzles, not moral guidance. But morality is not a cafeteria of personal choices – with every choice equally right and equally arbitrary, like picking a flavor of ice cream. We do not shape our own morality. It is morality that shapes our lives.

Take an example. A Massachusetts teacher – a devoted supporter of values clarification – had a sixth grade class which announced that it valued cheating, and wanted the freedom to express that value during tests. Her response? "I personally value honesty," she said. "Although you may choose to be dishonest, I will insist that we be honest on our tests here. In other areas of your life, you may have to be dishonest."

This is not moral neutrality. It is moral surrender. Our schools should not cultivate confusion. They must cultivate conscience.

In spite of conflicting signals – and in spite of a popular culture that sometimes drowns their innocence – most of our kids are good kids. Large numbers do volunteer work. Nearly all believe in God, and most practice their faith. Teen pregnancy and violence are actually going down. Across America, under a program called True Love Waits, nearly a million teens have pledged themselves to abstain from sex until marriage. Our teenagers feel the pressures of complex times, but also the upward pull of a better nature. They deserve our love and they deserve our encouragement.

And sometimes they show character and courage beyond measure. When a gun is aimed at a seventeen-year-old in Colorado – and she is shot for refusing to betray her Lord. When a seventeen-year-old student, during a madman's attack on a Fort Worth church, is shot while shielding a friend with Down's Syndrome – and continues to comfort her, even after her own injury. We are finding, in the midst of tragedy, that our children can be heroes too.

Yet something is lost when the moral message of schools is mixed and muddled. Many children catch a virus of apathy and cynicism. They lose the ability to make confident judgments – viewing all matters of right and wrong as a matter of opinion. Something becomes frozen within them – a capacity for indignation and empathy. You can see it in shrugged shoulders. You can hear it in the watchword of a generation: "Whatever."

Academics like Professor Robert Simon report seeing many students – nice, well-intentioned young men and women – who refuse to make judgments even about the Holocaust. "Of course I dislike the Nazis," he quotes a student, "but who is to say they are morally wrong?"

At the extreme, in the case of a very few children – lawless, loveless and lonely – this confusion can harden into self-destruction or evil, suicide or violence. They find no elevating ideals – from parents or church or school – to counter the chaos in their souls. "We laugh at honor," said C.S. Lewis, "and are shocked to find traitors in our midst."

But something is changing in this country. Perhaps we have been sobered by tragedy. Perhaps the Baby Boom generation has won some wisdom from its failures and pain. But we are no longer laughing at honor. "Values clarification" seems like a passing superstition. Many states have instituted real character education in their schools, and many more are headed in that direction. After decades of drift, we are beginning a journey of renewal.

Above all, we are relearning a sense of idealism for our children. Parents and teachers are rediscovering a great calling and a heavy burden: to write on the slate of souls.

We must tell our children – with conviction and confidence – that the authors of the Holocaust were evil men, and the authors of the Constitution were good ones. That the right to life, liberty and the pursuit of happiness is not a personal opinion, but an eternal truth.

And we must tell our children – with clarity and certainty – that character gives direction to their gifts and dignity to their lives. That life is too grand and important to be wasted on whims and wants, on getting and keeping. That selfishness is a dark dungeon. That bigotry disfigures the heart. That they were made for better things and higher goals.

The shape of our society, the fate of our country, depends on young men and women who know these things. And we must teach them.

I know this begins with parents. And I know that is easy for a politician to say. Mark Twain once commented, "To do good is noble. To instruct others in doing good is just as noble, and much easier." But the message of our society must be clear. When a man or woman has a child, being a father or mother becomes their most important job in life. Not all teachers are parents, but all parents are teachers. Family is the first school of manners and morals. And the compass of conscience is usually the gift of a caring parent.

Yet parents should expect schools to be allies in the moral education of children. The lessons of the home must be reinforced by the standards of the school – standards of safety, discipline and decency.

Effective character education should not just be an hour a week on a school's virtue of the month. Effective character education is fostered in schools that have confidence in their own rules and values. Schools that set limits, enforce boundaries, teach high ideals, create habits of good conduct. Children take the values of the adult world seriously when adults take those values seriously.

And this goal sets an agenda for our nation.

First, we must do everything in our power to ensure the safety of our children. When children and teenagers go to school afraid of being bullied, or beaten, or worse, it is the ultimate betrayal of adult responsibility. It communicates the victory of moral chaos.

In an American school year there are more than 4,000 rapes or cases of sexual battery; 7,000 robberies; and 11,000 physical attacks involving a weapon. And these are overall numbers. For children attending inner-city schools, the likelihood of being a victim of violence is roughly five times greater than elsewhere. It is a sign of the times that the same security company used by the U.S. Mint and the FBI has now branched out into high school security.

Surveying this scene, it is easy to forget that there is actually a federal program designed to confront school violence. It's called the Safe and Drug-Free Schools and Communities Act. The program spends about $600 million a year, assisting 97 percent of the nation's school districts.

What's missing from the program is accountability. Nobody really knows how the money is spent, much less whether it is doing any good. One newspaper found that federal money had gone to pay for everything from motivational speakers to clowns to school puppet shows to junkets for school administrators.

As President, I will propose major changes in this program. Every school getting this funding will report their results – measured in student safety. Those results will be public. At schools that are persistently dangerous, students will be given a transfer to some other school – a safe school.

No parent in America – no matter their income – should be forced to send their child to a school where violence reigns. No child in America – regardless of background – should be forced to risk their lives in order to learn.

In the same way, it is a federal crime for a student to bring a gun into any public school. Yet this law has been almost completely ignored by federal prosecutors in recent years. Of some 3,900 violations reported between 1997 and 1998, only 13 were prosecuted. It is easy to propose laws. Sometimes it is easy to pass laws. But the measure of our seriousness is enforcing the law. And the safety of our children merits more than lip service.

Here is what I'll do. We will form a new partnership of the federal government and states – called Project Sentry. With some additional funding for prosecutors and the ATF, we can enforce the law and prosecute the violators: students who use guns illegally or bring guns to school, and adults who provide them. And for any juvenile found guilty of a serious gun offense, there will be a lifetime ban on carrying or purchasing a gun – any gun, for any reason, at any age, ever.

Tougher enforcement of gun laws will help to make our schools safer. But safety is not the only goal here. The excellence of a school is not just measured by declines in robbery, murder, and aggravated assault. Safety is the first and urgent step toward a second order of business – instilling in all of our public schools the virtues of discipline.

More than half of secondary-school teachers across the country say they have been threatened, or shouted at, or verbally abused by students. A teacher in Los Angeles describes her job as "nine-tenths policeman, one-tenth educational." And many schools, intimidated by the threat of lawsuits, have watered down their standards of behavior. In Oklahoma, a student who stabbed a principal with a nail was suspended for three days. In North Carolina, a student who broke her teacher's arm was suspended for only two days.

In too many cases, adults are in authority, but they are not in control.

To their credit, many schools are trying to reassert that control – only to find themselves in court. Generations of movies from "The Blackboard Jungle" to "Stand and Deliver" cast as their hero the teacher who dares to bring discipline to the classroom. But a modern version of this drama would have to include a new figure in the story – the lawyer.

Thirty-one percent of all high schools have faced lawsuits or out-of-court settlements in the past two years. This is seriously deterring discipline, and demands a serious response.

In school districts receiving federal school safety funds, we will expect a policy of zero-tolerance for persistently disruptive behavior. This means simply that teachers will have the authority to remove from their classroom any student who persists in being violent or unruly. Only with the teacher's consent will these students be allowed to return. The days of timid pleading and bargaining and legal haggling with disruptive students must be over. Learning must no longer be held hostage to the brazen behavior of a few.

Along with this measure, I will propose a Teacher Protection Act to free teachers, principals and school board members from meritless federal lawsuits when they enforce reasonable rules. School officials, acting in their official duties, must be shielded from liability. A lifetime dedicated to teaching must not be disrupted by a junk lawsuit. We do not need tort lawyers scouring the halls of our schools – turning every classroom dispute into a treasure hunt for damage awards.

Safety and discipline are essential. But when we dream for our children, we dream with higher goals. We want them to love learning. And we want them to be rich in character and blessed in ideals.

So our third goal is to encourage clear instruction in right and wrong. We want our schools to care about the character of our children.

I am not talking about schools promoting a particular set of religious beliefs. Strong values are shared by good people of different faiths, of varied backgrounds.

I am talking about communicating the values we share, in all our diversity. Respect. Responsibility. Self-restraint. Family commitment. Civic duty. Fairness. Compassion. The moral landmarks that guide a successful life.

There are a number of good programs around the country that show how values can be taught in a diverse nation. At St. Leonard's Elementary School in Maryland, children take a pledge each morning to be "respectful, responsible, and ready to learn." Character education is a theme throughout the curriculum – in writing, social studies and reading. And discipline referrals were down by 70 percent in one year. At Marion Intermediate School in South Carolina, virtues are taught by studying great historical figures and characters in literature. Consideration is encouraged, good manners are expected. And discipline referrals are down by half in one year.

The federal government now spends $8 million on promoting character education efforts. My Administration will triple that funding – money for states to train teachers and incorporate character lessons into daily coursework.

We will require federal youth and juvenile justice programs to incorporate an element of character building.

Our government must get its priorities straight when it comes to the character of our children. Right now, the Department of Health and Human Services spends far more on teen contraception than it does on teen abstinence. It takes the jaded view that children are nothing more than the sum of their drives, with no higher goal than hanging out and hooking up. We owe them better than this – and they are better than this. They ask for bread, and we give them a stone.

Abstinence programs show real promise – exactly because more and more teenagers understand that true love waits. My Administration will elevate abstinence education from an afterthought to an urgent goal. We should spend at least as much each year on promoting the conscience of our children as we do on providing them with contraception.

As well, we will encourage and expand the role of charities in after-school programs. Everyone agrees there is a problem in these empty, unsupervised hours after school. But those hours should not only be filled with sports and play, they should include lessons in responsibility and character. The federal government already funds after-school programs. But charities and faith-based organizations are prevented from participating. In my administration they will be invited to participate. Big Brothers/Big Sisters, the YMCA and local churches and synagogues and mosques should be a central part of voluntary, after-school programs.

Schools must never impose religion – but they must not oppose religion either. And the federal government should not be an enemy of voluntary expressions of faith by students.

Religious groups have a right to meet before and after school. Students have a right to say grace before meals, read their Bibles, wear Stars of David and crosses, and discuss religion with other willing students. Students have a right to express religious ideas in art and homework.

Public schools that forbid these forms of religious expression are confused. But more than that, they are rejecting some of the best and finest influences on young lives. It is noble when a young mind finds meaning and wisdom in the Talmud or Koran. It is good and hopeful when young men and women ask themselves what would Jesus do.

The measure of our nation's greatness has never been affluence or influence – rising stocks or advancing armies. It has always been found in citizens of character and compassion. And so many of our problems as a nation – from drugs, to deadly diseases, to crime – are not the result of chance, but of choice. They will only be solved by a transformation of the heart and will. This is why a hopeful and decent future is found in hopeful and decent children.

That hope, of course, is not created by an Executive Order or an Act of Congress. I strongly believe our schools should reinforce good character. I know that our laws will always reflect a moral vision. But there are limits to law, set at the boundaries of the heart. It has been said: "Men can make good laws, but laws can not make men good."

Yet a president has a broader influence and a deeper legacy than the programs he proposes. He is more than a bookkeeper or an engineer of policy. A president is the most visible symbol of a political system that Lincoln called "the last best hope of earth." The presidency, said Franklin Roosevelt, is "pre-eminently a place of moral leadership."

That is an awesome charge. It is the most sobering part of a decision to run for president. And it is a charge I plan to keep.

After power vanishes and pride passes, this is what remains: The promises we kept. The oath we fulfilled. The example we set. The honor we earned.

This is true of a president or a parent. Of a governor or a teacher. We are united in a common task: to give our children a spirit of moral courage. This is not a search for scapegoats – it is a call to conscience. It is not a hopeless task – it is the power and privilege of every generation. Every individual can change a corner of our culture. And every child is a new beginning.

In all the confusion and controversy of our time, there is still one answer for our children. An answer as current as the headlines. An answer as old as the scriptures. "Whatever is true, whatever is honorable, whatever is right, whatever is pure, whatever is lovely, whatever is of good repute, if there is any excellence and anything worthy of praise, let your mind dwell on these things."

If we love our children, this is the path of duty – and the way of hope.

Position Paper
Education: The True Goal of Education

November 2, 1999

"Yes, we want our children to be smart and success-ful. But even more, we want them to be good and kind and decent. Yes, our children must learn how to make a living. But even more, they must learn how to live, and what to love. 'Intelligence is not enough,' said Martin Luther King, Jr. 'Intelligence plus character – that is the true goal of education.'"

Governor George W. Bush

EXECUTIVE SUMMARY

Governor Bush has developed a comprehensive three-part education policy, based upon his success in Texas. First, he announced initiatives to close the achievement gap between disadvantaged children and their peers by making schools accountable for results. Schools receiving federal funds that do not teach and will not change will have their federal funds transferred directly to parents to use for tutoring, charter schools, or another option.

Second, Governor Bush has called for creating a "culture of achievement" for all students. His plan will grant states unprecedented freedom from federal regulation in exchange for establishing an accountability system that includes high standards and annual testing to measure performance. Competition would be fostered by empowering parents with information on school performance, and by providing alternatives, such as charter schools and expanded Education Savings Accounts.

The third and final part of Governor Bush's education policy involves initiatives aimed at promoting school safety, classroom discipline, and character development:

To Improve School Safety, Governor Bush will:

- Hold states and districts receiving federal School Safety funds accountable for measuring and demonstrating improved safety.

- Require states and districts to provide all students in persistently dangerous schools with the option of transferring to a safe school.

- Create a uniform system for reporting on school safety and publish the results widely.

- Establish "Project Sentry," a federal-state partnership to prosecute juveniles who bring guns to school or use them illegally, and adults who provide them.

- Ban for life serious juvenile offenders from ever purchasing or carrying a gun.

To Increase Classroom Discipline, Governor Bush will:

- Expect states and districts to establish a "zero tolerance" policy on disruption, empowering teachers to remove violent or persistently disruptive students.

- Enact the "Teacher Protection Act" to shield teachers, principals, and school board members from meritless lawsuits arising from their efforts to maintain discipline.

- Lift legal barriers to information sharing between schools and law enforcement agencies.

To Promote Character Development, Governor Bush will:

- Increase character education funding and incorporate character-building lessons into federal youth programs.

- Establish the "American Youth Character Awards" to honor acts of character.

- Increase federal funding for abstinence programs to a level at least as high as that provided for teen contraception programs.

- Expand the role of faith-based organizations and charities in after-school programs.

School Safety, Discipline and Character

Governor Bush believes that the campaign for excellence in education must be accompanied by a renewed emphasis on character development. He recognizes that moral education must begin at home. But parents have the right to expect schools to be allies in the education of virtue. The lessons of the home must be reinforced by the standards of the school. To meet this challenge, Governor Bush is proposing initiatives to:

- Improve the safety of every child in every public school in America.

- Instill in all our public schools the virtues of discipline, empowering teachers to enforce discipline in their classrooms.

- Promote and honor character development.

Improving the Safety of America's Public Schools

Ensuring School Safety

The Safe and Drug-Free Schools Program (SDFS) is the largest source of federal funding to schools for state and local drug and violence prevention programs. It has provided more than $6 billion to 97 percent of the nation's school districts since its inception in 1986. The program currently provides states and local school districts with $600 million annually.

Unfortunately, SDFS lacks a mechanism to ensure accountability. Indeed, a 1998 *Los Angeles Times* investigation reported that SDFS money has been used by school districts to buy fishing poles, hire magicians, and fund puppet plays.

A 1997 GAO report found that "no overall evaluations of the Safe and Drug-Free Schools Program have been completed." The GAO also concluded that the lack of a uniform method for reporting on school safety made it difficult to maintain federal oversight of the program. Not surprisingly, General Barry McCaffrey, Director of the Office of National Drug Control Policy, has criticized the program for doing little except "mail out checks."

Meanwhile, too many schools in America remain unsafe, too many teachers are threatened by violence, and too many children fear for their safety:

- An estimated three million crimes are committed every year in or near the nation's 85,000 public schools.

- One-fifth of public high schools and middle schools reported at least one violent crime in 1996-1997, the most recent year for which data are available.

- Between 1993 and 1997, teachers were victims of 1,771,000 non-fatal crimes at school, including 1,114,000 thefts and 657,000 violent crimes.

- A 1995 study found that one in three male students attending inner-city schools had been shot at, stabbed, or injured with a weapon at or in transit to school.

To ensure that federal school safety funds achieve results, as President, Governor Bush will:

Hold States and Districts Accountable for Improving School Safety: States and districts receiving School Safety funds will be required to establish standards of school safety and report on safety levels on a school-by-school basis.

Require States and Districts to Provide All Students in Persistently Dangerous Schools with a Transfer to a Safe Alternative: Local education agencies will be required within three years to offer all students in persistently dangerous schools a transfer to a safe public or charter school in the same, or a nearby, district. If no space can be found, the district must use its federal education funding to support a transfer to a private school.

Call for the Creation of a Uniform Reporting System: To allow parents to assess comparative school safety, the federal government will devise a systematic method for reporting and evaluating violence in schools. Data from schools will be widely and regularly disseminated to parents, including posting information on the Internet.

Enforcing Juvenile Gun Laws

The federal Youth Handgun Safety Act prohibits anyone under the age of 18 from buying or carrying a handgun. This law also makes it a federal offense to sell or transfer a handgun or ammunition to a minor. In addition, the Gun Free Schools Act requires school districts to expel students who bring a firearm to school.

Unfortunately, these laws have not been aggressively enforced. Indeed, there have been astonishingly few federal prosecutions of juveniles who possess guns, or of the adults who provide guns to juveniles. In fact, from 1997 to 1998:

- Only 11 juveniles were federally prosecuted for possessing a handgun or handgun ammunition.

- Only 13 students were prosecuted under federal law for possessing a firearm in a school zone, though 3,930 were expelled for doing so.

- And only 13 adults were prosecuted under federal law for transferring a handgun or ammunition to a juvenile.

Moreover, no federal law exists to prevent serious juvenile offenders from purchasing or carrying a gun once they become adults. In contrast, adults convicted of a felony are prevented by law from ever again purchasing or carrying a gun in their lifetime.

Governor Bush has already called for more vigorous prosecution of gun offenses. In addition, to deter juveniles from illegally possessing guns and bringing them into schools, and to prosecute adults who provide guns to juveniles, Governor Bush will:

Establish "Project Sentry" to Enforce Federal Juvenile Gun Laws: This federal-state partnership will provide additional funding for state and federal law enforcement to establish local "Safe School Task Forces." These task forces will identify and appropriately prosecute, punish, and supervise juveniles who violate state and federal firearms laws. Each U.S. Attorney's Office would be required to dedicate one federal prosecutor as a "Project Sentry" Coordinator, to ensure juvenile offenders who pose a threat to fellow students are appropriately punished and deterred. The program will also make it a priority to increase prosecutions of gun dealers and adults who illegally purchase guns for juveniles, or who contribute to a person under 18 committing a crime of violence involving a gun.

Impose a Lifetime Ban on Gun Possession for Juvenile Offenders: Any person under the age of 18, who is found guilty of a serious gun or violent offense, will be banned for life from purchasing or carrying a gun.

Enforcing Discipline and Restoring Authority to Teachers

If schools are to set high standards of achievement for students, they must be able to maintain discipline within their classrooms. Persistently disruptive students detract from time that should be spent instructing others. Yet too many schools in America do not enforce codes of discipline, and teachers and principals are finding it increasingly difficult to maintain order because of legal constraints.

School districts are required by federal law to establish a zero tolerance policy for students that bring guns to school. Almost 80 percent of schools have chosen to establish zero tolerance policies for violence and tobacco use. However, not all schools have a zero tolerance policy for disruptive behavior, allowing teachers to remove from the classroom students who persistently disrupt class. As a result:

- Five out of six principals polled in 1997 said they spent too much time dealing with disruptive students.

- Sixty-five percent of public school teachers charge that discipline is a "serious" problem in their schools.

- Eighty-eight percent of teachers think that academic achievement would improve "substantially" if persistent troublemakers were removed from classes.

The problem of enforcing discipline has been compounded by the increasing incidence of lawsuits:

- In the last two years alone, almost one-third of all high school principals reported being involved in lawsuits or out-of-court settlements, versus only 9 percent ten years ago.

- Twenty percent of high school and middle school principals report spending 5-10 hours per week in activities to avoid litigation; six percent report spending as much as 10-20 hours a week doing the same.

- Ninety-nine percent of principals say their policy on reporting bad behavior has been modified because of liability costs and concerns.

Finally, federal laws that inhibit the appropriate exchange of information between school officials and local law enforcement officers make it difficult to take effective action against troublesome or violent students. In particular, schools are often unable to provide local law enforcement authorities with information that may help them prosecute a case because federal law severely restricts the circumstances under which such information can be shared.

As President, in order to empower teachers and principals to maintain discipline in the classroom, Governor Bush will:

Remove Barriers to Information Sharing Between Schools and Law Enforcement Authorities: As President, Governor Bush will propose changing federal law to make it easier for public school districts and local law enforcement authorities to share information regarding disciplinary actions and misconduct by students.

Require "Zero Tolerance" Policies for Violence and Persistent Misbehavior: States and districts that receive School Safety funds will be required to impose zero tolerance policies in all schools. While states and districts would be free to design their own policies, at a minimum they will be required to give teachers the authority to remove from the classroom students who engage in violence or persistent misbehavior. These students will be permitted to return to class only with the teacher's consent.

Enact the "Teacher Protection Act": The Teacher Protection Act will shield teachers, principals, and school board members acting in their official capacity from federal liability arising out of efforts to maintain discipline in the classroom, so long as they do not engage in reckless or criminal misconduct. Plaintiffs who bring meritless claims in federal court challenging teacher and principal disciplinary actions would be liable for attorneys' fees, incurred in the defense of the teachers and principals.

Encouraging Character Development and Moral Education

Character Education

Character education promotes the moral development of students by teaching universal virtues. Research indicates that character education can help improve behavior and academic achievement:

- A University of Illinois study of four schools using the "Positive Action" character development program found that the average number of incidents requiring disciplinary referral dropped by 74 percent after one year, and achievement scores improved by an average of 28 percentage points.

- Standardized test scores of students exposed to the "Responsive Classroom" program, which emphasizes good character, increased 22 percent on average, versus just three percent for students not participating in the program.

Though character education has traditionally been a component of American education, the number of schools teaching it has increased over the past few years. More than 70 percent of states support character education through federally funded pilot programs or legislative measures. However, federal funding for character development programs totaled about $8 million in grants for states or districts in FY 1999. In addition, federal regulations limit to 10 the number of states that can receive grants each year.

To encourage the adoption of character education in schools and in federal programs for students, Governor Bush will:

Increase Character Education Funding: As President, Governor Bush will increase funding for character education grants from $8 million to $25 million. These grants will be available to states and districts to train teachers how to incorporate character-building lessons and activities in student coursework. In awarding these grants, preference will be given to programs that contain accountability measures (i.e., that monitor a reduction in specific indicators such as cheating or thefts). In addition, he proposes removing the cap on the number of states that can receive character education funding.

Incorporate Character-Building Lessons into Federal Youth Programs: Appropriate federal programs affecting young people, including juvenile justice programs, will be required to teach character education to ensure that children in these programs are learning the importance of modeling good character.

Establish the "American Youth Character Awards" and Rally Support for Character Education: Students who distinguish themselves by acts of character will receive recognition through a presidential certificate. These awards will serve as a focal point for rallying faith-based organizations, youth-serving agencies and America's parents in an effort to restore traditional values in America's young people.

Abstinence Education

Numerous nationally recognized studies indicate that abstinence education works not only to reduce teen pregnancy and sexually transmitted diseases, but also to develop good character in young adults. Federal grants are available to establish abstinence programs in schools and community organizations throughout the country. However, the federal government spends twice as much on teen contraception programs (approximately $135 million per year through Title X, Medicaid, and the Adolescent Family Life program) as it does on abstinence education (approximately $62 million per year through Title V and Title XX).

Therefore, to emphasize the importance of character building through abstinence education, Governor Bush will:

Substantially Increase Funding for Abstinence Education: As President, Governor Bush will increase federal funding for abstinence education to a level at least as high as that provided for teen contraception programs.

After-School Programs

Studies indicate after-school programs help reduce drug use, teen pregnancy, and criminal behavior by providing supervised activities during the peak hours for juvenile crime. Many after-school programs, particularly those run by faith-based and community organizations, also incorporate character education into their curriculum.

Unfortunately, federal after-school programs tend to discourage the participation of faith-based groups and other community organizations. For example, the 21st Century Community Learning Centers program, which is one of the largest federal sources of funding for after-school activities, only schools are eligible to compete for funds. The Administration has recently proposed opening just 10 percent of the program's funding to competitive bidding.

In contrast, to encourage more after-school programs, Governor Bush will:

Open the Entire 21st Century Program to Competition: Governor Bush will introduce legislation to open 100 percent of the 21st Century program's funding to competitive bidding. This will allow youth development groups, local charities, churches, synagogues, mosques and other community and faith-based organizations to compete for these federal funds on an equal footing with schools. Preference will be given to partnerships between schools and these groups.

Fund New After-School Programs Using Certificates: Governor Bush will empower lower-income parents by providing certificates to help defray the cost of after-school activities of their choosing – whether run by a community group, a neighborhood church, or a local school. An additional $400 million a year will be added to the Child Care Development Block Grant to the states to help 500,000 low-income parents pay for an after-school program of their choice.

THE TEXAS EDUCATION RECORD

Governor Bush has made education his number one priority, both in focus and in funding. Working with the Legislature, he enacted key reforms based on three fundamental principles: local control, limited government and accountability for student performance and achievement.

Principles of Reform

Local Control

Governor Bush believes in aligning authority and responsibility at the local level. Power at the local level discourages excuses for failure and encourages accountability and enhanced student performance.

Limited Government

Governor Bush believes the state's role in education should be limited to setting measurable goals and then holding school districts accountable for achieving those goals. Today, Texas has four clear goals: excellence in math, science, English and social studies.

Accountability

Under Governor Bush's leadership, Texas has strengthened its accountability system into one of the nation's toughest. Texas now sets goals at the state level and rates individual campuses based on their ability to meet or exceed those goals.

Record of Success

Under Governor Bush, student achievement has improved dramatically, and teacher quality ranks first in the nation:

- Greatest Progress in the Nation: Texas is one of two states that has made the greatest recent progress in education, according to the National Education Goals Panel.

- Minority Students Rank Highest in Math: On the 1996 National Assessment of Education Progress (NAEP) in Mathematics, African-

American fourth-graders in Texas ranked first in the nation among African-American fourth-graders. Since 1992, African-American fourth-graders in Texas have made the greatest gains in math, and Hispanic fourth-graders have made the second greatest gains.

• <u>Students Score First and Second in Writing</u>: On the 1998 NAEP Writing Exam, African-American and Hispanic eighth-graders in Texas ranked first and second in the nation. Texas eighth-graders as a whole ranked fourth in the nation.

• <u>Students Improve Every Year on State Skills Test</u>: Under Governor Bush, the number of students passing all parts of the Texas Assessment of Academic Skills (TAAS) increased by 51 percent. The number of both minority students and economically disadvantaged students passing all parts of the TAAS increased by 89 percent.

• <u>First in Teacher Quality</u>: Texas ranked first in the nation in teacher quality, according to an independent evaluation by the Fordham Foundation.

Accomplishments

Governor Bush and the Texas Legislature have enacted a series of reforms to establish clear goals, return power to local communities and hold local school districts accountable for educating the children of Texas. Highlights:

• <u>Increased Funding for Education</u>: Texas has increased state funding for public schools by $8.3 billion, representing 56 percent of state spending increases during Governor Bush's tenure. State funding per pupil has increased 37 percent, and the state's financial commitment is making it possible for districts to build more than $5 billion worth of new classrooms in Texas.

• <u>Toughened the Texas Accountability System</u>: Under Governor Bush's leadership, Texas has developed its accountability system into one of the nation's strongest and most comprehensive to ensure that no child is left behind.

• <u>Insisted on Local Control</u>: In 1995, Governor Bush signed a new Education Code that decentralized public education and restored local control to schools.

• <u>Ended Social Promotion</u>: Governor Bush campaigned for and signed legislation ending social promotion in Texas' public schools. The initiative will help teachers identify and help students who have trouble learning in the earliest grades – when learning problems are easier to fix.

• <u>Implemented the Governor's Reading Initiative</u>: At Governor Bush's urging, the Legislature appropriated $82 million over a four-year period to help fund reading academies in Texas schools.

• <u>Promoted Early Childhood Education</u>: Under Governor Bush, Texas has made the largest investment in early childhood education in Texas history. The legislature appropriated $200 million for early education programs for low-income preschoolers, and $17 million to improve reading-readiness and Head Start – the first Texas investment ever in Head Start.

• <u>Offered Choice in Public Education</u>: The Texas Legislature, with the support of Governor Bush, authorized the creation of open-enrollment charter schools, including schools for "at-risk" youth. There are currently 168 charter schools approved in Texas.

• <u>Increased Teacher Pay</u>: The minimum salary for teachers increased 33 percent during Governor Bush's term in office, resulting in an average salary increase of $8,232.

Promoting School Safety and Character Education

In addition to improving students' achievement, Governor Bush's reforms have also promoted school safety and character education. Specifically, he has:

• <u>Created a Zero-Tolerance Policy for Bad Behavior in Texas Classrooms</u>: In 1995, Governor Bush signed the Safe Schools Act which created two new programs for disruptive students:

  • Juvenile Justice Alternative Education Programs (JJAEP), which serve expelled students who commit serious or violent offenses in counties with a population of 72,000 or more. Under the program, local juvenile justice boards operate the JJAEPs with guidance from local school districts.

  • Disciplinary Alternative Education Programs (DAEP), which serve students in all school districts who are removed from their regular classroom due to disruptive behavior or for committing felonies off campus. DAEPs may be located on or off campus.

- <u>Supported the Right Choices Initiative</u>: Governor Bush's "Lone Star Leaders" initiative focuses on key areas proven to boost kids' chances of making the right choices: (1) parental/family connectedness; (2) mentoring; (3) citizenship/character education; (4) abstinence; and (5) after-school programs.

- <u>Lone Star Kids of Character Initiative</u>: On October 22, 1999, Governor Bush awarded $900,000 in funding over a two-year period to support a character-building initiative for Texas schoolchildren. The initiative will be one of the largest and most comprehensive character development programs in the nation, providing practical tools to parents, educators, coaches, community and youth organization leaders, and others who want to instill strong character in young people.

Position Paper
Education: Reading First

March 28, 2000

> *"We have a national emergency. Too many of our children cannot read. Reading is the building block, and it must be the foundation, for education reform. That is why I will commit my Administration and the nation to the ambitious goal of ensuring that every disadvantaged child can read by the third grade."*
>
> *Governor George W. Bush*

EXECUTIVE SUMMARY

Governor Bush considers reading to be the gateway to all learning. Unfortunately, 68 percent of fourth-graders in America's poorest schools could not read at basic level in 1998. This tragedy is compounded by the fact that research has identified effective solutions to the literacy problem.

As President, Governor Bush will Commit His Administration and the Nation to the Ambitious Goal of Ensuring that Every Disadvantaged Child Can Read by the Third Grade. Specifically, He will:

- Establish the "Reading First" program to invest $5 billion over five years to conquer illiteracy among disadvantaged children.

- Reform Head Start by moving it to the Department of Education and refocusing it on its original purpose: early learning and pre-reading skills.

★　★　★

The Gateway to Learning

Governor Bush believes that reading is the gateway to all learning. He considers it a national tragedy that a majority of low-income fourth graders cannot read at grade level:

- In the highest-poverty schools, 68 percent of fourth-graders could not read at basic level in 1998, as measured by the National Assessment of Education Progress (NAEP) reading exam. In low-poverty schools, by contrast, more than three-quarters of fourth graders read at or above the basic level.

- The 1992 National Survey of Adult Literacy discovered that some 90 million Americans – nearly half the adult population – have severely limited literacy skills.

This situation is made even more tragic by the fact that research has identified effective solutions to the literacy problem. Indeed, recent studies conducted by the National Institute of Child Health and Human Development (NICHD), conclude that:

- Effective reading instruction involves a balanced approach, which includes explicit instruction in phonics and phonological awareness.

- An emphasis on phonics-based instruction is particularly important for disadvantaged children and others at risk for reading failure.

Success in Texas

Governor Bush put these solutions to work in Texas by setting a clear goal, providing flexible funding to local school districts, and by demanding results. Specifically, in January 1996, he set an ambitious goal: every Texas child must learn to read at grade level or better by the end of third grade, and continue to read at grade level or better throughout his or her schooling.

To help schools achieve this goal, Governor Bush and Texas leaders in 1997 gave educators the tools they need to improve reading performance:

- A rigorous, research-based core reading curriculum that is phonics-driven and emphasizes a back-to-basics approach.

- A new diagnostic tool, the *Texas Primary Reading Inventory*, to help K-2 teachers detect and correct reading problems early.

- New funding totaling $82 million over a four-year period to support "Reading Academies" – intensive schools-within-schools to teach reading programs that work.

- Training for teachers, involving more than 90 percent of Texas kindergarten teachers in an intensive summer training program.

- A commitment of more than $200 million for reading intervention programs – after-school, summer school, or in-school reading instruction.

As a result of these reforms, the percentage of third graders passing the Texas state skills test in reading increased by 13 percent in only two years. For low-income third graders, the passing rate improved by nearly 20 percent.

"Reading First" Initiative

Governor Bush believes that this model can work in local school districts nationwide. As President, he will commit his administration and the nation to the ambitious goal of ensuring that every disadvantaged child can read by the third grade. Others have announced similar goals, but they propose resources without reform.

Under Governor Bush's plan, new federal resources must be an instrument of reform, not another investment in failure. That is why he has proposed a comprehensive education reform plan that sets high standards and demands results in federal education programs, particularly those that serve disadvantaged students. His plan includes reforming Head Start by moving it to the Department of Education and returning it to its original purpose – early learning and pre-reading skills.

Reforming Head Start is the first step in fighting illiteracy. In addition, to ensure that every child has the best possible start toward the American Dream, Governor Bush will:

Establish the "Reading First" Program to Invest $5 Billion over Five Years to Conquer Illiteracy Among Disadvantaged Children: Governor Bush will increase federal funding to disadvantaged students by creating a $5 billion incentive fund for states to teach every child to read by third grade. States that choose to draw from this fund will be required to initiate the following:

- A reading diagnostic for students in K-2 to determine where students need help.

- A reading curriculum that includes elements based on the recent findings of the National Institute of Child Health and Human Development (NICHD) research on reading.

- Training for K-2 teachers in reading preparation.
- Reading intervention for K-2 students who are not reading at grade level.
- Ongoing state reading assessment for students in grades 3-8 linked to the state accountability system.

Education:
Strong Teachers, Strong Schools

Fritsche Middle School
Milwaukee, Wisconsin

March 30, 2000

Two days ago, in Virginia, I gave a speech on education. And I made the case, as I always do, for accountability. All true education reform insists on high goals for schools and high expectations for children. All true education reform measures results, praises success and confronts failure. Parents must know if learning is taking place. Teachers must know when students need help. Districts must know if the curriculum is working.

Accountability is the beginning of education reform – but it is not the end. Students, of every background, must be challenged by high standards. But they must also be prepared to meet them. And they will never be prepared if they cannot read. Reading is what turns a child into a student – the skill that makes all other skills possible.

And here we have a genuine national crisis. In the highest poverty schools, 68 percent of fourth graders could not read at basic level in 1998. In the last 15 years, 15 million students have graduated from high school without being able to read at basic level. More and more, we are divided into two nations. One that reads, and one that can't. One that dreams, and one that doesn't.

The problem of illiteracy is national in its impact. It requires a response national in reach.

So I have set a goal: Every American child will read by the end

of the third grade. And I have proposed a measure called Reading
First.

Reading First is a concentrated, systematic approach that
identifies early reading problems and gets children the best possible
help. It includes diagnostic tests to identify early reading challenges
in K-2. A curriculum based on sound research, including phonics.
Intensive training for teachers of early grades. And intervention to
give extra help to those having trouble reading, including summer
school and after school programs.

The message of Reading First is simple: We are going to have
high standards. But we are going to prepare children to meet those
standards. Accountability is not sink-or-swim. We want them to
succeed, and we will take practical steps so everyone enters the
accountability system on an equal footing. So that every third grad-
er has an equal chance.

Today, I want to make one additional point, and propose some
additional measures. Education reform depends on accountability.
Educational success depends on early reading. But all of this eventually depends on skilled teachers. Teachers with the commitment,
the training, the focus, the authority, and the freedom to challenge
their students and change their lives.

We trust teachers with the minds of our children. We should
also treat them like the professionals they are. This means professional development – giving them the best skills. And it means better pay and working conditions. This has been our goal in Texas.
We have increased teacher pay by an average of $8,000. We have
improved the teacher retirement system. We passed a zero tolerance law, giving teachers more control in the classroom. And we
have set high professional expectations for teachers, requiring them
to know their field.

Any movement of accountability should not just be a series of
demands on schools and teachers. It must be a partnership in a
common enterprise. As we ask more of teachers, we must do more

to help them.

My Administration will do so. And today I want to announce a four-point plan called "Strong Teachers, Strong Schools," designed to improve education by supporting our nation's teachers.

First, we will increase the opportunities for skilled men and women to enter the teaching profession. We have wonderful teachers, but many able, well-qualified people are barred from the profession because they don't have the time or money to get an education degree. This is a loss, for them and for the schools.

I intend to reinvigorate the "Troops to Teachers" program – bringing its budget from $2.4 million to $30 million. This program recruits talented, retired military personnel for teaching positions where the need is greatest. As Senator John McCain has often pointed out, these are men and women who have served their country, and want to do more for the next generation. They don't need two or three years of study to be qualified. They're ready to teach, and "Troops to Teachers" gives them that chance.

Second, we will expand the training opportunities for teachers.

In a way, every good teacher is still a student. Many teachers would like to study further in their fields. And reforms that raise standards often require new skills. To support this professional development, we will make $400 million in new money available for teacher training. In return for this funding, we will expect states to have high professional standards for their teachers.

Third, we will support teachers who enforce discipline in the classroom. Many teachers are wary of imposing discipline because they might be sued. In the last two years, 31 percent of all high schools have faced lawsuits or out-of-court settlements.

We're going to take litigation out of the learning process. I have proposed a Teacher Protection Act to free teachers from meritless lawsuits when they enforce reasonable rules. A lifetime dedicated to teaching should not be disrupted by a junk lawsuit.

In some schools, discipline problems are a serious roadblock to learning. Between 1993 and 1997, more than 1.7 million crimes were committed against teachers at school. Of these, more than a third were violent crimes. Some 88 percent of teachers believe that academic achievement would improve "substantially" in their schools if persistent troublemakers could be removed from class.

This is one area where teachers simply need more authority, and we will give it to them. In every school getting federal school safety funds, there will be a policy of zero tolerance for disruptive behavior. Teachers may remove any student who persists in being violent or unruly or disrespectful. And only when the teacher consents will they be allowed to return. Learning must no longer be held hostage to the brazen behavior of the few.

Fourth, we will treat teachers with more fairness. Every year, teachers spend an average of $400 of their own money to buy supplies needed in the classroom. But unlike, say, a business owner, they can't deduct those expenses from their taxes. We will change this, and allow teachers to deduct up to $400 a year for these out-of-pocket expenses.

These are some ways we can take the side of teachers. Making sure they are well-prepared, in control of their classrooms, protected from harassment, and treated more fairly. Education reform is empty if it does not take account of the needs of educators. Teachers are not the object of education reform, they are the engine of education reform. They have a high calling, and we must respect it.

One of my predecessors as governor was Sam Houston, who led an extraordinary life. He was a frontiersman, military officer, a U.S. senator, a governor of two states, even a president – back when Texas was independent. Before all this, he had been a teacher. And when it was all behind him, he observed that no office he had ever held, no honor he had ever earned, had given him greater satisfaction than being a teacher.

The teaching profession is still a great mission. And it can still bring great rewards. I will be a president who honors teachers in word and in law.

Position Paper
Education: Strong Teachers, Strong Schools

March 30, 2000

"Education reform is empty if it does not take account of the needs of educators. Teachers are not the object of education reform, they are the engine of education reform. They have a high calling, and we must respect it. As we ask more of teachers, we must do more to help them. My Administration will do so."

Governor George W. Bush

EXECUTIVE SUMMARY

Governor Bush believes that true education reform requires both local control and accountability. Thus, he is proposing an entirely new federal approach to education, granting states and local schools unprecedented freedom from regulation – in exchange for results.

But accountability should not merely place demands on schools and teachers. Rather, Governor Bush believes it should be a partnership: as government asks more of teachers, it should do more for teachers.

To Ensure Teachers Have the Commitment, the Training, the Authority, and the Freedom to Challenge their Students, Governor Bush Proposes a $2.9 Billion, Four-Point Plan Called "Strong Teachers, Strong Schools," which will:

- Increase funding for the Troops-to-Teachers program to help place additional, highly qualified teachers in the classroom.

- Combine existing and new funding into a flexible $2.4 billion grant program for teacher training and recruiting.

86

- Help teachers enforce discipline by requiring a "zero tolerance" policy on disruption and enact the Teacher Protection Act to shield teachers from meritless lawsuits.

- Establish a teacher tax deduction to help defray out-of-pocket classroom expenses.

Increasing Opportunities for Professionals to Become Teachers

Despite the fact that as many as two million new teachers may be needed in the next decade, many skilled individuals are prevented from entering the teaching profession because they do not have the time or resources to get a formal education degree or teaching certification. The Troops-to-Teachers program was designed in 1993 as a partial response to this problem, facilitating the placement of qualified military personnel in classrooms across the country by matching them with school districts that need more instructors, and by providing a stipend as they undergo training and certification.

A 1998 National Center for Education Information study found that more than 60 percent of Troops-to-Teachers participants were rated by administrators as "among the best," "well above average," or "above average." However, funding for the program has dropped from $65 million in its first year to only $2.4 million today.

Therefore, to increase opportunities for dedicated men and women who have served in the military to become teachers in underserved schools, Governor Bush will:

Increase Funding for the Troops-to-Teachers Program: As President, Governor Bush will increase funding for the Troops-to-Teachers program from $2.4 million to $30 million to help place additional highly qualified instructors in the classroom.

Expanding Training Opportunities for Teachers

Teachers will need new skills as educational reforms raise standards of achievement for students. However, while many teachers would like to pursue further studies in their fields, they lack the resources to do so. Many other teachers are not receiving the training they need to teach students in their designated subject areas. Indeed, so-called "out-of-field" teaching is becoming more the rule than the exception in certain areas:

- More than half of public school history teachers have neither a major nor a minor in history; similarly, more than half of the nation's public school physical science teachers neither majored nor minored in any of the physical sciences.

- Out-of-field teaching is particularly noticeable in high-poverty areas, where an estimated 43 percent of math instructors are teaching out-of-field, versus 27 percent of those teaching in low-poverty schools.

Unfortunately, under the current regime, states do not have the flexibility to use federal funds to address their specific teacher training, recruiting and hiring needs. Federal funding for teacher training remains modest, with $338 million in the Eisenhower Professional Development Grant Program. States also receive nearly $500 million through the Goals 2000 program, which has failed to realize its goal of improving teaching and professional development, and $1.2 billion in class size reduction money, of which only 25 percent can be used for teacher training.

Therefore, to increase flexibility for states to address their specific teacher training and recruiting needs, as President, Governor Bush will:

<u>Combine Existing and New Funding into a Flexible $2.4 Billion Grant Program for Teacher Training and Recruiting</u>: Existing federal funds for professional development, class size reduction, and the Goals 2000 program will be combined with $400 million of new money into a single, flexible $2.4 billion grant program to streamline certification, recruit and train teachers in their subject areas, and meet the specific needs of individual states. In return, states will be required to:

- Establish a teacher accountability system, which could include such measures as value-added assessment of teachers based on student results, differential pay, and subject-specific teacher testing.

- Help teachers master methods of instruction that have been shown to boost student achievement.

Supporting Teachers Who Enforce Classroom Discipline

Research confirms that teachers have a tremendous impact on student achievement, particularly for low-income students. Yet, in too many cases, teachers are not working in an environment conducive to learning. Violence is a threat for some, while others lack the authority they need to maintain discipline in the classroom.

Between 1993 and 1997, teachers were victims of 1,771,000 non-fatal crimes at school, including 1,114,000 thefts and 657,000 violent crimes. Nearly 65 percent of public school teachers charge that discipline is a "serious" problem in their schools, and about 88 percent think that academic achievement would improve "substantially" if persistent troublemakers were removed from classes.

The problem of enforcing discipline has been compounded by the increasing incidence of lawsuits. In the last two years alone, almost one-third of all high school principals reported being involved in lawsuits or out-of-court settlements, compared with only 9 percent ten years ago. And 99 percent of principals say their policy on reporting bad behavior has been modified because of liability costs and concerns.

Thus, to help teachers enforce discipline and shield them from meritless lawsuits, Governor Bush will:

Require "Zero Tolerance" Policies for Violence and Persistent Misbehavior: States and districts that receive federal school safety funds will be required to impose zero tolerance policies in all schools. While they will be free to design their own policies, at a minimum they will be required to give teachers the authority to remove from the classroom students who engage in violence or persistent misbehavior; these students will be permitted to return to class only with the teacher's consent.

Enact the "Teacher Protection Act" to Shield Teachers from Meritless Lawsuits: The "Teacher Protection Act" will shield teachers, principals, and school board members acting in their official capacity from federal liability arising out of their efforts to maintain discipline in the classroom, as long as they do not engage in reckless or criminal misconduct.

Treating Teachers More Fairly

Lastly, many teachers find it difficult to do their jobs because they lack the necessary courseware material, and/or supplies. Indeed, the National Education

Association estimates that the average teacher spends $400 a year of his or her own money on classroom materials needed for education. However, unlike business owners who are able to deduct business expenses, teachers who pay out-of-pocket for classroom supplies, training courses, or school-related activities lack the benefit of a corresponding tax deduction.

Therefore, in order to treat teachers more fairly, Governor Bush will:

<u>Establish a Teacher Tax Deduction to Help Defray Out-of-Pocket Classroom Expenses</u>: A new deduction will be established to cover expenses such as books, school supplies, professional enrichment programs and other training. All teachers would be able to deduct up to $400 of these expenses on their federal tax return, recouping a portion of their personal expenditures.

Position Paper
Education: Enhancing Education Through Technology
June 19, 2000

"We can harness technology to help close the achieve-ment gap, but technology alone cannot make children learn. Behind every wire and machine must be a teacher and a student who know how to use that tech-nology to help develop a child's mind, skills and charac-ter."

Governor George W. Bush

EXECUTIVE SUMMARY

Governor Bush believes that technology must be harnessed to close the educational achievement gap between disadvantaged students and their peers. However, the current federal investment in education technology neither demands accountability, nor provides flexibility to spur innovation. Thus, while many schools have been wired and equipped, too little attention has been paid to how technology can help children learn, too few teachers have been trained to use technology, and too little authority has been given to schools to meet their technology needs.

The real divide is in educational achievement, not just digital access. Technology is a tool, and the goal must be improved student performance. To achieve that goal, Governor Bush is proposing a set of reforms totaling $400 million over five years.

To Provide Schools Maximum Flexibility in Using Federal Education Technology Funds to Help Close the Achievement Gap, Governor Bush will:

- Establish a $3 billion "Enhancing Education through Technology Fund" by consolidating the FCC's Schools and Libraries program with eight Department of Education technology programs.

- Free states and schools from federal regulations to allow maximum flexibility in using federal funds for such purposes as teacher training, software purchase and development, and system integration.

- Continue to give priority to rural schools and schools serving high percentages of low-income students.

To Provide Schools More Information About the Uses of Technology for Improving Student Performance, Governor Bush will:

- Provide $65 million annually to the Department of Education's Office of Education Research and Improvement for universities and other research institutions to conduct research on which methods of education technology boost student achievement.

- Provide $15 million annually to establish the "Education and Technology Clearinghouse" to make available to schools and states information on effective education technology programs, best practices, and the latest research studies.

To Ensure Accountability in the Use of Federal Education Technology Funds, Governor Bush will:

- Require states to establish accountability measures for how education technology funds improve student achievement.

The Promise of Education Technology

"Education technology" generally refers to the use of computers and related equipment in schools. Used properly, technology offers the promise of individualized learning, provides access to rich reservoirs of information, and facilitates communication among students, teachers, parents and experts. For example, such technology is often used to drill students on particular skills and allow parents to monitor their child's progress from home; to create links with sister schools around the globe; and to enable simulations of math and science concepts.

Such applications can be a powerful means of boosting student achievement. In a 1999 study, the Princeton, New Jersey-based Educational Testing Service (ETS) found that eighth graders whose teachers used computers for "simulations and applications" performed better on the National Assessment of Education Progress (NAEP) exam than students whose teachers did not. Moreover, fourth and eighth-grade students whose teachers had received professional development in the use of education technology outperformed students whose teachers did not have such training.

Failings of the Federal Investment in Education Technology

The federal government invests approximately $3 billion in education technology through a wide range of programs. Among these is the Federal Communication Commission's (FCC) $2.25 billion Schools and Libraries ("E-Rate") program, which helps provide affordable access to advanced telecommunications services for all eligible schools and libraries in the United States.

The Department of Education currently spends over $730 million on eight programs under Title III of the Elementary and Secondary Education Act. These programs include: the Technology Literacy Challenge Fund, the Technology Innovation Challenge Grants, Star Schools, Software Development Program, Preparing Tomorrow's Teachers, Community Technology Centers, the Secretary Leadership Fund, and the Middle Schools Teacher Training Program.

These programs have sped the deployment of computer hardware and Internet access to our nation's schools: in 1994, only 35 percent of public schools had Internet access, by 1999, 95 percent of such schools did.

Lack of Focus on Results

It is far from clear, however, whether the federal investment in education technology is actually having an impact on student achievement. One reason for this is that the current administration tends to base success on how many computers are in the schools or how many classrooms are wired. A 21st Century Project study, "Federal Support for Technology in K-12 Education," stated: "[t]he benchmark set by President Clinton for getting a computer and an Internet connection into every classroom in the U.S. has no rational basis. It is mostly a political pledge, a slogan...." Similarly, the 1999 ETS study stated, "The purpose of providing technology to schools is to improve student academic performance and other educational outcomes, not to provide state-of-the-art equipment for its own sake."

Lack of Adequate Teacher Training

The ETS study also recommended that federal policymakers increase their efforts to ensure that teachers are properly trained to use computers and target teacher training efforts at high-poverty urban and rural schools. While spending on technology has increased 25 percent over the previous year, investment in teacher training has increased just 5 percent. According to another report, "the vast majority of K-12 teachers are novice or completely inexperienced Internet and computer users." The National Center of Education Statistics reports that only 20 percent of America's teachers feel prepared to use new computer applications and know how to integrate them into their classrooms.

High Administrative Costs and Inflexible Rules

In addition, the federal effort in education technology is balkanized, inflexible and administratively burdensome. If a school wants to receive funding for software development, it must fill out an application for the Software Development Program. If, instead, a school wants to receive funding for teacher training, it must fill out a separate application for the Middle Schools Teacher Training program.

The inflexible rules of the Schools and Libraries program are particularly onerous:

- The catalog of eligible equipment that can be purchased with E-rate funds is 36 pages long.

- The E-rate application and instructions are an additional 56 pages and take hundreds of hours to complete. Last year, the firm that distributes E-rate funds conducted two-day "regional training sessions" in seven cities, dedicated solely to teaching school administrators how to fill out these forms.

- The E-rate program requires more training to fill out federal forms than many schools provide in technology training for their teachers.

Furthermore, schools are being punished for minor technical errors. For example, the FCC denied millions of dollars in federal funding to hundreds of schools in Oklahoma and other states because the schools had listed on their applications a service provider employee as the primary contact instead of a school employee.

In addition to being prevented from using E-rate funds to purchase computer equipment, schools are also prevented from purchasing and installing as separate components either microwave or digital radio systems that can deliver high-speed Internet access at low cost. Finally, the inflexible rules penalize states such as Iowa and Washington that have already independently developed high-speed services.

Giving Schools Flexibility to Use Education Technology Funds

For several years the American Association of School Administrators, representing more than 14,000 superintendents and public school leaders, has called for "a single source of technology assistance." Establishing a single technology program would ensure that schools no longer have to submit multiple grant applications and incur the associated administrative burdens. Furthermore, a single program will facilitate comprehensive and integrated education technology strategies that target the specific needs of individual schools.

Therefore, in order to give schools increased flexibility in the use of federal education technology funds, as President, Governor Bush will:

Establish a $3 Billion "Enhancing Education Through Technology Fund:" Governor Bush will work with Congress to create this single fund by combining the FCC's E-Rate program and eight of the Title III education technology programs under the Department of Education.

Free Schools from Federal Restrictions and Red Tape: Governor Bush will remove detailed federal regulations, allowing schools maximum flexibility in using federal technology education funds for such activities as teacher training, software purchase and development, and system integration.

Continue to Give Priority to the Most Disadvantaged Schools: Governor Bush will ensure federal funds will be distributed based on need, giving priority to rural schools and schools serving high percentages of low-income students.

Providing Better Information on the Uses of Education Technology

Currently, the federal government provides education technology to public schools and libraries, but does not conduct research into the effectiveness of such technology in advancing learning and student achievement. Indeed, the 1999 ETS study concluded that "[u]nfortunately, for all the investment in educational technology, there is a surprising lack of hard data on its effects....the federal government does not collect national data expressly for the purpose of evaluating [how] educational technology [affects achievement]."

In addition, despite the fact that public and private efforts are providing more than $7 billion annually for education technology, there is far too little sharing of information among schools, educators, and research institutions about the most promising uses of technology to close the achievement gap. A recent survey by *Education Week* indicated that "educators are struggling to find high-quality software and web sites... [and] matching software instruction with state or district curricula is a moderate or big problem."

Therefore, to provide schools and educators better information about the uses of technology for improving student performance, Governor Bush will:

Provide $65 Million in New Funding Annually to the Department of Education's Office of Education Research and Improvement: The federal government will perform its basic research function by providing funding to universities and other research institutions to study ways in which education technology can boost student performance and close the achievement gap.

Provide $15 Million in New Funding Annually to Establish the "Education and Technology Clearinghouse:" The Clearinghouse will collect and disseminate information on effective, research-based education technology programs, best education technology practices, and the latest research studies.

Holding Schools Accountable for Education Technology Funds

In October 1999, Governor Bush proposed a comprehensive plan for accountability in education. In exchange for increased flexibility with federal education funds, states must establish high standards in core subject areas and must test students annually in grades 3-8 in math and reading using a state assessment. States will also be asked to participate in an annual NAEP exam, or its equivalent, for students in grades 4 and 8 in reading and math. Based on these measures, states that improve student performance will be rewarded with additional federal funds, while states that permit performance to decline will lose the administrative portion of their federal funding.

The federal government alone is expected to spend at least $30 billion over the next decade on K-12 education technology. In keeping with his overall education reform plan, Governor Bush will hold schools accountable for using those technology funds to improve student performance.

Therefore, to ensure that the federal investment in education technology boosts student achievement, Governor Bush will:

Require States to Establish Accountability Measures for How Education Technology Funds Improve Student Achievement: As part of the accountability systems that states will establish to demonstrate student performance, states will be required to set measures for how education technology improves such performance. Such accountability measures could include an assessment of the value added by education technology on student results.

Position Paper
Education: Improving Math and Science Education

June 20, 2000

"At this moment, we have a great national opportunity – to ensure that every child in every public school is challenged by high standards and has the opportunity to pursue their educational dreams. To fulfill these dreams and to meet the needs of the New Economy, we must make great strides in math and science education."

Governor George W. Bush

EXECUTIVE SUMMARY

Governor Bush is committed to creating a "culture of achievement" for all students in all subjects, including in math and science. The current state of math and science education in America, however, is inadequate to meet the high expectations of parents and the demand for qualified workers in the New Economy. America's math and science students lag behind their counterparts in many other countries, making America less competitive in the global marketplace.

Governor Bush has laid out a comprehensive education reform policy that gives schools increased flexibility with federal education funds in exchange for improvement in student achievement. To address specific problems in math and science education, Governor Bush is proposing reforms totaling $2.3 billion over five years to achieve three key goals.

To Enlist the Help of Colleges and Universities in Strengthening K-12 Math and Science Education, Governor Bush will:

- Establish a Math and Science Partnership Fund to promote partnerships between states and institutions of higher education to strengthen K-12 math and science curricula and teaching. The fund will make $1 billion available over five years.

- Require states participating in the Partnership Fund to meet clear accountability measures in boosting student achievement in math and science.

- Challenge major research universities to strengthen math and science education.

To Provide Incentives to High School Students to Take Advanced College Preparation Courses in Math and Science, Governor Bush will:

- Provide $1 billion over five years for enhanced Pell Grants to students who take college-level math and science courses in high school, allowing them an additional $1,000 to pay for college tuition.

To Encourage Math and Science Majors to Teach in Schools with a High Percentage of Low-Income Students, Governor Bush will:

- Provide $345 million over five years to increase from $5,000 to $17,500 the amount of student loans that may be forgiven for science, math, technology and engineering majors and minors who commit to teach in a high-need school for at least five years.

Demands of the New Economy

The New Economy is generating increased demand for workers with strong technical skills, but there is a decreasing supply of qualified individuals. The percentage of job applicants who lacked the reading and math skills needed to succeed on the job nearly doubled in the last two years, from 19 percent to 36 percent. And in 1999, one-tenth (350,000) of all computer-science related jobs were vacant. This was due in part to the fact that the total number of technical degrees awarded to U.S. citizens is only about 28,000 annually.

Congress raised the number of H1-B visas in 1999 to allow highly skilled immigrants to enter the country. Governor Bush has proposed a further increase to meet the short-term needs of U.S. high technology companies. However, the long-term solution to America's need for highly trained specialists is not immigration, but better education, particularly in the areas of math and science.

Math and Science Education Today

The current state of math and science education in America is not adequate to meet either the high expectations of parents or the demands of a competitive, global economy. Indeed, as the 1998 Third International Math and Science Study (TIMSS) demonstrates, the performance of America's students declines the longer students stay in school, compared with students in other industrialized countries. For example:

- While U.S. fourth graders outperformed all but one country on the TIMSS in science, U.S. twelfth graders only outperformed five, finishing 16th out of 21 nations taking the test.

- U.S. fourth graders outperformed their counterparts in 12 countries in math. By twelfth grade, however, U.S. students outperformed only two countries in math (Cyprus and South Africa).

- Even U.S. twelfth graders taking the most advanced coursework performed poorly, compared with their counterparts in other industrial nations. In physics, U.S. students ranked last; in advanced math they ranked next to last.

For minority and low-income students, in particular, there is a wide gap in math skills. On the most recent National Assessment of Education Progress (NAEP) in math, the average score for African-American and Hispanic eighth graders was below the basic level, which means they could add two-digit numbers but had difficulty with subtraction, multiplication and division problems beyond one-digit calculations.

As a result of these deficiencies, fewer students are entering college ready to learn at the college level. On average, 24 percent of entering college freshmen are required to take remedial math coursework. The math remediation rate for freshmen attending colleges with high minority attendance is 43 percent. High remediation rates mean students are less likely to complete college, particularly with a degree in math and science. While the overall number of students receiving bachelor's degrees has risen 6.7 percent since 1991, the number of students receiving degrees in computer science, engineering, mathematics and physics over the same period has declined 5 percent.

Obstacles to Math and Science Performance

There are three major causes for the poor performance of U.S. students in math and science. First, too few schools are offering challenging curricula and textbooks. A recent analysis by the American Association for the Advancement of Science evaluated middle school science textbooks and determined that most of them covered too many topics without developing any of them well. Many of the classroom activities in the books were either irrelevant to learning key science ideas or did not assist the student in relating to the principles being taught.

Second, too few students, particularly in high-poverty schools, are taking a rigorous course load. The Department of Education has determined that early success in algebra is the single most important predictor of degree attainment in college. Yet only one quarter of U.S. eighth graders are taking algebra. These figures are even lower for students in high-poverty schools, where only 16 percent of eighth graders are taking algebra.

An even smaller percentage of minority students are taking high-level math and science courses. For example, even though African-American and Hispanic students make up about 30 percent of public schools students, they comprise only 9 percent of Advanced Placement Calculus test-takers.

Third, too many math and science teachers, particularly in high-poverty schools, do not have adequate training in math and science:

- More than half of the nation's public school physical science teachers neither majored nor minored in any of the physical sciences.

- Out-of-field teaching is particularly noticeable in high-poverty areas, where an estimated 43 percent of math instructors are teaching out-of-field, versus 27 percent of those teaching in low-poverty schools.

The Need for High Standards and Accountability

Governor Bush believes the first step in boosting math and science achievement is to raise standards across the board. In exchange for increased flexibility with federal education funds, states must establish high standards in math, science, history, and English. Students in grades 3-8 should be tested annually in math and reading using a state assessment. The federal government will share in the cost of testing students and offer bonuses from a $500 million "Achievement in Education" fund to states and schools that:

- Close the achievement gap by raising the achievement of disadvantaged and minority students.

- Increase overall student performance.

- Increase opportunities for advanced academic achievement, by increasing, for example, the percentage of students who are deemed proficient on NAEP, raising SAT/ACT scores, and increasing the number of students who take and pass Advanced Placement and International Baccalaureate exams.

This accountability framework provides a foundation for improving student achievement. In addition, to address the specific problems in math and science education, Governor Bush will pursue reforms to meet three key goals.

Goal 1: Enlist the Help of the Higher Education Community

The Higher Education community is recognizing that it has a vested interest in working to improve elementary and secondary math and science achievement. Nearly 22 states have begun to form partnerships with colleges and universities for the purpose of raising math and science standards for students, providing math and science training for teachers, and creating innovative ways to reach underserved schools.

For example, in 1997 the University of Texas at Austin developed a program called UTEACH, which prepares math and science undergraduate majors to be teachers, increasing the number of teachers who hold degrees in math and science. The University of Texas has also launched a major initiative to train high school teachers to teach AP courses, and is developing on-line Advanced Placement courses to extend the reach of the AP program to high-need schools.

Similarly, the University of Texas at El Paso has collaborated with El Paso school districts and community groups since 1991 to boost science and math achievement, among other goals. As a result, high school science course enrollment has skyrocketed, led by a 96 percent increase in the percentage of high school juniors enrolled in chemistry since 1993. During this same time period, the percentage of all ninth-grade students taking Algebra I rose from 62 percent to nearly 100 percent. Since the 1992-93 school year, the number of students passing the state skills test in math increased by 137 percent for Hispanic students and by 130 percent for African-American students.

Governor Bush wants to encourage the development of similar partnerships in other states. Thus, to enlist the help of colleges and universities in strengthening K-12 math and science education, Governor Bush will:

Establish a "Math and Science Partnership Fund" to Encourage Partnerships Between States and Institutions of Higher Education: Governor Bush will allocate $1 billion over five years to the fund. States that access the fund will be required to sign partnership agreements with state colleges, universities, and community colleges to strengthen K-12 math and science education. These funds could be used by the states to defray the cost of the partnerships and involve other colleges and community colleges in their math and science initiatives. States and institutions of higher education, working primarily through mathematics and science research departments, would strive to:

- Strengthen the content of math and science standards.

- Develop scientifically rigorous research methods for math and science curricula.

- Recruit math and science majors or minors to teach in schools that lack qualified teachers.

- Provide effective, content-focused professional development to K-12 math and science teachers and administrators based on the more rigorous state standards.

- Increase the proportion of students completing a college preparatory curriculum.

- Develop online curriculum for AP courses for students whose schools do not offer AP courses, and offer college-level courses to high school students for college credit.

- Align high school graduation standards and assessments in math and science with standards and assessments used for college placement.

Require Partnership Goals to be Linked to Accountability Measures: States participating in the Partnership Fund will be required to boost student achievement in math and science as measured by:

- Student results on objective, state-selected assessments in math and science, particularly for low-income and minority students.

- Participation and passing rates on math and science AP exams.

- College placement and decreases in college remediation rates.

- The number of math and science majors entering the teaching profession.

Challenge Major Research Institutions to Strengthen Math and Science Education: Research universities receiving at least $18 million in federal grants annually would be challenged to sign a partnership agreement with their state to strengthen K-12 math and science education.

Goal 2: Encourage High School Students to Take College-Level Preparation Courses

Research clearly shows that taking a more rigorous curriculum in high school leads to higher achievement. For example, an analysis of the trends on the National Assessment of Educational Progress in math showed a direct correlation between taking rigorous courses in high school mathematics and performing at higher levels on standardized examinations. Likewise, a 1994 analysis by the College Board determined that students who take more challenging math and science courses in high school score higher on the SAT.

Taking a rigorous high school curriculum often has the additional benefit of counting toward college credit. AP exams are offered in most subjects, including in Calculus, Biology, Physics, Chemistry, and Computer Science. However, longitudinal data from the Department of Education's National Center for Education Statistics shows that low-income students are less than half as likely as high-income students to be taking a college preparation course.

Therefore, to encourage low-income students to take rigorous college preparation courses, Governor Bush will:

Offer Enhanced Pell Grants to Students Who Take Rigorous Math and Science Courses in High School: Today, more than half a million low-income entering freshmen are eligible to receive a Pell Grant worth an average of $3,000. Under Governor Bush's proposal, low-income Pell grant recipients who either passed AP math and science exams, or who took and passed college math and science courses while in high school, will be eligible to receive an additional $1,000 to pay for college tuition. The cost of this proposal would be $1 billion over five years.

Goal 3: Encourage Math and Science Majors to Teach in Low-Income Schools

Out-of-field teaching is particularly common in the subjects of math and science, where 27 percent of math instructors in low-poverty schools and 43 percent in high-poverty schools are teaching out-of-field. One reason it is difficult to recruit math and science majors to teaching is because non-teaching jobs for these majors pay more than teaching positions.

Among college graduates working full time in April 1997, the average annual salary was $34,000. Those graduates who had majored in mathematics, computer science or natural science were earning an average of $38,000 per year. By contrast, the average annual salary of teachers in 1997 was $25,600 and is frequently lower in poor school districts.

The 1998 re-authorization of the Higher Education Act created a loan forgiveness program to cancel up to $5,000 in student loans for instructors who committed to teach for five years. While this amount of loan forgiveness is a good incentive, it is not adequate to attract enough math and science majors to teach in high-need areas.

Therefore, as President, to encourage more in-field teaching in high-need areas, Governor Bush will:

<u>Increase the Amount of Student Loans That May be Forgiven for Science, Math, Technology and Engineering Students Who Agree to Teach in High-Need Schools</u>: The amount of forgivable guaranteed and direct loans would be increased from $5,000 to $17,500. Though instructors teaching other subjects could qualify for the expanded forgiveness, preference would be given to math and science majors and minors who agree to teach for five years in high-need schools. High-need schools would include those that teach a high percentage of low-income students or those in which there is a large proportion of out-of-field math and science teachers. The cost of this proposal would be $345 million over five years.

WHAT OTHERS SAY

"No candidate for President has ever looked so thoroughly, and understood so fundamentally, what ails our schools."

Lynne Munson, American Enterprise Institute

"...the Texas Governor has undertaken significant reforms in his state..."

Mark Barabak, <u>Los Angeles Times</u>, 4/6/00

"...and on national examinations, Texas schoolchildren have begun to show up their peers in other states. The trend has become so consistent that Texas' public school system, long among the nation's most troubled, is viewed today by educators as an emerging model of equity, progress and accountability."

Ethan Bronner, <u>The New York Times</u>, 5/28/99

"...reform plan is impressive...A Real Education President."

Checker Finn, Jr., <u>The Weekly Standard</u>, 9/20/99

"The number of students passing Texas' standardized tests has risen while Bush has been in office…"

Mark Mayes, <u>Lansing State Journal</u>, 5/5/00

"…all I can say is that in Texas, with regard to education, George Bush has managed to maintain the sort of system that ensures attention, support and achievement for minority and poor kids. While he has been governor, the gap between minorities and whites has closed rather remarkably."

Susan Navarro, Executive Director of the El Paso Collaborative for Academic Excellence (a nonprofit group in El Paso, TX)

"Bush was first out with tough education accountability proposals."

Mort Kondracke, <u>Roll Call</u>, 6/22/00

"Texas school children have been having rising test scores under George W. Bush."

Thomas Sowell, <u>Austin-American Statesman</u>, 9/11/99

"…he has promoted proposals to raise educational standards and provided school choice vouchers to parents whose children are in failing schools."

Donald Lambro, <u>Washington Times</u>, 4/12/00

"I laud him on making education a focus and turning up the flame on school reform."

Duren Cheek, <u>The Tennessean</u>, 9/3/99

"…The Texas education story is really one of the few success stories in the country. What you see in Texas is…all students' scores rising…the gap between minority kids and white kids closing, which demonstrates to us that all kids can achieve at high levels."

Amy Wilkins, Principal Partner at Education Trust, "NewsHour with Jim Lehrer", 6/6/00

PART II

A New Agenda for Compassion

The opening speech of this section, "The Duty of Hope," was also the first major address of my presidential campaign. Helping those in need must be at the center of our national agenda. And America's charities, faith-based organizations, and community groups must be at the center of that effort.

From Philadelphia to Detroit to Los Angeles, these groups are saving and changing lives in ways that government has never been able to match. As President, I will put the federal government on the side of these armies of compassion.

Throughout this campaign, I have said that the American Dream must touch every willing heart. This has very real meaning for Americans who endure discrimination; for immigrants who are made to feel unwelcome; for persons with disabilities who are denied full access to work and opportunity; for families who can't afford health care or a home of their own; for children lost in a failed child-welfare system. In each instance, government has a clear role: to ensure equality of opportunity and remove barriers formed by bigotry or indifference.

My Administration will apply conservative ideas and values to the hard and persistent issues facing our country. Compassionate conservatism has one great goal: to welcome all our people into the full promise of American life.

Duty of Hope:
Armies of Compassion

Front Porch Alliance
Indianapolis, Indiana

July 22, 1999

Everywhere I've gone in this campaign – from farms in Iowa
to Latino communities in California – I've carried one message.
Our country must be prosperous. But prosperity must have a purpose. The purpose of prosperity is to make sure the American
dream touches every willing heart. The purpose of prosperity is to
leave no one out... to leave no one behind.

We are a wealthy nation. But we must also be rich in ideals –
rich in justice and compassion and family love and moral courage.

I am an economic conservative. I believe we should cut taxes
to stimulate economic growth. Yet I know that economic growth is
not the solution to every problem. A rising tide lifts many boats –
but not all. Many prosper in a bull market – but not everyone. The
invisible hand works many miracles. But it cannot touch the
human heart.

The American Dream is so vivid – but too many feel: The
dream is not meant for me. Children abandoned by fathers.
Children captured by addiction and condemned to schools that do
not teach and will not change. Young mothers without self-respect
or education or the supporting love of a husband. These needs are
found everywhere, in cities and suburbs and small towns. But the
places where these problems are concentrated – from North
Central Philadelphia to South Central Los Angeles – have become

the ruins of communities. Places where despair is the easy path, and hope the narrow gate.

For many people, this other society of addiction and abandonment and stolen childhood is a distant land, another world. But it is America. And these are not strangers, they are citizens, Americans, our brothers and sisters.

In their hopes, we find our duties. In their hardship, we must find our calling – to serve others, relying on the goodness of America and the boundless grace of God.

The reality here is simple. Often when a life is broken, it can only be rebuilt by another caring, concerned human being. Someone whose actions say, "I love you, I believe in you, I'm in your corner." This is compassion with a human face and a human voice. It is not an isolated act – it is a personal relationship. And it works. The mentors in Big Brothers/Big Sisters – spending only a few hours a week with a child – cut first-time drug use by 50 percent and violent behavior by a third. The success of this fine program proves the obvious: in solving the problems of our day, there is no substitute for unconditional love and personal contact.

I was struck by the story of a gang initiation in Michigan. A 15-year-old boy was forced to stand and take two minutes of vicious beating from other members without fighting back. At the end, he was required to stand up and embrace his attackers. When asked why he submitted to this torture, he answered, "I knew this was going to hurt really bad, but I felt that if I could take it for just a couple of minutes, I'd be surrounded by people who loved me."

Imagine a young life that empty, so desperately in need of real love. And multiply it by millions. This crisis of the spirit creates an expanding circle of responsibility. Individuals are responsible to love our neighbors as we want to be loved ourselves.

Parents must understand that being a good mom or dad becomes their highest goal in life.

Congregations and community groups must fight for children

and neighborhoods, creating what Pope John Paul II calls, "a hospitable society, a welcoming culture."

A president has responsibilities as well. A president can speak without apology for the values that defeat violence and help overcome poverty. A president can speak for abstinence and accountability and the power of faith.

In the past, presidents have declared wars on poverty and promised to create a great society. But these grand gestures and honorable aims were frustrated. They have become a warning, not an example. We found that government can spend money, but it can't put hope in our hearts or a sense of purpose in our lives. This is done by churches and synagogues and mosques and charities that warm the cold of life. A quiet river of goodness and kindness that cuts through stone.

Real change in our culture comes from the bottom up, not the top down. It gathers the momentum of a million committed hearts.

So today I want to propose a different role for government. A fresh start. A bold new approach.

In every instance where my administration sees a responsibility to help people, we will look first to faith-based organizations, charities and community groups that have shown their ability to save and change lives. We will make a determined attack on need, by promoting the compassionate acts of others. We will rally the armies of compassion in our communities to fight a very different war against poverty and hopelessness, a daily battle waged house to house and heart by heart.

This will not be the failed compassion of towering, distant bureaucracies. On the contrary, it will be government that serves those who are serving their neighbors. It will be government that directs help to the inspired and the effective. It will be government that both knows its limits, and shows its heart. And it will be government truly by the people and for the people.

We will take this path, first and foremost, because private and religious groups are effective. Because they have clear advantages over government.

Sometimes the idea of compassion is dismissed as soft or sentimental. But those who believe this have not visited these programs. Compassion is not one of the easy virtues.

At InnerChange – a faith-based program run by Prison Fellowship inside a Texas prison – inmates are up at 5 a.m. and fill their days with work and study rather than soap operas. At Teen Challenge – a national drug treatment program – one official says, "We have a rule: If you don't work, you don't eat." This is demanding love – at times, a severe mercy. These institutions, at their best, treat people as moral individuals, with responsibilities and duties, not as wards or clients or dependents or numbers.

Self-control and character and goal-setting give direction and dignity to all our lives. We must renew these values to restore our country.

Many of these organizations share something else in common: A belief in the transforming power of faith. A belief that no one is finally a failure or a victim, because everyone is the child of a loving and merciful God – a God who counts our tears and lifts our head. The goal of these faith-based groups is not just to provide services, it is to change lives. And lives are changed. Addicts become examples. Reckless men become loving fathers. Prisoners become spiritual leaders – sometimes more mature and inspiring than many of us can ever hope to be.

In Texas, there is a young man named James Peterson, who'd embezzled his way into a prison term. But when he was offered parole, he turned it down, to finish the InnerChange course, which teaches inmates to rely on faith to transform their lives. As James put it, "There is nothing I want more than to be back in the outside world with my daughter Lucy, [but] I realized that this was an opportunity to ... become a living [witness] ... for my brothers [in prison] and to the world. I want to stay in prison to complete the transformation [God] has begun in me."

One example, but a miracle that is common. Sometimes our greatest need is not for more laws. It is for more conscience. Sometimes our greatest hope is not found in reform. It is found in redemption.

We should promote these private and faith-based efforts because they work. But we should also promote them because their challenges are often greater than their resources. Sometimes the armies of compassion are outnumbered and outflanked and outgunned. Visit Mission Arlington in Texas on a day they offer free dentistry, and people are often lined up at 3 or 4 in the morning. Or consider that only 3 percent of America's 13.6 million at-risk children now have mentors. These groups are widespread, but their scale, in some cases, is not sufficient.

It is not enough for conservatives like me to praise these efforts. It is not enough to call for volunteerism. Without more support and resources – both private and public – we are asking them to make bricks without straw.

So today I am announcing a series of proposals. And they are guided by some basic principles.

Resources should be devolved, not just to states, but to charities and neighborhood healers.

We will never ask an organization to compromise its core values and spiritual mission to get the help it needs.

We will keep a commitment to pluralism – not discriminating for or against Methodists or Mormons or Muslims, or good people of no faith at all.

We will ensure that participation in faith-based programs is truly voluntary – that there are secular alternatives.

And we will recognize there are some things the government *should* be doing – like Medicaid for poor children. Government cannot be replaced by charities – but it can welcome them as partners, not resent them as rivals.

Where do we start? Our nation is so prosperous that we can meet our current priorities and still take on new battles. We will strengthen Social Security and Medicare. We will fortify the military. We will cut taxes in a way that creates high-paying jobs. Yet there is another priority. In my first year in office, we will dedicate about $8 billion – an amount equal to 10 percent of the non-Social Security surplus – to provide new tax incentives for giving, and to support charities and other private institutions that save and change lives. We will prove, in word and deed, that our prosperity has a purpose.

My Administration will act in three broad areas:

First, we will encourage an outpouring of giving in America. Americans are generous with their time and money. But we can foster that generosity even further – creating fertile ground for the growth of charities.

Right now approximately 70 percent of all tax filers cannot claim the charitable tax deduction, because they do not itemize. We will give people who don't itemize the same treatment and incentive as people who do, rewarding and encouraging giving by everyone in our society, not just the wealthy.

We will provide for charity tax credits – credits which will allow individuals to give a part of what they owe in state taxes directly to private and religious institutions fighting poverty in their own communities. Individuals will choose who conducts this war on poverty – and their support won't be filtered through layers of government officials.

Second, we will involve the armies of compassion in some specific areas of need, to demonstrate how our new approach will work.

Here is an example. America has tripled its prison population in the last 15 years. That is a necessary and effective role of government – protecting our communities from predators. But it has left a problem – more than two million children who have one or both parents in prison. These are forgotten children – almost six

115

times more likely to go to prison themselves – and they should not be punished for the sins of their fathers. It is not only appropriate, it is urgent, to give grants to ministries and mentoring programs targeting these children and their families for help and support. My administration will start bringing help and hope to these other, innocent victims of crime.

As well, we will encourage and expand the role of charities in after-school programs. Everyone agrees there is a problem in these empty, unsupervised hours after school. But those hours should not only be filled with sports and play, they should include lessons in responsibility and character. So we will invite the Boys and Girls Clubs, the YMCA and local churches and synagogues to be a central part of after-school programs.

We will encourage private and religious charities to be more involved in drug treatment and maternity group homes. We will bring programs like InnerChange to four federal prisons, to test if its early promise is fulfilled. And we will set up a compassion capital fund, to identify good ideas transforming neighborhoods and lives and provide seed money to support them – helping to expand the scale of effective programs.

Third, we will change the laws and regulations that hamper the cooperation of government and private institutions. In 1997, Texas officials tried to close down faith-based drug treatment programs because they didn't fit the regulations. When challenged that these programs were effective, one official responded, "We're not interested in results, we're interested in complying with the law." We solved that problem in Texas. If I am president, federal workers in every department of my administration will know that we value effectiveness above red tape and regulation.

We will allow private and religious groups to compete to provide services in every federal, state and local social program. We will promote alternative licensing procedures, so effective efforts won't be buried by regulation. And we will create an advocate position – reporting directly to the President – to ensure that charities are not secularized or slighted.

I visit churches and charities serving their neighbors nearly everywhere I go in this country. And nothing is more exciting or encouraging. Every day they prove that our worst problems are not hopeless or endless. Every day they perform miracles of renewal. Wherever we can, we must expand their role and reach, without changing them or corrupting them. It is the next, bold step of welfare reform.

To take that step, our nation must get beyond two narrow mindsets. The first is that government provides the only real compassion. A belief that what is done by caring people through church and charity is secondary and marginal. Some Washington politicians call these efforts "crumbs of compassion." These aren't "crumbs" to people whose lives are changed, they are the hope of renewal and salvation. These are not the "crumbs of compassion," they are the bread of life. And they are the strength and soul of America.

There is another destructive mindset: the idea that if government would only get out of our way, all our problems would be solved. An approach with no higher goal, no nobler purpose, than "Leave us alone."

Yet this is not who we are as Americans. We have always found our better selves in sympathy and generosity – both in our lives and in our laws. Americans will never write the epitaph of idealism. It emerges from our nature as a people, with a vision of the common good beyond profit and loss. Our national character shines in our compassion.

We are a nation of rugged individuals. But we are also the country of the second chance – tied together by bonds of friendship and community and solidarity.

We are a nation of high purpose and restless reform – of child labor laws and emancipation and suffrage and civil rights.

We are a nation that defeated fascism, elevated millions of the elderly out of poverty and humbled an evil empire.

I know the reputation of our government has been tainted by scandal and cynicism. But the American government is not the enemy of the American people. At times it is wasteful and grasping. But we must correct it, not disdain it. Government must be carefully limited – but strong and active and respected within those bounds. It must act in the common good – and that good is not common until it is shared by those in need.

In this campaign, I bring a message to my own party. We must apply our conservative and free-market ideas to the job of helping real human beings – because any ideology, no matter how right in theory, is sterile and empty without that goal. There must be a kindness in our justice. There must be a mercy in our judgment. There must be a love behind our zeal.

This is where my campaign is headed. We will carry a message of hope and renewal to every community in this country. We will tell every American, "The dream is for you." Tell forgotten children in failed schools, "The dream is for you." Tell families, from the *barrios* of LA to the Rio Grande Valley: "*El sueño americano es para ti.*" Tell men and women in our decaying cities, "The dream is for you." Tell confused young people, starved of ideals, "The dream is for you."

As Americans, this is our creed and our calling. We stumble and splinter when we forget that goal. We unite and prosper when we remember it. No great calling is ever easy, and no work of man is ever perfect. But we can, in our imperfect way, rise now and again to the example of St. Francis – where there is hatred, sowing love; where there is darkness, shedding light; where there is despair, bringing hope.

Position Paper
Duty of Hope: Armies of Compassion

July 22, 1999

"We have always found our better selves in sympathy and generosity. Americans will never write the epitaph of idealism. It emerges from our nature as a people, with a vision of the common good beyond profit and loss. Our national character shines in our compassion."

Governor George W. Bush

EXECUTIVE SUMMARY

As President, Governor George W. Bush will commit himself and the nation to mobilizing the armies of compassion – charities and churches, communities and corporations, ministers and mentors – to save and change lives, as he has done in Texas. These groups are proving that real change comes from the bottom up, not the top down.

That is why Governor Bush envisions a different role for government – a role based on the belief that government should turn first to faith-based organizations, charities, and community groups to help people in need. Resources should be devolved, not just to the states, but to the charities and neighborhood healers who need them most and should be available on a competitive basis to all organizations – including religious ones – that produce results. This is the next bold step of welfare reform.

To Eliminate Barriers to Faith-Based Action and to Encourage an Outpouring of Giving, Governor Bush will:

- Expand "charitable choice" and remove barriers to the participation of faith-based groups in government programs.

- Establish an "Office of Faith-Based Action" in the Executive Office of the President.

119

- Expand the federal charitable deduction to people who do not itemize.

- Promote a new charitable state tax credit.

- Provide new incentives for corporate giving.

As President, Governor Bush Will Lead a Determined Attack on Need, Launching Initiatives to:

- Break the cycle of violence that grips the 1.3 million children of prisoners.

- Open federal after-school programs to community groups, churches, and charities.

- Create a "Compassion Capital Fund" to invest in charitable "best practices."

- Increase drug treatment funding and make faith-based and other non-medical drug treatment programs eligible for federal funds.

- Establish pilot "Second Chance" homes for unwed teenage mothers, and faith-based pre-release programs for prisoners.

- Make permanent the $5,000 adoption tax credit.

Sharing the Dream

America has never been more prosperous. But that prosperity is not shared by all. There is still too much poverty and despair amidst abundance. More than one out of six American families with children live with an income of $17,000 a year or less. There are roughly 14 million young people at risk of not reaching productive adulthood; more than two million children with a mother or father in prison; 520,000 children in foster care, more than one-fifth of whom are waiting to be adopted; and, in 1997, over one million babies were born to unwed mothers, 380,000 of whom were under the age of 20.

As President, Governor Bush will commit the country to rallying the armies of compassion nationwide, as he has done in Texas, to ensure no one is left behind as we enter the 21st century.

A Different Role for Government

Governor Bush believes real change comes from the bottom up, not the top down. Thus, in seeking to help those in need, his administration will look first to faith-based organizations, charities, and community groups that have a track record of success. This is the next bold step in welfare reform.

Governor Bush believes we should support private and faith-based efforts first and foremost because they work. But we should also promote them because the challenges they face are often greater than the resources they possess. He recognizes local efforts lack scale, good intentions often lack resources, and volunteerism alone is not enough. That is why he is proposing a different role for government based on these principles:

- Government should energize private action, not control it, by identifying what works and helping to bring good ideas to scale.

- Resources should be devolved, not just to the states, but to charities and neighborhood healers who need them most.

- Those resources should be made available through contracts, certificates or grants on a competitive basis to *all* organizations – including religious ones. This competition will spur innovation and better results.

- Organizations receiving resources should not be forced to compromise their core values and spiritual mission.

- Participation in faith-based programs should be truly voluntary, and secular alternatives should exist for beneficiaries.

- Government programs should be committed to pluralism – not discriminating for or against Christians, Muslims, or Jews – or good people of no faith at all.

As President, Governor Bush will follow these principles in mobilizing charities and churches, communities and corporations, ministers and mentors. He will dedicate about $8 billion in the first year of his presidency – or $38 billion over five years – to provide new tax incentives for giving, and to support charities and other private institutions.

Encouraging an Outpouring of Giving

Americans are a generous people. In 1998, charitable giving totaled $175 billion, an increase of nine percent over the previous year. However, when measured as a percent of gross domestic product, Americans give the same amount today (2.1 percent) as they did in 1971.

Thus, to stimulate additional charitable giving, as President, Governor Bush will propose initiatives to:

Expand the Federal Charitable Deduction: Under current law, only people who itemize deductions are allowed to claim a tax deduction for their charitable donations. About 80 million people – 70 percent of all filers – do not itemize. As President, Governor Bush will propose giving every taxpayer the ability to deduct his or her charitable donations. This change will generate billions of dollars annually in additional charitable contributions.

Promote a Charitable State Tax Credit: Governor Bush supports legislation that would provide a credit (of up to 50 percent of the first $500 for individuals and $1,000 for married couples) against state income or other taxes for contributions to charities addressing poverty and its impact. States would be able to designate the charities they want to target with the credit. States would also be permitted – at their option – to offset the costs of this credit by using money from the Temporary Assistance to Needy Families (TANF) program. This optional tax credit would give states additional flexibility in addressing human needs.

Permit Charitable Contributions from IRAs Without Penalty: Under current law, withdrawals from Individual Retirement Accounts are subject to income tax. This creates a disincentive for retirees to contribute some or all of their IRA funds to charity. Thus, Governor Bush supports legislation that would permit individuals over the age of 59 to contribute IRA funds to charities without having to pay income tax on their gifts.

Governor Bush believes corporations must be full partners in the effort to mobilize and strengthen our charities. As President, he will introduce legislation to:

Extend the New Charitable State Tax Credit to Corporations: Governor Bush will allow corporations to participate in the new Charitable State Tax Credit. Under his proposal, corporations will be eligible for a tax credit of 50 percent of the first $1,000 donated to charities dedicated to fighting poverty. In a nation with over five million corporations, this tax credit should help stimulate new partnerships between corporate and social entrepreneurs.

Raise the Cap on Corporate Charitable Deductions: Under current law, a corporation can deduct charitable donations until their value exceeds 10 percent of the company's taxable income. As President, Governor Bush will propose legislation to raise this cap to 15 percent, encouraging firms to raise their giving to charities that address human needs.

Provide Liability Protection for Corporate In-Kind Donations: The 1996 Good Samaritan Food Donation Act protects donors of foodstuffs to charities from liability, except in cases of gross negligence. The 1997 Volunteer Protection Act provided similar protection to individual volunteers. What is lacking is protection for corporate in-kind donations. Many charities, churches, and community groups need vehicles to transport the elderly, computers to educate children, and facilities to hold classes. To encourage such in-kind gifts, Governor Bush supports legislation limiting the civil liability of businesses that donate equipment, facilities, and vehicles to charitable organizations, except in cases of gross negligence.

Eliminating Barriers to Faith-Based Action

Social scientists have documented the power of religion to protect families and change lives. Studies indicate that religious involvement reduces teen pregnancy, suicide, drug abuse, alcoholism, delinquency, and crime. For example, over a decade's worth of "faith factor" research by Dr. David Larson of the National Institute for Healthcare Research and other scholars reveals that poor inner-city youth who attend church are only about half as likely to drop out of school, use drugs, or commit crimes as otherwise comparable youth without religion in their lives.

Similarly, grassroots inner-city outreach ministries have been credited by numerous leading social scientists with playing a major role in helping at-risk youth to avoid violence, achieve literacy, and find jobs. In short, faith-based charities and community groups are proving every day that religion, in the words of UCLA's James Q. Wilson, "creates an opportunity for personal transformation."

In recognition of the growing success of faith-based charities, the 1996 welfare reform bill, which replaced Aid to Families with Dependent Children with Temporary Assistance to Needy Families (TANF), contained a "charitable choice" provision. This provision allowed states to contract with religious organizations "on the same basis as any other non-governmental provider without impairing the religious character of such organizations." Despite this provision, the Administration continues to support regulations that hinder the ability of faith-based charities to provide needed services:

- On September 24, 1998, the U.S. Department of Agriculture notified the Salvation Army's Adult Rehabilitation Center (ARC) in Nashville, Tennessee, that it could no longer act as a food stamp agent, making low-cost, bulk purchases on behalf of the center's residents, because ARC was not certified as a "treatment center." Although the center protested that it was technically a church and provided no medical treatment, USDA forced it to withdraw from the food stamp program. The resulting increase in food costs has forced the center to curtail other services.

- The federal Community Development Block Grant program prohibits, as a general rule, CDBG assistance from being provided to "primarily religious entities for any activities, including secular activities." This prohibition has had a chilling effect on faith-based organizations' willingness to apply for federal funds. According to the executive director of the International Union of Gospel Missions, if these groups have to "strip" their programs of "moral and spiritual aspects, then they wouldn't be worth doing."

Governor Bush believes America must stop trying to eliminate poverty, crime, and addiction with one hand tied behind its back. Thus, he is committed to removing all remaining barriers to the participation of faith-based groups in government programs. As President, he will:

Expand "Charitable Choice:" Governor Bush is committed to making "Charitable Choice" explicitly applicable to all federal laws that authorize the government to use non-governmental entities to provide services to beneficiaries with federal dollars. Participation in faith-based programs should be truly voluntary. Faith-based organizations should be permitted to engage in inherently religious activities – as long as secular alternatives are also available, and those inherently religious activities are privately funded.

Eliminate Other Barriers to Faith-Based Action: Even if "Charitable Choice" is expanded across the board, barriers to the use of federal funds by faith-based groups will remain. Governor Bush believes a concerted effort to identify and remove all such barriers is needed. That is why he will:

- Establish an "Office of Faith-Based Action" in the Executive Office of the President: This office will identify barriers to faith-based action, serve as a national clearinghouse for information on effective faith-based groups, and assist faith-based organizations that need help with regard to federal action.

- <u>Encourage the Establishment of State Offices of Faith-Based Action</u>: Governor Bush will make federal matching funds available to encourage states to establish their own offices to facilitate faith-based action.

- <u>Promote Alternative Licensing Regimes</u>: As President, Governor Bush will promote alternative licensing regimes at the state and federal levels that recognize religious training as an alternative form of qualification.

Examples of the New Approach in Action

New incentives to encourage giving, combined with the elimination of barriers to charitable and faith-based action, form the essential foundation for attacking specific areas of need. The following are examples of just a few of the initiatives Governor Bush will launch as President – initiatives that illustrate a different and innovative approach to empowering the compassionate good work of private organizations and charities.

Children of Prisoners

The U.S. prison population has tripled in the past 15 years. On any given day there are 1.7 million people in prison. This has helped protect our communities from predators. But it has left an enormous problem: more than two million children who have a mother or a father – or both – in prison. Studies show that these children are six times more likely to be incarcerated than the average child.

As research by the University of Pennsylvania's John DiIulio and others has shown, too many of these children live in poverty and suffer from the lack of "loving, capable, responsible adults who can teach [them] right from wrong."

Governor Bush believes that these innocent victims of crime should have a special claim on our conscience and on our resources. Unfortunately, there are no federal funds specifically earmarked today for children of prisoners. Thus, as President, Governor Bush will:

<u>Launch an Initiative Directed at Children of Prisoners</u>: This program will make grants available on a competitive basis to faith-based and community groups committed to improving the life prospects of the low-income children of prisoners, through services ranging from church-run preschools to family-rebuilding programs for probationers and ex-prisoners.

After-School Programs

Studies indicate after-school programs help reduce drug use, teen pregnancy, and criminal behavior by providing supervised activities during the peak hours for juvenile crime. Unfortunately, some federal after-school programs tend to discourage the participation of faith-based groups and other community organizations. For example, under the 21st Century Community Learning Centers program, which is one of the largest federal sources of funding for after-school activities, only schools are eligible to compete for funds. The Clinton-Gore Administration has recently proposed opening just 10 percent of the program's funding to competitive bidding.

As President, Governor Bush will take a different approach and:

Open the Entire 21st Century Program to Competition: Governor Bush will introduce legislation to open 100 percent of the 21st Century program's funding to competitive bidding. This will allow youth development groups, local charities, and other community and faith-based organizations to compete for these federal funds on an equal footing with schools. Preference will be given to partnerships between schools and these groups.

Fund a New After-School Program Using Certificates: Governor Bush will empower lower-income parents by providing certificates to defray the cost of after-school activities of their choosing — whether run by a community group, a neighborhood church, or a local school. An additional $400 million a year will be added to the Child Care Development Block Grant to the states to help 500,000 low-income parents pay for an after-school program of their choice.

Best Practices

Thirty years of social policy have shown that often the most effective efforts have not been large, nationally-directed programs, but smaller, local initiatives. These initiatives are shaped by need, not by bureaucrats. Unfortunately, innovative practices tend to spread slowly because the social marketplace, unlike the commercial marketplace, has no "invisible hand" to promote good ideas, and few financing institutions to help take those ideas to scale.

Thus, to promote "best practices," as President, Governor Bush will:

Establish a Compassion Capital Fund: Governor Bush will establish the Compassion Capital Fund — a public/private partnership that will fund research into "best practices" among charitable organizations, support technical training in those practices, and provide start-up capital to qualified charitable organizations that wish to expand or emulate model programs. He will challenge the private sector to match federal funding of the program.

Drug Treatment

Studies show religion is a powerful tool in helping individuals overcome drug and alcohol addiction. However, government regulations tend to view addiction as a disease and prohibit or discourage the licensing of non-medical, faith-based treatment programs.

Governor Bush addressed this problem in Texas by signing legislation exempting programs that do not provide medical treatment, such as Teen Challenge, a nationally-recognized faith-based drug treatment program, from state licensing requirements. Since then, 38 non-medical, faith-based treatment programs have been established under alternative licensing arrangements.

As President, Governor Bush will:

Promote Results-Oriented Drug Treatment Programs: Governor Bush will make performance-based grants for drug treatment programs available to the states and ensure that non-medical, faith-based and community-based organizations are eligible to receive federal drug treatment funds on the same basis as any other organization.

Prison Ministries

The power of religion to transform lives has been demonstrated in programs that address everything from drug addiction to domestic violence. This power is now being used to harness change behind prison walls.

The State of Texas has permitted Prison Fellowship Ministries to take over a unit of the state prison in Sugar Land, Texas, and establish "InnerChange" – the nation's first, 24-hour-a-day, Bible and values-based pre-release program, aimed at helping inmates achieve spiritual and moral transformation. Prisoners voluntarily enroll in the program 12 to 18 months prior to release, and receive services for up to 12 months after release.

It is still too early to measure the effectiveness of the InnerChange program. However, there are some positive preliminary indications, and several states are considering implementing similar faith-based programs. To obtain more data on the effectiveness of these programs, Governor Bush will:

Provide Funding for Pilot Faith-Based Prison Programs: Funding for faith-based pre-release programs will be provided at four federal prisons. To generate substantial data on the efficacy of these programs, projects should be geographically diverse, and include facilities with different levels of security.

"Second Chance" Maternity Group Homes

In 1998, over 380,000 unwed mothers under the age of 20 gave birth in the United States. These mothers and their children face extraordinary odds in achieving success. Studies have shown that only about half of these mothers graduate from high school and 80 percent go on welfare. In addition, their daughters are more likely to have children out of wedlock themselves.

The 1996 welfare reform bill requires parents who are minors to live in an adult-supervised setting in order to receive welfare (TANF) funds. When a conventional adult-supervised setting is not available because of abuse or abandonment by the parent or guardian, federal law requires states to provide or assist in locating alternative living arrangements. Some states have turned to so-called "Second Chance" homes as the alternative. These homes provide young mothers with an opportunity to develop good parenting skills, finish school, and enter the workforce.

Unfortunately, many teenage mothers are placed in a virtually independent living environment because Second Chance homes are not easily available. Indeed, federal regulations currently do not allow federal funds to be used for the purchase or construction of a facility.

Governor Bush believes that to break the cycle of children having children the federal government should:

<u>Fund "Second Chance" Maternity Homes</u>: As President, Governor Bush will provide funding for pilot maternity group homes through a block grant to the states. The states will be authorized to make the funds available either as certificates to individuals, or as competitive grants to providers, who will be able to use the funds to purchase or operate a facility.

Foster Care

There are now 540,000 children in foster care, some 50,000 of whom are legally free for adoption now. Countless more children outside the foster care system are waiting to be adopted into loving families. Although the 1997 Adoption and Safe Families Act did much to move these children to safe adoptive homes, more needs to be done. For example, the cost of adoption still remains a major issue when couples decide to adopt. These costs also may prevent loving, low-income families from considering adoption at all. Thus, to make adoption more affordable, Governor Bush will:

Increase the Adoption Tax Credit and Make It Permanent: To help make adoption a more affordable option for families at any income level, Governor Bush will make permanent the current adoption tax credit, which would otherwise expire in 2001, and increase it from $5,000 to $7,500.

THE TEXAS RECORD

Governor's Faith-Based Task Force

In May 1996, Governor Bush created the "Governor's Advisory Task Force on Faith-Based Community Service Groups" to identify obstacles to faith-based groups and recommend ways Texas can create an environment in which those groups can thrive. In December 1996, Governor Bush signed an executive order directing Texas welfare-related agencies to permit religious-based organizations to compete for state contracts to provide welfare services without sacrificing their distinct religious character.

1997 Legislative Accomplishments

In 1997 the Legislature approved, and Governor Bush signed, several new laws based on recommendations from the Governor's Faith-Based Task Force. These laws encouraged churches, synagogues, and other faith-based groups to offer substance abuse treatment, welfare-to-work services, health care, crime-fighting programs, child care and other social services without jeopardizing their religious identity. The Legislature approved measures that:

- Exempt from state licensing and regulation those (non-medical) faith-based alcohol and drug treatment programs that rely exclusively on faith to change lives.

- Permit child care facilities that meet or exceed state standards to be accredited by private sector entities instead of being licensed and regulated by the state.

- Encourage state correctional agencies to use faith-based rehabilitation programs during and after imprisonment.

- Protect from legal liability those who donate medical devices in good faith to nonprofit health care providers.

1999 Legislative Accomplishments

During the recent legislative session, Governor Bush and state lawmakers continued efforts to help faith-based and charitable organizations deliver services to those in need. Legislative accomplishments included:

- The Texas Religious Freedom Restoration Act which, in response to hostile court cases, strengthens and protects the religious liberty of Texans and limits the government's ability to interfere with a citizen's free exercise of rights.

- A "Good Samaritan" bill that provides liability protections to health care professionals who donates charitable care to needy Texans.

- A law requiring the Texas Department of Human Services to designate certain employees as liaisons to faith-based organizations to promote community services for the needy.

- An exemption from state property tax for charities who help elderly citizens.

- A law directing Texas' 28 local workforce development boards to reach out to religious social ministries.

- A law permitting faith-based groups to acquire the state's surplus and salvage property.

"Charitable Choice" Under Governor Bush

The Personal Responsibility and Work Opportunity Reconciliation Act of 1996 included a landmark provision now commonly referred to as "Charitable Choice." Charitable Choice applies when states partner with faith-based and community organizations to deliver welfare services. Governor Bush issued an executive order urging state agencies to use this provision aggressively. And soon a resource guide and series of workshops will be utilized in Texas to train faith-based organizations how to access grants and submit proposals to deliver social services.

Under Governor Bush's leadership, Texas leads the nation in implementing Charitable Choice. Besides the religious groups all across Texas offering government-funded child care to the children of welfare mothers, other examples include:

InnerChange

InnerChange is the boldest experiment in criminal rehabilitation ever attempted in America. It's the nation's first-ever, 24-hours-a-day, Bible and values-based prerelease program, aimed at helping inmates achieve spiritual and moral transformation. Housed at the Jester II unit in Sugar Land, Texas InnerChange is a 3-phase, volunteer-led program that begins 12-18 months before release and continues on for 6-12 months of post-release aftercare to successfully re-integrate inmates back into society. InnerChange is a collaborative effort between Prison Fellowship Ministries, the Texas Department of Criminal Justice, and Houston-area churches.

Texas Youth Commission Pilot Faith-Based Ministry

This year, the Texas Youth Commission began a pilot faith-based dormitory project at the Gainesville State School facility. It's a 12-month structured program for juvenile inmates and their families and uses a spiritually-based curriculum that complements TYC resocialization programs.

Restorative Justice Ministries Network

In response to the Governor's call for faith-based solutions to rehabilitate offenders, the Restorative Justice Ministries Network formed to provide released inmates, via Texas churches and Christian businesspeople, with the tools they need to succeed and reintegrate back into society.

"Second Chance" Teen Parent Program

Governor Bush and the Texas Legislature created "Second Chance" group homes for unwed teen welfare mothers – run by faith-based and other private groups – to offer them a place to raise their child in a loving, structured environment, get an education and receive job training. The pilot program received $3.3 million in state funding and will serve teen mothers in four Texas counties: Dallas, Harris, Bexar, and Hildalgo. Buckner Children and Family Services, Baptist Children's Home Ministries, and Promise House, three prominent faith-based organizations, won state contracts to operate part of the program.

New Prosperity Initiative

West Side Ecumenical Ministry
Cleveland, Ohio

April 11, 2000

Governor Taft, Elving Otero – thank you both. It is good to be with you at the West Side Ecumenical Ministry, a moral and social leader in this community. One of the great privileges of running for president is the chance to visit groups like yours, seeing just how much good that people can do for one another with commitment and compassion and vision.

I have just come from another group here in Cleveland called El Barrio, where I had a chance to visit with its leader, Dr. Nelson Bardecio. Like you, El Barrio helps people in need – with occupational training, job placement, and after-school tutoring. And, like you, their calling is to spread not only the gifts of charity but the blessings of opportunity – helping people to make their own way in the world and to use their own gifts.

And that is the same message that brings me here.

To share with you my own vision of how – in every city, and every *barrio*, and all across our country – we can make opportunity not only a hope and a promise, but a living reality.

One hundred years ago, Booker T. Washington – born a slave, founder of the Tuskegee Institute, evangelist for an integrated America – was given an honorary degree by Harvard University. It was a recognition of his many accomplishments. A symbol of racial inclusion.

Yet Washington urged Harvard and a listening America to confront a great challenge. "The mansions on Beacon Street," he said, must "feel and see the need of the spirits in the lowliest cabin in the Alabama cotton fields [and the] Louisiana sugar bottoms." Each of these worlds, he explained, can give strength and vitality to the other. Both of these worlds must become one nation.

A century of achievement later, the challenge still echoes. Ours is an age of unmeasured prosperity.

Despite corrections and setbacks, the stock market continues its rise, and more Americans than ever own a share in its success. From the millionaire next door to the increasing affluence of the middle class, America is wealthier than it has ever been.

Yet, in this plenty, there is need. At the edges of affluent communities, there are those living in prosperity's shadow. The same economy that is a miracle for millions of Americans is a mystery for millions as well.

Americans who live in a world above welfare's assistance, but beneath prosperity's promise.

From the beginning of this campaign, I have said that prosperity must have a purpose. That our nation must close the gap of hope. Today, I want to expand on that agenda.

Our newspapers and television programs praise and profile the winners in our high-tech economy. But we must never become a winner-take-all society.

Our economy must also honor and reward the hard work of factory and field, of waiting tables and driving cabs – not just enterprise, but sheer effort, not just technology, but toil.

As President, I will be committed to the advancement of all Americans – including those who struggle.

Who are these Americans? There are at least three groups. Many are just beginning a life of work, liberated from dependence on welfare.

Four years ago, we replaced a system of cash benefits with work requirements and time limits. Across America, we have seen a 40 percent decline in welfare cases — 54 percent in my state of

Texas. And most who have left welfare are now working.

But those who have left welfare's grasp can still feel welfare's pull. Progress can come slow, and not without courage. The courage of long hours and small tips and big responsibilities – the hard journey to self-sufficiency.

One woman off welfare put it this way: "It's good to be working, but you're steady crawling."

The end of welfare should be the beginning of opportunity. We want entry-level jobs to lead to real economic progress. Welfare reform should not be the survival of the fittest. It should be the path to a better life.

Still others on the fringes of our prosperity are new Americans, who have come to this country with the same dreams as our ancestors.

I am the governor of a state with many immigrants. I see the challenges: language barriers, lack of education and housing. All the problems of a young workforce. Yet I also see the vitality, energy and determination of men and women for whom America is not just a country, but a promise. I see a powerful ethic of work and faith and family.

At one time, we called this the Puritan work ethic. Or the Protestant ethic. Now, we are finding it is the Asian ethic. The Hispanic ethic. The African ethic.

It is, in fact, the American ethic. And if we welcome these new Americans – into our economy and into our hearts – we will be enriched by their gifts.

And finally there are many struggling Americans who have never been on welfare and never seen an immigration line. On the outskirts of both poverty and prosperity, they live paycheck to paycheck. With little savings. No health insurance. They are found in rural areas, small towns and big cities. Their finances are fragile.

A job is lost, a husband leaves, and they are weeks from poverty.

In all these cases, it should be our goal to help those who are getting by to get ahead. We want them to build, for themselves. We want them to build the confidence of a middle class life – a margin of savings and skills. A margin of economic safety, that allows Americans to turn from daily struggle to greater goals.

The success of America has never been judged by the sum of its wealth.

America has been successful because it offers a realistic shot at a better life. America has been successful because poverty has been a stage, not a fate. America has been successful because anyone can ascend the ladder and transcend their birth.

Never in history has there been a nation with such a close connection between dreams and reality. The worker who in Europe had faced the bolted door of class found in America a door that opened wide onto an entire continent of opportunity.

And it is true today. *The Los Angeles Times* tells the story of the Mendoza family, Americans from Honduras. The husband drives for a courier service, the wife works as a caregiver, and they struggle on $27,000 a year. But once a month, they make a point of taking their two girls out to dinner. "The girls need to know how to behave, what to order in a nice restaurant," says their mother. "Someday they are going to have that in their lives."

The Mendozas take their girls to tutoring, and save for education. As Mrs. Mendoza says: "My girls will go to college."

This amazing certainty, this durable faith, is the silent strength of our country. And it must not be lost. This promised land must keep its promises.

Clearly there are some in our society who can't help themselves – the hardest core of need. People with severe mental and physical handicaps. People with no bootstraps to pull. These Americans require a safety net of care. Our nation should provide that safety net – and actively encourage charities and parishes and synagogues to add their support.

For the rest, we must have a "society of free work, of enterprise, of participation." Those are the words of Pope John Paul II. They are the substance of the American Dream.

This requires a healthy economy – rapid, non-inflationary economic growth. Such growth is not inevitable.

For our prosperity to continue, it must be actively expanded. And I have proposed a plan to do so. Less regulation. Less litigation. Lower taxes. Policies to create good, new jobs – to sustain our prosperity, and expand it.

But our prosperity is not enough. It is true that government can undermine upward mobility – as welfare once did. It is equally true that government – active but limited government – can promote the rewards of work. It can take the side of individual opportunity.

This is a higher and older tradition of my party. Abraham Lincoln argued that "every poor man should have a chance." He defended a "clear path for all." He financed colleges, welcomed immigrants, promoted railroads and economic development.

And, through the Homestead Act, he gave countless Americans a piece of land and a start in life. "Never in human history, before or since," says historian Paul Johnson, "has authority gone to such lengths to help the common people."

It is time for a New Prosperity Initiative that reflects the spirit of Lincoln's reforms. A plan to help remove obstacles on the road to the middle class. A plan to clear a path for all. Instead of helping people cope with their need, we will help them to move beyond it. With the same energy and activism that others have brought to expanding government, we must expand opportunity.

My New Prosperity Initiative begins with education – the constant focus of my campaign.

I have an agenda that brings high standards to low income schools. An agenda that says to failing schools: We will help you improve. But we will also require you to improve – to show results for the federal money. We will no longer ignore or excuse your failure. The stakes are too high. Jobs in America increasingly require reading and problem solving and computing. The quality of education is closely related to the quality of our jobs and the quality of our lives. So we must make all our schools into "engines of mobility."

Today I want to focus on four other areas – in addition to education. Four keys to upward mobility. We must increase the rewards of hard work. We must increase access to affordable health care. We must expand homeownership. And we must encourage savings and personal wealth.

First, we must change an oppressive tax system that punishes workers on the lowest rung of the economic ladder.

Picture a single mother with two children, working full-time, juggling all the responsibilities of home and work, and making $22,000 a year. Now picture a young corporate lawyer making ten times that much – $220,000 a year. Under the current tax code, that single mom actually pays a higher marginal tax rate than the lawyer does. In other words, just as she moves up and starts making more money, the federal government takes away nearly half of every dollar she earns through overtime and pay raises.

She is punished for working her hardest hours. This is unfair. It is unjust. And it must be ended.

Under my tax relief plan, she won't be paying that higher rate. In fact, she won't pay any federal income tax at all, and neither will six million other low income families. By reducing rates and doubling the child credit, my plan takes down the tollbooth to the middle class.

Our tax code, in the end, will be more progressive.

Today, the wealthiest taxpayers – those earning more than $100,000 – account for 62 percent of total income taxes paid. Under my plan, this will increase to 64 percent. For all other income groups, their share of the tax burden will fall.

In this year, you can expect to hear charges and counter-charges and attacks. But on taxes, I hope you'll remember this basic fact. Under today's tax code, a single-parent family of three starts paying federal income taxes at about $21,000 in income.

Under my plan, federal taxes for that family don't begin until $31,000. It used to be that my critics were against tax cuts for the rich. Now they're also against tax cuts for the poor. I welcome the debate.

Second, America must set a goal – a goal worthy of our nation. Every low-income, working family in America must have access to basic health insurance – for themselves and for their children.

Of all the bills we pay in life, medical costs are the most unpredictable, and can be the most expensive. For a family without health insurance, a single doctor bill can be a financial disaster.

I believe we can help these Americans.

We can start by making a basic health plan more affordable. As President, I will propose a Family Health Credit. This credit will pay for 90 percent of the cost of an insurance policy, up to $2,000 a year, for every family making less than $30,000.

Every family will be eligible that is not already covered by government programs or an employer plan.

This Family Health Credit will help to buy a basic policy. In most places in America, that means visits to a doctor, discounted prescriptions, and hospitalization. The basics, but enough to ensure against sudden poverty. And a lot more peace of mind.

We will also increase the number of good, lower-cost plans available to workers.

Small businesses should be allowed to buy insurance from a trade association, giving them the same purchasing power as a large company, and bringing down the cost. This means that a family restaurant, or a local hardware store, can insure their workers through, say, the National Restaurant Association, or the U.S.

Chamber of Commerce.

We will not nationalize our health care system. We will promote individual choice. We will rely on private insurance. But make no mistake: In my Administration, low-income Americans will have access to high quality health care.

Third, in the spirit of the Homestead Act, we will help many Americans to buy their first home. Just as Lincoln gave immigrants fresh from Europe a piece of land, we will help Americans to own a part of the American Dream.

Everyone who owns a home can remember that first day when the loan was approved, the check cleared and they stepped foot into their very own house.

It's different from renting. Suddenly you belong somewhere. Just like that, you're not just visitors to the community anymore but part of it – with a stake in the neighborhood and a concern for its future.

Looking at today's construction boom, it's easy to forget that many Americans are still waiting for this experience. The home-ownership rate among whites in America is 73 percent. Among African-Americans and Hispanics, it is 47 percent.

Right now the government offers help to low-income families, but mainly in the rental market. Through what's known as the Section 8 program, the federal government makes up the difference between fair-market rents and what a given family is able to pay.

This is a good aim, as far as it goes – but we should extend it further. Instead of receiving monthly voucher payments to help with the rent, I propose a path to ownership.

Under my plan, low-income families can use up to a year's worth of rental payments to make a down payment on their own house. And for five years after that, as they pay their mortgage and build equity, they can still receive housing support, just as they would if they were still renting.

It makes a lot more sense to help people buy homes than to

subsidize rental payments forever. They are not only gaining property but independence and the sense of belonging that ownership brings.

For the millions of low-income families not enrolled in Section 8, we will create a new program – called the "American Dream Down Payment Fund." When a low-income family is qualified to buy a house but comes up short on the down payment, we will help them. If they and the bank can come up with 25 percent of the down payment, the government will pay the rest, up to $1,500. This simple reform could help over 650,000 families in five years purchase homes.

I believe in private property. I believe in private property so strongly, and so firmly, I want everyone to have some.

In the same way, we can help people to build other assets, starting literally with money in the bank. The fourth key to upward mobility.

Those in the lowest 20 percent of income usually have savings of less than $1,000. Many coming off welfare have never had a personal bank account. But money in the bank builds confidence. It makes us agents of our own destiny.

Many people who are now successful can remember how hard it was to save – but how important it was to start. And we can help many Americans make that start. As President, I will propose Individual Development Accounts. If a low-income person is able to save up to $300, we will encourage banks, with a federal tax credit, to match that amount. The money can then be withdrawn tax free to pay for education, to help start a business or buy a home. This proposal should result in over one million new savings accounts.

For decades, our government tried to fight poverty by redistributing income, often leaving a legacy of dependence. The great promise of our time is to fight poverty by building the wealth of the poor. A home to anchor their family. A bank account to create confidence. And, I believe, a personal Social Security account, which would give millions of low-income Americans, not just a check, but an asset to own, a stake in our prosperity.

This account would not only better their lives, but could be passed to their children and grandchildren, giving them a better start in life. These are the tools of freedom and independence. And they should not belong to the prosperous alone.

In a depression, economic justice is a thundering demand. In good times, it is often a still, small voice. But we must listen. We must listen to a voice that says, "To whom much is given, much is required."

We must listen to a voice that says, "Let not the needy be forgotten, nor the hope of the poor be taken away."

In our society, it is easy to be secluded in success, in gated communities and separate schools. Yet our growing nation must not be allowed to grow apart. Since Lincoln, our national task has been to build a single nation – to cross boundaries of class and race and region. We have accepted a moral obligation to bring every American into the mainstream of opportunity. Because no one is a stranger. Because everyone is a neighbor and a citizen and a child of God.

I am reminded of Teddy Roosevelt's words: "For well or for woe we are knit together, and we shall go up or down together; and I believe that we shall go up and not down, that we shall go forward instead of halting and falling back, because I have an abiding faith in the generosity, the courage, the resolution and the common sense of all my countrymen."

It will be said of our times that we were prosperous.

But let it also be said of us that we used our wealth wisely. We invested our prosperity with purpose. We opened the gates of opportunity. And all were welcomed into the full promise of American life.

Position Paper
New Prosperity Initiative

April 11, 2000

"I propose a New Prosperity Initiative...A plan to help remove obstacles on the road to the middle class... Instead of helping people cope with their need, we will help them to move beyond it. With the same energy and activism that others have brought to expanding government, we must expand opportunity."

Governor George W. Bush

EXECUTIVE SUMMARY

Governor Bush believes that government should tear down barriers to the middle class for individuals and families caught between poverty and prosperity. The Governor's education reform plan does this by bringing high standards and accountability to low-income schools, turning them into "engines of mobility." Today, he is announcing his New Prosperity Initiative, which focuses on four other keys to upward mobility:

To Reward Work, Governor Bush's Tax Reform Plan will:

- Give the biggest percentage cuts to the lowest income earners, making the tax code more progressive.

- Help low-income families keep more of their earnings by creating a new, lower bottom rate of just 10 percent, and doubling the per-child credit to $1,000.

- Take 6 million families – one in five taxpaying families – off the income tax rolls.

To Provide Access to Affordable Health Care, Governor Bush will:

- Provide a health credit of up to $2,000 per family ($1,000 per individual) to cover 90 percent of the cost of health insurance for low-income, working Americans who are not covered by a government program or their employer. As income increases, the share of the cost covered by the health credit will decrease.

- Lower the cost of health insurance for small businesses and their employees by allowing these businesses to purchase more affordable policies through multi-state Association Health Plans.

- Strengthen the State Children's Health Insurance Program, giving states more flexibility to innovate and reach out to eligible people.

- Empower people through Flexible Savings Accounts and Medical Savings Accounts.

To Expand Homeownership, Governor Bush will:

- Reform HUD's Section 8 rental voucher program to permit recipients to use up to a year's worth of vouchers to finance the down payment on a home.

- Establish the "American Dream Down Payment Fund" to provide $1 billion of matching grants to lenders over five years to help as many as 650,000 low-income families, who are not enrolled in Section 8, to become homeowners.

To Build Savings and Personal Wealth, Governor Bush will:

- Support the creation of more than 1 million Individual Development Accounts (IDAs) by providing a tax credit to banks that match the savings of low-income earners, who can withdraw the matched funds tax free to finance a home, a business or education.

New Prosperity Initiative

The American economy has always been characterized by upward mobility. According to a study by the Federal Reserve Bank of Dallas, 95 percent of those individuals whose income placed them in the bottom fifth of the population in 1975 rose to a higher income class over the following 16 years. Over 50 percent of these people made it into the middle class or higher.

Similar studies suggest that the majority of today's low-income earners will also rise to the middle class. It may not be easy, but government can help. In order to accelerate their progress toward the middle class and to give all low-income earners increased opportunity, Governor Bush is committed to tearing down the major obstacles in their way. He has already announced his plan to remove one of the worst of these obstacles: schools that do not teach and will not change.

Governor Bush has proposed an education reform plan to turn failing schools into "engines of mobility" for low-income students. His plan is based on an entirely new federal approach to education, granting states and schools unprecedented freedom from regulation – in exchange for results. This requires generating pressure from above for high standards and accountability, and promoting competition from below to spur innovation and excellence.

Today, Governor Bush is announcing his New Prosperity Initiative, which focuses on four additional keys to ensuring upward mobility:

- Rewarding work by changing an oppressive tax code to give the biggest percentage tax breaks to the lowest income earners.

- Providing access to affordable health care.

- Expanding homeownership through down payment assistance.

- Building wealth by encouraging savings.

Rewarding Work Through Tax Cuts

The current tax code's high marginal rates act as a tollgate, limiting the access of low and moderate-income earners to the middle class. Because the benefit of the Earned Income Credit diminishes as workers earn more, many families face punitive marginal rates that serve as a powerful disincentive to work harder or invest more.

For example, a single mother with two children on the outskirts of poverty now loses almost half of any additional dollar she earns (taking into account social insurance taxes and state income taxes). In other words, the benefit of taking an extra training course or working an extra shift is cut in half by the government. As a result, a single mother with two children earning $22,000 a year faces a higher marginal tax rate than a lawyer earning $220,000. Lowering this barrier to the middle class is one of Governor Bush's top priorities.

Therefore, to increase access to the middle class for low-income individuals and families, Governor Bush's tax cut plan will:

Reward the Efforts of Low-Income Earners by Cutting Their Marginal Rate: Under the Bush tax plan, the marginal income tax rate will fall by over 40 percent for low-income families with two children, and by nearly 50 percent for families with one child, because the plan will:

- Create a New, Lower Bottom Rate of 10 Percent: The current 15 percent tax bracket will be cut to 10 percent for the first $6,000 of taxable income for singles, the first $10,000 for single parents, and the first $12,000 for married couples.

- Double the Per Child Credit to $1,000: The existing child tax credit will be increased from $500 to $1,000 per child.

These changes benefiting low-income earners account for almost half of the total cost of the Bush income tax cuts. While many other taxpayers will also benefit from these changes, they are the most powerful way to reduce the marginal rate on lower-income workers struggling to reach the middle class.

The Bush tax cut plan makes the tax code more progressive by providing the biggest percentage cuts to the lowest income earners. As a result, the share of the total tax burden shouldered by low- and moderate-income earners will decrease (from about 10 percent to slightly over 8 percent), while the share shouldered by those making more than $100,000 will increase (from less than 62 percent to more than 64 percent).

Another obstacle faced by low-income earners is mounting consumer debt, which has reached an all-time high of more than $1.4 trillion. Credit card debt alone totals over $600 billion, more than $2,000 for every man, woman, and child in the country. Low-income families often hold a disproportionately high amount of credit card debt.

By cutting marginal tax rates for low-income families, and by making the tax code more progressive, the Bush tax plan puts significantly more money into the hands of low-income individuals and families to pay their debts and meet their needs:

- A single mother with one child earning $18,500 will receive a $500 tax cut.

- A single mother with one child earning $22,000 will receive a $1,000 tax cut.

145

- A single mother with two children earning $32,000 will receive a $1,500 tax cut.

- Young people making just above the minimum wage will receive a $200 tax cut.

- A family of four will not pay any income taxes until $36,500, saving up to $1,750.

As a result, six million families – one in five taxpaying families with children – will no longer pay any federal income tax.

Providing Access to Affordable Health Care

Governor Bush's tax cut plan will provide low-income families with additional incentives to work and save, and more resources to meet their needs and pay their bills. But one of the largest potential bills faced by those on the road to the middle class is the bill for health care. For a family without health insurance, a single doctor bill can be a financial disaster.

People and families without health insurance are not only risking their financial health, they are also risking their physical health. Individuals without health insurance are less likely to have a primary care provider and to receive appropriate preventive care for themselves and their children.

It is for these reasons that Governor Bush is committed to providing all low-income Americans with the ability to choose a quality, affordable health care plan that meets their needs. To accomplish this objective, the Governor's New Prosperity Initiative focuses on:

- Providing access to health insurance for the uninsured through a refundable health credit.

- Promoting the development of more affordable private sector insurance plans.

- Empowering individuals with greater freedom of choice.

Providing Access for the Uninsured

In 1998, about 154 million Americans obtained health insurance through their employer, while about 34 million Americans received health insurance from public sector programs, such as Medicaid and the State Children's Health Insurance Program (S-CHIP). However, a growing number of Americans are falling into the gap between public sector coverage and private employer-based coverage.

According to recent census data, lower-income Americans are the most likely to be uninsured. As health insurance costs continue to rise and become a larger portion of a family's income, obtaining coverage is becoming even more difficult.

More than 80 percent of the uninsured are working Americans or their dependents. For many individuals and families who do not receive the benefit of tax-free, employer-provided insurance, purchasing a health insurance policy with after-tax dollars is too large a burden on their budget. According to the Employee Benefits Research Institute, individuals who must pay for health coverage with their own after-tax dollars are 24 times as likely to be uninsured than those with employer-provided coverage.

Low- and moderate-income individuals and families that are caught in the gap between government programs and employer-provided insurance need additional resources to afford health insurance. Thus, as President, Governor Bush will:

<u>Provide the Uninsured with a Refundable Health Credit to Purchase Health Insurance</u>: Individuals and families that do not receive employer-sponsored coverage and that are not eligible for public programs, such as Medicaid and S-CHIP, will receive a health credit of up to $1,000 per individual and $2,000 per family to cover up to 90 percent of the cost of health insurance. Those most in need will receive the most help:

- For individuals earning $15,000 or less, and families earning $30,000 or less, Governor Bush's health credit will cover 90 percent of the cost of coverage, and the recipient will contribute 10 percent.

- Thereafter, as a recipient's income increases, the government's share of the cost of coverage steadily decreases.

- For example, if a family earning $30,000 purchases a health insurance plan costing $2,222, the government will contribute $2,000 (90 percent), and the family will pay just $18.50 per month ($222 annually, or 10 percent).

- If a family earning $50,000 purchases the same $2,222 health plan, the government's contribution will be $667, and the family's contribution will be $129 a month ($1,555 annually, or 70 percent).

The credit can be used only for the purchase of health insurance, and can be advanced to the insurer when premiums are due.

Strengthening S-CHIP to Increase Access

The 1997 State Children's Health Insurance Program was intended to be a flexible block grant program. It was designed to allow states to expand Medicaid and/or develop new private sector programs to cover the 7.2 million uninsured children in families with incomes under 200 percent of the poverty level.

Unfortunately, S-CHIP has been burdened with regulations that restrict the ability of states to innovate. For example, states have been limited in their ability to perform adequate outreach so that all eligible children can be given the opportunity to be covered. The National Governors' Association concluded earlier this year that this limitation and other "prescriptive" regulations "will make it more difficult, if not impossible, for states to create new and innovative health care delivery systems for the 21st Century." It is for this reason that Governor Bush will:

Strengthen S-CHIP by Lifting Restrictions on State Flexibility: Governor Bush believes that the S-CHIP program should be returned to its original design as a more flexible block grant program. States will be given the freedom to innovate and expand coverage of the uninsured under S-CHIP so that more eligible people can be reached.

Promoting Affordable Small Business Health Plans

The road to the middle class for many low-income individuals leads through small businesses. Indeed, small businesses provide 67 percent of workers with their first job.

However, almost 60 percent of all workers without health insurance are employed by firms with fewer than 100 people or are self-employed. One of the key reasons for this is that small businesses and sole proprietors have to pay substantially more for health insurance plans than big businesses. Unlike large companies, small businesses do not enjoy the benefits of economies of scale and are unable to spread their risks over a large pool of employees. As a result, according to the National Federation of Independent Businesses (NFIB):

- Small businesses pay an average of more than $4,300 per family policy, versus an average of just $3,521 for Fortune 500 companies.

148

- More than 35 percent of NFIB members pay over $5,000 for a family policy.

Small businesses often have to pass some of these costs on to their employees, many of whom may opt to go uninsured. In fact, 7.3 million currently uninsured persons were offered employer-sponsored insurance, but declined, citing cost as the main reason.

To help these individuals and their employers purchase more affordable health insurance, as President, Governor Bush will:

<u>Support the Creation of Association Health Plans (AHPs)</u>: Association Health Plans will allow small businesses to band together, across state lines, to purchase insurance from bona fide trade associations, such as the Chamber of Commerce or the NFIB. AHPs will enjoy the benefits of economies of scale and a larger risk pool, and thus reduce the cost of health insurance for millions of small businesses and their employees.

Promoting Individual Choice

Two innovative products exist to help people manage their own health care needs: Health Flexible Savings Accounts (FSAs) and Medical Savings Accounts (MSAs). Unfortunately, each of these products is limited by current law.

FSAs are supplemental health coverage arrangements made available by many employers to their employees. FSAs allow workers to save a portion of their pre-tax wages for unexpected out-of-pocket expenses, such as vision and dental care, or for deductibles and co-payments that may be associated with an employer-provided health plan. About 22 million private sector employees took advantage of Flexible Savings Accounts in 1997.

However, under current law, FSAs have a "use-it-or-lose-it" feature that requires all funds in an individual's account to be spent annually. If any money remains in the account at year-end, it is forfeited back to the employer to cover administrative expenses. This creates a perverse incentive for working families to spend all the funds in the FSA, even if the medical services they purchase are only marginally beneficial.

Medical Savings Accounts work in combination with a high-deductible, catastrophic health insurance policy. MSAs allow people to build up tax-favored funds to cover out-of-pocket medical expenses. However, not only does the law authorizing MSAs expire this year, it imposes a variety of restrictions: the number of MSAs is currently capped at 750,000; employees are prevented from contributing to an MSA if their employer contributes; and MSA funds are limited to a percentage of the deductible of the related catastrophic insurance plan.

To promote greater freedom of choice and empower individuals to manage their own health care needs, as President, Governor Bush will:

<u>Permit Employees to Rollover Flexible Savings Accounts</u>: Under Governor Bush's plan, the current law will be changed to allow up to $500 of FSA funds to be carried over from one year to the next. This will encourage more efficient use of medical benefits and enable employees to more effectively meet their health needs.

<u>Expand and Reform Medical Savings Accounts</u>: The law and regulations governing MSAs will be changed to:

- Make MSAs permanent.

- Lift the 750,000 cap on the number of accounts.

- Allow all employers to offer an MSA, including as part of a cafeteria plan.

- Permit both employee and employer contributions.

- Lower the minimum deductible to $1,000 for an individual and $2,000 for family coverage, and permit contributions up to the deductible.

Expanding Homeownership

Homeownership has always been at the heart of the American dream. It is also central to the health of the U.S. economy and the wealth of families. Housing accounts for more than 22 percent of GDP. Americans spend about $1 out of every $3 in personal consumption on housing-related expenditures, and owner-occupied real estate comprises 21 percent of all household wealth.

Homeownership, and the stability it brings, yields a variety of social benefits:

- Homeowners are significantly more involved in their community than renters.

- Homeowners serve as officers of local improvement groups more often than renters.

- Homeowners' children are less likely to drop out of school.

Homeownership also increases savings. Mortgage payments, unlike rental payments, help build net worth because a portion of the payment goes toward building equity. In turn, as one's home equity increases, it becomes easier to finance an auto loan or a college education.

However, despite the fact that the U.S. homeownership rate is at a record 67 percent, not everyone has shared in that dream. While the rate of growth in homeownership is increasing faster among minorities and immigrants than among the population as a whole, less than 47 percent of African-Americans and Hispanics own homes, versus 73 percent of whites.

Providing Down Payment Assistance to Subsidized Renters

The biggest obstacle faced by low-income, first-time homebuyers is funding the down payment and closing costs. Surveys indicate that 43 percent of current renters cite these up-front costs as the number one barrier to homeownership.

Traditionally, the federal government has focused housing assistance on low-income renters – not first-time homebuyers – through programs such as the Department of Housing and Urban Development's (HUD) Section 8 voucher program. The House of Representatives recently passed "The American Homeownership and Economic Opportunity Act," which would help Section 8 renters purchase a home by allowing them to use their rental vouchers to finance a down payment and mortgage costs.

To encourage low-income recipients of Section 8 vouchers to graduate to homeownership, Governor Bush's New Prosperity Initiative will:

<u>Reform Section 8 by Allowing Recipients to Apply Their Rental Vouchers to Homeownership</u>: Governor Bush will support legislation authorizing local Public Housing Authorities to provide Section 8 renters with up to a year's worth of vouchers in a lump-sum payment to finance the down payment and closing costs on a house:

- Section 8 families will also be permitted to use vouchers to subsidize their monthly mortgage payments for up to five years. As their income increases, the subsidy will decrease.

- Families that receive down payment assistance will be required to complete a homeownership/financial management program, such as that offered by Habitat for Humanity and other non-profit groups.

Providing Down Payment Assistance to Other Low-Income Renters

Providing down payment assistance through Section 8 vouchers is only a partial solution to the problem of homeownership for low-income families. Existing federally-assisted housing programs reach only 25 percent of the roughly 17 million people who are eligible. The Section 8 voucher program itself reaches only 1.4 million families, and the wait for Section 8 vouchers can be several years or more in major metropolitan areas.

Thus, to help non-Section 8 renters become homeowners, as President, Governor Bush will:

Create the "American Dream Down Payment Fund:" This fund will provide $1 billion of assistance over five years to non-Section 8, low-income renters who aspire to homeownership. By leveraging the capital of banks and other private institutions, the fund could help over 650,000 low-income homebuyers:

- Assistance will be available to first-time homebuyers making less than 80 percent of the area median income.

- The fund will match a bank's contribution to a down payment, closing costs or a "soft" second mortgage on a 3 to 1 basis up to $1,500. For example, if a family is $2,000 short of a down payment, the government will provide 75 percent of the difference, if the bank provides the remaining 25 percent.

- The fund will be administered by state agencies.

Building Savings and Personal Wealth

The road from welfare to the middle class is not through consumption, but through saving and investment. Homeownership is one of the surest ways for families to build wealth. But given that less than half of all low-income families own a home, it is not surprising that a significant number of families have little or no savings:

- One-third of American households possess zero – or even negative – financial assets.

- Close to 50 percent of all children live in households with no net financial assets.

- Between 13 and 20 percent of Americans do not interact with a financial institution.

While the federal government encourages higher-income households to save through deductible mortgage interest payments and lower capital gains rates, it provides few incentives for low-income people to acquire wealth or save.

In response, the 1996 Welfare Reform law allowed states to incorporate matched savings accounts – so-called "Individual Development Accounts" (IDAs) – into their welfare programs. Subsequently, a number of IDA demonstration projects have been launched by non-profit organizations, such as the Corporation for Enterprise Development.

IDAs are designed to help low-income families accumulate wealth. Financial institutions, foundations, charities, community and faith-based groups match low-income depositors' savings up to a set amount annually. Depositors can then withdraw the funds for certain high-return investments, such as education, homeownership, and entrepreneurship.

Today, more than 5,000 low-income working people in 200 neighborhoods across the country are participating in IDA programs. Legislation has been introduced in the Congress to expand IDAs by providing a tax credit to financial institutions that match the savings of low-income depositors.

Governor Bush believes the private sector should take the lead in encouraging IDAs. However, to help accelerate their development, as President, he will:

<u>Support Legislation Encouraging Low-Income Families to Save and Invest Through Individual Development Accounts</u>: The IDA program envisioned by Governor Bush will provide $1 billion of tax credits over five years to sustain 1.3 million or more Individual Development Accounts:

- The program will provide a 50 percent tax credit to financial institutions that match deposits of up to $300 annually made by individuals making less than 60 percent of the area median income.

- Banks will receive a Community Reinvestment Act credit equal to 10 percent of matched contributions.

- Recipients will have full access to all IDA funds and will be able to withdraw the matching funds tax-free to buy a first home, start a new business, or pay for education. If participants want to use IDA funds for other purposes, they will be able to access only their own deposits, on a taxable basis.

- Governor Bush's previously announced Charitable State Tax Credit will be made available to encourage individual and corporate contributions to non-profit organizations that make matching grants and/or conduct financial education, monitoring, and administration for the IDA program.

Position Paper
Improving Long-Term Care for Senior Americans
May 10, 2000

> *"My goal is to make long-term care available and affordable, instead of a path to financial ruin...We have a system today where a person goes into a nursing home, and quickly consumes their life savings...In light of the expenses that could be involved, and the number of people likely to need long-term care, I will make affordable long-term care insurance – 'peace-of-mind' insurance – a priority."*
>
> *Governor George W. Bush*

EXECUTIVE SUMMARY

The need for long-term care is increasing. The number of individuals aged 65 or older is projected to double by 2030, due to the retirement of the Baby Boom generation. In addition, retirees are living longer lives due to medical advances.

To Make Long-Term Care Insurance More Affordable, as President, Governor Bush will:

- Make the cost of long-term care insurance fully deductible.

- Establish an additional personal exemption for home caregivers.

The Growing Need for Long-Term Care

By 2030, when the last of the Baby Boom generation reaches retirement, the number of individuals aged 65 or older is estimated to double from 35 million to nearly 70 million. At the same time, the life expectancy of these retirees is increasing. According to the Census Bureau, by the middle of this century over 40 percent of the people who reach age 65 will live to age 90.

As the baby boomers and their parents age, long-term care needs will become particularly acute. Between 2000 and 2030, the nursing home population will rise from 2.8 million to 5.3 million; total nursing home expenditures will rise from $69 billion to $330 billion.

Financing Long-Term Care Needs

Long-term care can be expensive. According to the American Council of Life Insurance, an assisted living facility can cost a person about $26,000 per year, two visits a day by a home health aide can cost more than $30,000 per year, and a stay in a nursing home can average $40,000 a year.

A recent survey found that 67 percent of the respondents were counting on having the cost of their long-term care needs covered by their existing health insurance plan or Medicare. Most private health insurance plans, however, do not cover long-term care needs, and Medicare covers only short-term, skilled nursing home care following hospitalization. Medicare also limits the coverage of home care to those who need rehabilitative services or physical therapy.

As a result, most long-term care costs are currently met through the Medicaid program and out-of-pocket expenditures. In fact, public funds pay for 62 percent of nursing home costs, while 31 percent comes from out-of-pocket funds. Only five percent are paid from private insurance sources. Under current trends, Medicaid expenditures will have to increase by 360 percent to $134 billion by 2030 to meet seniors' long-term care needs.

Making Long-Term Care Insurance More Affordable

While relatively few people rely on private insurance to cover nursing home costs, many affordable long-term care insurance plans are available. Congress requires these policies to meet certain basic standards:

- Policies may not limit or exclude coverage for certain illnesses and cannot be cancelled because of advancing age or deteriorating health.

- Premiums cannot increase because of advancing age.

- Policies must offer a non-forfeiture benefit: if a policy is cancelled or you let it lapse, some portion of your benefits will still be available.

- Policies must ensure inflation protection so that as costs rise, your benefit will keep pace with inflation.

The cost of these plans is surprisingly low compared to the price of a nursing home stay:

- For example, a 55-year-old man today would pay about $890 per year, or $74.16 a month, for a long-term care policy with a two-year nursing home benefit. If this man enters a nursing home at age 85, he will have paid premiums totaling $17,700 (in today's dollars). If he had been uninsured, the same two-year stay would have cost him $75,500 (again in today's dollars). As a result, having long-term care insurance means he saves $57,800.

- If the man in the example could have deducted his premium payments, he would have saved almost $200 annually (in today's dollars), making insurance significantly more affordable and attractive. Under current law, however, long-term care premiums can be deducted only by taxpayers who itemize and have medical expenses over 7.5 percent of their adjusted gross income.

Governor Bush is committed to making long-term care insurance available and affordable. As President, he will:

<u>Make the Cost of Long-Term Care Insurance Fully Deductible</u>: To provide an incentive for more people to purchase long-term care insurance, Governor Bush will provide a 100 percent above-the-line tax deduction for long-term care insurance premiums. Everyone will be eligible for the deduction, except for those who already receive employer-subsidized long-term care coverage. The total cost of the deduction is $5.1 billion over five years.

Easing the Burden of Home Care

While the costs of nursing homes and assisted living facilities are substantial, they do not include the full cost of caring for seniors who have physical or mental impairments. About 57 percent of the frail elderly rely solely on family and friends for care. In fact, a survey by the National Alliance for Caregiving found that 22 million American households have at least one member providing some unpaid assistance to a spouse, relative, or other person older than 50. In the future, it will not be uncommon for a 95-year-old to rely on assistance from a 90-year-old spouse, or a 65-year-old daughter.

Governor Bush is committed to easing the burden on those caring for relatives at home.   That is why, as President, he will:

<u>Establish an Additional Personal Exemption for Home Caregivers</u>: To alleviate some of the financial burdens associated with caring for family members at home, Governor Bush will establish an additional exemption for each elderly spouse, parent, or relative that a caregiver tends to in their home. The exemption is currently valued at $2,750 per person.   The total cost of the personal exemption is $2.3 billion over five years.

Position Paper
Strengthening the Health Care Safety Net
April 12, 2000

"Our society resolved long ago to provide a safety net for those in the most desperate circumstances: a safety net that includes income support, housing assistance, and health services...My Administration will work every day to extend the blessings of prosperity to all the people of our country. Even as we do so – even as we work to reduce the number of uninsured – we will continue addressing real needs in ways that have proven effective."

Governor George W. Bush

EXECUTIVE SUMMARY

Governor Bush's "New Prosperity Initiative" tears down barriers to the middle class for low-income earners and their families. It includes proposals to increase access to private sector health insurance, promote the development of affordable insurance plans, and ensure greater freedom of choice by empowering individuals to manage their own health needs.

To Strengthen the Health Care Safety Net for Those Most in Need – People Located in Medically Underserved and Remote Areas – Governor Bush's New Prosperity Initiative Will Include $4.3 Billion to:

- Increase the number of Community and Migrant Health Centers by 1,200 over the next five years.

- Reform the National Health Service Corps so that physicians are sent to the areas most in need.

- Establish a "Healthy Communities Innovation Fund" that will provide

$500 million in grants over five years to communities for the establishment of pilot programs or demonstration projects that target specific community health needs.

Expanding Community and Migrant Health Centers

Many of the nation's low-income uninsured people live in inner-city neighborhoods and rural communities – areas with few or no physicians or other health services. For these communities, access to health care is a critical need.

Currently there are 3,000 community-based primary care sites that serve as a health care safety net for more than 11 million patients, 4.4 million of whom are uninsured. They provide care on a discounted, sliding fee scale – seeing all patients, regardless of their ability to pay. According to the National Association of Community Health Centers, these facilities reach:

- One of every 6 low-income children (4.5 million).

- One of every 5 low-income births (400,000).

- One of every 10 uninsured persons (4.4 million).

- One of every 8 Medicaid recipients (3.5 million).

- One of every 12 rural residents (5.4 million).

- One of every 4 homeless persons (500,000).

Community health centers are a critical component of the American health care safety net and are being asked to provide care to a greater number of people every day. Nevertheless, there are areas in our country that still do not have access to any health care services. That is why, as President, Governor Bush will:

Increase the Number of Community and Migrant Health Centers by 1,200: Governor Bush will increase the budget for Community and Migrant Health Centers by $3.6 billion over five years in order to double the number of people they can serve. In addition, he will:

- Create a "best practices" clearinghouse so that Health Centers have access to information and data on efficient operations at centers across the country.

- Encourage Health Centers to partner with local hospitals and providers, managed care organizations, or other Community Health Centers to ensure a more stable health care delivery system and financial environment.

Strengthening the National Health Service Corps

Since 1972, through scholarship and loan repayment programs, the National Health Service Corps (NHSC) has placed over 20,000 health care providers in areas with a shortage of health professionals. Today, despite the fact that 1,300 NHSC physicians are serving over four million people in 4,000 medically underserved areas, the NHSC is meeting only 12 percent of the demand.

Moreover, a recent Government Accounting Office (GAO) report found that NHSC providers were not always being sent to those areas most in need for three reasons:

- First, the definition of a "Health Professional Shortage Area" tends to overstate the need for providers because it does not take into account non-physicians providing primary care, such as nurse practitioners, and Corps providers already practicing in the shortage area.

- Second, the NHSC does not have a system to take into account the more than 2,000 foreign physicians practicing in shortage areas under the J-1 visa waiver program. As a result, some areas have too many physicians, while others have too few.

- Third, the NHSC has no way to determine how many physicians will choose to remain in place after they complete their term of service.

Therefore, to ensure that the NHSC serves as many shortage areas as possible, Governor Bush will:

<u>Strengthen the National Health Service Corps</u>: Governor Bush will reform the NHSC placement process so that Corps physicians work in the neediest areas. Specifically, he will:

- Amend the definition of Health Professional Shortage Area to reflect other non-physician providers practicing in the area.

- Coordinate the Corps program with the J-1 visa waiver program to avoid overlap.

- Encourage physicians to participate in the NHSC by making scholarship funds tax free.

Healthy Communities Innovation Fund

In communities across the nation, local organizations are addressing health care needs in innovative ways. For example, the Texas Department of Health recently launched one of the largest school-based health promotion programs. The "Child and Adolescent Trial for Cardiovascular Health" (CATCH) was created in conjunction with the University of Texas' Houston School of Public Health with the objective of teaching children in grades three through five and their parents about healthy living. This includes teaching healthy lifestyle skills in class and serving healthier foods in the cafeteria. This program focuses on early prevention of cardiovascular disease, and is currently serving 5,000 ethnically diverse children.

Governor Bush believes it is important to encourage similar community-based innovation in the health care field. Therefore, as President, he will:

Establish the "Healthy Communities Innovation Fund:" This fund will provide $500 million in grants over five years to communities to implement pilot programs and demonstration projects that address targeted health risks, such as childhood and adult Type II diabetes. Grants will also be available to implement innovative technologies, such as telemedicine networks.

Position Paper

Renewing the Dream: A Plan to Increase the Supply of Affordable Homes

April 18, 2000

"Homeownership lies at the very heart of the American dream. But, in many communities, there is a shortage of good housing to buy. In some distressed neighborhoods – especially in urban areas – properties are available for redevelopment. Yet they sit vacant or abandoned, because private investors cannot make the economics work. So today I am announcing a proposal I call 'Renewing the Dream' – a new approach to expanding homeownership and renewing distressed areas."

Governor George W. Bush

EXECUTIVE SUMMARY

Governor Bush believes that homeownership is a key to upward mobility for low-income earners and their families. That is why his New Prosperity Initiative allows Section 8 rental vouchers to be used to fund homeownership. It provides an additional $1 billion of matching grants over five years to help low-income families who do not benefit from Section 8 to fund the down payment and closing costs on a new home.

But in many areas there is an insufficient supply of affordable homes. And too many inner-city neighborhoods are blighted by abandoned, vacant properties that provide a sanctuary for crime rather than a home for families.

To Renew Distressed Areas and Expand the Supply of Affordable Homes, Governor Bush will:

• Establish the "Renewing the Dream" program to provide $1.7 billion over the next five years in investor-based tax credits to encourage the reha-bilitation of housing or the construction of new affordable housing in dis-tressed communities.

The Need to Increase the Supply of Quality, Affordable Homes

In certain urban and rural communities, and on Native American land trusts, there is a shortage of affordable single-family homes. A recent survey found that more than one-third of all renters cited a lack of affordable housing as a major impediment to homeownership. Indeed, the homeownership rates for low-income households (52 percent), minority households (47 percent) and urban households (50 percent) are still well below the national average home-ownership rate of 67 percent.

Moreover, housing conditions for low-income homeowners are often poor. A 1999 HUD report found 2.2 million low-income households lived in housing with moderate to severe physical problems, much of which was located in inner-city areas.

Many communities, particularly in urban areas, have the challenge of rehabbing or redeveloping a large number of vacant and abandoned properties. One of the biggest obstacles to community revitalization is the gap between the cost of acquiring and rehabbing a home or constructing a new home, and the low market prices for homes in distressed areas. Absent some mechanism for bridging this gap, many properties are bound to sit vacant, harming surround-ing property values and posing a threat to public safety.

When communities are able to find entities that will bridge this financing gap, they have seen developers transform failed housing projects and vacant lots into new neighborhoods of homeowners:

- In Charlotte, North Carolina, a coalition of lenders, housing entities, and philanthropic organizations converted a number of duplexes into over 100 affordable homes in Genesis Park, which was known for having the highest crime rate in Charlotte. Because of grant money, homebuyers were able to buy a home for less than the cost of purchase and rehabil-itation. The HouseCharlotte Down Payment and Closing Cost Assistance program provided grants of up to $7,500, and the Charlotte-

Mecklenburg Housing Partnership provided 20 percent second mortgages.

- In Baltimore, the St. Ambrose Housing Aid Center and several partners acquired and renovated HUD foreclosures and vacant properties in the Waverly/Pen Lucy neighborhoods. While the average cost per unit was between $55,000-$60,000 per home, mortgages averaged only $40,000, and the subsidy per house ranged between $15,000-$20,000. The subsidies were paid by the partners and by a grant from the city of Baltimore.

The "Renewing the Dream" Tax Credit

Governor Bush understands that bridging the gap between development costs and market prices is a key to making homeownership a reality for many low-income Americans. Therefore, in order to provide an incentive for private investors to redevelop single-family housing or construct new single-family housing for low-income homebuyers, Governor Bush will:

Establish the "Renewing the Dream" Investor-Based Tax Credit: This credit is designed to encourage the renewal of distressed communities and increase homeownership opportunities for low and moderate-income families. The program will provide investors with a tax credit of up to 50 percent of project costs for eligible home rehabilitation or construction:

- Eligible areas will include census tracts at or below 80 percent of area median income, and Native American trust lands.

- Eligible homeowners will include families with income at or below 80 percent of area median income.

- The tax credit will be distributed by state agencies that will have the flexibility to tailor the program to local needs.

The "Renewing the Dream" program will be funded at $1.7 billion over five years, and is estimated to result in the rehabilitation or construction of 100,000 homes.

Removing Regulatory Barriers

Governor Bush believes that any effort to increase the supply of affordable low-income housing should be accompanied by a deregulation initiative.

Regulatory barriers can make it difficult to obtain a mortgage or increase the cost of building a home. It is estimated that an increase of 25 basis points on a mortgage can result in the denial of homeownership to 400,000 families. In turn, federal, state, and local regulations can drive up the price of a new home by 25 percent or more in a typical market.

A federal clearinghouse already exists to provide information on deregulatory practices, but it can be made more effective. Legislation recently passed the House of Representatives that would make the contents of the clearinghouse more accessible to state and local agencies. Thus, as President, Governor Bush will:

<u>Support an Initiative to Help States and Cities Identify and Remove Regulatory Barriers to Affordable Single-Family Housing</u>: Governor Bush will support legislation amending the existing federal clearinghouse on state and local "best practices" to make it more effective, including moving its contents on-line and making them more accessible to state and local agencies.

New Freedom Initiative

Alpha One Independent Living Center
Portland, Maine

June 15, 2000

Thank you. It's good to be here, and I want to thank Alpha One for hosting me today. Your work has made a difference for so many people.

The last several decades have brought great changes in the lives of Americans with disabilities. And all of us have gained a clearer understanding of the whole range of disabilities. Old misconceptions are being discredited. Old attitudes are slowly passing away, old barriers falling away. Our goal now is clear: to speed up the day when our country has removed the last barrier to full, independent, productive lives for every person, with or without disability.

This goal follows very naturally from the most basic American ideals: Equal treatment under law. Opportunity for all. Respect for the dignity and rights of every person. That is more than our creed as a nation. It is, to paraphrase Lincoln, our responsibility as citizens – our duty as brothers and sisters of a common country. America today is blessed with so many opportunities to strive and serve and succeed. All that citizens with disabilities ask is a chance to use their own gifts, and to make their own contribution.

Many doors were opened ten years ago, when Congress passed the Americans with Disabilities Act. I support the ADA, and I am very proud that my father's signature made it the law of the land.

Because of the ADA, discrimination against a person with a disability is not just unkind or cruel or wrong: It is an infringement of federal law, and a violation of civil rights.

Because of the ADA, millions of Americans can now compete for jobs once denied them; enter buildings once closed to them; travel in buses and trains once unequipped for them. For those who have visual or hearing impairments, for those who use walkers or wheelchairs, or have mental retardation or mental illness, we have become a more hospitable society. Ten years after the ADA became law, we are a better country for it.

But the banning of discrimination is just the beginning of full participation. Barriers remain. There are steps we can and should take to remove these barriers.

In that spirit, I am proposing today a New Freedom Initiative to ensure that all Americans with disabilities, whether young or old, have every chance to pursue the American dream – to use more of their own skills, and make more of their own choices. We must do everything we can to ensure that more Americans with disabilities can live independently, hold jobs, and take part in the life of their communities. My Administration will act in three specific areas.

First, we will promote independent living.

As you know, the wonders of technology are nowhere more gratefully received than among those who have disabilities. In millions of lives, assistive technology is helping to defeat dependence and frustration and isolation: Text telephones for those with hearing impairments. Computer monitors with Braille display for those with visual impairments. Infrared pointers for people who can't use their hands – allowing them to use a computer by pointing at functions on the monitor or keyboard. Special software to help people with mental retardation learn how to read and write. Lighter wheelchairs and artificial limbs.

My Administration will be a champion of assistive technology and universal design principles. Through Rehabilitation

Engineering Research Centers, the federal government is a leader on assistive technology research. We will make this research a higher priority, and we will triple the current funding.

In addition, there are several thousand small businesses that have innovative ideas for assistive technology, but lack the means to bring them to market. So we will form a technology transfer fund to enable these firms to bring promising technology to the people who need it.

Thousands of people who require assistive technology cannot afford it. Alpha One was among the first to address this challenge, by working with banks and the state of Maine to arrange affordable financing for those in need. Congress has also recognized this problem by creating a low-interest loan program for those in need. My Administration will increase by tenfold the resources available for this program.

Education is another key to independent living. The Individuals with Disabilities Education Act guarantees children with disabilities a free and appropriate public education that meets their needs. I support the IDEA and its goals. And in meeting those goals, the federal government must pay its fair share.

Independent living should also include greater opportunities for homeownership. To provide such opportunities, we'll reform the section eight rental program. For the first time, a section eight recipient who has a disability will be able to use up to a year's worth of rental vouchers to finance the down payment on a home of their own, and continue using vouchers to pay the mortgage.

Second, we will help citizens with disabilities to claim their rightful place in the workforce.

Under the ADA, workplaces are less forbidding than they once were. Every day, millions of Americans with disabilities travel miles from home to work at full-time jobs. For others, this is impossible – and until recently, few alternatives were available to them.

All this is changing. Today more than 40 million Americans

work out of their homes during all or most of the week, plugged into the company network by telephone, fax, and computer. For families across America, this change has brought great convenience and flexibility. But for those with disabilities, it's nothing less than a revolution – opening a world of new opportunities and potential.

As with assistive technology, sometimes the last limitation is simple affordability. To overcome it, my Administration will create an Access to Telecommuting Fund. We will spend 20 million dollars in federal matching funds to enable Americans with disabilities to buy computers and other equipment necessary to telecommute.

I will ask Congress to change the tax treatment of computers and Internet access supplied by employers for use in the home. Making these a tax-free benefit will supply an added incentive to hire employees with disabilities who telecommute.

To create even more work opportunities, I will issue an executive order to fully and swiftly implement the recently-passed "Ticket-to-Work" law. As it is, many people with disabilities are reluctant to take a job, even a telecommuting job, for fear of losing their disability benefits and health coverage. This is a choice they should not be forced to make.

Third, we will help Americans with disabilities to gain fuller access to community life.

Every law depends on good faith in observance, and consistency in enforcement. The fact is that some requirements of ADA have yet to be fulfilled. This is especially true for people who face mental illness and mental retardation.

In the *Olmstead* case last year, the Supreme Court ruled that, wherever possible, persons with mental illness are entitled to live in the "most integrated" community settings rather than in institutions. This ruling, however, has not been completely carried out. As President, as I have as Governor, I will sign an executive order committing my Administration to the implementation of the *Olmstead* decision.

I am committed to fully enforcing the ADA. And to extend compliance even further, we will devote an additional five million dollars per year for technical assistance to small businesses to meet all requirements of the law.

We must remember that many activities of civic life are still difficult for people with disabilities. Even voting can be a hardship for them, as also for the elderly. I will work with Congress to make polling places and the voting process easier for seniors and those with disabilities.

We can also assist organizations that, while exempt from the ADA, are trying to observe it anyway. Most notable are churches, synagogues, and mosques, which want nothing more than to open their doors to all. Often, they just don't have the money. This has left many Americans with disabilities unable to worship alongside their families and neighbors. Also left out are those who would like to be active in clubs and community groups. How can they feel welcome if they can't even enter the building?

My Administration will seek $10 million each year to aid religious and civic groups in making their facilities more accessible. Over time, this will help make ramps and elevators even more common – a sign not only of more accessible buildings, but of a more welcoming society.

Next month, we mark Independence Day. A few weeks later, on July 26th, comes the tenth anniversary of the Americans with Disabilities Act. For many across America, that day in 1990 is remembered as a personal independence day – the day the law recognized their rights and full standing as citizens of the United States.

People with disabilities confront hardship every day of their lives. To me, that leaves our society with a simple choice – whether to add to that hardship, or to try to lessen it. Whether to answer that challenge with indifference, or with generosity of spirit.

With ADA, we gave our answer. We set for ourselves a permanent standard to live by, and to govern by. I make this pledge today: in my Administration we will honor that standard. We will not tolerate unfair barriers or unfair treatment for Americans with physical or mental disabilities. We will press on, until everyone has a chance to contribute – until every citizen shares in the full promise of American life.

Position Paper
New Freedom Initiative

June 15, 2000

"I am proposing today the New Freedom Initiative to ensure that all Americans with disabilities, whether young or old, have every chance to pursue the American dream – to use more of their own skills and make more of their own choices. We must do everything we can to ensure that more Americans with disabilities can live independently, hold jobs, and take part in the life of their communities."

Governor George W. Bush

EXECUTIVE SUMMARY

Governor Bush believes that all Americans should have the opportunity to learn and develop skills, engage in productive work, choose where to live, and participate in community life. Too often, however, people with disabilities are trapped in bureaucracies of dependence and are denied the tools and access necessary for success.

In Texas, Governor Bush has increased opportunities for individuals with disabilities, ranging from committing additional resources for community-based services and encouraging employment, to increasing access to public facilities and making appointments to state boards, commissions, and the Texas Supreme Court. As a presidential candidate, Governor Bush has worked to make his campaign accessible to people with disabilities. To continue these efforts to expand opportunities for Americans with disabilities, Governor Bush proposes the following new initiatives totaling $1.025 billion over five years:

To Increase Access to Technology for Americans with Disabilities and Promote Independence, Governor Bush will:

- Triple the Rehabilitative Engineering Research Centers' budget for assistive technologies, create a new fund to help bring assistive technologies to market, and increase tenfold the funding for low-interest loan programs to purchase assistive technologies.

- Work with Congress to increase funding for special education with the goal of meeting the federal obligation under the Individuals with Disabilities Education Act.

- Focus Title I funds on earlier grades to identify children with disabilities, and invest $5 billion over five years to establish the "Reading First" program.

- Reform HUD's Section 8 rental voucher program for people with disabilities to permit recipients to use up to a year's worth of vouchers to finance the down payment on a home.

To Further Integrate Americans with Disabilities Into the Workforce, Governor Bush will:

- Provide $20 million in federal matching funds to states to guarantee low-interest loans for individuals with disabilities to purchase computers and other equipment necessary to telework from home.

- Support legislation making a company's contribution of computer and Internet access for home use by employees with disabilities a tax-free benefit.

- Provide $100 million in matching grants and $45 million for pilot programs to promote innovative transportation solutions and increase access to alternate forms of transportation.

- Sign an Executive Order to support effective and swift implementation of the "Ticket-to-Work and Work Incentives Improvement Act" giving Americans with disabilities the ability to choose their own support services and maintain their health benefits when they return to work.

- Support full enforcement of the Americans with Disabilities Act, and provide new resources for technical assistance, to help small businesses comply with the Act.

To Increase Access for Americans with Disabilities into Community Life, Governor Bush will:

- Sign an Executive Order supporting the most integrated community-based settings for individuals with disabilities, pursuant to the Supreme Court decision in *Olmstead*.

- Create a National Commission to recommend reforms of the mental health service delivery system.

- Support improving access to the polls and ballot secrecy for people with disabilities.

- Provide $10 million in matching funds annually to increase the accessibility of organizations that are currently exempt from Title III of the ADA, such as churches, mosques, synagogues, and civic organizations.

Challenges and Opportunities for Americans with Disabilities

Today, there are over 54 million Americans with disabilities, a full 20 percent of the U.S. population. Almost half of these individuals have a severe disability, affecting their ability to see, hear, have speech understood, walk, or perform other basic functions of life. In addition, there are over 25 million family caregivers and millions more who provide aid and assistance to people with disabilities.

Beyond the numbers, disabilities can affect a person's ability to engage in major life activities. Recent data show that Americans with disabilities continue to face obstacles in education, employment, income, political participation, and participation in community life:

- One out of five adults with disabilities has not graduated from high school, compared to less than one of ten adults without disabilities.

- Among adults with disabilities age 18 to 64, only 29 percent work full- or part-time, compared to 79 percent of those without disabilities.

- In 1997, over one-third of adults with disabilities lived in a household with an annual income of less than $15,000, compared to only 12 percent of those without disabilities.

- Only 69 percent of adults with disabilities socialize with close friends, relatives or neighbors at least once a week, while 84 percent of adults without disabilities do, and approximately one-third of adults with disabilities go out to a restaurant once a week, while 60 percent of those without disabilities do so.

- Six out of ten adults with disabilities were registered to vote in the 1996 presidential election, compared with almost eight out of ten adults without disabilities. Voter registration services from government or community agencies have been offered to only a small percentage of adults with disabilities.

Progress has been made over the last two decades – most prominently with the passage of the Americans with Disabilities Act of 1990 – to improve access to employment, public accommodations, commercial facilities, telecommunications services, housing, schools, and polling places. However, much more needs to be done. To increase choices and opportunities to Americans with disabilities, Governor Bush has proposed a comprehensive package of initiatives to meet the following three goals.

Goal 1: Increase Access to Technology and Promote Independence

Assistive and Universally Designed Technologies

The National Council on Disability (NCD) has stated, "for Americans without disabilities, technology makes things easier. For Americans with disabilities, technology makes things possible." Assistive and universally designed technology can significantly enhance the quality of life for many of America's 54 million Americans with disabilities.

The NCD has found that federal policies often act as a barrier to the development and dissemination of assistive technology. As the NCD recently reported, "these barriers translate into poor quality of life for people who need the assistive technology they cannot get…[federal assistive technology policies] are a maze of conflicting definitions, eligibility criteria, philosophical models, and requirements for access to assistive technology."

Factors that limit access to assistive technology include:

- Inadequate funding for research;

- Lack of effective coordination among federal agencies and between the private and public sectors; and

- Insufficient incentives to help Americans with disabilities acquire assistive technology.

As President, Governor Bush will work to remove these barriers to assistive technology so that every American has the opportunity to fully participate in society.

Increase Investment in Assistive Technology R&D

Rehabilitative Engineering Research Centers (RERCs) funded through the National Institute on Disability Rehabilitative Research (NIDRR) are recognized as conducting some of the most innovative and high impact assistive technology research in the federal government. Each RERC focuses on a specific area of research, such as information technology access, prosthetics and orthotics, and technology for children with orthopedic disabilities. Increased funding would widen and deepen areas of research specifically targeted to people with disabilities.

Therefore, to increase the investment in these high impact programs, as President, Governor Bush will:

<u>Triple the Research Budget of the Rehabilitative Engineering Research Centers (RERC)</u>: As President, Governor Bush will triple the funding from $11 million to $33 million per year for advanced research in the development and application of assistive technology.

Improve Federal Coordination and Private-Public Partnerships

NIDRR is the most important agency dealing with assistive technology research and development in the federal government, accounting for 50 percent of appropriated funds for such purposes. However, it has failed to serve as an effective coordinating body because the Interagency Committee on Disabilities Research (ICDR) housed within NIDRR has no real authority. As part of Title II of the Technology Assistance Act of 1998, Congress authorized, but did not appropriate, funds for ICDR to coordinate the federal efforts to promote assistive technology.

There are nearly 2,500 companies working to bring assistive technologies to millions of Americans with disabilities. Many companies, however, cannot make the necessary capital investments until they have information concerning the market for a particular assistive technology. According to the Chief of the

Commercial Technology Office at NASA, "the end result is that while the necessary technology may exist in many cases, the private sector is often not able to apply it to serve the needs of many disabled Americans."

To improve the coordination of federal research in and commercial development of assistive technology, as President, Governor Bush will:

Fund the Interagency Committee on Disability Research (ICDR): Governor Bush will provide $3 million in new funding annually to the ICDR to increase its ability to coordinate the federal effort. These improvements will be achieved by hiring staff who will prioritize immediate assistive and universally designed technology needs in the disability community, as well as by fostering information transfer and collaborative projects between the federal laboratories and the private sector.

Establish a New "Assistive Technology Development Fund:" Housed under the ICDR, this $5 million annual fund will help underwrite technology demonstration, testing, validation and market assessment to meet specific needs of small businesses, with minimal paperwork and turnaround times.

Increase Access to Assistive Technology

Assistive technology is often prohibitively expensive. Personal computers configured with assistive technology can cost anywhere from $2,000 to $20,000. Micro-loan programs for interest rate buy-downs or loan guarantees are powerful tools to enable people with disabilities to buy the technology they need to be independent and productive. In a recent national survey, 61 percent of respondents who participated in such programs said they could not have otherwise afforded the product.

Congress has recognized the value of low-interest loans, authorizing $25 million for such programs in Title III of the Assistive Technology Act of 1998. Only $4 million was appropriated in FY2000, however. According to the National Council on Disability, "the availability of low-interest or even no-interest loans to people with disabilities through Title III would significantly increase the availability of a whole host of [assistive technology] devices, equipment, and services to people who currently have little or no access to [assistive technology]." Such incentives and loans lead to more productive lives for people with disabilities, while lessening the financial burdens on society.

Therefore, as President, Governor Bush will:

<u>Increase Funding for Low-Interest Loan Programs to Purchase Assistive Technology</u>: Funding for the federal low-interest loan program to purchase Assistive Technology will be increased from $4 million to $40 million annually. These grants must go to a state agency in collaboration with a bank or non-profit groups to guarantee loans and lower interest rates.

Education for Children with Disabilities

Originally passed by Congress in 1975, the Individuals with Disabilities Education Act (IDEA) ensures that children with disabilities would have a free and appropriate public education that would meet their needs.

The federal government has not been providing sufficient funding for the IDEA. By not providing the necessary federal IDEA funds, the program has become a large unfunded mandate on state and local governments and is failing to meet the needs of children with disabilities.

Governor Bush believes that no child should be left behind, including those with disabilities. Therefore, as President, Governor Bush will:

<u>Work with Congress to Increase Funding for Special Education with the Goal of Meeting the Federal Obligation under the IDEA</u>: Governor Bush would set the goal of increasing funding for the IDEA to reduce the unfunded mandate on the states and increase educational assistance to students with disabilities.

Governor Bush also believes it is equally important to emphasize preventative efforts to identify children with special needs. Early detection of needs will greatly benefit children by giving them the assistance they need, while reducing costs to local, state and federal government. To further these efforts, as President, Governor Bush will:

<u>Focus Title I Funds on Earlier Grades</u>: Students in K-12 will still be eligible for Title I, but Title I funds will focus on students in the elementary grades, where math and reading difficulties can be corrected before children are diagnosed as needing special education services.

<u>Establish the "Reading First" Program to Invest $5 Billion over Five Years</u>: Governor Bush will increase federal funding to low-income students, including those with disabilities, by creating a $5 billion incentive fund for states to help teachers detect and correct reading problems early, with the goal of teaching every child to read by third grade.

Homeownership for People with Disabilities

Rental assistance for Americans with disabilities is provided by a program known as Section 8 of the Housing Act of 1937, administered by the U.S. Department of Housing and Urban Development (HUD). Residents are provided Section 8 vouchers so they can afford rental payments for public housing. Nearly one-quarter of all Section 8 vouchers are given to individuals with disabilities under the age of 62.

Homeownership has always been at the heart of the American dream. Individuals with disabilities should not be bound to a government program that only allows them to rent. Instead, individuals with disabilities who are recipients of Section 8 vouchers for rental payments should be given the opportunity to buy a home.

To empower individuals with disabilities who receive Section 8 vouchers with more tools for independence, as President, Governor Bush will:

<u>Reform Section 8 to Allow Recipients Who are Disabled to Apply Their Rental Vouchers to Homeownership</u>: Governor Bush will support legislation allowing local Public Housing Authorities to provide recipients of Section 8 vouchers who are disabled with up to a year's worth of vouchers in a lump-sum payment to finance the down payment and closing costs on a home.

Goal 2: Integrate Americans with Disabilities into the Workforce

Promoting Telework

With the advent of widespread Internet access and innovative computing and web-based technologies, it is possible for significant numbers of workers with disabilities to do their jobs seamlessly from home.

The computer and Internet revolution has not reached as many people with disabilities as the population without disabilities. Only 25 percent of people with disabilities own a computer, compared with 66 percent of U.S. adults. And only 10 percent of people with disabilities have access to the Internet, compared to over 40 percent of U.S. adults. The primary barrier to wider access is cost. Computers with adaptive technology can cost as much as $20,000, which is prohibitively expensive for many individuals. The median income of Americans with disabilities is far below the national average.

Many companies have decided to give new computers and Internet access to their employees for home use. Many more are looking to do so. The value of the computer and the Internet provided, however, are treated under the tax code as a taxable fringe benefit, forcing companies to withhold income tax to reflect the tax value of the donation. Employees are also concerned about the loss of pay.

To help Americans with disabilities purchase teleworking tools, encourage companies to contribute these items, and ensure that federal regulations promote, rather than impede, the growth of telework, Governor Bush will:

Create the "Access to Telework" Fund: Governor Bush will provide $20 million in federal matching funds annually to states to guarantee low-income loans for people with disabilities to purchase equipment to telecommute from home.

Make a Company's Contribution of Computer and Internet Access for Home Use by Employees with Disabilities a Tax-Free Benefit: The value of a computer, software and peripheral equipment provided to employees with disabilities would be excludable from income. This proposal is estimated to cost $75 million annually.

Access to Affordable Transportation

Access to affordable transportation is another barrier to work for Americans with disabilities. One-third of people with disabilities report that inadequate transportation is a significant problem. In 1997, the Director of *Project Action* stated that "access to transportation is often the critical factor in obtaining employment for the nation's 25 million transit dependent people with disabilities." More must be done to test new transportation ideas and to increase access to alternate means of transportation, such as vans with accessibility lifts, modified automobiles, and ride-share programs.

To support the development of innovative transportation initiatives and increase access to alternate methods of transportation, as President, Governor Bush will:

Promote Innovative Transportation Solutions for People with Disabilities: Governor Bush will provide $45 million in funding over three years for ten pilot programs run by state or local governments in regional, urban, and rural areas. Governor Bush will work with Congress to evaluate the effectiveness of the pilot programs and encourage the expansion of successful initiatives.

Help Create a Network of Alternate Transportation Through Community-Based and Other Providers: Governor Bush will establish a competitive, $100 million matching grant program to promote access to alternative methods of transportation which will be open to Centers for Independent Living, Assistive Technology Centers, vocational rehabilitation centers, and other community-based organizations.

Ticket-to-Work

Throughout his campaign, Governor Bush has supported the "Ticket-to-Work and Work Incentives Improvement Act of 1999," which will give Americans with disabilities both the incentive and the means to seek employment. Now that the bill has been signed into law, Governor Bush is calling for its swift implementation.

Today, there are more than 7.5 million Americans with disabilities receiving benefits under federal disability programs. According to a recent Harris Survey, 72 percent of the disabled want to work. However, because of perverse disincentives in federal law, less than one percent of those receiving disability benefits enter the workforce.

Prior to the "Ticket-to-Work" law, a recipient's impairment made him or her unable to engage in any substantial work activity, thereby creating a disincentive to seek employment. In order to continue to receive disability payments and health coverage, the prior law required that a recipient could not engage in any substantial work, creating an enormous disincentive to seek employment.

Governor Bush supports swift implementation of the new law in order to:

- Provide Americans with disabilities with a voucher-like "ticket" that allows them to choose their own support services, including vocational education programs and rehabilitation services.

- Extend Medicare coverage for SSDI beneficiaries so they can return to work without the fear of losing health benefits.

- Expand Medicaid eligibility categories for SSI recipients so that they can continue to receive benefits even after their income, resources, or medical condition improves.

To increase opportunities for individuals with disabilities to enter the workforce, as President, Governor Bush will:

<u>Sign an Executive Order to Support Effective and Swift Implementation of "Ticket to Work:"</u> The Executive Order will direct federal agencies to swiftly implement the law giving Americans with disabilities the ability to choose their own support services and to maintain their health benefits when they return to work.

Compliance with Americans with Disabilities Act

When the Americans with Disabilities Act (ADA) was signed into law by President Bush on July 26, 1990, it was the most far reaching law advancing access, workforce integration, and independence for Americans with disabilities. The law gives civil rights protections to individuals with disabilities that are like those provided to individuals on the basis of race, sex, national origin, and religion.

To encourage small businesses to comply with the ADA, legislation was signed into law in 1990 to provide a credit for 50 percent of eligible expenses up to $5,000 a year. Such eligible expenses include assistive technologies. Unfortunately, many small businesses are not aware of this credit.

Governor Bush believes that the Americans with Disabilities Act has been an integral component of the movement toward full integration of individuals with disabilities, but recognizes that there is still much more to be done. He also recognizes that to further integrate individuals with disabilities into the workforce, more needs to be done to promote ADA compliance and financial incentives among small businesses. That is why, as President, Governor Bush will:

Support ADA and Provide Technical Assistance to Help Small Businesses Comply: Governor Bush will support full enforcement of the Americans with Disabilities Act, and provide $5 million annually for technical assistance to help small businesses comply with the Act, serve customers, and hire more people with disabilities.

Promote the Awareness and Utilization of Disabled Access Credit (DAC): The DAC, created in 1990, is an incentive program to assist small businesses in complying with the ADA. The DAC provides a credit for 50 percent of eligible expenses up to $5,000 a year, including expenses associated with making their facilities accessible and with purchasing assistive technologies. Utilization of the credit has been limited because small businesses are often not aware of it.

Goal 3: Increase Access into Community Life

Commitment to Community-Based Care

On June 22, 1999, the Supreme Court decided *Olmstead v. L.C.*, holding that the ADA requires the placement of persons with mental disabilities in a community setting wherever possible. The Court concluded that "unjustified isolation," i.e., institutionalization when a doctor deems community treatment

182

equally beneficial, "is properly regarded as discrimination based on disability."

Olmstead has yet to be fully implemented. Governor Bush supports community-based services, and, under his administration, funding for such programs in the State of Texas has increased by more than $1.7 billion, a 72 percent increase. In response to the *Olmstead* decision, on September 29, 1999, Governor Bush signed Executive Order GWB 99-2, calling for compliance with *Olmstead* through an immediate review of all services and support systems for Texans with disabilities and removal of barriers to community placement.

Governor Bush believes that community-based care is critically important to promoting maximum independence and to integrating individuals with disabilities into community life. That is why, as President, Governor Bush will:

Sign an Executive Order Supporting Swift Implementation of the *Olmstead* Decision: Governor Bush will enter an Executive Order supporting the most integrated community-based settings for individuals with disabilities, pursuant to the *Olmstead* decision, and calling for the identification and removal of barriers to community placement.

Direct the National Institute of Mental Health and the Substance Abuse and Mental Health Services Administration to Coordinate New Research Initiatives and Innovative Pilot Programs to Support Such Reforms: To ensure that the states come into compliance with *Olmstead* by instituting mental health reforms, Governor Bush will direct the National Institute of Mental Health and the Substance Abuse and Mental Health Services Administration to coordinate research initiatives and innovative pilot projects to further support such reforms.

Improve Coordination of Mental Health Programs

Currently, there are over 13 federal agencies that oversee mental health policies, funding, laws and programs including: the Substance Abuse and Mental Health Services Administration, Office of Personnel Management, Social Security Administration, National Institute of Neurological Disorders and Stroke, Department of Housing and Urban Development, Department of Justice, and Department of Labor.

These disparate agencies are doing valuable work, but they could be much more effective, efficient, and less duplicative if they were better coordinated. For instance, the Stanley Foundation Research Programs recently reported that the National Institute for Mental Health (NIMH) dedicates only 36 percent of its research funds to support basic and clinical research on severe mental illness.

With coordination, the competitive advantage of each agency could be leveraged so that the agency would provide the most needed and suitable service in the framework of federal efforts to address mental health. That is why, as President, Governor Bush will:

Create a National Commission on Mental Health Services: The National Commission would study and make recommendations for improving America's mental health service delivery system, including making recommendations on the availability and delivery of new treatments and technologies for individuals with severe mental illness.

Access to the Political Process

There are over 35 million voting-age persons with disabilities, but currently people with disabilities register to vote at a rate that is 16 percentage points less than the rest of the population and vote at a rate that is 20 percent below people without disabilities. If people with disabilities voted at the same rate as those without disabilities, five million more votes would have been cast in the last presidential election.

According to the National Organization on Disability, low voter turnout among people with disabilities is due to both accessibility problems at voting locations and the lack of secrecy and independence when voting. The most recent Federal Election Commission (FEC) report states that at least 20,000 of the nation's more than 120,000 polling places are inaccessible to people with disabilities.

Governor Bush recognizes that full integration into society must include access to and participation in the political process. That is why, as President, he will:

Support Improving Accessibility to Voting for Americans with Disabilities: Governor Bush will support improved access to polling places and ballot secrecy. He will work with Congress to address the barriers to voting for Americans with disabilities.

Access to ADA-Exempt Organizations

Title III of the Americans with Disabilities Act of 1990 opened countless businesses and public accommodations to people with disabilities by mandating that such places be made accessible. For constitutional and other concerns, however, Title III exempts many civic organizations (such as Rotary and Lions Clubs) and religious organizations from its requirements of full access.

Americans with disabilities should be able to be fully integrated into their communities, and civic and religious organizations are vital parts of those communities. Too many private clubs, churches, synagogues and mosques are inaccessible or unwelcoming to people with disabilities. As a result, people with disabilities are often unable to participate as fully in community or religious events as are people without disabilities.

Many organizations and congregations want to be open to all, but have limited resources to ensure accessibility.

Governor Bush believes that we should make every effort to ensure that Americans with disabilities have every opportunity to be integrated into their communities. Therefore, as President, Governor Bush will:

Establish a National Fund to Provide $10 Million in Matching Grants for Accessibility Renovations for ADA-Exempt Organizations: To assist private clubs and religious organizations in making sure their facilities are fully accessible and to expand access for all, Governor Bush will propose legislation to provide $10 million in annual federal matching grants to ADA-exempt organizations making renovations or accommodations to improve accessibility. Because the grants would go to all ADA-exempt organizations, irrespective of whether they are religious or secular, they would comport with the Supreme Court's test for constitutional neutrality.

Position Paper
Strong Families, Safe Children

July 11, 2000

"Our children are our greatest treasures and embody hope for the future. We must do everything we can to ensure that every child grows up in a safe, stable and loving family... and that our child welfare system actually advances this goal."

Governor George W. Bush

EXECUTIVE SUMMARY

Governor Bush believes that every child deserves to live in a safe, permanent and loving family. The federal-state child welfare system has failed to achieve this. The current system does too little to support and preserve families. At the same time, the system also leaves too many abused and neglected children languishing in foster care or other temporary living arrangements. The result is that countless children are growing up without the chance to fulfill their dreams.

In Texas, Governor Bush has strengthened efforts to keep families together and to protect children from abuse and neglect. In cases where children cannot remain in the home, he has also streamlined adoption laws to allow children to be adopted into loving families as quickly as possible. The number of children legally free for adoption more than doubled during 1996 to 1999; the time children spend waiting for adoption has been cut nearly in half over the last decade; and adoptions increased 175 percent from 1996 to 1999.

To expand efforts nationwide to protect our children, Governor Bush proposes the following reforms totaling $2.3 billion over five years.

To Encourage States to Help Families in Crisis, as President, Governor Bush will:

- Provide states an additional $1 billion over five years for preventative services to keep children in, or return them to, their homes, whenever safely possible.

To Ensure that Children in Foster or Adoptive Homes Live in Safe and Stable Environments, Governor Bush will:

- Require states to conduct criminal background checks on prospective foster and adoptive parents and close existing loopholes permitting states to opt out of such requirements.

- Create the presumption that "permanence" for children in the child welfare system means returning to a safe and stable biological family or, when a judge deems that impossible, finalized adoption. This will help prevent most children from spending their formative years in foster or other temporary care.

To Further Encourage Adoption and to Help Those Children Who Remain in Foster Care Until the Age of Majority, Governor Bush will:

- Provide $1 billion over five years to increase the adoption tax credit from $5,000 to $7,500 to families for non-reimbursable expenses associated with the adoption of a child. Governor Bush will also work with Congress to make the adoption tax credit permanent.

- Provide $300 million over five years for vouchers to young people who have "aged out" of foster care. These vouchers can be up to $5,000 for each young person to use for college tuition or vocational training.

The Plight of Children

America knows that foster care is failing the very children it is designed to protect. There are more than 540,000 children in government-paid foster care, some 50,000 of whom are legally free for adoption now. This substitute care

187

population is growing at a rate 33 times greater than the U.S. child population in general. For each of the years from 1983 to 1993, more children entered than exited substitute care.

Tragically, one in four foster children remains in foster care for at least three to five years; in every state, there are children who have been in foster care for more than seven years. A foster child lives, on average, with three different families; experiencing ten or more placements into different homes is not uncommon.

The costs are especially high for young people who leave the system at age 18 (or another age determined by the state) without having been adopted. According to a Westat, Inc. study, two-and-one-half to four years after young people left foster care, "46 percent had not completed high school, 38 percent had not held a job for more than one year, 25 percent had been homeless for at least one night and 60 percent of young women had given birth to a child." In addition, the study found that "forty percent had been on public assistance, incarcerated or a cost to the community in some other way." One study showed that, in New York City alone, more than 60 percent of the homeless population in municipal shelters are former foster children. These statistics should alarm anyone who is concerned with the plight of America's most vulnerable children.

Federal-State Child Welfare System

The current child welfare system has three primary goals – to ensure children's safety; to create permanency in children's living arrangements; and to promote healthy child development. The financing mechanism of the current system, however, does not always advance these goals. The most significant resources, measured either by absolute level or by growth rates, are provided for the removal and placement of children outside their own homes. Limited funding is provided for services that could either prevent a child's removal from his or her family or support timely family reunification in cases in which temporary removal is necessary. States may be able to better promote child safety, permanency, and well-being by using federal funds for preventative services.

The Social Security Act provides federal funds to the states for child welfare, foster care, and adoption activities. Overall, such funds are divided into two sections – one for child protection services (Title IV-B Child Welfare Services and Promoting Safe and Stable Families Programs) and one for the removal of children and their temporary placement outside of the home (Title IV-E Foster Care and Independent Living Programs). Adoption programs are also funded by Title IV-E.

Child welfare programs include funds for prevention programs to help children at high risk of abuse and neglect, and for related services. These funds are authorized and appropriated and sent to the states in the form of grants. In contrast, most of the foster care and adoption funds are entitlements, whereby the federal government has a binding obligation to make payments to any person or entity that meets the eligibility criteria. This has resulted in a significant disparity in funding between child welfare programs on the one hand, and foster care and adoption programs on the other. For example, in 1999, federal funding for child protection and prevention services totaled $600 million, while funding for foster care, adoption assistance and independent living was $4.6 billion. The Congressional Budget Office expects spending on removal and placement programs to average nine times as much as spending on services and prevention between 1999 and 2003.

Moreover, because the growth of funds for prevention services has been so restricted, states often do not have enough money to provide the services that could either prevent children's removal from their families or support timely reunification in cases in which temporary removal is necessary.

Helping Families in Crisis

States should have the resources to help keep children with biological families, if safe and appropriate, or to place children with adoptive families. If a state takes preventative efforts to help families in crisis, the prospects for children to live in a permanent home are enhanced. A child will remain with his or her biological parents or will be removed and placed in temporary foster care. Attempts can be made to return the child from foster care back to the home. If the state can show that such preventative efforts have failed to safely keep the child in, or return the child to, their home, judges are more likely to terminate parental rights, making the child legally free for adoption.

Therefore, to give states additional resources to help families in crisis, as President, Governor Bush will:

Provide States an Additional $1 Billion Over Five Years for Preventative Services: Governor Bush will provide $200 million annually to the Title IV-B Child Welfare Services and Promoting Safe and Stable Families Programs in order to keep children in, or return them to, their homes whenever safely possible. This represents a 33 percent increase in annual funding for these programs.

Ensuring Safe and Stable Homes for Children

In 1997, the Adoption and Safe Families Act "ASFA" (P.L. 105-89) was signed into law. Under ASFA, states are required to provide procedures for criminal records checks for any prospective foster or adoptive parent before such parent may be approved for placement of any child. The procedures require that prospective foster or adoptive parents not be approved if a criminal record check: 1) reveals a felony conviction for child abuse or neglect, for spousal abuse, for a crime against children (including child pornography), or for a crime involving violence, including rape, sexual assault or battery; or 2) reveals a felony conviction for physical assault, battery, or a drug related offense, if the felony was committed within the past five years.

ASFA, however, allows states to opt out of these criminal background checks by either passing a state law that exempts the state from these new requirements, or if the governor of the state provides written notice to the Secretary of Health and Human Services that the state has elected to be exempt from these requirements. Moreover, Congressional testimony indicates that, many states will have to change their laws to ensure that foster or adoptive parents are not approved if a criminal record check reveals a felony conviction.

To ensure that children in foster or adoptive homes live in safe and stable environments, as President, Governor Bush will:

<u>Require All States to Conduct Criminal Background Checks on Prospective Foster and Adoptive Parents</u>: Governor Bush will review the Adoption and Safe Families Act and its exceptions on criminal background checks to close existing loopholes allowing states to opt out of its requirements. He will also work with Congress to ensure perspective foster or adoptive parents cannot pass criminal background checks if they have a felony conviction at any time before or during the current five-year limit.

Foster care is supposed to provide children a temporary home until they can be reunited with their biological families or placed permanently in an adoptive family. Current law, however, equates a permanent family setting (such as a biological or adoptive family) with long-term foster care or institutional placement. As a result, the current system encourages states to allow children to languish in foster care. Although Governor Bush recognizes that foster care may be the only option for some children, all efforts should be made to place children in permanent families.

Therefore, to ensure that as many children as possible are reunited with their families or placed quickly through adoption, as President, Governor Bush will:

Set the Goal that "Permanence" for Children in the Child Welfare System Means Returning to a Safe and Stable Family or Finalized Adoption: Governor Bush will work with Congress to define permanence as returning to a safe and stable biological family or, when a judge deems that impossible, finalized adoption by a family whose home-study has been completed. This will help prevent many children from spending their formative years in foster homes or other temporary care, without reducing financial support for such care when necessary.

Encouraging Adoption and Helping Children Who Leave Foster Care

In 1996, Congress passed and the President signed into law a tax credit designed to increase the number of adoptions. The provision provides a $5,000 tax credit to families for expenses associated with the adoption of a child. The provision also provides a $5,000 exclusion from income for employer provided assistance.

There are more than 50,000 children legally free for adoption (i.e. termination of parental rights has occurred) in the United States. While parents do not need to be given financial incentives to welcome children into their loving homes, the costs of adoption can be high and many parents need help defraying those costs. Domestic public agency adoptions can include up-front fees and expenses up to $2,500 or more. Costs of adoption can include everything from agency and application fees to post-placement counseling, and legal fees.

Therefore, to encourage more adoptions, as President, Governor Bush will:

Increase the Adoption Tax Credit: Governor Bush will work with Congress to make the adoption tax credit permanent and increase it from $5,000 to $7,500. The credit will cover non-reimbursable expenses associated with the adoption of a child. The total cost of increasing this credit will be $1 billion over five years.

Some 20,000 children who reach the age of majority this year are still in foster care. After they leave the foster care system, many of their futures are quite dim. After "aging out" of foster care, 27 percent of males and 10 percent of females were incarcerated within 12 to 18 months; 50 percent were unemployed, 37 percent had not finished high school, 33 percent received public assistance, and 19 percent of females had given birth to children. One study found that before leaving foster care, 47 percent of children were receiving some kind of counseling or medication for mental health problems; but that number dropped to 21 percent after leaving care.

191

To help children who are still in the foster care system when they reach the age of majority, Governor Bush will:

Provide $300 Million over Five Years for Vouchers to Young People Who "Age Out" of Foster Care: Governor Bush will work with Congress to ensure that young people who are about to leave the foster care system will be able to obtain federal funds to develop skills to lead independent and productive lives. These vouchers can be up to $5,000 for each young person to use for college tuition or vocational training.

Position Paper
Project ChildSafe

May 12, 2000

> *"Having child safety locks on every new gun sold is not enough. My goal is to make child safety locks available for every single one of the 65 million handguns in America."*

> *Governor George W. Bush*

The Need for Child Safety Trigger Locks

In the past two years, the gun control debate has focused on federal legislation to require child safety triggerlocks on all new handguns. Governor Bush has indicated that if Congress passed such legislation, he would sign it as President.

Governor Bush believes that parents have the ultimate responsibility to keep locks on guns and to monitor their children. Nevertheless, Governor Bush believes that the government should help parents protect their kids by providing child safety locks for handguns.

There are currently an estimated 65 million handguns in America. While the proposed federal legislation requires only new handguns sold to have safety locks, it does nothing for the 65 million handguns already in circulation.

Project ChildSafe

As President, Governor Bush will launch Project ChildSafe, a federal-state-local partnership to ensure child safety locks are made available for every single handgun in America.

The program would provide $75 million a year for five years in federal matching funds with the goal of providing free child safety locks to every handgun owner in America:

- The standard cost of a safety lock is typically around $10 each. Therefore, locks for all 65 million handguns would cost a total of $650 million.

193

- Each year for five years, the federal government will provide $65 million to states and local governments on a dollar-for-dollar matching basis. At the end of those five years, the total matched amount will be $650 million.

- An additional $10 million a year for five years will go to administrative costs and advertising, to make sure all parents are aware of the program and can access it.

- The annual federal matching funds will also be available to match private contributions by organizations seeking to assist in the goal of providing locks for every handgun in America.

- The money will be distributed annually by the Department of Justice, and the locks themselves will be distributed by local municipalities, counties, or private organizations.

- There will be a national 800-number for all parents to call to get their free locks.

Position Paper
Reforming the INS

June 26, 2000

"Latinos have come to the United States to seek the same dreams that have inspired millions of others: they want a better life for their children. Family values do not stop at the Rio Grande River. Latinos enrich our country with faith in God, a strong ethic of work and community and responsibility. We can all learn from the strength, solidarity, and values of Latinos...Immigration is not a problem to be solved, it is the sign of a successful nation. New Americans are not to be feared as strangers, they are to be welcomed as neighbors."

Governor George W. Bush

EXECUTIVE SUMMARY

Governor Bush's goal is a more inclusive, compassionate America, where every person is respected. He believes legal immigrants are the future and the changing face of America, and should be welcomed as a sign of America's success.

Too often, however, new immigrants are treated as suspects and strangers, not welcomed as neighbors. One reason for this is the structure, culture, and policies of the Immigration and Naturalization Service (INS). The INS has two conflicting missions: to secure America's borders against illegal immigrants, and to serve those coming to America by legal means. Its policies also tend to keep families apart unnecessarily, forcing them to wait while a slow bureaucracy processes paper.

To Help Change the Character of the INS and to Make America More Welcoming to New Immigrants, as President, Governor Bush will:

- Restructure the INS, splitting it into two agencies: one to deal with enforcement, and one to deal with service.

- Encourage family reunification for legal immigrants by allowing visits by spouses and minor children of permanent residents.

- Improve INS service by proposing that every INS immigration application be processed within 180 days of submission.

Governor Bush will also propose an additional $500 million over five years to improve INS service and provide INS employees with performance-based incentives.

Changing the Structure and Character of the INS

Immigrants come to America seeking a better life for themselves and their children. Governor Bush believes immigration is not a problem, but a sign of the continuing appeal of the American dream.

Yet, the reality is that too often new immigrants are denied the respect they deserve. They are welcomed not with open arms, but by a bureaucracy that views them with suspicion, treats them with indifference, and burdens them with long lines and slow service.

A significant reason for this is the fact that the INS itself has two distinct responsibilities: enforcement and service. Unfortunately, the two roles often conflict, and frequent complaints have been raised that each function bleeds over into the other. Border enforcement is often criticized as unfocused, and the service component frequently appears adversarial and authoritarian. A legal immigrant working to get his or her immigration paperwork processed need not be greeted by a uniformed officer with a badge, and should not be treated like a criminal or a suspect.

These inherent conflicts are exacerbated by INS policy. For example, a legal permanent resident, who tries to bring his or her spouse or minor children to America, now confronts a policy that frustrates family reunification. Once that permanent resident's spouse or minor children apply to emigrate permanently, they are immediately ineligible for even a tourist visa while their applications for permanent residency are being processed. As a result, families of legal permanent residents can be kept apart for years, because the INS will not allow them even to visit while their applications are pending.

To help change the character of the INS and to make America more welcoming to new immigrants, as President, Governor Bush will:

Restructure the INS into Two Agencies: Governor Bush will support legislation to divide the INS into two separate agencies: one to deal with the enforcement components of border protection and interior enforcement, and another to deal with the service components of naturalization. Both agencies will be headed by an Associate Attorney General for Immigration Affairs, who will supervise both functions, and make sure that the agencies are taking consistent legal and policy approaches.

Allow Spouses and Minor Children of Permanent Residents to Visit: Governor Bush will change the INS policy so that spouses and minor children of legal permanent residents are allowed to apply for visitor visas while their immigration applications are pending. He will reverse the presumption that such family members will violate their terms of admission, and will encourage family reunification for legal immigrants.

Improving Service to New Immigrants

Currently, the INS takes 3-5 years or more simply to process an immigration application. In California, federal delays in processing adjustment of status applications have averaged 52 months; in Texas, federal delays in processing have averaged 69 months; in Arizona, 49 months; in Illinois, 37 months. There is no justification for processing to take 3-5 years; an INS properly focused on service would move much faster.

Therefore, to improve the focus of the INS on service and to reduce the delays in INS processing of immigration applications, as President, Governor Bush will:

Propose a 6-Month Standard for Processing Immigration Applications: Every INS immigration application should be fully processed within 180 days of submission. To meet this 6-month standard, and to fundamentally alter the approach of the INS, Governor Bush will:

- Work to change the culture of the INS to emphasize service for new immigrants. Splitting the INS into two agencies, one focused exclusively on service, should help effect this change.

- Introduce performance-based incentives for INS employees to process cases quickly, and make customer satisfaction a priority. These reforms will be part of Governor Bush's overall plan to make government more citizen-centered and to reform the civil service.

- Propose an additional $500 million over 5 years to fund new INS personnel and increased employee incentives to provide quality service to legal immigrants.

NAACP Annual Convention

Baltimore, Maryland

July 10, 2000

I'm pleased to be here. I'm also reminded of what the great Jackie Robinson once said when President Kennedy did something that upset him. Robinson said that he was sure the President was a "fine man" – but he reserved the right to change his opinion.

For those who support me – I see one or two here – I hope you won't change your opinion. For those who don't, I hope you take Jackie's position as your own and give me the chance to tell you what is in my heart.

The history of the Republican Party and the NAACP has not been one of regular partnership. But our nation is harmed when we let our differences separate us and divide us. So, while some in my party have avoided the NAACP, and while some in the NAACP have avoided my party, I am proud to be here today. And this dialogue is so important, if I am elected President, I will be back next year as well.

I am here today because I believe there is much we can do together to advance racial harmony and economic opportunity.

But before we get to the future, we must acknowledge our past. In the darkest days of the Civil War, President Lincoln pleaded to our divided nation to remember that, "We cannot escape history...[that] we will be remembered in spite of ourselves." One hundred and forty years later, that is still true.

For our nation, there is no denying the truth that slavery is a blight on our history. And that racism, despite all our progress, still exists today.

For my party, there's no escaping the reality that the Party of Lincoln has not always carried the mantle of Lincoln.

Recognizing and confronting our history is important. Transcending our history is essential. We are not limited by what we have done, or what we have left undone. We are limited only by what we are willing to do.

Our nation must make a new commitment to equality and upward mobility for all our citizens.

This is a great moment of national prosperity. But many still live in prosperity's shadow. The same economy that is a miracle for millions is a mystery to millions as well.

From the beginning of this campaign, I have said that prosperity must have a purpose. The purpose of prosperity is to ensure that the American Dream touches every willing heart. We cannot afford to have an America segregated by class, by race or by aspiration. America must close the gap of hope between communities of prosperity and communities of poverty.

We have seen what happens when African-American citizens have the opportunity they have earned and the respect they deserve. Men and women once victimized by Jim Crow have risen to leadership in the halls of Congress. Professionals and entrepreneurs have built a successful, growing African-American middle class.

It must be our goal to expand this opportunity – to make it as broad and diverse as American itself. And this begins with enforcing our civil rights laws.

Discrimination is still a reality, even when it takes different forms. Instead of Jim Crow, there is racial redlining and profiling. Instead of "separate but equal," there is separate and forgotten. Strong civil rights enforcement will be a cornerstone of my

Administration. We will not close our eyes to the truth.

We must also confront another form of bias – the soft bigotry of low expectations in education.

Several months ago I visited Central High School in Little Rock, where African-Americans confronted injustice and white Americans confronted their conscience. In 43 years, we've come so far in opening the doors of our schools.

Yet today we have a challenge of our own: while all can enter our schools, many are not learning there. There is a tremendous gap of achievement between rich and poor, white and minority. This, too, leaves a divided society. And whatever the cause, the effect is discrimination.

My friend Phyllis Hunter, a teacher in Texas, calls reading "the new civil right." Equality in our country will remain a distant dream until every child, of every background, has a chance to learn and strive and rise in the world. No child in America should be segregated by low expectations... imprisoned by illiteracy... abandoned to frustration and the darkness of self-doubt.

But there is reason for optimism. A great movement of education reform has begun in this country, built on clear principles: Raise the bar of standards. Give schools the flexibility to meet them. Measure progress. Insist on results. Blow the whistle on failure. Provide parents with options to increase their influence. And don't leave any child behind.

I believe in these principles. I have seen them turn around troubled schools in my state. I've seen them bring hope into the lives of children – inspiring confidence and ambition. I'm especially proud that the performance of minority students in my state is improving at one of the fastest rates in the country. African-American fourth-graders in Texas have better math skills than any other state.

We can make the same kind of progress at the national level. A central part of my agenda is changing Title I to close the achievement gap. All students will be tested. Low-performing schools will have three years to produce results. If they do not, then these resources will go directly to the parents.

Every child can learn. Every child in this country deserves to grow in knowledge and character and ideals. Nothing is more important to our prosperity and goodness than cultivated minds and courageous hearts. As W.E.B. Du Bois said a century ago, "Either the United States will destroy ignorance, or ignorance will destroy the United States."

Education is the essential beginning – but we must go further. To create communities of promise, we must help people build the confidence and faith to achieve their own dreams. We must put government squarely on the side of opportunity.

This is a higher and older tradition of my party. Lincoln argued that "every poor man should have a chance." He defended a "clear path for all." He financed colleges, welcomed immigrants, promoted railroads and economic development. Through the Homestead Act, he gave countless Americans a piece of land, a start in life.

I have proposed a New Prosperity Initiative that reflects the spirit of Lincoln's reforms. A plan to remove obstacles on the road to the Middle Class. Instead of helping people cope with their need, we will help them move beyond it.

We must provide a Family Health Credit that covers 90 percent of the cost of a basic health policy for low-income families.

We must make it possible for more people to become home-owners, to own a part of the American Dream. So we'll allow low-income families to use up to a year's worth of Section 8 rental payments to make a down payment on their own home – then use five years of those payments to help with the mortgage.

We'll start an American Dream Down Payment Fund, matching individual savings for the down payment on a home.

Behind all these proposals is a simple belief: I believe in private property. I believe in private property so strongly, I want everyone to have some. This promised land must keep its promises.

Education helps the young. Empowerment lifts the able. But there are those who need much more. Children without role models. Young people captured by gangs or addiction or despair.

Government can spend money, but it cannot put hope in someone's heart or a sense of purpose in their lives. This is done by caring communities – by churches and charities that serve their neighbors because they love their God. Every day they prove that our worst problems are not hopeless or endless. Every day they perform miracles of renewal.

What we need is not something new, but something old and proven: the transforming power of faith. In the words of a writer who visited the Mott Haven section of the Bronx: "the beautiful old stone church ... is a gentle sanctuary from the terror of the streets outside."

In city after city, for the suffering and the hurting, the most hopeful passageway is the door to the house of God. We are going to extend the role and reach of charities and churches, mentors and community healers, in our society. As President, I intend to rally these armies of compassion in the neighborhoods of America.

I will lift the regulations that hamper private and faith-based programs. I will involve them in after-school programs, maternity group homes, drug treatment, prison ministries. I have laid out specific incentives to encourage an outpouring of giving in America. Supporting these men and women – the soldiers in the army of compassion – is the next, bold step of welfare reform.

Here's an example. More than a million children have one or both parents in prison. These are forgotten children – almost six times more likely to go to prison themselves. And they should not be punished for the sins of their fathers. We should give grants to ministries and mentoring programs that offer support to these children. Let us bring help and hope to these other innocent victims of crime.

I'm not calling for government to step back from its responsibilities, but to share them. We'll always need government to raise and distribute funds, monitor success and set standards. But we also need what no government can provide: the power of compassion and prayer and love.

These are some of my goals for America – to help make opportunity not only a hope and a promise, but a living reality.

The NAACP and the GOP have not always been allies. But recognizing our past and confronting the future with a common vision, I believe we can find common ground.

This will not be easy work. But a philosopher once advised: "When given a choice, prefer the hard." We will prefer the hard because only the hard will achieve the good. That is my commitment. That is our opportunity.

One Nation, One People

Simon Wiesenthal Center
Los Angeles, California

March 6, 2000

It is a special honor to be with you today, and to visit this place of remembrance and hope and vigilance. Here we remember the past – including its crimes and cruelties. Here, we imagine the future – as a place where intolerance and hatred have no place in the policies of government, or the souls of citizens.

I am pleased to be with friends of the Wiesenthal Center – people committed to the spread of justice and tolerance and people dedicated to a safe and secure Israel. I join you in this important cause.

All of you are supporting a great work. For more than a generation now, the Wiesenthal Center has fought against anti-Semitism and all forms of bigotry. Not just here, but around the world.

More than 50 years ago, a member of the Nazi SS told Simon Wiesenthal that it wasn't worth telling the story of the death camps – because no one would ever believe such things were possible. Yet now we do not just believe, now we know. We know because Simon Wiesenthal and many others have preserved truths that must never be lost to memory, or sacrificed to revisionism.

Our century has revealed both the durability of human hate, and the durability of human hope. In the Holocaust, we saw unending hate and undying hope. Anti-Semitism once destroyed the moral foundations of one of the most educated nations on earth. It is a fact that barbarism can appear even in the most outwardly civilized society. Tolerance can never be assumed. It must always be taught.

We must teach our children to respect people from all walks of life. We must teach our children to respect people whose skin is of a different color. We must teach our children to respect those whose ancestry or religion is different from their own. Finally, we must teach our children that we are one nation, one people, all American.

There is a contest of light and shadow in every nation, in every generation. Intolerance is not merely a problem of the past. Racism finds new targets, and reopens old wounds. Hate groups recruit on the Internet and warp the souls of children. We are called by conscience to set our hearts against all assaults on human dignity. You have answered that call – along with many other Americans.

There are two great pillars of tolerance in this country.

One is the American tradition itself. The unbreakable guarantees of the Constitution. The echoing ideals of the Declaration of Independence. Our commitment to tolerance and equality under law emerges from the very nature of our country. That commitment has never been completely fulfilled, but it must always be pursued. For all its flaws, I believe our nation is chosen by God and commissioned by history to be a model to the world of justice and inclusion and diversity without division. These are American convictions. Defending them is America's calling. And they must be passed intact to America's children.

The other pillar of tolerance is faith.

The teaching of our tradition is simple and permanent: "Love your neighbor as yourself." Not just because this promotes the peace and good order of society. But because this is the proper way to treat human beings created in the image and likeness of God.

Many Americans, of many backgrounds, share the same conviction. We don't believe in tolerance in spite of our faith. We believe in tolerance because of our faith.   And it leads us to condemn all forms of religious bigotry.

But a leader must do more than hold this conviction. He must give it voice. And he must give it force. That is my commitment to the people of this country. Every American must know they are equally American – no matter their culture, race or religion. And those who practice intimidation and violence will have a determined enemy in the President of the United States.

This place bears the name of a man who has never tired in righting wrongs and seeking justice. It is monument to the power of truth over falsehood. Your work is always urgent, and always unfinished. Thank you for your commitment, and for your welcome today.

WHAT OTHERS SAY

"If it were a movie it would deserve an Oscar.

"If it were theatre it would deserve a five-star rating in the travel guides.

"But it was none of those…it was…Gov. George W. Bush…making his first major policy address.

"Bush has [a] detailed plan to expand the role of the faith-based charities and other community groups committed to help the needy.

"Bush deserves high marks for…help[ing] those who have been left behind…it may take…Bush to restore middle-class America's faith in government's ability to help those who need help the most."

Clarence Page, <u>Chicago Tribune</u>, 7/25/99

"Bush's program would make finding a permanent home for kids a priority – whether that means with their biological parents or in an adoptive home..."

Karen Gullo, AP, 7/11/00

"Bush programs would help the disabled...Laudable goals...a detailed plan...after spending more than a half-hour with Governor Bush, he convinced me he'll support the ADA. What's more, he has a real grasp of issues facing people with disabilities."

John M. Williams, Business Week Online, 6/21/00

"...George W. Bush deserves praise for announcing a plan to help lower-middle class families buy homes."

Louis Winnick, The New York Times, 4/22/00

" Tax credits are the right cure for low-income families without health insurance...Single mothers trying to get off welfare, and minority working families – particularly Hispanic families – stand to benefit the most from the Bush initiative."

Grace-Marie Arnett, The Galen Institute, 4/13/00

"Roman Williams, an NAACP member from Montgomery, Ala., said he was impressed with Bush's forthright approach...'He seems like he wants to bridge the gap, that he is sincere.'"

Terry M. Neal and Michael A. Fletcher, Washington Post, 7/11/00

"Daniel Hawkins, Jr., vice-president for federal and state affairs at the National Association of Community Health Centers...graded his [health] proposal an 'A-Plus-Plus. This trumps anything...It is a bold and innovative and creative plan to get significant amounts of care out there at a relatively low cost.'"

Todd J. Gillman, Dallas Morning News, 4/13/00

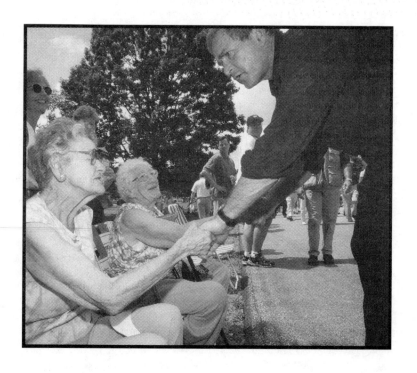

PART III

Strengthening Social Security and Medicare

For 65 years now, Social Security has been a defining commitment between generations. By any measure, it is the most successful social program ever undertaken by the federal government. Social Security's promise of retirement income was joined 35 years ago by Medicare's health guarantees. This program, too, was founded on an ethic of respect for the dignity of all seniors.

Too often, the long-term challenges faced by both these essential programs have been ignored or exploited for political purposes. In the last eight years, opportunities for bipartisan reform were squandered, causing needless worry among seniors and cynicism among the young.

We must strengthen both these programs with needed reform, based on bipartisan cooperation.

In the speech that follows, I deal with Social Security in clear terms, outlining the principles I will follow as President. For those now on Social Security – or near retirement – nothing will change. Our government will keep its commitments. And I will lead bipartisan reform that puts Social Security on a sound footing for the future, offering young Americans more options to build wealth and retirement security.

My approach on Medicare is similar: answering pressing problems with clear principles of reform, so all seniors have the health care they deserve from doctors they choose. Under my plan, all seniors will have access to a prescription drug benefit through Medicare; they will make their own health care decisions; and the health care safety net will always be in place for those in need.

A Defining American Promise

Rancho Cucamonga Senior Center
Rancho Cucamonga, California

May 15, 2000

Today, I want to talk with and about the elderly – about the challenges they face and the contributions they make. About the policies of our government and the values of our society.

Senior Americans are not one more interest group, one more voting bloc to be polled, pandered to, or written off.

They are our parents and grandparents, our neighbors, coworkers and friends, passing through a stage of life that awaits each of us. How we treat them reflects the deepest commitments of our society. How we treat them reflects something about ourselves – whether we honor and appreciate life in all its seasons.

Meeting our commitment to the elderly begins with economic security.

America made this commitment almost exactly 65 years ago – in August of 1935. A person born the year Social Security came into being is now eligible for its benefits.

Life before Social Security could be harsh. A woman who grew up in rural Alabama described the fate of senior citizens this way: "They sent them over the hill to the poorhouse. I was a little girl but I can remember. All they did was lay up there and die."

Sixty-five years later, we can declare: Social Security is the single most successful government program in American history. Without it, more than half of all seniors would live in poverty. For millions – for parents and grandparents with little or no savings – it is the difference between destitution and dignity.

Social Security is a defining American promise, and we will not turn back.

This issue is a test of government's capacity to give its word and keep it, to act in good faith and to pursue the common good.

And Social Security is also a test of presidential candidates – a measure of seriousness and resolve. Too many times, Social Security has been demagogued to frighten the elderly for political advantage. Too many candidates have traded on the problems of the system instead of correcting them, shoving them off for others to handle – to some future generation, some other president and some other Congress.

I am here with a message for America, and to put my opponent on notice. The days of spreading fear and panic are over. The days of delaying, dividing and demagoging are over. When I am elected, this generation and this President will save Social Security.

We are nearing Social Security's greatest test. Eight years from now, the massive baby-boomer generation will begin drawing benefits. Their lives will be long and healthy. And within two decades, there simply won't be enough younger workers to pay the benefits earned by the old.

If we do nothing to reform the system, the year 2037 will be the moment of financial collapse. The system will be insolvent, with deficits in the trillions of dollars, requiring either a massive cut in benefits or a massive increase in taxes.

At a time for leadership – for long-term thinking – my opponent proposes a band-aid approach. He says: "If it ain't broke, don't fix it." But in the lifetime of some people in this room, it will be broke, and we must fix it. With every day of delay this becomes more difficult. For eight years, the Clinton-Gore Administration has failed to act. And now Al Gore wants to pass the burden on to future generations. The Gore plan will eventually require either a 25 percent increase in income taxes – the largest in our history – or a substantial reduction in benefits.

But there is good news. There is a new attitude in Washington that shows that reforming Social Security can and must be bipartisan. Recently I met with Senator Bob Kerrey – a Democrat who is a leader for Social Security reform. Senator Kerrey, and Senator Moynihan, both Democrats, and Senator McCain, a Republican, recently had a press conference to discuss common principles of reform. They proposed an innovative framework for members of Congress to work together on this issue – a framework that includes a bipartisan commission.

I support a bipartisan commission, because it will help pave the way to a consensus on reform. We can already see the emerging outlines of a consensus – led by people like Senators Breaux, Gregg, Grassley, and Gramm... Congressmen Kasich, Archer, Shaw, Kolbe and Stenholm. As President, I will build on that momentum, with some clear principles.

First, we must not change Social Security for those now retired, or nearing retirement. Let me put this plainly. For those on Social Security – or close to receiving it – nothing will change. Government has made a commitment, and you have made your plans. These promises will be honored. Yet, without reform, younger workers face a great risk – a lifetime of paying taxes for benefits they may never receive. The reforms I have in mind will actually increase their retirement income.

Second, all Social Security funds in the federal surplus must stay where they belong – dedicated to Social Security. In my economic plan, more than $2 trillion of the federal surplus is locked away for Social Security. For years, politicians in both parties have dipped into the trust fund to pay for more spending. And I will stop it.

Third, the payroll tax must not be raised. We cannot tax our way to reform.

Fourth, reform should include personal retirement accounts for young people – an element of all the major bipartisan plans. The idea works very simply. A young worker can take some portion of his or her payroll tax and put it in a fund that invests in stocks and bonds. We will establish basic standards of safety and soundness, so that investments are only in steady, reliable funds. There will be no fly-by-night speculators or day trading. And money in this account could only be used for retirement, or passed along as an inheritance.

Right now, the real return people get from what they put into Social Security is a dismal two percent a year. Over the long term, sound investments yield about a six percent return. Investing that four percent difference, over a lifetime, can show dramatic results. A worker who invests even a limited portion of his or her paycheck could, over a career, end up with hundreds of thousands of dollars for retirement.

The American securities markets, over time, have been among the most reliable investments in the world. Through the Great Depression, a World War, and 11 recessions, the overall stock market has never lost money over any 20-year period. It is the best, safest way to build personal wealth. That's why teacher pension plans and private business retirement plans all across America invest in such funds.

Some in Washington call this idea risky. But here are some simple questions you should ask them: Do they own stock themselves? Is that part of their own retirement plan? Does it make them feel more secure, or less, to own investments? Clearly, they don't think this is risky for themselves. People in Washington see it as an opportunity. Yet it is an opportunity they would deny to others.

Every federal worker is offered a personal account to help improve their retirement – 1.3 million have these accounts. Al Gore, who calls these bipartisan proposals risky, has a substantial amount of his family's money invested in the stock market. If he is building his own retirement security in the market, why does he object to young Americans doing the same?

Consider this simple fact: Even if a worker chose only the safest investment in the world – an inflation-adjusted U.S. government bond – he or she would receive twice the rate of return of Social Security.

There is a fundamental difference between my opponent and me. He trusts only government to manage our retirement. I trust individual Americans. I trust Americans to make their own decisions and manage their own money.

Let me be clear. Personal accounts are not a substitute for Social Security. They involve only a limited percentage of the payroll tax so the safety net remains strong. Let me say this again: For those who are retired or near retirement, there will be no changes at all to your Social Security. But we can and must give younger workers the option of new opportunities.

Personal accounts build on the promise of Social Security – they strengthen it, making it more valuable for young workers. Senator Moynihan, Democrat, says that personal accounts take the system to its "logical completion." They give people the security of ownership. They allow even low-income workers to build wealth, which they will use for their own retirement and pass on to their children. Some plans would match the contributions of low-income workers to their personal accounts. That is also an idea we should consider.

Senator Kerrey, also a Democrat, recently said: "It's very important, especially for those of us who have already accumulated wealth, to write laws to enable other people to accumulate it, and arrive where we are." Ownership in our society should not be an exclusive club. Independence should not be a gated community. Everyone should be a part-owner in the American Dream.

Within the framework of these principles, we can keep Social Security strong and stable. We can keep our commitments. We can avoid tax increases. And millions of Americans will have an asset to call their own. This is the best thing about personal accounts. They are not just a program, they are your property. And no politician can take them away.

As our society grays, we must keep our commitments. But we must also set new goals. Our nation has a vital interest – a moral interest – in making retirement a time of security and health and contribution.

Last week, I visited with a group of senior citizens in Davenport, Iowa, and outlined my plan to make long-term care available and affordable, instead of a path to financial ruin. Soon I'll be offering proposals to encourage senior volunteerism, and to fight diseases of the aged. But today let me focus on one more issue – another issue where partisanship is blocking progress.

Our nation must reform Medicare – and, in doing so, ensure that prescription drugs are affordable and available for every senior who needs them. As with Social Security, Medicare reform must be guided by clear tenets.

Medicare must be preserved as an entitlement for all who qualify. Seniors on Medicare should have access to the latest medical technology. Medicare must offer comprehensive coverage for low-income seniors, including prescription drugs. And any reform must ensure the solvency of Medicare.

Seniors deserve a wider scope of coverage, and they deserve to have more choices among health plans. Over the last few years, both Republicans and Democrats have embraced these goals. Yet despite the best efforts of leaders like Senator Frist, Congressman Thomas, Senator Kerrey and Senator Breaux, the Clinton-Gore Administration has blocked bipartisan Medicare reform.

When I am President, I will lead Republicans and Democrats to reform and strengthen Medicare and set it on firm financial ground.

And I make this pledge to seniors: Every senior will have

access to prescription drug benefits.

Prescription drugs are becoming the treatment of choice. Drugs are often more cost-effective than surgery or hospitalization, with fewer risks and better results. And the picture gets better year by year. By one estimate, suppliers are now working on more than 600 new medicines to treat the causes of disability among seniors.

But prescription drugs can be expensive. The average senior already pays $450 each year in out-of-pocket drug expenses. Twelve percent of Medicare beneficiaries have drug bills of $1000 or more. Ninety-eight percent of health plans today offer some form of prescription drug benefit. Yet Medicare does not. And this must change.

A bipartisan approach is already gaining support in Congress. Under this model, every person on Medicare could choose a plan with a prescription drug benefit. And for low-income seniors, Medicare itself would cover the whole cost of the plan – including prescriptions.

This is a realistic reform – balancing personal and public responsibilities. Just as important, it keeps government out of the business of setting prices or dictating treatments, which it must never do.

Our society is aging, and this brings new responsibilities. In our time, we must reform and strengthen the programs on which many seniors depend. But we must also renew the values that inspired these programs – the values of a generous and welcoming society.

Our seniors contribute goods and gifts only they can offer. Sometimes these goods register on the economic scales, in second careers. And sometimes they escape the measure of economics – in the lessons they teach to their grandchildren, and the love they give.

I think of my own parents, my busy mom, and my 75-year-old father who parachutes from airplanes. Both are examples of the active, important lives that many older Americans are living. Mom and Dad are the greatest possible blessing at this stage in our own lives, and in the lives of our children.

Modern medicine has lengthened the years allowed us. But, as President Kennedy said, "It is not enough for a great nation merely to have added new years to life – our objective must also be to add new life to those years."

When leaders build the health and security of older Americans, our nation gains their talents and shows its values. We are enriched by their skills, and we show the respect they have earned. It is a daily opportunity, and an ancient obligation: Honor thy father and mother.

Our seniors have blessings to give. And our nation has promises to keep.

Position Paper

A Defining American Promise: Strengthening Social Security and Medicare

May 15, 2000

"Senior Americans are our parents and grandparents, our neighbors, co-workers and friends... I am here with a message for America, and to put my opponent on notice. The days of spreading fear and panic are over. The days of delaying, dividing and demagoging are over. When I am elected, this generation and this President will save Social Security and Medicare."

Governor George W. Bush

EXECUTIVE SUMMARY

Governor Bush believes that the nation has a vital interest – a moral interest – in ensuring that retirement is a time of security and health for America's seniors. That is why his new agenda for older Americans begins with preserving – and modernizing – Social Security and Medicare.

Social Security is a defining American promise that Governor Bush is determined to keep. But it can be saved for future generations only if it is reformed. Because the system taxes younger workers to pay the benefits of retired workers, it will generate huge deficits as the Baby Boom generation swells the ranks of retirees over the next three decades, eventually becoming insolvent in 2037. Under the Clinton-Gore administration, which has avoided Social Security reform, the present value of these deficits has risen from $1.8 trillion to $2.9 trillion, or $28,000 per household.

220

As President, Governor Bush will Build a Bipartisan Consensus to Save Social Security on the Basis of Six Key Principles:

- Modernization must not change existing benefits for retirees or near-retirees.

- The Social Security surplus must be locked away only for Social Security.

- Social Security payroll taxes must not be increased.

- The government must not invest Social Security funds in the stock market.

- Modernization must preserve the disability and survivors components.

- Modernization must include individually controlled, voluntary personal retirement accounts, which will augment the Social Security safety net. These accounts will earn higher rates of return, have parameters of safety and soundness, and help workers build wealth that can be passed on to their children.

Governor Bush will also reform and strengthen Medicare on a bipartisan basis. Medicare is a 1965 health care delivery system that has not kept pace with 21st century medicine. Moreover, it faces insolvency in 2025, due to the same demographic changes that are threatening Social Security.

As President, Governor Bush will Build on Recent Bipartisan Efforts and Seek Medicare Reform Based on these Principles:

- Medicare's current guarantee of access to seniors must be preserved.

- Every Medicare recipient must have a choice of health plans, including the option of purchasing a plan that covers prescription drugs.

- Medicare must cover expenses for low-income seniors.

- Reform must provide streamlined access to the latest medical technologies.

- Medicare payroll taxes must not be increased.

- Reform must establish an accurate measure of the solvency of Medicare.

★ ★ ★

Challenge and Opportunity

The graying of America is often portrayed as a demographic time-bomb. The challenges presented by an aging population are, of course, significant. But Governor Bush believes that the graying of America also presents an opportunity – an opportunity to affirm the dignity of every life and to reaffirm the social compact between the elderly, government, and future generations. That compact is embodied in two successful programs that will not survive these demographic changes unless they are reformed: Social Security and Medicare.

The challenges to Social Security and Medicare posed by an aging population arise from three basic factors: the increasing life expectancy of the elderly, the impending retirement of the Baby Boom generation, and the resulting decline in the ratio of workers to retirees.

When Social Security was established in 1935, the average life expectancy was 61. When Medicare was established in 1965, the average life expectancy was 70. Today, the average life expectancy is 76 and increasing. Moreover, many seniors live far beyond the average. Indeed, about 1.4 million Americans are currently in their 90s, and another 64,000 are 100 or older.

The increase in life expectancy is compounded by the approaching retirement of the Baby Boom generation (those born between 1946 and 1964). There are 77 million Baby Boomers in America. In just eight years, the first of these will reach 62, becoming eligible for Social Security benefits. Three years later, in 2011, the Boomers will start turning 65, becoming eligible for Medicare.

As a result of the increase in life expectancy and other demographic factors, the ratio of workers to retirees has been declining. When the Baby Boomers begin to retire, that ratio will shrink precipitously. For example, in 1945, the payroll taxes of 42 workers supported the benefits of each retiree. Today, the payroll taxes of over 3 workers support the benefits of each Social Security recipient, and by 2030 that ratio will shrink to just 2 to 1. (See Chart 1.) The demographic changes are so dramatic that it is impossible to rely solely on economic growth to maintain the solvency of Social Security.

Saving Social Security

The Old Age and Survivors Insurance and Disability Insurance program (Social Security) is one of the most successful programs in U.S. history. Enacted in 1935, Social Security has dramatically reduced poverty among seniors. In 1960, 35 percent of older Americans lived in poverty. Today, less than 11 percent live below the poverty line.

Chart 1

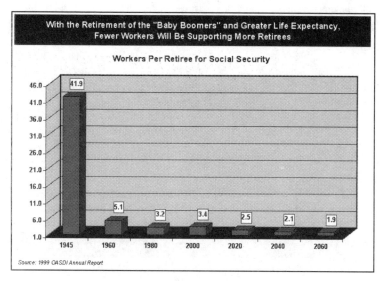

With the Retirement of the "Baby Boomers" and Greater Life Expectancy, Fewer Workers Will Be Supporting More Retirees

Workers Per Retiree for Social Security

Source: 1999 OASDI Annual Report

However, after 65 years of service, the program needs to be modernized to meet the challenges posed by the pressures of an aging population. These pressures will inevitably generate cash flow deficits, as the benefits owed to older Americans exceed the payroll taxes collected from younger workers. In addition, these pressures are steadily worsening workers' return on their Social Security investment. Social Security reform that addresses these issues will also strengthen the economy as a whole.

Approaching Deficits

Social Security is based on a "pay-as-you-go" structure. Payroll taxes collected from workers are used to pay benefits to retirees. If the ratio of workers to retirees is high enough, the system produces a surplus, as it has done since 1983. Currently, Social Security is projected to run a surplus until 2025. The surplus will total over $2 trillion in the next decade alone.

The Social Security surplus has been routinely "borrowed" by the federal government to pay for various programs. In turn, the U.S. Treasury deposits bonds or "IOUs" in the Social Security trust fund. While these IOUs are deemed to be "assets" of the Social Security system, they cannot be used to pay for current benefits. They represent a promise by the Treasury to repay the system, from general revenues, what it has borrowed, plus interest. To meet this promise, the government must eventually raise taxes, cut spending, or borrow more from the public.

As the Baby Boomers retire, the number of Social Security beneficiaries will nearly double, rising from 44.8 million today to 82.7 million in 2030. In turn, the ratio of workers to retirees will decline significantly. As a result, by 2025 the amount of Social Security benefits owed annually to retirees will exceed income into the system. (See Chart 2.) The resulting deficit will grow over time and the trust fund will become insolvent in 2037. Under the Clinton-Gore Administration, the present value of these deficits has already increased 60 percent – from $1.8 trillion in 1992 to $2.9 trillion today (according to the Social Security actuaries), or roughly $28,000 per U.S. household.

Chart 2

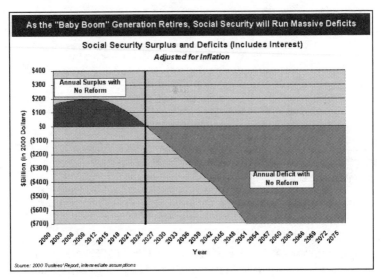

Financing the Deficits

There are only a few ways to finance Social Security's cash flow deficits:

- First, the deficits could be financed by increasing payroll taxes by up to

50 percent, or by cutting Social Security benefits by up to 30 percent. Social Security taxes have increased 21 times and benefits have been cut. Indeed, Social Security payroll taxes have increased from 2 percent in 1937 to 12.4 percent today. (See Chart 3.) As a result, nearly 80 percent of working families already pay more in payroll taxes than in income taxes.

• Second, as Vice President Gore proposes, the deficits could be concealed by issuing more government bonds, or IOUs, to the Social Security trust fund. Under the Gore plan, the government would issue $34 trillion in additional bonds beginning in 2011 – at least three years after the next president leaves office. Eventually, the Social Security Administration will need the cash and will call the bonds. At that point, the government would have to raise income taxes by 25 percent – the largest tax increase in history – to pay off the bonds.

• Third, instead of dramatically raising taxes or cutting benefits, individual workers could be permitted to establish personal retirement accounts. By allowing younger workers to invest a portion of their payroll taxes in stocks and bonds, these accounts will generate higher rates of return, thus helping to increase retirement income for younger workers.

Chart 3

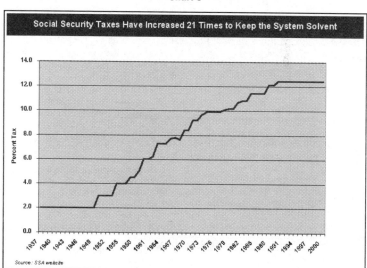

Social Security Taxes Have Increased 21 Times to Keep the System Solvent

Source: SSA website

Declining Rates of Return

Over time, changing demographics and the maturation of the pay-as-you-go system have forced changes in Social Security. In order to shore up the system, benefits have been cut and taxes have been raised. As a result, today's workers can expect a return of less than 2 percent after inflation. (See Chart 4.)

A worker retiring this year will now have to live until age 90 just to break even on his or her contribution to Social Security. A worker retiring in 2020 will have to live past 100 to break even. (See Chart 5.)

In addition to worsening rates of return, the current structure of the Social Security system impedes, rather than enhances, wealth creation. Because it is a "tax and transfer" system, workers do not accumulate wealth as they would in an investment-based system. In fact, the unfunded liability of Social Security is $8.8 trillion – about $84,000 per household.

Whereas a worker's contribution to his or her 401(k) plan is invested in income-producing assets, that same worker's contribution to Social Security is simply paid out as a benefit to a retiree. This represents a huge opportunity cost in the form of foregone wealth creation. As a result, one third of Americans have no positive net worth – despite paying over 12 percent of their income into the Social Security system.

Principles of Social Security Reform

Governor Bush believes that today's prosperity provides an opportunity to preserve Social Security for senior Americans, while building wealth for younger Americans. The inevitable math of demographic change means that each year reform is delayed, the more difficult this task becomes.

However, returning Social Security to a sound financial footing should not be a partisan effort. Thus, Governor Bush will reform Social Security by building on bipartisan reform efforts in Congress, with a few clear principles:

- **Principle #1: Modernization Must Not Change Social Security Benefits for Retirees or Near-Retirees**. Social Security represents a solemn commitment that must be kept. Thus, Governor Bush believes that reform must not affect anyone currently receiving Social Security benefits – or anyone close to receiving them.

- **Principle #2: The Current Social Security Surplus Must Be Protected by a "Lock Box."** Governor Bush's economic plan requires the entire $2 tril-

Chart 4

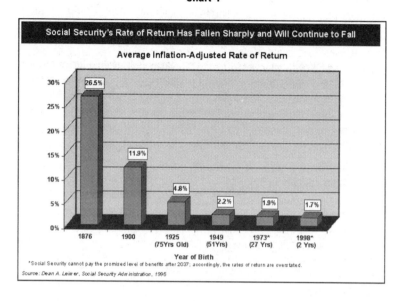

Social Security's Rate of Return Has Fallen Sharply and Will Continue to Fall

Average Inflation-Adjusted Rate of Return

*Social Security cannot pay the promised level of benefits after 2037; accordingly, the rates of return are overstated.
Source: Dean A. Leimer, Social Security Administration, 1995

Chart 5

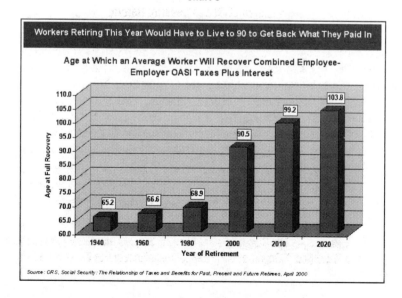

Workers Retiring This Year Would Have to Live to 90 to Get Back What They Paid In

Age at Which an Average Worker Will Recover Combined Employee-Employer OASI Taxes Plus Interest

Source: CRS, Social Security: The Relationship of Taxes and Benefits for Past, Present and Future Retirees, April 2000

lion Social Security surplus to be preserved solely for Social Security. Unlike the current administration, which has spent $295 billion of the Social Security surplus on other programs, Governor Bush will commit to securing the current surplus through a lock box.

- **Principle #3: Social Security Payroll Taxes Must Not Be Increased.** The payroll tax is a regressive tax on productive activity. It hits hardest those at the lowest end of the economic spectrum. Raising it merely lowers the expected rate of return for current workers. Governor Bush believes that reform must treat all generations fairly. Thus, he rejects any plan that punishes struggling families by increasing taxes.

- **Principle #4: Government Must Not Invest Social Security Funds in the Stock Market.** Virtually all proposals recognize that one key to reform is to incorporate investment-based options, which would provide an opportunity for higher rates of return. Governor Bush believes that the investment decisions must reside with individual workers and retirees, not the federal government.

- **Principle #5: Modernization Must Preserve Social Security's Disability and Survivors Components.** Social Security is much more than a retirement program. It also provides critical benefits to survivors and disabled workers. For example, in 1999 over 6 million workers and family members received $51 billion in Social Security disability benefits. These disability benefits are currently funded by 1.7 percentage points of the total 12.4 percent payroll tax. Governor Bush believes that reform must preserve the existing safety net for survivors and disabled workers.

- **Principle #6: Modernization Must Include Individually Controlled, Voluntary Personal Retirement Accounts, Which Will Augment the Social Security Safety Net.** Governor Bush agrees with every major bipartisan proposal that modernization must allow workers to invest a portion of their payroll taxes in personal retirement accounts, consistent with parameters of safety and soundness. Because of the impact of compound interest, which Albert Einstein called the most powerful force in the universe, diversified personal retirement accounts will grow rapidly. The accounts can be expected to earn nearly 6 percent after inflation – almost three times what Social Security now provides. (See Chart 6.) Many personal account proposals have the added benefit of allowing workers to choose their own retirement age.

Chart 6

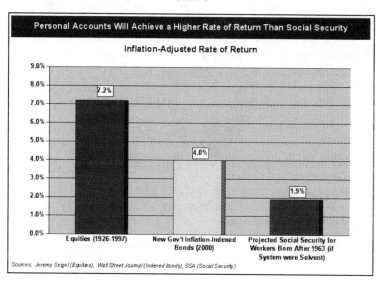

Personal Accounts Will Achieve a Higher Rate of Return Than Social Security

Inflation-Adjusted Rate of Return

Equities (1926-1997): 7.2%
New Gov't Inflation-Indexed Bonds (2000): 4.0%
Projected Social Security for Workers Born After 1963 (if System were Solvent): 1.9%

Sources: Jeremy Seigel (Equities), Wall Street Journal (Indexed bonds), SSA (Social Security)

Chart 7

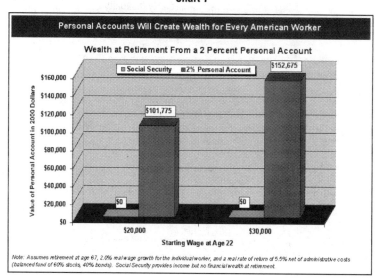

Personal Accounts Will Create Wealth for Every American Worker

Wealth at Retirement From a 2 Percent Personal Account

Value of Personal Account in 2000 Dollars

Starting Wage at Age 22

$20,000: Social Security $0; 2% Personal Account $101,775
$30,000: Social Security $0; 2% Personal Account $152,675

Note: Assumes retirement at age 67, 2.0% real wage growth for the individual worker, and a real rate of return of 5.5% net of administrative costs (balanced fund of 60% stocks, 40% bonds). Social Security provides income but no financial wealth at retirement.

Personal retirement accounts would also build wealth, particularly for lower-income Americans. For example, if a 22-year-old earning $20,000 a year were permitted, as some bipartisan proposals advocate, to invest two percent of her payroll taxes in a personal account involving a mix of stocks and bonds, that account would be worth over $100,000 at retirement. (Assumes only 2 percent wage growth; See Chart 7.) The various reform proposals differ as to the percentage of payroll taxes that may be invested – but all would build significant wealth. These accounts would be owned by workers, used exclusively for retirement benefits, and could be passed from one generation to the next.

Reforming Medicare

Just as Social Security sought to ensure retirees' economic well being, Medicare was designed to ensure retirees' physical well being. Enacted in 1965, Medicare today provides health insurance for over 39 million people aged 65 years and over and certain disabled individuals. The traditional Medicare program has two basic components:

- Part A (Hospital Insurance): Provides individuals who paid the Medicare payroll tax with premium-free care in hospitals, skilled nursing facilities, hospices and some home care. Part A is financed primarily (87 percent) by payroll taxes, shared equally by employers and employees.

- Part B (Physician Insurance): Provides coverage to individuals for physician services, outpatient hospital care, and certain other medical services not covered by Part A. Part B is financed 75 percent by general revenues and 25 percent by beneficiaries who pay a premium of $45.50 per month.

Medicare Parts A and B collectively cover only 53 percent of the typical senior's health costs. The remaining costs include premiums for so-called "Medigap" insurance, which is designed to cover some of the costs that Medicare does not. But even most Medigap plans do not protect against financial exposure from the cost of outpatient prescription drugs, yearly physical exams, some preventive tests, and routine hearing, eye or dental care.

To help extend the scope of coverage, the Balanced Budget Act of 1997 created the Medicare+Choice program, which allowed private insurance companies to offer coverage to seniors who would otherwise be covered by Medicare. Many of these plans include prescription drug benefits. However, since the government reimburses the private companies on a per-capita basis,

Medicare+Choice is not offered in many rural areas and smaller cities where the reimbursement rate is low.

Despite Medicare's many successes in providing health care to seniors, the system now faces serious challenges, both in terms of its financial solvency and the scope of its benefits.

Approaching Insolvency

On the surface, Medicare appears to be financially sound. This is because the government measures Medicare's solvency solely by the fiscal health of the Part A (Hospital Insurance) Trust Fund. This creates the opportunity to increase the appearance of solvency merely by shifting costs from Part A to Part B. For example, the 1997 Balanced Budget Act transferred the costs for home health care from Part A to Part B, which was deemed to extend Medicare solvency by six years.

Unfortunately, both Part A and Part B are facing increasing financial pressures that cost shifting may disguise, but cannot solve. Since Part A is largely funded by payroll taxes, its financial solvency is being undermined by the same demographic changes that are undermining Social Security:

- The impending retirement of the Baby Boomers will greatly increase the number of Medicare beneficiaries. In 1970, 20 million Americans were eligible for Medicare. Today, there are 39 million, and by 2030 there will be 76 million.

- The ratio of workers to beneficiaries is declining. Currently there are 4 workers for every Medicare beneficiary; by 2030, there will be barely 2 workers for every beneficiary.

As a result, according to the intermediate assumptions of the Medicare Trustees, payments to beneficiaries from the Part A Trust Fund will exceed its income in 2010, and exhaust the fund's assets entirely by 2025. At the same time, payments from Medicare Part B, which is financed primarily from general revenues, have been growing about 5 percent faster than the economy as a whole – leaving fewer and fewer federal dollars to support other government programs. Thus, the only way to keep the Medicare system financially sound is to increase taxes by at least 20 percent – or reform the system.

Lack of Prescription Drug Coverage

Just as the growth in retirees is outstripping the resources of the system,

231

so, too, are rapid advances in medicine outstripping the scope of Medicare coverage. As Senator John Breaux (D-LA) has noted, "Medicare is still a 1965 health care delivery system trying to keep pace with 21st century medicine."

Today's medical science relies increasingly on prescription drugs to treat disease and reduce health care costs. In the last decade alone, 370 new medicines have been developed to fight cancer, heart disease, diabetes, Parkinson's, Alzheimer's, depression and arthritis.

However, unlike 98 percent of health plans today, Medicare does not offer a prescription drug benefit or a cap on out-of-pocket expenses. As a result:

- One-third of Medicare beneficiaries pay for prescription drugs out-of-pocket or go without them. The remaining two-thirds have prescription drug coverage mainly through employer-provided retiree benefits, Medicaid or Medigap insurance.

- Senior citizens pay an average of $450 per year in out-of-pocket drug expenses.

- Twelve percent of Medicare beneficiaries have drug expenses of $1,000 or more per year.

Failure to Provide Access to Medical Advances

In addition to its failure to provide adequate prescription drug coverage, Medicare is also slow to provide seniors with access to new medical technology. Indeed, Medicare's procedures for adding new technologies to the benefits package have not been fundamentally overhauled since the program was established in 1965. The result is that many seniors are denied state-of-the-art care routinely covered by private insurers. For example:

- Medicare still does not cover the use of Positron Emission Topography (PET), a unique diagnostic imaging technique approved by the FDA, for many of the indications that have been reimbursed by private insurance companies for almost a decade, such as brain tumors and epilepsy.

- Medicare does not cover the use of ultrasound technology to stimulate the healing of broken bones, despite the fact that it was approved by the FDA in 1994, has a 91 percent healing rate, and is currently being reimbursed by over 800 private insurers and health plans.

- Medicare does not reimburse for certain widely used early detection and preventive tests, such as cholesterol screenings and annual physical exams. Even though a test for prostate cancer had been on the market since early 1990, Congress had to pass a law in 1997 to approve Medicare payment.

Bureaucratic Complexity, Fraud and Abuse

The need for Medicare reform arises not only from the program's precarious finances and outdated coverage, but also from the complexity of the Medicare bureaucracy itself.

The Health Care Financing Administration (HCFA), which administers Medicare, annually publishes:

- Over 132,000 pages of regulations – three times longer than the U.S. Tax Code; and

- Over 10,000 different prices for medical care in 3,000 counties.

Medicare providers maintain that the program's burdensome regulations force them to take time away from patient care to comply with excessive and complex paperwork. Worse, an increasing number of physicians are opting to no longer treat Medicare patients. The problem is so significant that HCFA now has a study underway.

Excessive administrative complexity makes Medicare prone to fraud and abuse. In 1999, the Inspector General determined that Medicare made $13.5 billion in improper payments. But, due to the complexity of the system, it is often difficult to tell where honest mistakes end and fraud begins. As Dr. Robert Waller, Chairman Emeritus of the Mayo Foundation has testified, "The public has been led to believe that the Medicare system is riddled with fraud, when, in reality, complexity is the root of the problem."

Principles of Medicare Reform

The National Bipartisan Commission on the Future of Medicare was created as part of the 1997 Balanced Budget Act. The 17-member commission was led by Senator John Breaux, a Democrat, and Representative Bill Thomas, a Republican. The commission introduced a reform plan modeled after the Federal Employees Health Benefit Program, which provides benefits to approximately 9 million federal employees and their families and retirees. The plan called for a new solvency test based on the total cost of the program, guaranteed protections for low-income seniors, and a choice of government-approved and supported plans.

Unfortunately, the Bipartisan Commission fell one vote short of the 11 votes necessary to approve the proposed reform plan. All four of the Clinton-Gore appointees voted against the bipartisan recommendation.

Subsequently, bipartisan legislation was introduced in the Senate by Senators Breaux (D-LA), Frist (R-TN), Kerrey (D-NE) and Hagel (R-NE). Although not identical, the Commission's proposal and the Senate legislation have many common elements.

As President, Governor Bush will seek to reform Medicare by building on these recent bipartisan efforts. In particular, he is committed to ensuring that reform expands the scope of coverage, improves the system's financial stability, and reduces bureaucratic complexity.

Thus, Governor Bush believes that Medicare reform must adhere to these basic principles:

- **Principle #1: Medicare's Current Guarantee of Access to Seniors and the Disabled Must be Preserved.** Everyone who qualifies for Medicare must continue to automatically receive benefits. Moreover, Medicare recipients must be allowed to keep their current Medicare plan or choose the health plan that best fits their health care needs.

- **Principle #2: Every Medicare Recipient Must Have a Choice of Health Plans, Including the Option of Purchasing a Plan that Covers Prescription Drugs.** All Medicare recipients should be given the opportunity to choose a comprehensive health plan that best reflects their health care needs, including a plan that provides coverage of outpatient prescription drugs.

- **Principle #3: Medicare Must Cover Expenses for Low-Income Seniors.** In order to keep our commitment to low income seniors, a reformed Medicare program must cover the entire cost of a health plan, including prescription drug expenses.

- **Principle #4: Medicare Must Provide Access for Seniors to the Latest Medical Advances, and Streamline Its Regulations.** The government must reform its methods for approving new technology and devices to give seniors access to state-of-the-art treatment. In addition, regulations must be simplified to minimize mistakes and ease the burden on physicians and other medical providers.

- **Principle #5: Medicare Payroll Taxes Must Not Be Increased.** Medicare must be saved and strengthened through reform – not through tax increases on working families and individuals.

- **Principle #6: Reform Must Establish a New Solvency Test Based on Total Program Costs for Part A and Part B.** Instead of measuring Medicare's solvency solely by the fiscal health of the Part A (Hospital Insurance) Trust Fund, costs for Part B (Physician Insurance) should be included as well. This more honest presentation of Medicare's solvency will preclude shifting costs from Part A to Part B merely to increase the appearance of Medicare's solvency. This "unified" measure of the financial health of the program should encompass all payroll taxes, general revenues, and premiums so that current and future beneficiaries are adequately protected and that appropriate action by Congress can be triggered.

Position Paper
Building on the Promise of Social Security: Personal Retirement Accounts

May 16, 2000

> *"Personal accounts build on the promise of Social Security – they strengthen it, making it more valuable for young workers. They give people the security of ownership. They allow even low-income workers to build wealth, which they will use for their own retirement and pass on to their children."*
>
> Governor George W. Bush

> *"[Governor Bush] has proposed what would be the logical completion of the Social Security system."*
>
> Senator Daniel Patrick Moynihan (D-NY)

The Benefits of Personal Retirement Accounts

Virtually all bipartisan proposals in Congress to reform Social Security enable individuals to invest in personal retirement accounts. The benefits of personal retirement accounts are as follows:

Saving Social Security

Social Security is facing new challenges – people are living longer, large numbers of "Baby Boomers" will begin to retire in 2008, and the number of workers for every retiree is declining. There are only a few ways to keep Social Security solvent and to protect the retirement income of all Americans. Instead of dramatically raising taxes or cutting benefits, Social Security could be strengthened by permitting individuals to invest some of their contributions in personal retirement accounts.

Higher Rates of Return than Social Security

For most workers, Social Security will be the largest investment of their life. Personal retirement accounts would provide higher rates of return on their contributions. On average, workers born after 1963 can expect a mere 1.9 percent real return on their Social Security investment (the total amount of payroll taxes they have paid during their working years). As the Social Security system veers toward insolvency in 2037, the average rate of return on their Social Security investment will decline further. In contrast, a balanced portfolio of stocks and bonds can be expected to return about 6 percent after inflation.

Vice President Gore has proposed a new retirement account that is completely separate from Social Security. Under his proposal, workers must first pay 12.4 percent of their wages into a system that promises a low, or even negative, return. To take advantage of his accounts, workers must then put up even more of their hard-earned income before they are allowed to take advantage of higher returns and compound interest.

Building Retirement Assets

Personal retirement accounts will permit workers to accumulate wealth by saving and investing their own funds, and enjoying the benefits of compound interest. As an example, if a 22-year-old making $20,000 annually were permitted, as some bipartisan proposals advocate, to invest 2 percentage points of her payroll taxes in a personal account involving a mix of stocks and bonds, that account would be worth over $100,000 at retirement (net of inflation; assumes only 2 percent wage growth). The various reform proposals differ as to the percentage points of payroll taxes that may be invested – but all would build significant wealth.

Leaving Assets for Future Generations

Unlike Social Security, individuals would own the assets in their personal retirement accounts and could bequeath them to their children. Such accounts would also ensure greater fairness for beneficiaries who do not live until the Social Security retirement age.

Freedom from Political Risk

Personal accounts would create secure retirement income free from polit-

237

ical risk. Under the current system, individuals do not have any legal right to the amount of money they contribute in payroll taxes. Congress can reduce Social Security benefits or increase taxes on benefits at any time. Social Security taxes have increased 21 times and benefits have been cut to keep the system solvent.

Diversification and Safety

By investing in personal retirement accounts, workers can diversify their retirement savings, thereby enhancing returns and decreasing risk. For example, individuals could invest in a mixed fund of equities and bonds.

Bipartisan proposals in Congress establish parameters to ensure the safety and soundness of personal retirement account investments.

Other Retirement Systems Give Workers Flexibility

Unlike Social Security, many retirement plans give workers the flexibility to invest a portion of their wage income in income producing assets. Employees of for-profit and non-profit organizations often have 401(k) plans that enable them to build up tax-deferred income in diversified investments. Some state and local governments have withdrawn from, or not elected to participate in, the Social Security system altogether and have established for their employees investment based retirement accounts. Employees of the federal government may choose to invest a portion of their wages in a "Thrift Savings Plan," consisting of common stocks, government securities, corporate bonds or some combination of such investments. Today, over 86 percent of employees in the Federal Employment Retirement System invest a portion of their income in the Thrift Savings Plan. (See Chart 1.)

Enhance Personal Savings and Freedom to Retire

People are saving less money than at any period since the Great Depression. (See Chart 2.) Personal retirement accounts may help stimulate savings for retirement. Workers would be likely to make extra contributions as they watch their accounts grow. Personal retirement accounts also give individuals the freedom to retire on their own terms.

Chart 1

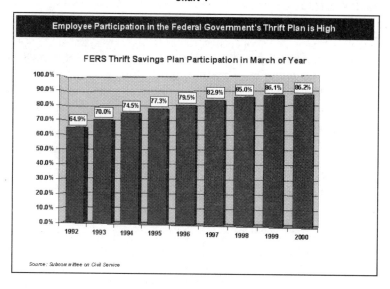

Employee Participation in the Federal Government's Thrift Plan is High

FERS Thrift Savings Plan Participation in March of Year

Source: Subcommittee on Civil Service

Chart 2

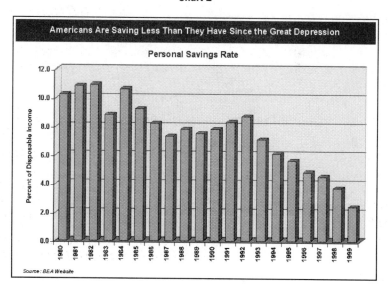

Americans Are Saving Less Than They Have Since the Great Depression

Personal Savings Rate

Source: BEA Website

Benefits to the Economy

Personal retirement accounts would not only increase retirement income and help stabilize the Social Security payroll tax, but would also substantially increase national savings and the gross domestic product. An increase in national savings means more available capital, better jobs and higher living standards.

WHAT OTHERS SAY

"Meanwhile, Bush won praise for his Social Security plan from a surprising source-New York Democratic Senator Daniel P. Moynihan, who is seen as one of Social Security's best friends. Moynihan said Bush's plan to let workers invest some of their Social Security is 'a very serious proposal' and 'the logical completion of the Social Security system' because it will give retirees 'a little wealth.'"

**Christopher Francescani and Deborah Orin,
New York Post, 4/30/00**

"Bush has a record of bi-partisanship in Texas and he indicated that he would apply the principle in trying to reform Social Security."

Mort Kondracke, Roll Call, 5/04/00

"Social Security...must be modernized...Gov. Bush has been admirably willing to argue against the status quo."

Editorial, <u>National Review</u>, 5/01/00

"...Mr. Bush's proposal to let workers voluntarily invest...into their own safe, long-term investment accounts, makes sense."

Donald Lambro, <u>Washington Times</u>, 5/04/00

"The people who would benefit most are poor people who do not have the ability to save...With private accounts, it is your money, and when you die you can pass it on to your families. So, the proponents of private accounts say that this would give wealth creation to poor people – that they do not now have an ability to save money that they don't otherwise have – and give them some way of passing on some wealth to their families."

Jim Angle, Special Report with Brit Hume, 5/1/00

"Bush also advocated a bipartisan approach to improving Medicare, the federal health insurance program for senior citizens. Bush in the past has voiced support for a Medicare reform plan outlined by a bipartisan commission last year. The plan would extend Medicare coverage through the Federal Employees Health Insurance Program but also would open more private markets for alternative health care coverage. Medicare would cover the cost for low-income individuals..."

R.G. Ratcliffe and Bennett Roth, <u>Houston Chronicle</u>, 5/16/00

"...Gov. George W. Bush... proposed a fundamental change in the retirement system that would allow workers to choose how to invest some of their payroll taxes."

Alison Mitchell and James Dao
<u>The New York Times</u>, 5/16/00

"Gov. Bush's plan puts the 'security' back in Social Security and, for that, small business applauds him," declared Jack Faris, president of the National Federation of Small Business, which has been advocating the creation of personal retirement accounts with Social Security funds."

Tim Nickens and Sara Fritz, <u>St. Petersburg Times</u>, 5/16/00

"...the current Social Security system is broken...Mr. Bush's proposal... is the only viable option."

Editorial, <u>Washington Times</u>, 5/05/00

"I am particularly encouraged by the emphasis that Governor Bush placed on the need for bipartisan cooperation to address the issue of Social Security."

Charles Stenholm (D-17th TX), 5/14/00
Statement on Gov. Bush's Social Security speech

"...Mitchell [professor at the Wharton School], praised Bush for taking the 'very courageous' step of advocating such major changes in Social Security."

Glenn Kessler, <u>Washington Post</u>, 5/16/00

"Allowing workers to invest part of their payroll tax into stocks and bonds could be one of the best ways ever to help the working class to build wealth."

Editorial, <u>Atlanta Journal-Constitution</u>, 5/17/00

"When George Bush says, 'I trust Americans to make their own decisions and manage their own money,' He is reminding them of the value of freedom – and choice."

Editorial, <u>Seattle Times</u>, 5/22/00

PART IV

Economy, Environment and Entrepreneurship

Government does not create wealth. Wealth is created by the entrepreneurial spirit of hard-working Americans. But government can help create an environment in which that spirit flourishes – an environment that promotes innovation, risk-taking and equal opportunity. This principle underlies the speeches and statements that follow, which cover a range of issues concerning our economy and quality of life.

In my speeches on tax reform, I've often noted that single mothers on the outskirts of poverty face higher marginal tax rates than people earning ten times as much. I've met with some of these single moms, and heard of this unfair burden firsthand. It is one of the many problems with a tax code that too often punishes honest effort and ambition.

I've met with farmers and small business owners who, with all their struggles, must also fear the impact that the death tax will one day have on their families. In California, I've spoken with high-tech entrepreneurs who must contend with excessive litigation. In cities across America, I've seen bleak, unsightly brownfields too long neglected because of ill-advised government policies.

All of these are things easily overlooked in times of prosperity: a mounting tax burden on families, junk and frivolous lawsuits, needless regulations hindering new industries, small farmers barely getting by, and a natural environment in need of wise stewardship.

My Administration, however, will not ignore them. We will provide tax reform based on fairness, not favoritism. We will help America's small farmers, encourage the high-tech innovation of the New Economy, and enhance the quality of our air and water with policies based on sound science.

A Tax Cut with a Purpose

Greater Des Moines Chamber of Commerce
Des Moines, Iowa

December 1, 1999

From the first day of this campaign, I have been deeply grateful for the warmth and welcome of this state.

Today, I want to share my tax cut plan with you, and with America. A tax cut designed to sustain our nation's prosperity – and reflect our nation's decency.

For nearly twenty years, with rare exceptions, our economy has been strong. America's long economic boom has defied all prediction and precedent.

Twenty-five years ago, experts talked about "limits to growth." We were advised to lower our expectations and ration our dreams. Ten years ago, we were told our country could not compete with the rising economic powers of the world. That we were slipping into the second rank and the second rate.

In America, however, pessimists are seldom prophets. Instead of finding barriers, we have crossed boundaries. Instead of decline, we have seen economic growth beyond all expectation. Consider one fact: For the last 17 years the American economy has created jobs at a pace equal to one new General Motors every four months.

This is a miracle, but not a mystery. The momentum of today's prosperity began in the 1980s – with sound money, deregulation, the opening of global trade and a 25 percent tax cut. And the economic growth of the 1980s provided the venture capital for the technology revolution of the 1990s – creating new wealth out of silicon and genius.

Along the way we have confirmed some truths and discarded some dogmas. Government can be an ally of enterprise – by creating an environment that rewards work and inspires investment. But government does not create wealth. Wealth is the economic measure of human creativity and enterprise. The success of our economy is not a tribute to politicians, hungry for praise. It is a tribute to the effort and risk-taking of Americans. It is a tribute to the power and possibilities of freedom.

But, for America, progress must be more than productivity, and success more than wealth. Even in the best of economic times, we expect more from our country. We want our free society to be a just society.

Everywhere I've gone in this campaign – from farms in this state to Latino communities in California and New York – I've talked about prosperity with a purpose. We want our prosperity to endure. But the purpose of prosperity is to ensure the American dream touches every willing heart – reaches every man or woman who works for a better life.

This is the strength and example of America. Our political system is unique – but so is our economic system. We prize competition and limited government. But we must have other priorities that give direction to our prosperity: social mobility and family and equal opportunity and the entrepreneurial spirit.

We believe in the profit motive – and in the Golden Rule. We are a land of rugged individualists – who are committed to a common good. We want a prosperity as broad and diverse as America itself.

So my tax cut plan is not just about productivity, it is about people. Economics is more than narrow interests or organized envy. A tax plan must apply market principles to the public interest. And my plan sets out to make life better for average men, women and children.

Here are the key elements:

- I will double the current child credit to $1,000 per child.
- I will replace the current five rate tax structure of 15, 28, 31, 36 and 39.6 percent with four, lower rates: 10, 15, 25 and 33 percent.
- I will expand the charitable deduction, allowing taxpayers who do not itemize their returns to deduct contributions.
- I will increase the annual contribution limit on Educational Savings Accounts from $500 to $5,000, and expand them beyond college, down to Kindergarten.
- I will eliminate the death tax.
- I will restore the 10 percent tax deduction for two-income, married couples, greatly reducing the marriage penalty.
- I will eliminate the Social Security earnings test – an unfair burden on working retirees.

These proposals, behind the dry numbers, represent and promote the enduring values of our nation.

Let's start where the need is greatest: with social mobility for hard working American families. We need a tax system that makes it easier, not harder, to join the ranks of the middle class. Half the revenue cost of my income tax cuts goes to financing two changes which I believe are vital for encouraging upward mobility.

I propose we cut the current 15 percent tax bracket by a third – to a 10 percent rate – for the first $12,000 of taxable income for married couples. It's worth recalling that when the income tax was started in 1913, it was intended only for the very rich. It had a top bracket of just 7 percent, then raised to 15 percent. It never occurred to anyone back then to tax the lowest income groups at high rates. But the current tax code does just that. Today, waitresses, store clerks and janitors are paying higher tax rates than were paid by the Morgans, Vanderbilts and Rockefellers of another era.

I also plan to double the child credit to $1,000. This, combined with lower tax rates, can completely eliminate taxes for a four person family earning $35,000 – a tax cut of over $1,500. Many two-income families making $50,000 a year will see their income taxes cut by half.

Single parents will also see their taxes cut drastically. Today, a single parent with one child earning $25,000 per year pays almost $1,500 in income taxes. I will cut that by over two-thirds – over $1,000.

It is not just the amount of taxes that matters, it's also what the economists call a taxpayer's marginal rate: the taxes we pay on every extra dollar we earn. That rate determines the incentives to work.

Under current tax law, for example, a single waitress supporting two children on an income of $22,000 faces a higher marginal tax rate than a lawyer making $220,000. As she moves up, the federal government starts taxing her income at the same time it is reducing her Earned Income Credit benefit. She can work overtime. She can earn a raise. Yet when all taxes are considered, half of her new earnings are taken away. In other words, the hardest hours of labor are taxed at the highest rates.

Under my plan, she will pay no income tax at all. And she will be joined by 6 million other low- and moderate-income, working families, who will be removed from the tax rolls entirely. That is one of every five families in America with children.

We will take down the tollgate on the road to the middle class.

My second goal is to treat the middle class itself with greater fairness.

I propose that we establish a basic principle: No middle-class family should face a federal income tax rate higher than 25 percent.

Many middle class families are working three jobs: his, hers and the full time job of caring for their children. The tax rate cuts and child credit increases in my plan will help. But given their burdens, these families do not need a marriage tax as well. So I propose we restore the marriage tax relief that Ronald Reagan passed in 1981. For a two earner couple, each making $30,000, this will mean eliminating their marriage tax penalty of over $760.

Our society has taxes on alcohol and tobacco and gambling. We call them "sin taxes." But the tax burden on families is a "virtue tax" – discouraging the most important commitments and obligations of life. Under my tax cut plan, families will be rewarded, not punished, for being families.

Securing this measure of fundamental fairness for the middle class accounts for one-third of the revenue cost of my income tax changes.

Third, my plan will encourage entrepreneurship – the path to prosperity taken by so many minorities, women and young people.

Across America, more than one in five jobs is created by a business that didn't exist a decade ago. And the story of this success is written in many hands. Between 1987 and 1997, the number of Hispanic-owned businesses more than tripled... African-American and Asian-owned businesses more than doubled. Since the 1970s, women's share of small business ownership increased from five percent to 38 percent.

One basic problem: Many of these hard working risk-takers find that government expects to be a partner in their success – sharing none of the risks, but nearly half of the profits.

Let us lay down another basic principle: No one in America should have to work more than 4 months a year to pay the IRS. The federal government, in peacetime, has no business taking more than 33 percent of anyone's paycheck. After all, the entrepreneurs of America create jobs, take risks and make their profits with honor. My tax cut plan will expand their ranks by encouraging American enterprise, not penalizing it.

Setting the top tax rate at 33 percent will take about one dollar of every six of the revenue cost of my income tax reductions. Entrepreneurs and small business owners are also singled out for punishment by the estate tax – better known as the "death tax."

Right now, as every farmer knows, inheriting a family business generally means inheriting a tax, on assets over $650,000, of between 37 and 55 percent. Family businesses often can't afford this. They may have assets, but lack ready cash. Many inherited businesses fail. In nine of ten cases, the heirs list the death tax as a major cause.

The death tax penalizes those who want to build on the wealth created by their family. It impedes economic growth by seizing the capital needed to make small businesses flourish. It can tax wealth three times over – in the earning, in the transfer, and in the sale of an asset.

When a man or woman builds a business, they are also leaving a legacy. Their death should not mean the end of their life's work. This tax violates virtually every principle of common sense and free enterprise – and I intend to abolish it.

Fourth, my plan takes the side of compassion and giving – because a prosperous society must be a generous society.

A rising tide lifts many boats, but not all. Many prosper in a bull market, but not everyone. In the most affluent country of history, there are still people in need of help and hope. And there are private and religious groups in every community willing to provide both – saving children from gangs, rescuing people from addiction, caring for women in crisis.

Yet it is not enough for conservatives like me to praise these efforts. It is not enough to call for volunteerism. Without more support and resources, both private and public, we are asking them to make bricks without straw.

Most of these groups depend on charitable contributions. Yet today 70 percent of tax filers cannot claim the charitable deduction, because they do not itemize. Under my plan, people who don't itemize will be given the same treatment and incentive as people who do, rewarding and encouraging giving by everyone in our society, not just the wealthy.

Finally, we must treat the elderly with dignity.

Our "greatest generation" deserves our greatest respect.

This begins by keeping our word. We must protect Social Security benefits for those who receive them... reserve the Social Security surplus for Social Security itself... while giving young workers of today new options like personal retirement accounts. A reform that would strengthen the system and give workers a larger share in the economic growth of America.

Respecting seniors also means respecting their abilities. Our current system places little value on the economic potential of senior citizens, as if their productive years were just a fading memory. Under today's "earnings test," as it's known, many Social Security recipients who continue to work lose anywhere from 33 to 50 percent of their benefits. An effective tax rate of up to 70 percent.

I happen to know two senior citizens very well. And neither of them shows much inclination to withdraw from productive life. One of them, at the age of 64 was elected President of the United States. At 75, he jumped out of an airplane. Both today keep busy. But my parents are just one example of the millions of skilled and experienced seniors who still have a lot to offer their community and their country.

Congress has made some adjustments in this earnings test. My plan eliminates it entirely – a change that will help millions of seniors. The law should not hinder our seniors from making their own choices and working as long as they want – all while fully receiving the Social Security benefits they have already earned.

These five priorities – social mobility, middle class families, entrepreneurship, charity and the elderly – mark a very different direction from that of the current Administration. It has increased the level of taxes. And the percentage of national income we now pay in federal income taxes is the highest since the Second World War, when America had eight million men under arms. Yet the President and Vice President insist that tax cuts are a "risky" proposition.

I do not accept the assumption that it is somehow "risky" to let taxpayers keep more of their own money.

What is risky is when politicians are given charge of a surplus. There is a strong temptation to spend it. And, in Washington, that temptation is overwhelming. A government with unlimited funds soon becomes a government of unlimited reach.

There are only two things that can be done with a surplus. It can be used by government, as the President proposes. Or it can be used by Americans, to save and build and invest. As you can see from this tax plan, I have made my choice. I choose the creation of wealth, over the care and feeding of government.

I am always amazed when I hear politicians say government cannot "afford" a tax cut. May I remind them that government does not "pay" for anything: The people pay for government. The question is not how much government can afford to give to taxpayers. The question is how much the taxpayers can afford to give to government.

Low tax rates are a powerful economic tool to promote a higher standard of living for all Americans. They can be the difference between renting or buying a home, paying or postponing a debt, saving for college or worrying you won't be able to help your children.

Yet I also believe in tax cuts for a another practical reason: because they provide insurance against economic recession.

Sometimes economists are wrong. I can remember recoveries that were supposed to end, but didn't. And recessions that weren't supposed to happen, but did. I hope for continued growth – but it is not guaranteed. A president must work for the best case, and prepare for the worst.

There is a great deal at stake. A recession would doom our balanced budget. It would leave far less money to strengthen Social Security and Medicare. But, if delayed until a downturn begins, tax cuts would come too late to prevent a recession. Putting more wealth in the hands of the earners and creators of wealth – now, before trouble comes – would give our current expansion a timely second wind.

Our times allow a substantial tax cut. Integrity requires that it also be a realistic and responsible tax cut.

My plan is realistic because it avoids meaningless 15-year budget projections. It is not based on inflated growth estimates.

It is easy to build false hopes with false numbers. But this is not daring, it is deception. It is not boldness, it is cynicism. And Americans see through it.

For me, tax cutting is not some abstract cause. I have a plan, but I also have a record. I have actually done the work of passing tax cuts. Of persuading Democrats and Republicans to join in the two largest tax reductions in Texas history – nearly $3 billion returned to taxpayers.

My tax cut plan for America is responsible because it sets priorities. It reserves all the Social Security surplus for Social Security itself. None of it will be used either for new spending or tax reductions. My plan balances the budget. It funds needed priorities, including defense and education. It reduces the national debt. And it ensures that the excess – the rest of the surplus – is returned to the American people, who earned it and deserve it.

These, then, are the basic ideas that guide my tax policy: lower taxes for all, with the greatest help for those most in need. Everyone benefits – while the highest percentage tax cuts go to the lowest income Americans.

This plan is judicious in approach – using real numbers. And just in effect – helping real people.

I believe this is a formula for continuing the prosperity we've enjoyed, but also expanding it in ways we have yet to discover. It is an economics of inclusion. It is the agenda of a government that knows its limits and shows its heart.

For many years "sharing wealth" was a code word for redistribution – the project of government planners and social engineers. With the best intentions, they actually added to the sum of suffering.

My economic vision goes in the opposite direction. I believe our sustained prosperity now permits us to use the tools of the free market to promote the goals and values we share as a nation: independence, accountability, faith in the good judgement of citizens, confidence in their ability to compete, and charity for those who cannot.

How fortunate we all are to live in an age and a country where effort is rewarded, freedom prized and opportunity shared. Now let us press on, making the most of this chance given to no other nation in no other time – building a country rich not only in goods, but in goodness, and not only the envy of the world, but its inspiration.

Position Paper
A Tax Cut with A Purpose

December 1, 1999

"My tax cut plan is not just about productivity, it is about people. Economics is more than narrow interests or organized envy. A tax plan must apply market principles to the public interest. And my plan sets out to make life better for average men, women and children."

Governor George W. Bush

EXECUTIVE SUMMARY

Governor Bush's Bold Approach to Tax Cuts

Federal taxes are the highest they have ever been during peacetime. Americans now work more than 4 months a year on average to fund government at all levels. High taxes unfairly limit the participation of low-income earners, middle-class families, and seniors in today's prosperity, and act as a success tax on entrepreneurs. That is why Governor Bush is proposing a bold tax cut plan that will not only ensure continued prosperity – and leave the Social Security surplus untouched – but give that prosperity a purpose.

Governor Bush's tax plan focuses on cutting marginal tax rates, a powerful way to raise standards of living. The Bush tax plan will replace the current five-rate tax structure of 15, 28, 31, 36, and 39.6 percent with four lower rates: 10, 15, 25 and 33 percent. This would mean lower taxes for all Americans, providing $460 billion of tax relief over 5 years.

The highest percentage cuts will go to those taxpayers with the lowest incomes:

- A family of four making $35,000 a year will receive a 100 percent income tax cut.

- A family of four making $50,000 a year will receive a 50 percent income tax cut.

- A family of four making $75,000 a year will receive a 25 percent income tax cut.

Overall, the marginal income tax rate on low-income families will fall by over 40 percent, and six million American families – one in five taxpaying families with children – will no longer pay any income tax at all.

Governor Bush's Tax Cuts Focus On Five Priorities

To Increase Access to the Middle Class for Hard-Working Families, Governor Bush's plan will:

- Cut the current 15 percent tax bracket to 10 percent for the first $6,000 of taxable income for singles, the first $10,000 for single parents, and the first $12,000 for married couples.

- Double the child tax credit to $1,000.

To Treat All Middle Class Families More Fairly, Governor Bush's Plan will:

- Cut the maximum marginal tax rate for the middle class to 25 percent (versus the current maximum rates of 28 and 31 percent).

- Greatly reduce the marriage penalty by restoring the 10 percent deduction for two-earner families, allowing them to deduct up to an additional $3,000.

- Raise the threshold for the phase-out of the child tax credit from $110,000 to $200,000 for married couples, and from $75,000 to $200,000 for single parents.

To Encourage Entrepreneurship and Growth, Governor Bush's Plan will:

- Cap the top marginal tax rate at 33 percent (down from the current 39.6 percent).

- Eliminate the death tax.
- Make the Research and Development tax credit permanent.

To Promote Charitable Giving and Education, Governor Bush's Plan will:

- Extend the deduction for charitable contributions to the 80 million taxpayers that do not itemize, and raise the cap on corporate giving.
- Increase the annual contribution limit on Education Savings Accounts from $500 to $5,000 per child.

To Allow Seniors to Work Without Penalty, Governor Bush's Plan will:

- Eliminate the Social Security earnings test.

Governor Bush's Tax Reforms Make the Tax Code Fairer

Governor Bush's income tax cuts will benefit all Americans, but they are especially focused on low and moderate income families:

- Roughly $3 out of every $6 returned to taxpayers would finance changes that help low income families gain access to the middle class: the new 10 percent bracket and the doubling of the child tax credit.
- $2 out of every $6 returned to taxpayers would finance changes that treat middle class families more fairly: the new 25 percent bracket, marriage penalty relief, and the higher phase-out threshold for the child tax credit.
- $1 out of every $6 returned to taxpayers would go to entrepreneurs and creators of wealth.

Governor Bush's Tax Cut Plan Preserves the Social Security Surplus

Governor Bush's tax cuts will be financed exclusively out of the non-Social Security surplus:

- Governor Bush supports Social Security "lock box" legislation, which would wall off the Social Security surplus from the rest of the budget.

The Relationship Between Taxes and Economic Growth

Governor Bush recognizes that continued economic growth will require a coordinated economic plan that preserves Social Security and Medicare, reduces the national debt, eliminates outdated regulations, controls the growth of government spending, deters frivolous lawsuits, embraces free trade, and promotes monetary policies that keep inflation low.

One of the most powerful tools the federal government has to raise standards of living is to lower marginal tax rates. That is why Governor Bush's tax plan focuses on cutting marginal rates where they impose the greatest obstacle to economic well-being. His tax plan promotes the values that make the American economy second to none: access to the middle class, family, equal opportunity, and the entrepreneurial spirit.

Limited Government and Lower Taxes Promote Growth

Economic studies comparing countries over long periods of time have confirmed that excessively large governments, and government distortion of markets, tend to lower economic growth. The reason is clear: large governments require high taxes, and high taxes distort markets. In developed economies, large governments are also correlated with lower per capita income and higher unemployment. (See Chart 1.)

Chart 1

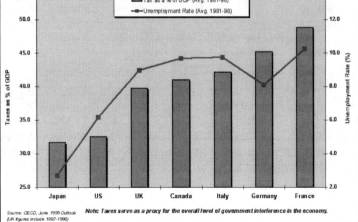

These academic studies indicate that wealth is created by hard-working, risk-taking individuals, not government programs. Countries with low taxes, limited regulation, and open borders grow faster, create more jobs, and enjoy higher standards of living than countries with bigger, more centralized governments and higher taxes. Thus, it is no coincidence that the technology revolution is being led by the United States. And it is no accident that the United States has significantly less unemployment than other nations. America is simply a freer country. If people are given the freedom to create, they do. If people are given a stake in the outcome, they succeed.

Cutting Marginal Tax Rates Raises the Standard of Living

The marginal tax rate is the tax on each additional dollar of income. The lower the marginal rate, the greater the incentive to find a better job, to save for the future, or start a new business. Lower marginal tax rates also encourage households to save, which in turn increases the funds available for capital formation. Equally important, lower tax rates leave more resources with innovative entrepreneurs, instead of funding government bureaucracies.

The foundation for today's prosperity was laid in the 1980s through the reduction of marginal tax rates, the taming of inflation, the opening of global markets, the restructuring of corporations, and the winning of the Cold War. Under strong leadership, the malaise and stagflation of the 1970s melted away into the prosperity of the 1980s. And the economic growth of the 1980s provided the venture capital to seed the technology revolution of the 1990s. (See Chart 2.)

The turning point for the economy came on August 13, 1981, when President Reagan signed into law the largest tax cut in American history. The 25 percent across-the-board cut in income taxes, combined with prudent deregulation and anti-inflation monetary policy, helped unleash the longest economic boom in the 20th century. Since 1982, over 40 million jobs have been created and the Dow Jones Industrial Average has surged from less than 1,000 to over 10,000 today. The roaring economy briefly slowed in 1990, when the Gulf War began. It regained steam in the spring of 1991, and surged ahead in 1997 under the power of the technology revolution. The economic and strategic victories of the 1980s created a strong economy and permitted a downsizing of defense, which together generated today's budget surplus.

Chart 2

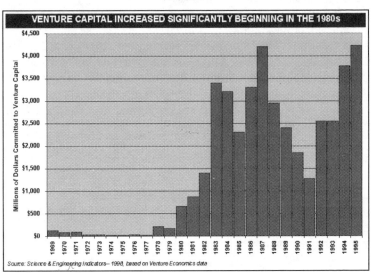

VENTURE CAPITAL INCREASED SIGNIFICANTLY BEGINNING IN THE 1980s

Source: Science & Engineering Indicators–1998, based on Venture Economics data

The Need to Cut Today's Record High Taxes

Federal income taxes have risen dramatically in the 1990s. (See Chart 3.) Today, federal taxes from all sources are the highest they have ever been during peacetime. Even worse, taxes at all levels of government absorb 36 percent of net national product.

Because of the unprecedented economic growth our country is experiencing, the current high level of taxation is generating ever-larger surpluses. Lawmakers are using these surpluses to fuel the growth of the federal government. In contrast, Governor Bush believes that a government with unlimited funds becomes a government with unlimited reach. Thus, as President, he would leave excess tax money with the people who earn it.

Access to the Middle Class

High marginal tax rates act as a tollgate, limiting the access of low and moderate income earners to the middle class. The belief that any worker, with enough effort, can join the middle class is at the heart of the American Dream. But when government attempts to help the poor by simply redistributing

Chart 3

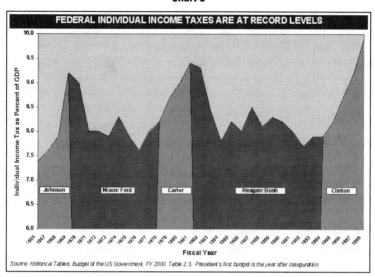

FEDERAL INDIVIDUAL INCOME TAXES ARE AT RECORD LEVELS

Source: Historical Tables: Budget of the US Government, FY 2000. Table 2.3. President's first budget is the year after inauguration

income, it often undermines incentives to work harder and earn more.

For example, because the benefit of the Earned Income Credit diminishes as a worker's income increases, a single mother with two children on the outskirts of poverty will lose half of any additional dollar she earns (taking into account social insurance taxes and state income taxes). The benefit of taking an extra training course or working an extra shift is cut in half by the government. As a result, a single mother with two children earning $22,000 a year faces a higher marginal tax rate than a lawyer earning $220,000. Lowering these barriers to the middle class is one of Governor Bush's top priorities.

The Success Tax

The tax cuts of the 1980s helped generate the venture capital that is now fueling the growth of the Internet and other technologies. New technologies are boosting productivity and economic growth by helping companies achieve new efficiencies. In this environment, entrepreneurship has become the path to prosperity for many minorities, women, and young people. Yet, today's high marginal tax rates tend to penalize continued innovation and business formation and expansion.

High marginal tax rates inhibit entrepreneurial activity because they act as a success tax, claiming a larger share of income from flourishing enterprises, while the government shares little of the risk of loss. For most entrepreneurs, income taxes reduce their companies' cash flow – the money businesses need to expand, buy more equipment, and hire more workers.

To ensure continued innovation, Governor Bush believes the tax system should be revised to restore incentives for success. In this period of revolutionary technological change, the government should leave as many resources as possible with the entrepreneurs and companies that are generating new ideas, better jobs, and greater wealth.

The Tax Burden on Families

The current level of taxes is so high that, on average, families now pay more in total taxes than they spend on housing, food, and clothing combined. These high taxes force families to work harder each year to fuel a growing government. Indeed, on average, Americans now work over four months of the year to fund government at all levels.

This high tax burden strips families of resources needed to solve their most pressing problems. Every family faces different challenges: some need better childcare, some need tutoring for their children, and others need a greater variety of after-school programs. Government cannot tailor its programs to the needs of each family. That is why Governor Bush believes that the best way to help all families is to let each family keep more of its income – and spend it as it deems appropriate.

The Debt Burden on Working Americans

Consumer debt has reached an all time high and now approaches $1.4 trillion. Credit card debt alone totals nearly $600 billion, more than $2,000 for every man, woman, and child in the country. Because auto loans and other forms of debt are also at all time highs, just servicing consumer debt takes a bigger share of income than ever before. Tax relief would give families the ability to pay off their debt without cutting critical family investments, such as quality childcare, medical check-ups, or adequate computers.

A Timely Second Wind

The current high level of taxation provides little or no insurance against a potential economic downturn. Economic history teaches the importance of keeping an eye on the horizon, especially when the economy is performing well. That is why Governor Bush advocates cutting taxes now: the best way to ensure that prosperity continues is to put more wealth in the hands of the entrepreneurs and creators of wealth. A tax cut will give the economy a timely second wind.

The Tax Cut Plan of Governor Bush

Governor Bush's tax cut plan would convert the income tax code into a simpler, flatter, and fairer tax system. His approach focuses on reducing marginal rates to spur and sustain economic growth. Lower marginal rates will give all workers the freedom to succeed, raising standards of living generally. Accordingly, under the Bush tax cut plan, the current five-rate tax structure of 15, 28, 31, 36, and 39.6 percent would be replaced with four lower rates: 10, 15, 25 and 33 percent.

This new, flatter rate structure would mean lower taxes for all working Americans. Because Governor Bush believes that a free society must also be a just society, the highest percentage cuts would go to those families and individuals with the lowest incomes. (See Chart 4.)

Recognizing that prosperity should have a purpose, the Bush tax cut plan focuses on five priorities.

Priority 1: Increasing Access to the Middle Class

The current tax code's high marginal rates serve as a barrier to the middle class for many low income families. Because the benefit of the Earned Income Credit diminishes as workers earn more, many families face punitive marginal rates that serve as a powerful disincentive to assume extra responsibility at the office, work an extra shift, take technical training, or invest in a higher educational degree.

Thus, to provide a greater reward for those who make the sacrifices needed to move ahead, one-half of the revenue cost of the Bush income tax cuts would finance changes designed to help low-income families enter the middle class. Specifically, Governor Bush's tax cut plan would:

Substantially Lower the Marginal Tax Rate for Low-Income Parents: Under the Bush tax cut plan, the marginal income tax rate would fall by over 40 percent for low-income families with two children, and by nearly 50 percent for families with one child. (See Chart 5.) This results from two key changes in the tax code:

- The current 15 percent tax bracket would be cut to 10 percent for the first $6,000 of taxable income for singles, the first $10,000 for single parents, and the first $12,000 for married couples; and

- The existing child tax credit would be doubled to $1,000 (and count against the AMT).

Chart 4

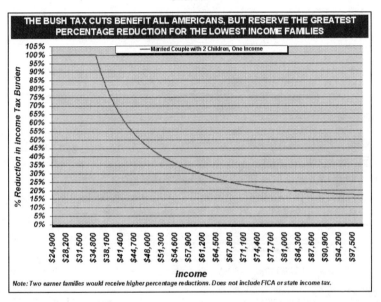

THE BUSH TAX CUTS BENEFIT ALL AMERICANS, BUT RESERVE THE GREATEST PERCENTAGE REDUCTION FOR THE LOWEST INCOME FAMILIES

Married Couple with 2 Children, One Income

% Reduction in Income Tax Burden

Income

Note: Two earner families would receive higher percentage reductions. Does not include FICA or state income tax.

As a result of these changes, six million families – one in five taxpaying families with children – would no longer pay any federal income tax (see Chart 6).

Priority 2: Treating All Middle Class Families More Fairly

Governor Bush believes it is imperative to ease the excessively high tax burden on middle class and upper middle class families – a burden that robs families of precious time together and resources to address pressing needs. As a result, one-third of the revenue cost of the plan's income tax cuts is related to changes that treat these families more fairly. These changes make the tax code

Chart 5

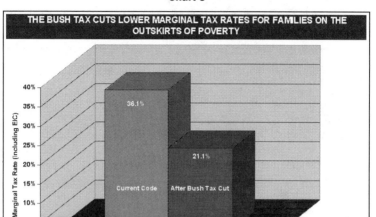

THE BUSH TAX CUTS LOWER MARGINAL TAX RATES FOR FAMILIES ON THE OUTSKIRTS OF POVERTY

Marginal Tax Rate (including EIC)

36.1%

21.1%

Current Code

After Bush Tax Cut

Single Parent with 2 Children Earning Between $21,300 and $30,600

Note: Marginal tax rate excludes FICA and state income taxes.

pro-children and pro-marriage. Specifically, Governor Bush's tax cut plan would:

Cut the Maximum Marginal Rate for the Middle Class to 25 Percent: A new, lower maximum marginal tax rate of 25 percent would be established for the middle class. This 25 percent rate would apply to married couples with taxable income over $43,050, and to singles with taxable income over $25,750. Currently, these taxpayers face a marginal rate of 28 or 31 percent.

Greatly Reduce the Marriage Penalty: The marriage penalty would be cut by restoring the deduction for two-earner families. This would allow the lower-earning spouse to deduct 10 percent – up to $3,000 – of the first $30,000 of income. If each spouse earned $30,000, the marriage penalty would drop from $763 under the current code to $0 under the Bush code. On average, the two-earner deduction would eliminate roughly half of the marriage penalty for couples with combined incomes between $50,000 and $100,000. The marriage penalty would be further mitigated by the effect of the new, lower maximum rate of 25 percent, which would reduce the portion of the marriage penalty that derives from a progressive rate structure.

Chart 6

THE BUSH TAX CUTS REMOVE OVER SIX MILLION LOWER AND MODERATE INCOME FAMILIES FROM THE FEDERAL TAX ROLLS		
	Minimum Income Before Paying Income Taxes	
Filing Status	**Current Tax Code**	**After Bush Tax Cuts**
Married Filers:*		
Married with 1 Child	$18,800	$26,200
Married with 2 Children	$24,900	$36,500
Single Filers:		
Head of Household w/ 1 Child	$15,200	$21,900
Head of Household w/ 2 Children	$21,300	$31,300
Single Filers	$7,100	$7,100
TOTAL FILERS REMOVED FROM THE TAX ROLLS:		**6 MILLION**

*Assumes two earner family with top earner making 75% of their combined income.
Note: Does not include EIC, FICA, or state income taxes. (Based on 2002 filer data estimates).

Raise the Threshold for the Phase-Out of the Child Credit: The starting point for the phase-out of the child tax credit would be raised from $110,000 to $200,000 for married couples, and from $75,000 to $200,000 for single parents.

As a result of these changes, a family of four earning $50,000 would receive about a 50 percent tax cut (returning over $1,900), and a family of four earning $75,000 would receive about a 25 percent tax cut (returning over $2,500).

Priority 3: Encouraging Entrepreneurship and Growth

Reducing marginal tax rates is the best way to promote economic growth through the tax code. Reducing the top rate in particular would spur entrepreneurial activity and help attract the best workers from around the globe to America. Governor Bush believes it is critical to reduce taxes on entrepreneurial success in order to help expand the economy through innovation. That is why one-sixth of the cost of the Bush income tax cuts would go to eliminating the success tax on entrepreneurs and creators of wealth. Specifically, the Bush tax cut plan would:

Cut the Top Marginal Tax Rates: The maximum marginal tax rates of 36 and 39.6 percent would be cut to 33 percent. This large reduction should provide a powerful economic stimulus to the economy over time.

High marginal tax rates are not the only limitation on wealth creation and risk-taking. The death tax also impedes economic growth because much of the capital formation in America occurs through estates. More capital means more tools and higher incomes for all workers. Since the marginal federal tax rate on savings can reach 73 percent (the 40 percent top income tax rate combined with the effect of the 55 percent top death tax rate), the death tax can also create a disincentive for seniors who want to save for their children or grandchildren.

The punitively high death tax falls most heavily on small businesses and family farms that are land rich but cash poor. According to a 1993 survey, nine of ten successors whose family businesses failed within three years of the owner's death listed the death tax as a contributing factor.

Finally, by encouraging tax avoidance through trusts and life insurance, the death tax may actually lower income tax revenue more than it raises death tax revenue. The tax has created an entire industry of lawyers and accountants. Compliance costs can reach 65 cents for every dollar raised in revenue, making this one of the most inefficient federal taxes.

Governor Bush believes that the bias of the death tax against the family farm and family business is the antithesis of the American Dream. Accordingly, the Bush tax cut plan would:

Eliminate the Death Tax: Eliminating the death tax would allow family farms and businesses to be passed from one generation to the next without having to break up or sell the assets to pay a punitive tax to the federal government. As a result, wealth would be taxed once – when it is earned, not again when entrepreneurs and senior citizens pass the fruits of their labors to the next generation.

A final impediment to innovation and economic growth is the uncertainty surrounding whether the current Research and Development tax credit will continue to exist. The R&D tax credit was originally enacted in 1981 and provides companies with a 20 percent tax credit for incremental R&D expenditures. According to one study, the credit yields a 31 percent return on investment – more than twice the rate of typical incentives. However, extensions of the tax credit have resulted in three gaps in coverage, two of which were retroactively filled. The on-again, off-again nature of the tax credit impedes long-term research. Thus, the Bush tax cut plan would:

Make the R&D Tax Credit Permanent: To create an environment that rewards investment in innovative technologies, the existing Research and Development tax credit would be made permanent. This should spur the sustained, long-term investment in R&D that America needs to develop the next generation of critical technologies – both civilian and military.

Priority 4: Promoting Charitable Giving and Education

Governor Bush believes that a prosperous society must be a generous society. Since the tax code first began in 1913, the law has recognized the importance of encouraging charitable giving by providing a deduction. Today, however, 70 percent of all filers – about 80 million people – cannot deduct their charitable donations because they do not itemize deductions. Thus, to encourage an outpouring of giving, the Bush tax cut plan would:

Expand the Federal Charitable Deduction: As President, Governor Bush will propose giving every taxpayer the ability to deduct his or her charitable donations. This change will generate billions of dollars annually in additional charitable contributions.

Permit Charitable Contributions from IRAs Without Penalty: Under current law, withdrawals from Individual Retirement Accounts are subject to income tax. This creates a disincentive for retirees to contribute some or all of their IRA funds to charity. Thus, Governor Bush supports legislation that would permit individuals over the age of 59 to contribute IRA funds to charities without having to pay income tax on their gifts.

Raise the Cap on Corporate Charitable Deductions: Under current law, a corporation can deduct charitable donations until their value exceeds 10 percent of the company's taxable income. As President, Governor Bush will propose legislation to raise this cap to 15 percent, encouraging firms to increase their giving to charities that address human needs.

Governor Bush's tax cut plan would also generate more resources for education. His plan recognizes that whether their children attend public, private, religious, charter or home schools, parents need funds to pay fees, buy books and supplies, cover transportation costs, and pay for tutoring and special needs. Thus, to empower parents with additional education resources, Governor Bush's tax cut plan would:

Expand Education Savings Accounts: Governor Bush would allow families or individuals with incomes up to $150,000 (or single earners with annual incomes up to $95,000) to contribute up to $5,000 annually per child into education savings accounts. Parents will be permitted to withdraw funds tax free (i.e., without being taxed on any gain or interest earned) to use for education-related purposes – from Kindergarten to college.

Priority 5: Allowing Seniors to Work Without Penalty

Social Security recipients who continue to work lose a portion of their benefits due to the Social Security earnings test. Those who are age 62 to 64 lose $1 of benefits for every $2 they earn over $9,000, and those who are age 65 to 69 lose $1 of benefits for every $3 they earn over $15,500. This work penalty adds between 33 and 50 percentage points to the already high marginal rates in the income tax code. For this reason, the earnings test discourages Social Security beneficiaries from working. Thus, the Bush tax cut plan would:

Repeal the Social Security Earnings Test: According to the Social Security actuaries, eliminating the work penalty would have little impact on the long-run financial status of the Social Security trust fund. By encouraging seniors to work longer, the repeal of the earnings test would boost Social Security tax revenue, increase general tax revenue, and decrease Medicare payments. Over time, these factors would more than offset the increase in Social Security benefits.

Distributional Impact of Governor Bush's Tax Cuts

Governor Bush's tax cuts would reduce income taxes for all Americans, but would especially benefit lower and middle-income families. For example, under the current code, a typical married couple with two children begins paying federal income taxes when their earnings reach $24,900. Under the Bush tax cut, this family would not begin paying taxes until its earnings reached $36,500. Similarly, under the current code, a single mother with two children begins paying taxes when she earns as little as $21,300. But under the Bush plan she would not become a taxpayer until her earnings reached $31,300 a year (see Chart 6). Many other lower-income taxpayers will see their income taxes slashed by over 50 percent. More affluent Americans also receive a tax cut, but they will also shoulder a larger portion of the federal income tax burden (see Chart 7). The result is an income tax burden that is fairer, yet lowers income taxes for all taxpayers.

Chart 7

UNDER THE BUSH TAX CUT PLAN, LOWER AND MIDDLE INCOME FAMILIES WILL SHOULDER LESS OF THE INCOME TAX BURDEN		

Tax Burden by Income Bracket for 2004

	PERCENT OF TOTAL INCOME TAXES PAID		Percent Cut In Income Tax Burden
	Current Tax Code	After Bush Tax Cuts	After Bush Tax Cuts
Less than $10,000	-0.9%	-1.1%	100.0%
$10,000 to $20,000	-1.0%	-1.4%	100.0%
$20,000 to $30,000	2.2%	1.9%	28.3%
$30,000 to $40,000	4.1%	3.8%	20.1%
$40,000 to $50,000	5.4%	5.1%	17.9%
$50,000 to $75,000	14.6%	14.2%	15.8%
$75,000 to $100,000	13.6%	13.4%	14.6%
$100,000 to $200,000	22.8%	23.2%	12.1%
$200,000 and over	39.1%	40.9%	9.7%
Total, All Taxpayers	100.0%	100.0%	

Note: Distribution assumes that the Bush Plan is fully phased-in. Does not include the charitable deduction or the expansion of the education savings accounts, but does include EIC payments.

Impact of Governor Bush's tax cuts on representative taxpayers:

- Single parent making $22,000 with 1 child: 100% reduction ($1,000)

- Single parent making $32,000 with 2 children: 95% reduction ($1,500)

- Married couple, each making $18,000, with 2 children: 100% reduction ($1,700)

- Married couple, each making $35,000, with 2 children: 35% reduction ($2,600)

- Married couple with one earner making $100,000, with 1 child: 15% reduction ($2,300)

Locking Up the Social Security Surplus

Governor Bush is committed to ensuring that all of Social Security's money is preserved for Social Security. That is why he is a strong supporter of Social Security lock box legislation, which would wall off the Social Security surplus from the rest of the budget. The lock box would ensure that all Social Security money is dedicated to paying benefits to current and future recipients and to modernizing the program for future generations. Thus, as President, Governor

Bush would finance his tax cuts exclusively out of the "on budget," or non-Social Security surplus.

Financing Governor Bush's Tax Cuts

Governor Bush's tax cut plan would return $460 billion to taxpayers over five years, fitting easily within the projected on-budget surplus. His income tax cuts will be phased in over five years, and the repeal of the death tax will be phased in over eight years.

Agriculture:
The Heart of Our Economy

Dallas Center, Iowa

September 1, 1999

We've got our work cut out for us. But hard work is what the American farmer knows best.

Agriculture is not just one industry among many. It is the heart of our economy. And it symbolizes some of the best and finest things about our nation: independence, hard work, risk-taking and sacrifice.

Farmers contribute to the wealth of America. But – with their commitment to faith, family and the land – they also contribute to the character of our country. I am honored to be the Governor of the second largest farm state. And I know when farmers hurt, we must help.

Today, the American farmer is facing a crisis – especially here in Iowa.

The problems are complicated, involving every kind of adversity, from bad weather to closed markets. But our response must be simple and direct.

First, we must get farmers the emergency assistance they need, in the form of direct payments. And, unlike last year's emergency aid, the help must come in time to meet the emergency.

The 1996 Farm Bill brought a lot of changes into the lives of farmers. In the long term, it promises much good – as farmers rely less on government control of supply and more on market demand.

But this is today, not the long term, and we owe it to farmers to see them through the transition.

Second, we must reform the crop insurance system. At present only 60 percent of cultivated land is covered. Some crops and livestock aren't covered at all. And where coverage is available, the government's premium structure can make adequate coverage unaffordable. We need to change that. We need to cover more crops, to reform the government premium structure, and to encourage insurers to develop new methods of risk-management.

Third, we should create tax-deferred savings accounts that allow farmers to safeguard against downturns in the farm economy – permitting them to set aside a substantial percentage of their farm income for future needs. Down the road, these accounts will help in the tough years, like this one.

Next, some serious tax reform is in order – and it should begin with the death tax.

It has always amazed me that while trying to help farmers on one end through agriculture policies, the government punishes small farmers on the other end with this destructive tax. We make it impossible for families to carry on one generation after another, and then we wonder why America's small farms are vanishing.

Today death taxes on farms run as high as 55 percent, forcing many farmers to sell off land or equipment just to pay the government. It is bad policy, unwise and unfair. We must phase out death taxes on farms until this burden is eliminated.

In Texas, in my first term, we enacted one of the strongest property-rights laws in the nation. As President, I would follow the same policies.

I know that farmers are on the front lines of advances in technology. This has led to new products and increased productivity. That is why I support value added processing. That is why I support ethanol to clean our air. And that is why we need to continue to support innovative uses for agricultural products, in the United

States and abroad.

These are some of the things that must be done here at home, in changing the policies of our own government. More complex are the problems farmers face abroad, in exporting to foreign markets. Americans account for just four percent of the world's population. Clearly the farmer's greatest challenge – and opportunity – is to gain ground in the markets that feed the other 96 percent.

American farmers are without rival in their ability to produce and compete. Often the only thing that stands in your way are trade barriers built by foreign governments and tolerated by this Administration. They will not be tolerated in my Administration.

The next president must reclaim the authority of the executive to negotiate new trade agreements. Every president from 1975 to 1994 has had that fast-track authority, until this president let it lapse. It is a powerful tool in prying open foreign markets, and never have we needed it more.

To foreign governments, the next president must also carry a simple and unequivocal message: We will no longer tolerate favoritism and unfair subsidies for your national industries. We want to compete, and compete on level ground.

I favor the so-called "single undertaking" approach to the next round of trade negotiations. That's diplomatic talk, and let me translate: Agriculture won't be left behind. I will use all the leverage at our disposal to open agriculture markets worldwide.

The next president must send an even more direct message to our European trading partners. Today, the European Union has a moratorium on the import of all but a handful of biotech crops. Yet the rules state clearly that health and safety regulations must be based on sound science. And study after study has shown no evidence of danger.

As President, I will have strong relations with the European Union. But I will not stand for unfair trade barriers. And that is what these objections to our biotech crops really are. They are trade barriers pure and simple – unfounded in science, unjustified in law, and unfair in practice.

Just as we oppose trade barriers abroad, however, we can not impose them on ourselves. Unilateral sanctions on agricultural exports only punish our own farmers, while helping our competitors. We are too good a people to use food as a weapon. In my Administration, we will end this practice.

Finally, there is one other piece of unfinished business on the topic of trade. On the right terms, I believe we should bring China into the World Trade Organization as quickly as possible.

Earlier this year, when the Chinese tried to enter the WTO, their negotiators made some major concessions – agreeing to dramatically increase their purchases of bulk commodities like corn and wheat. The limits on corn imports, for example, would have risen from 250,000 metric tons to 7.2 million metric tons.

On top of that, China agreed to reduce tariffs on agricultural products, even below what most of our trading partners impose.

I have some serious concerns about China's record as a trading partner. But these were serious concessions, a good sign, and we should have taken them up on it. Bringing China within the rules of the world trading system is in China's own interest. More importantly it is in ours, because America's best export is freedom.

Crises come and go, but commitments do not. And these are my commitments to you. In our high-tech economy, with everything changing so quickly, I think there is a tendency to take the agriculture industry for granted. In a way, this is a tribute to farmers: America has long been the agricultural center of the world, and many just assume it will always be so.

But this will not always be true, unless we support American farmers as they have supported us. The American people have always been able to count on you. Now it is time that you, the farmers of America, were able to count on us.

Position Paper
Agriculture: The Heart of our Economy

"The American spirit shines bright in America's farmers: independent, hard working, entrepreneurial, with faith in their families, their labor and their land. In this downturn in the farm economy, we must provide farmers with the means to weather change. And we must fight hard to expand existing export markets – and pry open new ones – to fuel the future growth of the farm economy."

Governor George W. Bush

The U.S. Farm Sector

Agriculture is at the heart of the U.S. economy. The entire food and fiber sector – including agricultural production, transportation, and marketing – accounts for 13 percent of our nation's economic production. According to the American Farm Bureau, agriculture is the nation's largest employer, with more than 22 million people working in some phase of the industry, from growing food and fiber to selling it at the supermarket. Future prosperity of the U.S. farm sector depends in large part on expanding global markets for U.S. products:

- The U.S. leads the world in agricultural exports, with $53.7 billion in 1998, which generated an agricultural trade surplus of $16.7 billion.

- Nearly every state benefits from the income generated by agricultural exports, and nineteen states have exports of $1 billion or more.

As trade becomes an ever more important segment of the agriculture economy, Governor Bush is committed to opening markets and to finding new avenues for American products and American values.

Response to the Current Crisis

The 1996 Farm Bill reversed decades of supply control management, and unleashed U.S. farmers to plant in response to market demand, not government programs. After a period of growth, the farm economy has now weakened due to increased global production and slack demand, principally in Asia.

As the farm sector moves toward market-driven production, Governor Bush believes the government should help farmers adapt to a global market-place by providing them with a strong safety net and the means to manage the cyclical downturns in the farm economy. That is why Governor Bush supports:

Additional Emergency Assistance to Help Farmers Make the Transition to a Market-driven Regime: The farm sector has been hit hard by the impact of large supplies and low prices. USDA economic projections for 1999 suggested continued low prices for several major farm commodities, such as cotton, corn, soybeans, and livestock, and further contraction of overseas markets. That is why Governor Bush supported additional emergency assistance, in the form of direct payments, consistent with the principles in the 1996 Farm Bill, to ensure that the move toward a market-oriented farm policy continues.

Reform of the Crop Insurance Program: Under the current crop insurance program, 60 percent of cultivated land is covered by crop insurance. Governor Bush believes we must make it a priority to develop a crop insurance program that better reflects farmers' risk management needs, including policies that cover more commodities, including livestock, offer a wider variety of plans, more comprehensive coverage, and affordable premiums. At the same time, we should encourage the private sector to continue to develop new risk management tools, like the Crop Revenue Coverage and Revenue Assurance programs, which were developed in Iowa, and are now available in six states.

Tax Incentives

Governor Bush understands that "saving for a rainy day" has a literal meaning for farmers and ranchers. What they need are new tools to help them manage through cyclical downturns. That is why Governor Bush supports:

Incentives to Encourage Farmers and Ranchers to Establish Tax-Deferred Accounts to Help Manage Fluctuations in Farm Income: Creation of farm and ranch risk management accounts would permit farmers to reserve a substantial percentage of their net farm income in a tax-deferred account. These funds could be held in the account for several years and drawn upon in years of declining income to help farmers offset operation expenses and to purchase supplies for the next production cycle.

Eliminate the Estate Tax for Family Farms and Ranches: Estate taxes can destroy family-owned farms, ranches, and small businesses, when the tax – which can be as high as 55 percent – forces farmers and ranchers to sell land, buildings or equipment to pay the government. That is why Governor Bush's tax cut plan calls for eliminating the estate tax to allow farms, ranches and other small businesses to be passed, intact, from one generation to the next.

New Technologies

Farmers are on the front lines of the new "knowledge-based" economy. Advances in technology are leading to new products, increased productivity, and more environmentally friendly farming. For the U.S. agricultural economy to remain competitive, we must support projects that will generate new exportable goods. That is why Governor Bush supports:

- Agriculture Research and Education Activities that help develop technologically advanced farm products for market here in the United States and for export to our world partners.

- Permanent Extension of the Research and Development Tax Credit.

Ethanol and Alternative Uses of Agricultural Products

Governor Bush is committed to the continuing search for innovative uses for agricultural products, especially environmentally beneficial uses. That is why he supports ethanol. Ethanol helps our farmers and makes our air cleaner.

Governor Bush believes we need to accelerate our search for innovative uses for farm products. For example, research into biomass technology could develop efficient fuels and other chemicals from virtually any plant or plant product. This type of research could become even more important for fuels like ethanol, given emerging evidence regarding the potential environmental damage from the fuel additive MTBE (methyl tertiary butyl ether). As President, he would encourage the development of new technologies for cost-effectively producing ethanol, bio-diesel fuel and other bio-fuels and products.

Regulation

Governor Bush recognizes that burdensome regulations have a real cost impact to the farm economy. That is why Governor Bush believes that regulations should be based on the best science and common sense, and solutions should involve local input, wherever possible.

Private Property Rights

Governor Bush understands that private property is fundamental to our way of life and the backbone of our economy. In his first term as Governor of Texas, he signed one of the strongest private property rights laws in the nation. As President, Governor Bush would require that the federal government carefully evaluate the impact of regulatory initiatives on private property rights. In the event that the government, acting on behalf of all citizens, asks private landowners to refrain from utilizing land, Governor Bush believes that the landowners should receive just compensation for their loss.

Livestock Price Reporting

Governor Bush believes that in order to ensure a healthy agricultural economy we must guard against potential anti-competitive practices. He recognizes that increased concentration is a growing concern among farmers and ranchers. He believes that ensuring transparent and accurate price reporting is important to ensure a competitive market. That is why Governor Bush supports the livestock industry's efforts to work together to formulate a policy that guarantees accurate, fair, and open price reporting. As President, his administration will diligently work to maintain competitive markets and ensure that existing anti-trust laws are enforced.

Kyoto Protocol

Efforts to improve our environment must be based on the best science. Scientific data show average temperatures have increased slightly during this century, but both the causes and the impact of this slight warming are uncertain. Changes in the Earth's atmosphere are serious and require much more extensive scientific analysis. Governor Bush opposes the Kyoto Protocol: it is ineffective, inadequate, and unfair to America because it exempts 80 percent of the world, including major population centers such as China and India, from compliance. America must work with businesses and other nations to develop new technologies to reduce harmful emissions.

Food Quality Protection Act

Governor Bush supports the 1996 Food Quality Protection Act (FQPA). He recognizes, however, that the FQPA presents many challenges, and believes that several key concerns need to be addressed in its implementation:

- The Environmental Protection Agency and other agencies should proceed to implement the new law in a manner that does not disrupt farmers' access to safe crop protection products.

- New requirements under the FQPA should not be implemented in a manner that restricts the use of valuable crop protection tools unless viable alternatives are available.

International Trade

Governor Bush is committed to free trade. He will work to tear down barriers everywhere and will use every available tool to combat unfair trade practices. Governor Bush is confident that America's best is the best in the world. To lead the world on trade and open markets for U.S. farmers, Governor Bush believes we must:

<u>Pass Presidential Trade Negotiating Authority to Negotiate Market-Opening Agreements</u>: Every President since Ford has had this authority, which the Clinton-Gore Administration let expire in 1994; since then, the Administration has been unable to renew this important tool for trade negotiations. This has not only hobbled the Administration's ability to pry open foreign markets, but undermined America's fundamental ability to lead global market-opening efforts. As President, Governor Bush will work with Congress to renew presidential trade negotiating authority.

<u>Open Global Agricultural Markets</u>: The recent failure to initiate a new trade round in Seattle underscores the administration's lack of leadership on trade. As President, Governor Bush will work to launch a new trade round that will level the agricultural playing field once and for all by completely eliminating agricultural export subsidies and tariffs worldwide.

<u>Eliminate Barriers to Safe Food</u>: In 1999, 50 percent of the soybeans, 40 percent of the cotton, and about one-third of the corn produced in the U.S. was genetically modified. The European Union, however, imposed a moratorium on the import of new biotech crops. Additionally, despite a ruling of the World Trade Organization, the European Union continues to ban the import of U.S. beef treated with growth hormones. World Trade Organization rules clearly state that

health and safety regulations must be based on sound science. As President, Governor Bush will fight to ensure that U.S. products are allowed entry into the European Union and require them to use accepted scientific principles in enacting their regulations.

Exempt Food from Unilateral Trade Sanctions and Embargoes: Unilateral trade sanctions are rarely effective in achieving their foreign policy goals, and often force U.S. businesses and farmers to lose market share to foreign competitors. That is why Governor Bush believes that, if sanctions are used, they should be directed at the offending government, not innocent populations, and food and medicine exports should be exempt from any new unilateral sanctions.

Admit China to the World Trade Organization: Governor Bush believes that on the right terms, admitting China to the World Trade Organization is in America's interest. It will provide U.S. farmers, ranchers, and businesses access to a growing market, and will help introduce American values along with American products.

THE TEXAS RECORD

As the Governor of the second-largest agriculture producing state, Governor Bush has led Texas in implementing innovative policies to support the continued growth of the farm sector. Specifically, Governor Bush:

- Signed into law the "Agriculture and Rural Development Act," which created the state's first comprehensive agriculture policy.

- Appropriated $25 million in emergency spending and $50 million in cost sharing assistance to aid with boll weevil eradication, providing over 23,000 producers with support during an especially difficult crop season.

- Signed into law "The Young Farmer Loan Guarantee Program," that expanded the Texas Agriculture Financing Authority to provide $225 million in loan guarantees to assist in rural development and value-added agriculture production.

- In his first term, Governor Bush led the successful fight for passage of one of the strongest laws on private property rights in the

Environment:
Reform Plan for Brownfields

U.S. Gypsum
Aliquippa, Pennsylvania

April 3, 2000

For seven years, this land around us sat contaminated and unused. And it might have remained so for years to come. With the leadership of Governor Ridge and local authorities, it has been cleaned up and redeveloped – preserving open space, and providing local jobs and tax revenue. It took more than good intentions and a good cause to accomplish this. It took good laws.

Brownfields are one of many environmental challenges facing our country. And every environmental issue confronts us with a duty to be good stewards. As we use nature's gifts, we must do so wisely. Prosperity will mean little if we leave to future generations a world of polluted air, toxic lakes and rivers, and vanished fields and forests.

Most Americans share this conviction. The debate today is how best to balance our needs of growth and progress with regard for the natural world we inherited and the world we leave to posterity.

Brownfield redevelopments – like this one – represent the cooperative spirit and results-oriented approach that, under my presidency, will guide our nation's environmental agenda.

Today, an estimated 450,000 brownfields tarnish the landscapes of communities throughout the United States. Typically they are abandoned industrial facilities, like this one, polluted and unused because of rigid, complex regulations – and fear of Superfund liability for anyone having anything to do with contaminated properties.

The Superfund law passed in 1980 was intended to clean up the nation's worst hazardous waste sites in five years. Twenty years later, the job is not done. Billions of dollars have been squandered for lawsuits and lawyers and consultants. The average length of a Superfund cleanup is eight years and fewer than half of Superfund sites have been cleaned up at all. Not only has Superfund been slow and costly, but also the complexity of the law itself has been an obstacle to state and local efforts to clean up brownfields.

Fear of liability and complex regulations have discouraged good faith efforts to clean up our environment.

Most brownfields are located in urban areas with high poverty rates, high crime rates, and high unemployment. By making cleanup of abandoned sites so expensive and so complicated, Superfund leaves these places with nothing – no new businesses, no new jobs, and the same old contamination.

What's more, the old system of mandate, regulate, and litigate only sends potential developers off in search of greener pastures – literally. Instead of hassling with sites that might be subject to Superfund liability, developers simply move on to "pristine" sites farther out in the country or the suburban fringe. Brownfields get passed over, while greenfields get paved over, furthering urban sprawl.

That's what happens when old ways have become so entrenched, when people get so attached to the process, that they lose sight of the goal. In response to this failure at the federal level, some 35 states have developed voluntary programs that are cleaning up thousands of brownfield sites faster and more effectively, and with less litigation, than under the Superfund program.

When I became Governor five years ago, there were several thousand brownfields sitting idle across Texas – and no ongoing effort or incentive to clean them up. I signed the Texas Voluntary Cleanup Program into law, protecting future developers from liability for past contamination, and providing technical support to encourage cleanups.

Our reforms have made a difference. Since we created the new program, Texas has cleaned up 451 brownfield sites – improving the environment, restoring more than $200 million in property value to local tax rolls, and revitalizing communities across the state.

Thanks to similar reforms here in Pennsylvania, 634 brownfield sites have been cleaned up since 1995.

These successful state programs show that America needs a different vision, where what counts is what you do, not what you promise. The old vision distrusts markets, distrusts local government, distrusts solutions that don't originate in Washington, D.C.

Washington's command-and-control mindset is an obstacle to reform. The solution is not to eliminate the federal role in protecting the environment; the solution is reform.

Reform that encourages innovative solutions. Reform based on common sense and the best science. Reform that sets high standards, and gets results.

As part of my reform agenda, I announce today a six-point plan to strengthen the successful state approach to brownfield cleanup and redevelopment.

First, I will direct the EPA to set high standards for brownfield redevelopment – while simultaneously allowing states the flexibility to find the best ways to meet those standards.

Second, the federal government must focus its efforts and work with states and the private sector to encourage the use and development of the best science. New technologies are being developed that will help communities clean up contamination faster and more effectively. For example, at the University of Texas, scientists are using microbes in soil and water to break down the chemical bonds of contaminants, making them harmless.

The federal government must evaluate various cleanup methods and new technologies, and provide states and communities with the information they need to clean up brownfields in the fastest, most effective way.

Third, I will continue to fund the federal grant program that has provided millions of dollars for the environmental assessment and inventory of brownfield sites. But I will reform the Brownfields Cleanup Revolving Loan Fund.

This program was intended to help communities clean up brownfields – but it has become so bogged down in regulations that only two sites have been cleaned. I will continue the funding, but cut the red tape by sending the money directly to the states as block grants for brownfield cleanup and redevelopment programs.

Fourth, I will work with Congress to provide liability protection at the federal level for potential redevelopers of brownfield sites. Developers who had nothing to do with polluting a site should not face future liability for past damage. Good public policy should encourage developers to purchase and clean up brownfields, rather than leaving the land contaminated and unused.

Fifth, current tax incentives to encourage brownfield redevelopment are set to expire December 31, 2001. I will make the provision permanent.

And finally, I will end the double standard that has the federal government acting as environmental enforcer – while at the same time causing pollution that violates those very laws.

While states clean up brownfields, the federal government has yet to clean up much of the contamination it has caused – from the thousands of gallons of raw sewage that flows untreated into the lakes and streams of Yellowstone National Park, to an EPA lab that contaminated groundwater with mercury.

America should not have two sets of rules – one for government, a different one for people. As President, I will direct active federal facilities to comply with environmental protection laws by which we all must live. The Clinton-Gore Administration has not required federal agencies to live up to the federal government's own standards; I will turn the federal government from the country's worst polluter into a good neighbor.

With real leadership – with a new vision of conservation and a new spirit of cooperation, America can make great strides toward a healthier environment, and thereby earn the gratitude of future generations.

Position Paper
Brownfield Cleanup and Redevelopment

April 3, 2000

"Prosperity will mean little if we leave to future generations a world of polluted air, toxic lakes and rivers, and vanished fields and forests. Most Americans share this conviction. The debate today is over how best to apply it. The old system of mandate, regulate, and litigate only sends potential developers off in search of greener pastures – literally. Brownfields get passed over, while greenfields get paved over. Washington's command-and-control mindset is an obstacle to reform. The solution is not to eliminate the federal role in protecting the environment; the solution is reform. Reform that sets high standards, and gets results."

Governor George W. Bush

EXECUTIVE SUMMARY

The federal Superfund statute has prevented the cleanup and redevelopment of the nation's 450,000 brownfields – mostly abandoned industrial or commercial facilities in urban areas – by scaring away potential investors and developers who fear being caught in the maze of Superfund regulation, liability, and litigation. In response, 35 states, including Texas, have developed innovative brownfield cleanup programs. Governor Bush is announcing today a six-point reform plan to strengthen the successful state approach to brownfield cleanup and redevelopment:

To Ensure Brownfield Cleanups Protect Human Health and the Environment, While Enabling Affordable Cleanups and Economic Growth, Governor Bush will:

- Direct the EPA to establish high standards for brownfield cleanups that will provide more flexibility than the current Superfund standards.

To Remove Legal Obstacles that Prevent Brownfield Cleanups, Governor Bush will:

- Provide redevelopers with protection from federal liability at brownfields cleaned up under state programs that meet high federal standards.

To Assist States and Local Communities to Gain the Technical Know-How to Clean up Brownfields, Governor Bush will:

- Focus the efforts of the federal government on developing cleanup techniques and new cleanup technologies.

To Make Federal Brownfield Financial Assistance More Effective, Governor Bush will:

- Reform the Brownfield Cleanup Revolving Loan Fund by cutting red tape and block granting funds to the states.

To Provide Incentives that Spur More Brownfield Cleanups, Governor Bush will:

- Extend permanently the brownfield cleanup tax incentive that is scheduled to expire on December 31, 2001.

To End the Double Standard that has the Federal Government Acting as Environmental Enforcer While, at the Same Time, Polluting the Environment, Governor Bush will:

- Direct active federal facilities to comply with all environmental protection laws and hold them accountable.

The Importance of Brownfield Cleanup and Redevelopment

A brownfield is an abandoned or underutilized industrial or commercial property, typically located in an urban area, where redevelopment is complicated by possible environmental contamination and potential liability. The General Accounting Office (GAO) estimates there are 450,000 brownfields in the United States.

Spurring more effective and efficient cleanup and redevelopment of brownfields is an important environmental initiative because it:

- Removes environmental hazards from communities;

- Revitalizes communities by returning property to local tax rolls; and

- Relieves pressure to develop pristine open space and farmland.

The U.S. Conference of Mayors, in its February 2000 brownfields survey, *Recycling America's Land*, calls for a "national commitment to recycle the thousands of brownfields in America's cities." Of the 231 cities that participated in the survey:

- 210 cities responded that they have more than 21,000 brownfields occupying more than 81,000 acres of land; and

- Collectively, they estimate that brownfield cleanup and redevelopment would generate up to $2.4 billion in new tax revenue in their cities.

Superfund's Failure

The federal Superfund statute – which Al Gore cites as one of his greatest legislative accomplishments – was passed by Congress in 1980 to ensure that the worst contaminated sites in the country would be promptly cleaned up. However, Superfund has failed in its mission:

- First, it has proven both expensive and inefficient. According to the GAO, of the 1,231 Superfund sites, only 595 have been cleaned up as of June 30, 1999. Moreover, while Superfund was expected to cost $5 billion and complete all cleanups in less than five years, actual Superfund spending has exceeded $30 billion and the current average length of cleanups is eight years.

- Second, Superfund has promoted costly litigation. According to studies done by RAND, 36 percent of the $11 billion spent by the private sector on Superfund in the first ten years of the program went not to clean up contaminated sites, but to pay consultants' and lawyers' fees and other litigation costs.

- Third, Superfund has actually had a chilling effect on brownfield cleanup, because a brownfield can be subjected at any time to Superfund and its complex regulations and liability scheme. This uncertainty has scared off many potential investors, redevelopers and new owners of brownfields.

State and Local Brownfield Innovation

Taking matters into their own hands, 35 states have developed innovative brownfield programs that are cleaning up thousands of brownfield sites across the country more quickly and more effectively – and with less litigation – than under Superfund. These programs set high cleanup standards tailored to particular contaminants and the end use of the site, and provide liability protection for new owners and operators of brownfields. These innovative efforts have demonstrated significant success:

- Texas' Voluntary Cleanup Program, signed by Governor Bush, has resulted in cleanups at 451 brownfields and has restored more than $200 million to property tax rolls since 1995.

- Pennsylvania's Land Recycling Program has resulted in cleanups at 634 brownfields since 1995.

- Illinois' Site Remediation Program has resulted in cleanups at 541 brownfields since 1989.

- Michigan's Site Reclamation Program has resulted in cleanups at over 700 brownfields since 1995.

The Role of the Federal Government in Brownfields Cleanup and Redevelopment

As President, Governor Bush will seek meaningful environmental reform designed to strengthen the successful state and local approach to brownfield cleanup and redevelopment. That reform will be based upon his belief that the federal government should set high standards to give states and local communities the freedom to innovate and develop new solutions to environmental challenges, and then hold them accountable for results. Accordingly, Governor Bush is proposing a six-point plan to spur more brownfield cleanups and redevelopments in every state in the country.

Proposal 1: Set High Federal Standards for Brownfield Cleanups

There is no "bright line" distinction between what makes a contaminated site a brownfield or a Superfund site, as the listing of contaminated sites on the Superfund National Priority List is a bureaucratic decision made by the EPA. The fact that a brownfield can at any time be subjected to Superfund and its complex regulations, one-size-fits-all cleanup standards, and liability scheme has scared off many potential developers and new owners and operators of brownfields.

Governor Bush believes that the federal government has an important, yet limited, role in brownfield cleanup. It should set high standards, while encouraging innovation at the state and local level in meeting those standards. Thus, as President, Governor Bush will:

Establish High Standards for Brownfield Cleanups and Give States Freedom to Innovate: Governor Bush will direct the EPA to establish high standards for brownfield cleanups that fully protect human health and the environment, while enabling affordable cleanups and economic growth. These standards will provide greater flexibility than the current Superfund standards to spur more cleanups. Standards will be set for cleanup levels of particular contaminants, and the standards will take into account what the end use of the brownfield will be. For example, a brownfield that is being cleaned up and redeveloped to house a school will have a higher cleanup standard than a brownfield that will be demolished, capped and have a manufacturing plant built on top of it. States will be given the freedom to innovate and develop programs that meet these high standards, without EPA interference.

Proposal 2: Provide Liability Protection to Brownfield Cleanups Meeting High Federal Standards

A critical obstacle to brownfield cleanup and redevelopment is the lack of liability protection at the federal level for present or future owners or operators of redeveloped brownfield sites. Under Superfund's legal framework, current owners of a contaminated property can be held liable for all or part of the cost of cleanup, no matter whether they contributed to the contamination or how small their contribution was.

To address the liability concerns of developers and new owners and operators of brownfields, state brownfield programs offer reassurance that the state will not hold them liable for contamination caused by others. However, this does not prevent the EPA from exercising its authority under Superfund to intervene and subject the property to future federal environmental enforcement. As a result, thirteen states (including Texas) have entered into Memoranda of Agreement with the EPA that stipulate once a brownfield has been cleaned up to an acceptable standard under the state's brownfield program, the EPA will intervene only if there is an imminent and substantial threat to public health or the environment. However, the value of these MOAs has been questioned because they are not legally binding.

Governor Bush believes that the better solution to the liability problem is to reform the Superfund statute itself. Thus, as President, he will:

<u>Urge Congress to Provide Protection from Federal Liability at State-Approved Brownfield Cleanups</u>: Governor Bush will urge Congress to pass legislation removing federal Superfund liability at brownfields that are cleaned up under state programs that meet the new high federal standards. Once an eligible state certifies a brownfield cleanup as complete, the developer and future owners and operators of the redeveloped brownfield will enjoy protection from both state and federal liability.

Proposal 3: Focus the Efforts of the Federal Government on Developing New Cleanup Techniques and Technologies

Part of the challenge facing communities as they clean up brownfields is finding the best methods of removing the contamination from the property. Often states and local communities do not have the resources or expertise to develop new cleanup techniques and technologies to remove contamination faster and more effectively. Therefore, as President, Governor Bush will:

<u>Focus the Efforts of the Federal Government on Developing Cleanup Models and New Cleanup Technologies</u>: Governor Bush will direct the federal government to employ the best science to establish methods to clean contaminated brownfields, develop models for cleanups and new cleanup technologies, and provide this information to states and local communities – and then permit them to clean up and redevelop brownfields without bureaucratic delay.

Proposal 4: Reform the Brownfields Cleanup Revolving Loan Fund

According to the U.S. Conference of Mayors survey, one of the most significant impediments to brownfield cleanup and redevelopment is the lack of funds available for actual cleanups.

In 1997, the EPA launched the $35 million Brownfields Cleanup Revolving Loan Fund (BCRLF), which provides grants of up to $500,000 over five years to assist communities to capitalize loan funds for the actual cleanup of brownfields. A total of 68 BCRLF grants have been awarded.

However, the BCRLF has been criticized because, of the 68 grants awarded under the program, only two have produced actual financing for brownfield cleanups. The reason for the failure of the BCRLF is that the program is bogged down in regulations and red tape. Cleanups financed by loans under this program are governed by Superfund's one-size-fits-all cleanup standards and regulations, which are more bureaucratic and inflexible than those of the states' brownfield programs. In addition, the funds cannot be used to clean up certain contaminants, such as petroleum.

While it makes economic sense for the private sector to clean up and redevelop many brownfields without government assistance, Governor Bush recognizes the cost of cleaning up certain brownfields may exceed the value of the property.

Thus, to provide funding to help clean up brownfields that might otherwise go uncleaned for economic reasons, Governor Bush will:

Reform the $35 Million Brownfields Cleanup Revolving Loan Fund by Block Granting the Funds to the States: Governor Bush will reform the BCRLF by sending the funds directly to the states in the form of block grants to distribute as grants or loans to communities to finance brownfield cleanups. Cleanups financed under the program will be regulated by the more flexible, successful state brownfield programs.

Proposal 5: Permanently Extend the Expensing of Brownfields Cleanup Costs

Under the Taxpayers' Relief Act of 1997, Congress permitted taxpayers that clean up brownfields to make certain cleanup costs fully deductible in the year in which they are incurred, rather than having to capitalize the costs and depreciate them over 39 years, as is the case with other expenditures that increase the value or extend the useful life of a property. However, this brownfield cleanup tax incentive, which costs about $150 million a year, is scheduled to expire on December 31, 2001. Therefore, as President, Governor Bush will:

Extend Permanently the Brownfield Cleanup Tax Incentive: Governor Bush will urge Congress to permanently extend the brownfield cleanup tax incentive to spur more cleanups across the country.

Proposal 6: Require Federal Facilities to Meet Federal and State Environmental Standards

The federal government is considered the nation's worst polluter. The GAO has estimated that the cost of cleaning up the 165 federal sites listed on Superfund's National Priority List (NPL) is about $300 billion. Moreover, the pace of cleanups has been slow. According to the EPA, by FY 1992, six federal sites had been cleaned up and removed from the NPL; by FY 1997, only two more federal sites had been cleaned up and removed from the NPL. Many federal sites have been on the NPL for over 10 years, including Rocky Flats in Colorado, Oak Ridge Reservation in Tennessee, and Hanford in Washington.

In addition to the federal sites listed on the NPL, about 60,000 non-NPL federal sites across the country have been identified as having violated environmental protection laws. For example, in the past two years, tens of thousands of gallons of raw sewage have flowed untreated into lakes and streams from Yellowstone National Park. Similarly, an EPA lab in Massachusetts was found several years ago to be leaching mercury into the groundwater.

Governor Bush will expect the federal government to lead by example. He believes it is time to end the double standard that has the federal government acting as enforcer of the nation's environmental laws, while at the same time causing pollution that violates those laws. Therefore, as President, Governor Bush will:

Require Federal Facilities to Meet All Environmental Standards: Governor Bush will direct active federal facilities not currently listed on the NPL to comply with the environmental protection laws that apply to private facilities, and he will hold those federal facilities accountable for any action that violates environmental protection laws.

Environment:
Building Conservation Partnerships

Sand Harbor State Park
Lake Tahoe, Nevada

June 1, 2000

The American West has been called the "native home of hope," and today we are in one of its greatest landmarks. There is so much beauty here – everywhere around us the touch of our Maker's hand. We need to preserve places like this, to appreciate and to protect them. It will take work and ingenuity and cooperation, but I believe that it can be done. We will need inspiration as well – and that, too, is all around us.

Since the days of Teddy Roosevelt, there has been a consensus that Americans have a common interest in protecting our natural lands and watersheds. As President, I will speak for that great national goal. It is our duty to use the lands well, and sometimes not to use them at all. It is our responsibility as citizens, but more than that, it is our calling as stewards of the earth.

The federal government has a crucial role to play in conservation – particularly in managing our national forests, our park system, wilderness areas, and national wildlife refuges. At its best, the federal government can lend support to local and state conservation efforts. A good example is right before us. The federal government can and should cooperate in the effort to preserve the beauty and clarity of Lake Tahoe.

We have a national consensus about the importance of conservation. But problems arise when leaders reject partnership, and rely solely on the power of Washington – on regulations, penalties, and dictation from afar. Unfortunately, this is exactly what we've seen over the last seven years. We have seen millions of acres of land declared off-limits and designated national monuments – just like that, with no real public involvement and no regard for the people affected by these decrees. And we have seen a steady decline in funding for the state and local component of the Land and Water Conservation Fund. For three decades, this Fund had provided needed resources for state and local conservation efforts.

This Washington-centered mindset breeds resentment and needless conflict. It creates a false choice, overlooking private and local conservation efforts. The federal government and the states, local communities and private landowners, must respect and work with one another to preserve our natural heritage.

It's time to build conservation partnerships between the federal government and state governments, local communities and private landowners.

This is the approach we've taken in Texas. All but three percent of the land in our state is privately owned. And yet we have remarkable biological diversity – thousands of animal and plant species, and a greater variety of birds than any other state.

Our challenge has been to protect both the claims of nature and the legal rights of private property owners. And we have succeeded – not by antagonizing people, but by inviting them to become part of the solution.

With sound conservation policies, we turned landowners across the state into avid and knowledgeable conservationists. We proved that private land management is an effective way to ensure wildlife and habitat conservation.

Nearly ten million acres in Texas – an area larger than most New England states – are under wildlife management plans. Under our Private Lands Enhancement Program, Texas provides technical assistance to landowners who want to make conservation a priority.

And the Texas Landowner Incentive Program encourages that choice – helping landowners in 16 separate counties enhance habitat for rare species, even while continuing to farm and ranch on their land.

Thanks to this common-sense approach, the Aplomado Falcon was spared from extinction. Hardly seen in the United States since the 1950s, this magnificent creature now has a chance – owing to private and local conservation efforts. This is a testament to the potential for private stewardship everywhere.

We can learn from these successes, and the successes of other states – like Wyoming, where revenue from the sale of wildlife permits goes to funding youth-led conservation projects. Or Utah, where the state has partnered with private landowners and conservation groups to protect the watershed on a 7,000-acre working ranch – thereby securing the water supply of local residents. Or Colorado, where landowners who donate conservation easements receive a tax credit.

In all these efforts, we see the future of conservation. What is the federal role? To provide the scientific and financial resources to help states, local communities and private landowners preserve land and wildlife. To provide flexibility, decentralization, and positive incentives to involve more Americans in the responsibility of conservation. And at the end of the day it will require leadership – a president who will set a new tone in Washington. A president who will reach across partisan lines and bridge political differences. That's what I intend to do.

I will seek to fully fund the Land and Water Conservation Fund – to its authorized level of $900 million. I will propose that half of those funds be devoted to state and local conservation. I am pleased that there is bipartisan progress in Congress to support these efforts.

Of that $900 million, I will ask that $50 million be used to help states set up Landowner Incentive Programs, similar to ours in

Texas. And $10 million for a Private Stewardship Program – making grants available to individuals and groups engaged in private conservation.

I will establish the President's Awards for Private Stewardship, to recognize outstanding examples of private stewardship, and to publicize innovative techniques in natural resource management.

I will seek an additional tax incentive to encourage private conservation. Some such incentives already exist in the tax code, but only if the land is given away. Many private landowners want their property to be conserved, but are in no position to give it away. Under my proposal, the seller would receive a 50 percent break on his or her capital gain if the land is sold for conservation purposes.

Finally, I will ask Congress to abolish the death tax. This tax often leaves citizens with no choice but to sell farmland or open space to developers to meet their tax bill – when they would much rather pass it along intact for future generations to enjoy.

The demands of development have sometimes been harsh on the natural world and its inhabitants. Some fear that places like this are scenes from a passing world. But it need not be so – if we bring to conservation the same vision and ingenuity we bring to development. This is a responsibility all of us should welcome – to protect gifts that all of us should appreciate.

Position Paper:
Building Conservation Partnerships

June 1, 2000

> *"Since the days of Teddy Roosevelt, there has been a consensus that Americans have a common interest in protecting our natural lands and watersheds. As President, I will speak for that great national goal. It is our duty to use the lands well, and sometimes not to use them at all. It is our responsibility as citizens, but more than that, it is our calling as stewards of the earth."*
>
> Governor George W. Bush

EXECUTIVE SUMMARY

In addition to its role as manager of our National Parks System, National Forests, National Wildlife Refuges and Bureau of Land Management holdings, the federal government should provide the scientific and financial resources to help states, local communities and private landowners conserve wildlife habitat, watersheds and open space. The United States has a long and proud history of local and private stewardship, which is best accomplished through cooperative efforts among federal and state government, local communities and conservation groups, and private landowners. Governor Bush is proposing a five-point plan to provide resources for conservation and encourage more Americans to take an active role in protecting natural resources and wildlife:

To Ensure Conservation of America's Natural Resources and Facilitate State and Local Conservation, Governor Bush will:

- Fully fund the Land and Water Conservation Fund and provide 50 percent for state and local conservation efforts.

To Establish Positive Incentives for Private Landowners and Local Communities to Preserve Land and Protect Rare Species, Governor Bush will:

- Provide matching grants for states to establish a Landowner Incentive Program to help private landowners protect rare species while engaging in traditional land management practices, and establish a Private Stewardship Grant Program to provide funding for private conservation initiatives.

To Encourage Private Conservation, Governor Bush will:

- Establish the President's Awards for Private Stewardship to recognize and honor the best examples of private conservation.

To Encourage the Protection of Environmentally Important Land for Conservation Purposes, Governor Bush will:

- Create a tax incentive to provide capital gains tax relief for private landowners who voluntarily sell their land for conservation purposes.

To Make it Easier for Private Landowners to Pass their Land, Intact to the Next Generation, Governor Bush will:

- Eliminate the estate tax.

The Federal Conservation Legacy of Theodore Roosevelt

Theodore Roosevelt was the first American President to awaken the American consciousness to the importance of conservation. It was Roosevelt who noted, "The nation behaves well if it treats the natural resources as assets which it must turn over to the next generation increased, and not impaired, in value."

Beginning with Roosevelt and the establishment of the National Forest Service at the turn of the century and continuing through the enactment of the Endangered Species Act in 1973 and beyond, the federal government has played a primary role in the conservation of land and water. As a result, Americans today share a proud conservation legacy, which is best symbolized by the 378 units – including the 55 National Parks – of the National Park System, which cover approximately 83.6 million acres.

The Successes of Private Conservation

While federal conservation efforts may be better known, private conservation has long been a driving force behind American habitat and wildlife conservation. In the 1890s, the first land conservation trusts emerged through private sector efforts. Today, The Nature Conservancy estimates that there are more than 1,000 local land trusts in America, and they continue to form at the rate of one a week.

One of the greatest success stories of private conservation in the 20th century is the preservation of the nation's wetlands, which came in response to the damage done by the drought of the Dust Bowl Era. Programs such as the Duck Stamp, which raised revenue for conservation of wetlands, grew out of a broad coalition of people with a personal interest in preserving wetlands – sportsmen, private conservation groups, and state wildlife agencies. Today, private, nonprofit foundations manage at least one million acres of wildlife refuges for a wide variety of species and operate at least 11,000 duck-hunting clubs that protect between five to seven million acres of wetlands.

Private conservation is necessary because:

- Almost two-thirds of all land in the United States is privately owned; and

- About 75 percent of endangered species reside on private land.

Private conservation works because it recognizes that people who live and work in and around open spaces have a personal stake in the future of their own backyards. These local stakeholders are the ones who know the land best and care about the places and ways of life they are attempting to conserve.

The Role of State Government and Local Communities in Encouraging Local and Private Conservation

Over the past decade, states and local communities have recognized the potential of private conservation to go beyond the minimum established land and wildlife protection programs. In general, these state and local programs embody four main principles:

- Prioritizing problem-solving over process;

- Encouraging innovation through the use of positive incentives rather than the threat of punishment;

- Understanding the need to balance the competing interests and goals of traditional land management practices, like farming and ranching, and environmentalism; and

- Recognizing private property rights.

For example:

- In Texas, the Private Lands Enhancement Program provides technical assistance to landowners wanting to include wildlife management considerations in their land use practices. Under the program, wildlife biologists from the Texas Parks and Wildlife Department work one-on-one with private and public land managers to develop management plans for preserving or enhancing habitat. Today, nearly 10 million acres in Texas are under wildlife management plans.

- In Wyoming, the state has developed the Coordinated Resource Management strategy, comprised of voluntary, landowner-initiated, problem-solving teams that use science, common goals and consensus to resolve natural resource issues. Currently, there are over 65 local teams that are using this public-private approach to resolve natural resource issues at the local level. The state is also applying the CRM strategy to watershed planning in an effort to resolve water quality issues.

- In the Northern Forests of New England, New York and Vermont, The Conservation Fund, local land trusts, private donors, and timber investors have worked together to conserve over 200,000 acres of private lands with conservation easements on lands previously owned by Champion International. Valuable wildlife habitat, critical watersheds, spectacular vistas and premier outdoor recreational opportunities will be protected on these working landscapes, while the economic benefits of local jobs will help sustain neighboring communities for the long term.

The Role of the Federal Government in Encouraging Conservation Partnerships

Governor Bush believes that protecting our natural resources will require cooperation among federal, state and local governments, conservation organizations and private landowners. As President, Governor Bush will ensure that the federal government provides adequate resources to protect our natural resources and plays an active role in facilitating local and private conservation. Accordingly, Governor Bush is proposing a five-point plan to build cooperative conservation partnerships between the federal government and state governments, local communities and private landowners.

Proposal 1: Fully Fund the Land and Water Conservation Fund and Provide 50 Percent for State and Local Conservation Efforts

Thirty-five years ago, Congress created the Land and Water Conservation Fund (LWCF), one of the most successful and far-reaching pieces of conservation legislation in America's history. The LWCF, which is principally funded from the revenues from oil and gas drilling on the outer continental shelf, is designed to fund federal, state and local conservation, natural resource protection and outdoor recreation.

At their peak in fiscal year 1978, appropriations from the LWCF nearly reached their authorized level of $900 million annually. By 1997, the LWCF had provided a total of $5.6 billion to purchase new federal park and recreation lands and about $3.2 billion in matching grants to states and local communities for the creation, development and improvement of over 37,000 parks and outdoor recreation facilities across the country.

Over time, however, the federal government has rarely maintained full funding for the LWCF's federal component, and has forgotten its vital state and local conservation function. For example, funding for the federal component was less than half of the authorized amount in five out of the last six fiscal years. Moreover, the state and local portion of the LWCF has significantly declined from approximately one-third of all appropriated funds since the law was implemented in 1965, to no funds in the last five fiscal years.

Governor Bush believes more should be done to protect natural resources and build cooperative conservation partnerships between federal and state governments, local communities and private landowners. Therefore, as President, Governor Bush will:

<u>Fully Fund the Land and Water Conservation Fund and Provide 50 Percent of the LWCF for State and Local Conservation</u>: Governor Bush will encourage reinvestment in America's natural resources by fully funding the LWCF. Governor Bush will also require that 50 percent of the $900 million LWCF be

provided for state and local conservation. In spending the federal portion of the LWCF, Governor Bush will require that federal land purchases be made from willing sellers, and any federal conservation initiative will include the input and participation of local, affected communities and stakeholders. Governor Bush will emphasize the use of a wide range of innovative conservation tools beyond traditional land acquisition, including technical and financial assistance to landowners, rehabilitation of existing land holdings, conservation easements and the purchase of development rights. The LWCF is currently funded at almost $500 million (all federal). This proposal to nearly double LWCF funding will cost about $2 billion over five years.

Proposal 2: Provide Resources to Encourage Private Land and Wildlife Conservation

In 1997, Texas launched the Landowner Incentive Program, an innovative government program – the first of its kind in the nation – that offers incentives for private landowners to protect rare species and restore habitat while engaging in traditional land management practices, like farming and ranching.

The goal of the Landowner Incentive Program is to provide incentives and encourage stewardship as an effective means of achieving rare species conservation on private lands. This incentive program is particularly important since about 75 percent of endangered species reside on private land, and about 97 percent of Texas is privately owned. Regulatory programs, like the Endangered Species Act (ESA), can only prevent landowners from engaging in activities that may harm an endangered species; such programs cannot require private landowners to do more to restore habitat for such species. The disincentive built into the ESA for landowners to become private stewards of wildlife is what Michael Bean of Environmental Defense has called the "Achilles heel" of the ESA.

The Texas Landowner Incentive Program recognizes that to recover rare species that are dependent on private lands, cooperative efforts to restore habitat are essential. To be eligible for the Landowner Incentive Program in Texas, a private landowner must show that the proposed project will contribute to the enhancement of at least one rare species or its habitat. Participating landowners work with state biologists to assess the progress of their conservation efforts. They may receive up to $10,000 a year for as long as five years, but they are expected to contribute at least 20 percent of the total cost of the project.

The Landowner Incentive Program has made impressive gains, benefiting almost 30 rare species in 16 Texas counties. Funded projects include Lesser

Prairie Chicken habitat restoration in the Panhandle, rare plant propagation in the Hill Country, Ocelot habitat restoration in the Lower Rio Grande Valley, and Attwater's Prairie Chicken habitat restoration on the coastal plains.

As the Governor of a state where 97 percent of the land is privately owned, Governor Bush recognizes that conservation in the 21st century will require a range of tools, including providing technical and financial assistance for landowners to encourage private stewardship. He believes offering positive incentive programs to assist private landowners in protecting and managing rare species can have a direct and positive impact on the conservation of such species. Therefore, as President, Governor Bush will:

Encourage States to Establish a Landowner Incentive Program: Governor Bush supports devoting $50 million of the federal portion of the Land and Water Conservation Fund to provide matching grants to states to establish their own Landowner Incentive Programs. These state programs will provide technical and financial assistance to private landowners all across the country and will help them enhance habitat for rare species, while continuing to engage in traditional land management practices.

One obstacle facing individuals and local groups interested in land and wildlife conservation is the challenge of raising the necessary funds to purchase land or enhance habitat. That is why, as President, Governor Bush will:

Establish a Private Stewardship Grant Program: Governor Bush supports devoting $10 million of the federal portion of the Land and Water Conservation Fund to establish a Private Stewardship Grant Program. Individuals and groups engaged in local, private conservation will be able to apply for a grant to help fund their projects. A diverse panel of representatives from state and federal government, conservation organizations, agriculture interests and the science community will assess the applications and make recommendations on grant winners to the Secretary of the Interior, who will award the grants.

Proposal 3: Recognize and Honor the Best Examples of Private Conservation

America owes a debt of gratitude to every private citizen and local conservation group who, in the spirit of Theodore Roosevelt, devotes time, resources and energy to enhancing the natural world. All too often, however, all that is reported are the rare cases where individuals do not act as good stewards of the land or protectors of wildlife.

Private citizens who excel in habitat management and wildlife conservation should be recognized, and the best examples of sound natural resource management practices should be promoted. Most importantly, the important role of America's private landowners in the future of natural resources conservation should be emphasized. Therefore, as President, Governor Bush will:

Establish the President's Awards for Private Stewardship: The purpose of these awards will be to recognize outstanding examples of private stewardship in every state. It will also serve as a way to publicize innovative techniques in natural resources management, encourage more people to get involved in private conservation, and build trust between private individuals and public servants in the field of conservation. Nominations will be accepted from every state wildlife or natural resources protection agency, and every year, the President will issue up to 50 of these awards.

Proposal 4: Create a Conservation Tax Incentive for the Sale of Land

Incentives for private conservation currently exist in the tax code, but only for charitable contributions. For example, a private landowner may place his land in a perpetual conservation easement, giving up the development rights to the land, and may donate the easement to a non-profit conservation group or government agency. The landowner continues to hold the title to the land, but may deduct the value of the donated easement from his income tax liability.

There any many landowners, however, who cannot afford to donate land in perpetuity for conservation purposes. Moreover, when the most ecologically sensitive land goes on the market, it is often lost to development because conservation groups do not have the financial resources to compete with a developer.

Governor Bush believes it is necessary to provide an incentive to private owners of ecologically important land to sell it for conservation purposes, while making it easier for conservation groups to make a financially attractive offer on land with the most important conservation value. Therefore, as President, Governor Bush will:

Provide Capital Gains Tax Relief for Sales of Land for Conservation Purposes: Governor Bush supports excluding 50 percent of any gain realized from private, voluntary sales of land or interests in land for conservation purposes. The land must be used to protect wildlife or plant habitat or open space for agriculture, outdoor recreation or scenic beauty to qualify for the tax incentive. The annual cost of this conservation tax incentive is $66 million, but The

Nature Conservancy estimates that this incentive would protect land valued at approximately $100 million a year, thereby leveraging the federal investment.

Proposal 5: Eliminate the Estate Tax

The estate tax is an impediment to private conservation, as it has often led to the breaking up and development of family farms and ranches, open spaces and habitat for many species of plants and wildlife. The estate tax, which can be as high as 55 percent, serves as a powerful disincentive for cash-poor but land-rich individuals – particularly farmers and ranchers – who are forced to sell a portion of their land, sometimes to developers, to pay the tax. That is why, as President, Governor Bush will:

Eliminate the Estate Tax: The elimination of the estate tax will make it easier for private landowners to pass their land, intact, from one generation to the next. The cost of eliminating the estate tax is $55 billion over five years. This has already been included in Governor Bush's tax plan.

Environment:
Earth Day 2000 Statement

April 21, 2000

This weekend, millions of Americans will observe the 30th anniversary of Earth Day and celebrate the tremendous progress we've made as a nation in protecting our environment and preserving our vast natural resources. Today, our air and water are cleaner; wolves have been reintroduced into Yellowstone Park after decades of absence; and the bald eagle has been brought back from the brink of extinction. And in 1995, we achieved a status of "no net loss of wetlands." All this has occurred despite rapid population and economic growth.

Long before the first Earth Day, Theodore Roosevelt became the first American President to awaken the American consciousness to the importance of environmental preservation. It was Theodore Roosevelt who noted, "The nation behaves well if it treats the natural resources as assets which it must turn over to the next generation increased, and not impaired, in value."

As an avid outdoorsman, I know all our prosperity as a nation will mean little if we leave future generations a world of polluted air, toxic waste and vanished wilderness and forests. Environmental stewardship is a trust, not a license. No one wants to live in communities that are polluted or environmentally unsafe. Yet no one wants governmental power to go unchecked, with individual rights and private property counting for nothing. So we must work to inspire public stewardship, and we must be careful and conscientious in our use of our natural resources.

The United States is entering a new era of environmental policy that requires a new philosophy of public stewardship and personal responsibility. Our current regulatory system dates back to the first Earth Day. That system has produced immense benefits, but experience has taught that it has serious shortcomings as well. It encourages Americans to do just the bare minimum, it breeds wasteful litigation, and it fails to reward innovation and real results. Further environmental progress will require better policies that build on what we have learned – producing a new era in which high federal standards are based on the best science, and market-based incentives and private innovation produce results that meet and exceed those standards. Economic prosperity and environmental protection can and must go hand-in-hand; indeed they are inseparable parts of the same story of human progress.

A successful 21st century environmental policy will require a leader who can reach across partisan lines and bridge political differences. The environmental changes facing us are contentious issues that will require strong leadership. As President, I will be committed to improving the quality of our environment, and I will work with both Republicans and Democrats to achieve our environmental goals.

High Tech:
Taking the Side of Innovation

Agenda 2000
Phoenix, Arizona

October 18, 1999

This summer in Silicon Valley, I faulted the Clinton Administration for opposing limits on Y2K litigation, for imposing barriers on encryption technology, and for opposing a permanent tax credit for research and development. Since then, the Administration has reversed itself on Y2K litigation, reversed itself on encryption exports, and reversed itself on tax credits for R&D. Now that's what I call responsive government! If I had only known they were going to grant me three wishes, I might have asked for something else.

With this Administration, wisdom comes so rarely, we should not complain when it comes late. There is a difference between last-minute concessions and enthusiastic support – between reaction and initiative. And your industry these past seven years has spent enough time worrying about what might come next from Washington. If I am President, I will always take the side of innovation over litigation, and private initiative over federal regulation.

I'm here today to talk about policy, but also to share what's in my heart.

I'm running for president because our country must be prosperous. But prosperity must have a purpose. The purpose of prosperity is to make sure the American dream touches every willing heart. The purpose of prosperity is to leave no one out... to leave no one behind.

Prosperity is not a given, and governments do not create it. Wealth is created by Americans – by creativity and enterprise and risk-taking. These are the hallmarks of the high tech industry, where the great engine of wealth has become the human mind – creating value out of genius.

The role of government is to create an environment where businesses and entrepreneurs and families can dream and flourish.

We'll be prosperous if we reduce taxes. I'll have a plan that reduces marginal rates to create jobs, but a plan that also helps struggling families on the outskirts of poverty.

We'll be prosperous if we reduce the regulations that strangle enterprise. And I will do what I did in Texas: fight for meaningful, real tort reform.

We'll be prosperous if we embrace free trade. I'll work to end tariffs and break down barriers everywhere, entirely, so the whole world trades in freedom. The fearful build walls. The confident demolish them. I am confident in American workers and farmers and producers. And I am confident that America's best is the best in the world.

Our current technology export system just doesn't work. The Administration seemed to concede this last month when, after years of talk and delay, it reversed itself on the sale and export of encryption technologies. Now the industry will have to wait and see how this new policy actually takes shape – whether it truly frees our technology exports, or whether it simply adds a few more layers of bureaucracy.

My policy as President would be to safeguard genuine military technology, while letting Americans sell what is already widely available elsewhere.

I support congressional efforts to reauthorize the Export Administration Act. The final bill must include a change in the criteria governing high-tech exports. Export controls that do not serve any clear national-security purpose will be eliminated. The new set of controls will no longer be based on technical specifications. Instead, we will guide our decisions by the availability of technologies in mass markets and foreign markets.

Our best companies have felt frustrated that they cannot sell some of their products abroad – even when equivalent technology is sold by foreign competitors. Those controls aren't serving the cause of America's security – they are a disservice to America's economic strength.

I will also form an advisory board answering directly to the President on all matters relating to high tech exports. Too often, the federal government's export policies are arbitrary and irrational – overtaken by the very technology they attempt to regulate. Yesterday's supercomputer is today's laptop. Yet current rules don't take this into account. And there has been too little opportunity for America's high tech exporters to make their case about what should be restricted and what should not. This advisory board – the President's Technology Export Council – will give you that opportunity. It will work quickly, with a simple mandate: Wherever there is no security interest at stake, exports will be permitted. Wherever security is truly at stake, exports will be barred, with serious penalties for violations. And we will work to renew the cooperation of our allies in this effort.

There need not be any conflict between America's security interests abroad and our economic interests. We just need to be smart enough and flexible enough to distinguish between the technologies that guide enemy missiles and the technologies that animate children's games.

There is an irony here. While this Administration has restricted high-tech exports – fearing these products might fall into the wrong hands – it has done little to develop our own military technologies here at home. They have actually cut our research and development investment by almost a billion dollars a year.

Last month in South Carolina I outlined my plans for the

transformation of our military. America now has a tremendous opportunity – given few nations in history – to extend the current peace into the far realm of the future. This opportunity is created by a revolution in the technology of war. Power is increasingly defined, not by mass or size, but by mobility and swiftness. Influence is measured in information, safety is gained in stealth, and force is projected on the long arc of precision-guided weapons.

This revolution perfectly matches the strengths of our country – the skill of our people and the superiority of our technology. The best way to keep the peace is to redefine war on our terms.

Central to that goal is a greater emphasis on research and development. Step one is to commit an additional $20 billion dollars to defense R&D between the time I take office and 2006. Step two is to encourage long-term private investment in research and development by making the R&D tax credit permanent.

As it is, high-tech companies are often hesitant to undertake long-term research projects because they cannot count on that tax credit. It might be renewed, it might not. Yet it is exactly this kind of sustained, long-term R&D our country needs to gain the next generation of critical technologies – both military and civilian. If we as a nation wish to continue to enjoy strong economic growth, continued military superiority, and unrivaled technological leadership, then we must reverse this decline in R&D and invest in our future.

So America will be prosperous if we do the right things. But prosperity alone is simple materialism. Prosperity must have a greater purpose. The success of America has never been proven by cities of gold, but by citizens of character. Men and women who work hard, dream big, love their family, serve their neighbor. Values that turn a piece of earth into a neighborhood, a community, a chosen nation.

That dream is so vivid – but too many are saying: The dream is not for me. Kids who turn schoolyards into battlefields. Children who corrupt their wills and souls with drugs, who limit their ambitions by having children themselves. Failed schools are creating two societies: one that reads and one that can't; one that dreams and one that doesn't.

These are burdens on the conscience of a successful nation. The next President must close this gap of hope. It is the great challenge to America's good heart.

I want to be a president who sets a tone, a direction, an agenda. I will be an activist President, who sets goals worthy of a great nation. I won't use my office as a mirror to reflect public opinion. And I'll be guided by conservative principles. Government should do a few things, and do them well. Government should not try to be all things to all people.

My first goal is to usher in the responsibility era. An era that stands in stark contrast to the last few decades, when the culture has clearly said: If it feels good, do it. If you've got a problem, blame someone else. Each of us must understand we are responsible for the choices we make in life.

We're responsible for the children we bring into the world. We're responsible to love our neighbor as we want to be loved ourselves

The prosperous need to be generous. It is a responsibility that comes with success, as many of you realize. The amazing prosperity of the new economy must be applied to a higher purpose. Economic entrepreneurs need to become social entrepreneurs, using their creativity to help reform schools and confront poverty.

And we must pass this message of responsibility to our children – teach them there are right choices in life and wrong choices in life. Drugs will destroy you. Alcohol will ruin your life. And having a child out of wedlock is a sure fire way to fall behind. We'll love the babies. But the message must be clear: It is not the definition of a man to father a child out of wedlock and say, "They're not my problem, they're yours."

Some people think it's inappropriate to draw a moral line. Not me. For our children to have the lives we want for them, they must learn to say yes to responsibility, yes to family, yes to honesty and work. I have seen our culture change once in my lifetime, so I know it can change again.

Government can help. We can write laws to give schools and principals more authority to discipline children and protect the peace of classrooms. We must encourage states to reform their juvenile justice laws. We must say to our children, "We love you, but discipline and love go hand in hand, and there will be bad consequences for bad behavior."

But changing our culture requires more than laws. Cultures change one heart, one soul, one conscience at a time. Government can spend money, but it can't put hope in our hearts or a sense of purpose in our lives. This is done by churches and synagogues and mosques and charities that warm the cold of life. A quiet river of goodness and kindness that cuts through stone.

So my second goal – one of the biggest jobs for the next president – is to rally these armies of compassion that exist in every community. To nurture. To mentor. To comfort. To perform their commonplace miracles of renewal.

As President, I will lift the regulations that hamper them. I will involve them in after-school programs, maternity group homes, drug treatment, prison ministries. I will lay out specific incentives to encourage an outpouring of giving in America. Supporting these men and women – the soldiers in the army of compassion – is the next, bold step of welfare reform. Because changing hearts will change our entire society.

And my third goal: We should make a solemn commitment in this country: That every child will be educated. That no child will be left behind.

This is urgent in our New Economy. Our nation must have a workforce prepared to seize new opportunity. In the short-term, America should be able to benefit from the immigration of skilled workers. The limit on H-1B visas should be raised.

But the long-term solution is better schools with higher standards. I've seen what works in Texas. Measure progress. Insist on results. Blow the whistle on failure. Emphasize early reading, early intervention, math and science instruction. End social promotion. Above all, don't give up on anyone.

I believe that children, not systems, are sacred. I believe that the educational oligopoly has little incentive to reform itself. That's why I believe in charter schools and choice to challenge the status quo.

Everyone must have a first rate education, because there are no second rate children, no second rate dreams.

You've heard me talk about compassionate conservatism. These goals are what I mean.

It is conservative to cut taxes. It is compassionate to let people keep more of their own money to save and give and build.

It is conservative to reform welfare by insisting on work. It is compassionate to take the side of charities and churches that confront the suffering which remains.

It is conservative to confront illegitimacy. It is compassionate to offer practical help to women and children in crisis.

It is conservative to insist on education standards, basics and local control. It is compassionate to make sure that not one single child gets left behind.

I am proud to be a compassionate conservative. I welcome the label. And on this ground I'll take my stand.

It is the ground I've stood as Governor of Texas, a job I really love. I know it isn't the same as being president. But if Texas were a country, it would be the 11th largest economy in the world. And I've had some successes. We passed the two biggest tax cuts in Texas history. We reformed our welfare and tort laws. We improved test scores for all the children in our schools, especially African-American and Hispanic kids.

I've learned to lead. I know how to set a clear agenda and get results.

I've learned you can not lead by dividing people. I'm a uniter not a divider. And I know my most important responsibility is when I put my hand on the Bible, I will not only swear to uphold the laws of our country. I will swear to uphold the dignity of the office of President of the United States of America.

This country is hungry for a new style of campaign. Positive. Hopeful. Inclusive. A campaign that attracts new faces and new voices.

A campaign that unites all Americans toward a better tomorrow.

We will prove that someone who is conservative and compassionate can win without sacrificing principle. We will show that politics, after a time of tarnished ideals, can be higher and better. We will give our country a fresh start after a season of cynicism.

We have a long way to go, but we are starting. And I hope you'll join me.

Position Paper
High Tech: Taking the Side of Innovation

"Governments don't create wealth. Wealth is created by Americans – by creativity and enterprise and risk-taking. The great engine of wealth has become the human mind – creating value out of genius. The role of government is to create an environment where business-es and entrepreneurs and families can flourish."

Governor George W. Bush

EXECUTIVE SUMMARY

Americans have always been leaders in technology, and technology has always played an integral part in our nation's history. But in an unprecedented way, technology is taking center stage in the American economy.

Governor Bush is committed to ensuring an environment – at home and abroad – in which innovation and entrepreneurship can flourish. In Texas, he has encouraged high technology by creating tax incentives for research and development, passing strong measures to end frivolous lawsuits, and integrating technology into schools. As a result, Texas leads the nation in high tech job growth and ranks second in high tech employment and exports. Governor Bush will bring this record of success to the White House and strengthen the New Economy by focusing on three key goals.

To Lift Barriers to Innovation and Fight Efforts in the United States and Overseas to Impose New Obstacles, Governor Bush will:

- Fight to achieve meaningful, real tort reform.

- Pursue an international agenda that supports America's high technology companies, tearing down barriers to trade and innovation.

- Develop a tough-minded, common sense export control system.

320

To Help Maintain a Workforce Prepared to Seize the Opportunities of the New Economy, Governor Bush will:

- Increase the limit on "H1-B" visas.

- Reform the nation's public schools by raising standards, measuring progress, and blowing the whistle on failure.

- Give schools unprecedented flexibility in using federal education technology funds.

- Improve math and science education, and bring education technology from the classroom to the community.

To Establish a Stable Environment that Encourages Research and Innovation in the Private Sector and the Military, Governor Bush will:

- Enact a permanent tax credit for research and development.

- Strengthen research and development in the military.

- Promote the growth of responsible biotechnology.

Technology and the Economy

Technology is taking center stage in the U.S. economy:

- The high technology elements of the economy accounted for over one-third of real economic growth in the United States between 1995 and 1998.

- In 1999, Internet-related companies generated more than $500 billion in revenue in the United States and were responsible for 2.3 million jobs.

- The Internet Economy is projected to be worth $1 trillion by 2001.

To create an environment – at home and abroad — in which U.S. businesses, entrepreneurs, and families can flourish, Governor Bush will set three main goals for the high technology sector.

Goal 1: Lift Barriers to Innovation and Fight Efforts in the United States and Overseas to Impose New Obstacles

The world is changing and so must the attitude of government. To ensure the competitiveness of American's high tech sector, Governor Bush will:

<u>Fight to Achieve Meaningful, Real Tort Reform</u>: Governor Bush understands that many America's most innovative technology companies are startups and small businesses that are particularly vulnerable to frivolous and junk lawsuits. Thus, as President, he will fight to achieve what he did in Texas: meaningful, real tort reform. Governor Bush has offered a comprehensive plan to end the stream of frivolous and junk lawsuits that clog our courts, threaten our economy, and delay justice for the deserving.

<u>Pursue an International Agenda that Supports America's High Technology Companies</u>: Governor Bush understands that to be prosperous America must embrace free trade. As President, he will fight to tear down the international barriers to innovation that have already been raised, and work to ensure that new ones are not erected. Among other things, he will work to:

- Make the Internet a duty and tariff-free zone worldwide.

- Tear down non-tariff barriers to trade in information technology.

- Step up efforts to combat piracy of American ideas and intellectual property.

- Promote the development of internationally compatible standards for e-commerce.

<u>Develop a Tough-Minded, Common Sense Export Control System</u>: This system will safeguard military technology, while allowing U.S. companies to sell technology that is readily available in the commercial market. The current system of export controls is broken. Too often it penalizes U.S. high tech companies by controlling technology that is widely available from other countries, while failing to prevent unique technology from falling into dangerous hands. Moreover, controls often lag behind technological developments. And because the international regime for coordinating export controls was disbanded under

the Clinton-Gore Administration, the United States now frequently finds itself trying to single-handedly prevent the diversion of sensitive technology.

Governor Bush is committed to developing a tough-minded, common sense export policy – a policy that places a priority on safeguarding our national security, while recognizing that the competitiveness of our high technology sector is itself a critical component of that security. Such a policy must consist of several key elements:

- First and foremost, we must strengthen America's intelligence and counterintelligence capabilities to staunch the theft of sensitive military technology at home, and identify threats abroad before they arise.

- Second, we must allow American companies to sell products in the international marketplace when those products are readily available from their foreign competitors. That means easing export controls on computers and encryption products that can already be purchased on the open market. At the same time, as the use of encryption programs increases, American law enforcement must always have the resources to stay ahead of the criminal use of that technology.

- Third, as the Cox Report recommends, the United States must lead its allies in establishing new, binding rules to prevent the export of sensitive military technology. The United States must no longer be alone in keeping dangerous technologies and products away from those who do not wish us well.

Goal 2: Maintain a Workforce Prepared to Seize the Opportunities of the New Economy

The new "knowledge-based" economy depends upon a skilled and educated workforce. To ensure that America's high tech companies have access to the best employees, Governor Bush will:

<u>Maintain the Competitiveness of U.S. High Tech Companies by Allowing Them to Recruit More Workers with Special Skills Through an Increase in "H-1B" Visas</u>: Temporary, highly skilled workers are admitted under H-1B visas, which are currently limited to 115,000 annually. However, nearly one million high tech jobs will go unfilled this year, costing the U.S. economy $105 billion. To meet the immediate needs of the nation's high tech companies for computer engineers, software programmers, and technicians, Governor Bush supports a significant increase in the cap on H-1B visas.

Reform the Schools That Do Not Work and Will Not Change by Raising Standards, Measuring Progress, and Blowing the Whistle on Failure: The long-term solution to a shortage of prepared workers is not immigration. It is education. Governor Bush believes in the power of high standards and high hopes. That is why he has proposed a comprehensive education reform plan that gives states and schools unprecedented freedom from federal regulation – in exchange for results. He will reward states that succeed in closing the educational achievement gap between disadvantaged students and their peers, impose consequences for failure, and provide parents with information and choices.

Give Schools Unprecedented Flexibility in Using Federal Education Technology Funds: While the federal government has invested billions of dollars in education technology, it is not clear whether this investment is improving educational achievement. Thus, Governor Bush will establish a $3 billion "Enhancing Education through Technology Fund" that schools can use to train teachers to use technology, purchase and develop software, and integrate systems. In addition, Governor Bush will invest $400 million over 5 years to boost research into how technology can improve student achievement and to create a clearinghouse so states and local governments can exchange best practices.

Improve Math and Science Education: The current state of math and science education in America is inadequate to meet the high expectation of parents and the demand for qualified workers in the New Economy. Thus, as President, Governor Bush will invest $2.3 billion to strengthen math and science curricula. He will also provide incentives to high school students to take advanced college preparation courses in math and science, and to encourage math and science majors to teach in poor schools.

Bring Education Technology from the Classroom to the Community: Governor Bush will invest $400 million to establish and strengthen community technology centers around the country. More than 60 percent of Americans who use such centers come from families with incomes under $15,000, and only 11 percent of the families have home Internet access. According to a National Science Foundation survey, community technology centers have a positive impact on learning for over 80 percent of attendees.

Goal 3: Establish a Stable Environment that Encourages Research and Innovation in the Private Sector and the Military

Governor Bush understands that America needs sustained, long-term investment in R&D to develop the next generation of critical technology, both civilian and military. To encourage research and innovation, Governor Bush will:

Support a Permanent Tax Credit for Research and Development: The Research and Experimentation Tax Credit encourages long-term investment in research by high technology companies and thereby strengthens America's technological leadership. Since its inception in 1981, the benefits of the credit have been undercut by its temporary, on-again, off-again nature, which confuses and disrupts corporate planning. This year, Congress took a step in the right direction by passing a five-year extension of the credit. As President, Governor Bush will lead the Congress to make the credit a permanent part of the U.S. tax code.

Strengthen Research and Development in the Military: A substantially greater emphasis on research and development will be required to ensure that our military is fully prepared to meet future challenges and to realize the full promise of new technology. As President, Governor Bush will increase the defense R&D budget by $20 billion from FY 2002-FY 2006 and will direct the Secretary of Defense to earmark at least 20 percent of the total procurement budget for acquisition programs that propel America generations ahead in military technology.

Promote the Growth of Responsible Biotechnology: Biotechnology has brought enormous change to the world, revolutionizing medicine, agriculture, and industry, while helping fuel a continued economic boom. As President, Governor Bush will stand firmly for the protection of intellectual property, pursue health care reform that keeps pharmaceuticals free from price controls, and fight to open markets for U.S. bioagriculture products.

THE TEXAS RECORD

High Tech Leadership

During Governor Bush's term in office, Texas has led the nation in high-tech job growth. Between 1995 and 1998, over 97,200 high-tech jobs were created, making Texas second in the nation for high-tech employment. Texas also ranks second in the nation in high tech exports.

More than 90 percent of Texas public schools now have Internet access, and all 57 community colleges are receiving state technology grants. In addition, Texas has emerged as a national biotechnology leader, employing over 50,000 in the industry and receiving over $900 million in NIH grants in 1998.

High Tech Initiatives

Under Governor Bush's leadership, Texas:

- Cut the state Internet access and data processing tax.

- Created an E-Government Task Force to evaluate opportunities to interact with citizens, universities, and other states online.

- Enacted legislation to provide legal protections for companies that make good faith efforts to address Y2K-related problems.

- Passed comprehensive tort reform measures that will discourage frivolous and junk lawsuits by limiting punitive damage awards, making joint and several liability more fair, and increasing sanctions for those filing frivolous lawsuits. As a result, Texans have enjoyed $2.9 billion in insurance rate reductions.

In 1996, Governor Bush created the Science and Technology Council to devise a strategic plan to ensure Texas remains at the forefront in high-tech job growth. As a result, Governor Bush and the Texas Legislature acted on the Council's recommendations and:

- Provided a research and development tax credit to help Texas attract high-skilled, high-paying jobs.

- Increased funding from $2 million to $21 million for the high school Advanced Placement program to increase the number of high school graduates with high level math and science skills. The increased funding will provide more classes per high school, reduce the cost of the test for low income students, and provide teacher training.

- Developed a statewide technology curriculum for community colleges to better prepare students for the demands of the high technology employment.

WHAT OTHERS SAY

"…a different kind of Republican – one willing to offer sizable tax reductions for the working poor, proposing to take 6 million Americans off the tax rolls by cutting the lowest tax rate to 10 percent from 15 percent."

William Neikirk, <u>Chicago Tribune</u>, *12/02/99*

"…It was great, and I'm a lifelong Democrat,' said Carmela Brown, 60, a former treasurer of the Iowa Democratic Party and local hospital executive. 'He hit on every single tax that is discouraging to Americans…Who can resist a message of a more sensible tax scheme?'"

Todd J. Gillman, <u>Dallas Morning News</u>, *12/02/99*

"...the Texas governor's [environmental] record is far better than activists allow. Governor Bush has tackled environmental problems creatively, with a new approach that emphasizes cooperation over conflict.

"...Texas actually led the nation in reducing toxic releases in 1997, the most recent year for which figures have been reported."

Lynn Scarlett, *The New York Times*, 5/9/00

"Mr. Bush recently proposed his own...plan to encourage conservation through grants and tax credits. Environmentalists praised Mr. Bush's proposal to fully fund the Land and Conservation Fund..."

Andrew Cain, *Washington Times*, 6/28/00

"[George W. Bush] was obviously out here yesterday...in Silicon Valley and Palo Alto. A huge turnout...Gordon Moore, the co-founder of Intel, Ray Lane, the president of Oracle, John Chambers, CEO of Cisco Systems, all clapping...or jumped onto the Bush bandwagon...[T]here were several issues he outlined including increasing the number of visas for skilled workers, very important to Silicon Valley...easing restrictions on exporting computer systems overseas... There were several other issues like that which all came forward and really for the first time I think Silicon Valley could see that they have a real choice..."

**Tony Perkins, Editor-in-Chief, Red Herring
CNNfn, "Digital Jam," 7/2/99**

"George W. Bush...is committed to opening international markets to our farm products, enhancing value-added agriculture and restoring profitability to farmers."

Former Iowa Governor Terry Branstad

"Governor George W. Bush this week revealed a compelling platform for the cleanup and redevelopment of so-called "brownfields"—former industrial sites that have significant, though not severe pollution."

Editorial, *New York Post*, 4/9/00

"The most important work of the next American President will be nurturing today's painfully earned prosperity. With the tax-cut proposal he unfurls today, George W. Bush sends his strongest signal to date that he understands this challenge. . . Mr. Bush is proposing an economic agenda worthy of a new President."

Editorial, <u>Wall Street Journal</u>, 12/01/99

"Brian Halla, chief executive of National Semiconductor, said: 'People talk about the administration coming out here once every few months in the last few years, but I can tell you that Governor Bush can walk the walk and talk the talk'...Bob Herbold, chief operating officer at Microsoft."

**Richard Wolffe, "Bush Woos Silicon Valley,"
<u>Financial Times</u>, 7/2/99**

"I've been impressed with Governor Bush's program for agriculture...His emphasis on expanding markets and reduced regulation is the kind of leadership North Dakota farmers are looking for."

Susan Larson of Gilby, North Dakota

PART V
Reforming Our Government

For too long, the institutions of government have become insulated from common sense and removed from the people. At the same time, the conduct and tone of politics – both during and after elections – have brought out the worst in both parties.

The speeches that follow make an appeal for reforming government. In providing services, government should be as responsive and innovative as the private sector. The court system should serve the interests of all the people, not just trial lawyers. Campaign finance laws should be reformed to end abuses of power and restore public trust in the election process. Finally, and most important, we need leadership that sets a new tone in Washington – a tone of bipartisanship, civility, and fair dealing.

As a governor, I've worked with Democrats and Republicans to serve the public interest. So have many other governors across America. I know that a President can set the tone of our nation's capital, and I will bring that spirit of cooperation to Washington, D.C.

Government Reform:
A New Approach

Civic Coliseum Plaza
Knoxville, Tennessee

June 8, 2000

It has been almost a year since my campaign began. Since that first trip to Iowa, I have laid out my agenda for America both at home and abroad.

My goals for America are clear. To make sure that every child is educated, by returning high standards and accountability to public schools.

To bring more economic growth and opportunity, by reducing the income tax burden on all Americans – especially those aspiring to the middle class.

To keep our commitment to elderly Americans, and generations to come, by saving and strengthening Social Security.

To keep the peace, by building a national missile defense, modernizing our military, and establishing clear principles for the use of our power in the world.

These are things that must be done, the nation's pressing business.

Today I want to talk about the way we conduct the nation's business. Many Americans believe that Washington's way of doing things just isn't working. That government's purposes are too often forgotten, and opportunities too often squandered – resulting in too few results.

In so many ways, America in the year 2000 is the picture of

success. Our economy is more competitive than ever – more efficient. Our technologies are marvels of creativity. Throughout the private sector, we're seeing what people can accomplish with strong leadership, clear goals, fair dealing, and cooperation.

This could hardly be said of the federal government. There is too much argument in Washington and not enough discussion. Too much polling and not enough decision making. Too much needless division, not enough shared accomplishment. Not enough final acts and resolutions, and lasting achievements.

There is blame enough to go around. I do not dismiss the serious disagreements that are part of politics, but the reality is that Americans look upon this spectacle and don't like what they see. They know that this is not the way the world's great power should conduct its affairs. I agree with them. It's time for change.

Consider, by contrast, many of our state and local governments, where the best ideas and boldest reforms of the last decade have taken place. All across America, governors, state legislators, and city officials have laid partisan differences aside and done what they were elected to do – serve the people.

In New York City, Mayor Rudy Giuliani brought order and civility back to the streets – cutting crime rates by 50 percent.

In Cleveland, Mayor Michael White's bipartisan leadership has led to a revitalized downtown area and a higher quality of life similar to Mayor Ash, here in Knoxville.

In Wisconsin, Governor Tommy Thompson led bipartisan reform and proved that welfare dependence could be reversed – reducing the rolls in his state by 91 percent similar to Governor Sundquist, here in Tennessee.

In Texas, we never lack for partisan battles. Texas is a two-party state where tough politics comes naturally. But when it counts, we work to put the public interest first. In my first term as governor, I worked with a Democratic legislature to reform education, the legal system, juvenile justice, and welfare. These were joint accomplishments of a Republican governor and a Democratic legislature.

Politics has not been my career. And what I've learned in the private sector has proven true in government: a little good will goes a long way. Good will is earned by respecting your opponents, telling the truth, and leaving yesterday's quarrels behind.

And if good will is to prevail, a leader must set the right tone. A leader guided his convictions, not by the counsel of his pollster. A strong leader sets his mind to solving problems, not settling scores. Every successful mayor and governor understands this. And so should the next President.

With just seven months until the end of his term, we will leave our current President to the judgment of history. What matters now is whether the bitterness that now prevails in Washington will continue after his term.

There is a clear choice in this campaign, and the people are seeing it in the kind of tone we set, and how we talk about the big issues facing America. Take Social Security, for example. Recently I laid out a plan, a framework, to guide bipartisan reform in social security, to increase its value and keep our commitments to the elderly. There will be reasonable disagreements on this important issue. Surely, all can agree that this is a serious matter requiring the best efforts of both parties.

And yet all we have heard from my opponent are the familiar exaggerations and scare tactics. Ideas he doesn't share are never just the other side of an issue: They are "radical" or "reckless" ideas. Proposals he disapproves of are never just arguable; they are always "risky schemes."

This kind of unnecessary rhetoric is characteristic of the tone in Washington. It's the war-room mentality – the hostile stance, the harsh charges, the lashing out at enemies. We have had eight years of this, and eight years is enough.

We need a clean break from the recent past. It is time for leadership that sets a new tone – a tone of respect and bipartisanship.

A president can do this. He can refrain from personal attacks, and treat members of both parties with respect. He can reach across the partisan aisle and work with all for the good of the country.

In this same spirit, there are some practical steps we can take to change Washington. I am proposing today a set of six specific reforms relating to the budget process, pork-barrel spending, and nominations.

First, the budget process. I will propose that the federal budget be passed by both Houses of Congress and signed by the President into law.

As it is now, the President and Congress work separately on their own budget proposals. Only very late in the year do these two branches begin working together on the details. Often their separate budgets are just a prelude to battle. A joint budget resolution signed by the legislative branch and the executive branch would start the process on the right footing, encouraging cooperation, and early agreement on fundamentals.

I also support a law putting the entire budget and appropriations process on a biennial basis, as is done in my state and 20 others.

If the discord in Washington never seems to end, this is partly because the budget process never seems to end. Lawmakers spend more than half of their time each year wrangling over budget resolutions, reconciliation bills, and appropriations bills. And often, as many legislators will tell you, they've hardly had time to examine the bills before the vote is taken.

By putting the process on a two-year schedule, we allow more time for thoughtful debate on the whole range of issues facing the Congress – better oversight of the bureaucracy, confirmations, and other long term concerns.

I will also propose a bill ending the annual threat of shutting down the government.

These threats have given both parties some moments we all prefer to forget. Disagreements have become deadlocks, the entire budget process resulting in no budget at all. Americans have had to watch federal agencies close for business and national parks and monuments turn away visitors.

These standoffs have undermined public confidence in government. To ensure that the government does not shut down again, here is what I propose.

If an appropriations bill is not signed by October first of the new fiscal year, affected programs would continue to be funded at the level of the President's budget, or the previous year's level as approved by Congress – whichever is lower.

Behind this reform is the simple principle that, above and beyond the quarrels of the moment, the United States government has certain basic commitments, and those commitments must be kept.

Next, I will address a longstanding source of public irritation and outrage – the wasteful habit of pork-barrel spending.

It's often said that one politician's "pork" is another's vital project, one district's "corporate welfare" another district's vital federal investment. But we need a more objective definition of "vital."

This confusion is the source of too much waste, and too much haggling, bargaining, and resentment in Washington. We have all heard examples of wasteful spending, such as the $250,000 to research caffeinated chewing gum. Or the $750,000 for grasshopper research. New examples come along every year. The process never seems to change.

I support the establishment of a bipartisan commission to eliminate pork throughout the federal government.

There is bipartisan support for such a commission, including the backing of Senators McCain, Thompson, Abraham, and

Lieberman. But such an idea needs a presidential push, which I will give it. This panel will submit to Congress a list of all spending projects deemed frivolous and unnecessary. The Congress will then cast a simple "up" or "down" vote. No amendments, no back-scratching, no logrolling.

Further, to bring fiscal discipline to the budget, I will ask Congress to pass line-item veto legislation.

The Supreme Court has made clear how such legislation can pass constitutional muster. Congress cannot give the President a permanent line-item veto. But it can give the President authority to decline to spend wasteful appropriations. As President, I will seek that constitutional authority. And I will use it to prevent spending that fails to serve the public interest. And I will use the unspent money to pay down the national debt.

These reforms can take some of the friction out of our national politics – and justify greater public confidence in Washington. But they are reforms of procedure only. In the end, only the spirit of the lawmakers themselves can bring real change to Washington. Above all else, we must call a truce to politics as combat – where differences of principle give rise to unprincipled attacks on character.

A good place to start is the nomination and confirmation process.

The Constitution empowers the President to nominate officers of the United States, with the advice and consent of the Senate. That is clear-cut, straightforward language. It does not empower anyone to turn the process into a protracted ordeal of unreasonable delay and unrelenting investigation.

Yet somewhere along the way, that is what Senate confirmations became – lengthy, partisan, and unpleasant. Often they are occasions for pushing larger agendas, having nothing to do with the merits of the nominee. At some memorable low points, hearings have become a gauntlet of accusation, interest-group warfare, and public humiliation. This has done enough harm to the process.

The President and the Senate have a joint responsibility here. The President must be prompt in submitting his nominations, and the Senate prompt in acting upon them.

Starting next January, I will make the prompt submission of my presidential nominees a top priority. And I will ask the Senate to act on each nominee I submit within 60 days. I would ask Republicans and Democrats in the Senate to follow this standard regardless of who may be elected next November.

Public service is an honorable calling, and there are many now serving in Washington who view it just that way. But their voices are easily drowned out in the din of battle. Instead, the agenda is determined – the tone set – by the loud, the aggressive, the contentious.

This should not be the spirit of Washington. This is no way to encourage good people to serve, and no way to build a legacy of accomplishment.

None of us can control how others will conduct themselves. But each of us can control our own actions and our own words. As President, I will set a new tone in Washington. I will do everything I can to restore civility to our national politics – a respect for honest differences, and a decent regard for one another.

Position Paper
Government Reform: A New Approach
June 8, 2000

"We need a clean break from the recent past. It is time for leadership that sets a new tone – a tone of respect and bipartisanship. A president can do this. He can refrain from personal attacks, and treat members of both parties with respect. He can reach across the partisan aisle and work with all for the good of the country. In this same spirit, there are some practical steps we can take to change Washington. I am proposing today a set of six specific reforms relating to the budget process, pork-barrel spending, and nominations."

Governor George W. Bush

EXECUTIVE SUMMARY

Governor Bush believes that leaders should focus on solving problems, not settling scores. Yet partisan strife has become a way of life in Washington. Progress on vital national issues, such as Social Security and health care reform, has been stalled by brinkmanship. The result has been an erosion of citizen confidence in government.

In contrast, Governor Bush has repeatedly reached across the aisle on a bipartisan basis in Texas to pass vital legislation, ranging from a new Texas Code of Education to civil justice reform. Governor Bush is committed to bringing this spirit of bipartisan leadership to Washington and restoring confidence in government.

To Promote Bipartisan Cooperation in the Budget Process, Governor Bush will:

- Adopt biennial budgeting to promote long-range planning and to allow budget decisions to be made in non-election years; alternating years would be used for oversight.

- Require a Joint Budget Resolution, signed by the President, to promote early agreement on an overall budget framework.

- Enact legislation to prevent government shutdowns, allowing the government to stay open even if an appropriations bill is not signed by October 1st of the new fiscal year.

To Restore Trust in Government and Eliminate Pork Barrel Spending, Governor Bush will:

- Support a bipartisan Commission to Eliminate Pork Barrel Spending, whose recommendations will be presented to the Congress for a straight "up or down" vote on the entire package.

- Seek line item veto legislation, fully constitutional, allowing the President to defer indefinitely unnecessary spending and use the savings to pay down the national debt.

To Minimize Delay and Division Over Presidential Appointments, Governor Bush will:

- Make the prompt submission of presidential nominees a top priority, and challenge Congress to act within 60 days of the submission of presidential nominees for the new Administration, regardless of who is elected President in 2000.

Restoring Trust and Civility to Government

In recent years, the federal government has been wracked by partisan strife. Progress on vital national issues, such as health care and Social Security reform, has been stalled by brinkmanship. As a result, citizen confidence and trust in government has eroded. Indeed, a recent ABC News/Washington Post survey found that only 30 percent of those responding said they "trusted" the federal government to do "what is right" all or most of the time.

In contrast, many state and local governments have succeeded in laying aside partisan differences to advance the public interest. As a Republican governor who has worked with a Democratic legislature, Governor Bush has repeatedly reached across the aisle on a bipartisan basis to pass legislation:

- Governor Bush worked with the Democratic Chairman of the House Public Education Committee to enact a new Texas Code of Education, which eliminated unnecessary bureaucracy, restored local control to schools, set clear goals, and held districts accountable for results.

- Governor Bush worked with Democrats and Republicans to restructure the Texas Workforce Commission, consolidating 28 programs in 10 different state agencies into one agency, and devolving power to local workforce boards headed by local businesses. The resulting model was used as a template for federal workforce reform legislation in 1998.

- And in 1995, by working closely with a Democratic Lieutenant Governor, Governor Bush and the Texas Legislature passed a tort reform package that limited punitive damage awards, reformed the deceptive trade practices act, limited forum shopping, and curbed frivolous suits.

None of this bipartisan spirit is possible without leadership, and a president, above all, can provide that leadership. To create this spirit of bipartisanship in Washington, and to restore trust in government, Governor Bush will propose a set of specific reforms aimed at three perennial problems: the budget process, pork-barrel spending, and the process for approving presidential nominations.

Reforming the Budget Process

Every year, Congress battles over the budget, and each year the battles seem to get bloodier. While no procedural change can substitute for a commitment to bipartisan cooperation, Governor Bush believes there are several practical reforms that can blunt the partisan edge of budget negotiations.

Biennial Budgeting and Appropriations

The current annual budget cycle has proven to be time-consuming and inefficient, regardless of which party is in control of Congress. Only twice in the last 50 years has the Congress enacted all 13 appropriation bills by the end of the fiscal year. Under the imminent threat of a budget shutdown, leaders make hasty decisions simply to keep the government running.

In contrast, under a biennial budget, funding decisions would be made in non-election years to help de-politicize the process. Lawmakers could devote more time to finishing the appropriations bills on time because the next year would be free for other legislative business.

In addition, government agencies would receive more stable funding, which would facilitate longer-range planning. Indeed, according to Lee Hamilton, former Democratic Representative and currently Director of the Woodrow Wilson Center, moving to "biennial budgeting would also free up time that could be used by Congress and the executive branch to focus more on long-term strategic thinking."

Unfortunately, biennial budgeting recently failed to pass the House on a very close vote. Twenty-one states, however, including Texas, use biennial budgeting.

As President, to blunt the partisan edge of budget negotiations and give lawmakers more time for forward thinking, Governor Bush will:

Introduce Legislation to Adopt Biennial Budgeting and Appropriations: Government spending decisions would be made every two years, leaving the alternating year to be used for effective oversight of the federal agencies and systemic review.

Require a Joint Budget Resolution

The budget process should allow our leaders to determine the overall fiscal course for the federal government. But under current law, neither the President's budget nor the Congressional budget has the force of law. As a result, the existing process discourages cooperation and encourages posturing. The Congress writes budgets that implicitly ignore the President's power to sign and veto laws, and the President crafts budgets that ignore the Congress' power to write legislation. There is little incentive for the President and Congress to reach early agreement on the broad outlines of a budget package, thus increasing the chance of a "train wreck" at the end of the process.

In contrast, a joint budget resolution would recognize that the two branches of government must cooperate. A joint resolution requires the President's signature and has the force of law. This joint budget resolution would set the overall level of appropriations, mandatory spending, taxes, and debt reduction in a simple document. It would bring the President into the process at an early stage and, together with biennial budgeting, would help restore order to the budget process.

To maximize the opportunity for bipartisan cooperation on the budget, as President, Governor Bush will:

<u>Seek Legislation to Require a Joint Budget Resolution Signed by the President</u>: The joint budget resolution would set the overall level of appropriations, mandatory spending, taxes, and debt reduction into law. This would encourage the two branches of government to agree on an overall fiscal strategy before specific tax and spending bills are written.

Preventing Government Shutdowns

Under the present system, when appropriators cannot agree, and when Congress and the President remain at loggerheads, the government can shut down altogether. Most recently, for example, the federal government shut down (except for "essential functions") two times in the period from November 14, 1995, to January 8, 1996, while Congress and the President wrestled with the budget.

Fortunately, good suggestions exist for limiting this predictable trouble spot. Since the budget impasse of 1995, several Members of Congress, including Senators McCain, Domenici, and Thompson, have each sponsored bills that would prevent future government shutdowns.

Therefore, to prevent partisan "train wrecks" over the budget, Governor Bush will:

<u>Seek Legislation Preventing Government Shutdowns</u>: If an appropriations bill is not signed by October 1 of the new fiscal year, affected programs would continue to be funded at the lower of the President's budget or the prior year's level. This legislation would apply to each of the 13 appropriations bills, and to any omnibus bill. It would remove incentives for the President or the congressional leadership to use the leverage of "shutting down government" to achieve

spending objectives they could not otherwise obtain through the normal appropriations process.

Eliminating Pork Barrel Spending

Challenging the Politics of Pork Barrel Spending

A perennial criticism of the federal government is that the annual budget contains too much "pork barrel spending." The persistence of pork erodes citizen confidence in government, and skirmishes over pork contribute to personal and partisan divisions. While many have observed that "one man's pork is another's essential service," there are some consistent characteristics of what fairly qualifies as pork.

According to the nonpartisan Citizens Against Government Waste, most pork barrel spending can be identified as having at least two of the following seven characteristics:

1. It was requested by only one Chamber of Congress;

2. It was not specifically authorized;

3. It was not awarded competitively;

4. It was not requested by the President;

5. It greatly exceeded the President's budget request or the previous year's funding;

6. It was not the subject of congressional hearings; or

7. It serves only a local or special interest.

Items frequently cited as pork include $250,000 for research on caffeinated chewing gum (FY 1999) and $750,000 for grasshopper research in Alaska (FY 1999).

While many will debate the precise definition of pork, few will dispute that it is persistently difficult to strip from the budget. What is needed is a bipartisan mechanism to eliminate pork barrel spending. Senator McCain, along with Senators Thompson, Lieberman, and Abraham, has proposed just such a mechanism – a bipartisan commission to identify and eliminate pork initiatives.

Therefore, to help restore citizen confidence in government, Governor Bush will:

Endorse Legislation Calling for a Bipartisan Commission to Eliminate Pork Barrel Spending: The legislation would create a bipartisan legislative commission to identify and propose for reduction or elimination non-entitlement government spending. The recommendations from the Commission would be presented to the Congress through legislation calling for an "up or down" vote on the entire package.

Line Item Veto Authority

The longer-term solution to the problem of unnecessary pork barrel spending is to empower the President to act directly to stop it through the line item veto. The governors of 43 of the 50 states already have this authority, and at least eleven Presidents since the Civil War – Ulysses Grant, Rutherford Hayes, Chester Arthur, Franklin Roosevelt, Harry Truman, Dwight Eisenhower, Richard Nixon, Gerald Ford, Ronald Reagan, George Bush, and Bill Clinton – have publicly called for giving the President line item veto authority. Similarly, Governor Bush would support a constitutional amendment giving the President this authority. Because the amendment process is by design long and cumbersome, he also supports immediate legislation providing for equivalent authority for the President to limit wasteful and pork barrel spending.

In April 1996, Congress passed and the President signed the Line Item Veto Act. Two years later, in 1998, the Supreme Court declared the Act unconstitutional because it "g[ave] the President the unilateral power to change the text of duly enacted statutes." At the same time, however, the Court acknowledged that there were fully constitutional ways to accomplish the same result.

From the Nation's founding, the President has had the authority – if Congress so delegates it – to decline to spend appropriated sums. However, this authority was curtailed in 1974, when Congress passed the Impoundment Control Act, which restricted the President's authority to decline to spend appropriated sums.

The Line Item Veto Act of 1996 attempted to return some of that authority, but did so by allowing the President to permanently and irreversibly prevent an appropriation from having any "legal force or effect." Because this was tantamount to a "repeal" of a duly enacted law, the Court struck it down. But, as Justice Scalia noted in dissent, "[h]ad the Line Item Veto Act authorized the President to 'decline to spend' any item of spending contained in the Balanced Budget Act of 1997, there is not the slightest doubt that authorization would have been constitutional."

In order to increase the President's authority to limit unnecessary pork spending, Governor Bush will:

Propose Fully Constitutional Line Item Veto Legislation Linked to Paying Down the National Debt: Governor Bush will propose legislation giving the President the authority to decline to spend amounts appropriated for discretionary budget authority. Such deferrals will be allowed whenever the President determines the deferrals will not impair essential government functions and will not harm the national interest. All savings from such deferrals will be used to pay down the national debt.

Expediting Presidential Nominations

In recent years, the process of presidential nominations and confirmations has become increasingly lengthy, partisan, and unpleasant, resulting in fewer people being willing to enter into high-level government service. As one recent nominee famously remarked, "[i]t is nasty and brutish without being short."

Under President Reagan, 11 percent of nominations took over 6 months to confirm; under President Bush, 25 percent took over 6 months; under President Clinton, 44 percent took over 6 months. Moreover, under President Clinton, 49 percent of appointees described the confirmation process as "confusing," and 25 percent as "embarrassing." This acrimony and delay causes the country to go without senior government officials – especially sub-cabinet officials – for extended periods of time, and it discourages good people from entering public service in the first place.

Governor Bush believes that a bipartisan effort should be made to improve the nominations process – regardless of which party wins the White House later this year. Thus, to minimize delay and divisions over presidential nominations and to help restore confidence in government, as President, Governor Bush will:

Make the Prompt Submission of Presidential Nominees a Top Priority, and Challenge Congress to Act on Those Nominees Within 60 Days: Governor Bush believes that 60 days is a reasonable and achievable goal for Senate action on nominees. Indeed, from 1964 to 1984, 48 percent of all presidential nominees were through the confirmation process in one to two months. The Senate can and should do so, Governor Bush believes, regardless of who is elected President in 2000.

Getting Results From Government

Carpenter's Hall
Philadelphia, PA

June 9, 2000

Thank you. I'm pleased to be here, and I appreciate the invitation. It is especially good to be in the host city of my party's national convention.

It will be a great honor to receive the Republican nomination, and to carry my message all across this country. I intend to win this election on the strength of a positive, optimistic vision of America's future – a vision that unites us around common ideals. I will go to Washington with a reform agenda – a set of ideas to make government work for citizens, and move America forward.

My goals for America are clear. My goals are to make sure that every child is educated, by returning high standards and accountability to public schools.

To bring more economic growth and opportunity, by reducing the income tax burden on all Americans – especially those aspiring to the middle class.

To keep our commitment to elderly Americans, and generations to come, by saving and strengthening social security.

To keep the peace, by building a national missile defense, modernizing our military, and establishing clear principles for the use of our power in a changing world.

All of these reforms will require a departure from old ways of government. Each will depend on reforms in government itself.

Yesterday, I spoke about the way business is conducted in Washington – the tone of the nation's capital and the spirit of the political process. I offered ideas that represent a new approach to the people's business – ideas that will restore confidence in government, and return a measure of civility and decency to the national debate.

Today my subject is the everyday operations of government and attitudes of the federal government towards its customer – how it goes about its business and how it treats the people it is obligated to serve.

The strategy can be found in the private sector. Never before have private businesses been so quick to change and adapt – so accountable to the customer. In the private sector we see innovation and competition and a focus on results. Ideas and information are proving as valuable as machinery and factories. Custom design is replacing mass production. Services once delivered in days now come in seconds. Technology and information have created a remarkable age where time and distance have shrunk to almost nothing.

The effect of all this is clear: more choices, more information, and more power for the citizens and local communities.

This new culture has extended its reach into some levels of government, which are transforming the way they do business.

In Houston, the city's school system has partnered with a private education company to help the most troubled students. Under the agreement, if students' reading and math scores don't improve, the firm must continue to help these students at no cost to the city.

In Pennsylvania, Governor Ridge has reformed public contracting. The state now uses online auctions to buy bulk commodities like rock salt or coal, eliminating the shadow of favoritism and influence that has always haunted government contracting.

Indianapolis has put 80 municipal services – from trash collection to airports – up for competitive bidding. So far, taxpayers have saved hundreds of millions of dollars. And the services are better.

In Virginia, instead of standing in line for hours, drivers can renew their licenses over the Internet.

Across America, people are learning about this trend of reform. Yet it appears largely to have escaped the notice of the federal government.

Today, when Americans look to Washington, they see a government slow to respond. Slow to reform. And ignoring all the changes going on around it. At times the government is irrational, running things without any standard of what is necessary, or even what was intended.

When an elderly patient is denied Medicare reimbursement for a simple procedure, it takes almost two years to process an appeal. Part of the reason may be that there are 132,000 pages of Medicare regulations, making decisions for provider and patient alike.

Federal education policy can be even more bewildering. It is so complicated that there are 788 programs to carry it out. And there's actually a federal committee trying to figure out who's doing what in these 788 programs. The committee's been at work for 17 years now. Maybe it's become an example of the problem it set out to solve.

The federal government is also responsible for the safety of our nation's food supply. The way things work now, there's one agency that inspects cheese pizza. There's another that inspects pepperoni pizza. There is one agency that inspects food grown outside the United States. Another that inspects food grown here inside the United States. Apparently, the revolutionary idea that maybe these functions could be combined hasn't dawned on anyone yet.

Americans hear examples like this and conclude, quite reasonably, that government is out of touch, that it is too big and it spends too much. That is true. But size and inefficiency are not the only problems our federal government faces. Our government in Washington acts in a way that loses the people's confidence – the confidence that John F. Kennedy called the basis of effective government.

You may recall that the present Administration came to Washington promising to change all this, to clear away the clutter of bureaucracy and streamline the system. They called their idea a National Performance Review to "reinvent government."

At last report, they had, in the vice president's words, "created a government that works better and costs less." But that doesn't square with the facts. The General Accounting Office looked into some of these claims of big savings. Of those reviewed by the GAO, two-thirds had no evidence to back them up.

The Administration claims to have reduced the number of low- and mid-level workers in the federal government. As it turns out, many positions have been eliminated – but the layers of middle and senior managers have multiplied. We now have Washington offices crowded with people bearing titles like "associate principal deputy assistant secretary" or "principal deputy to the deputy assistant secretary."

My point here is that for all the Administration's rhetoric about reinvention, they never ask fundamental questions about the purpose of government – what it is doing, or whether it should be doing it at all. At a time when private businesses are turning to leaner management teams, Washington keeps adding new managers. They haven't re-invented government bureaucracy – they've just reshuffled it.

Throughout this campaign, I have set forth policies that capture my vision of government reform. They are guided by three principles: government should be citizen-centered, results-oriented, and, wherever possible, market-based.

In my Administration, government will be an ally of the new

economy. Government will rely more on the good judgment and common sense of the people themselves. Government will give citizens more options, and fewer orders. Government will respect the people, and answer to them. This is, after all, what the term "public service" is supposed to mean.

My education reforms would empower parents, school districts, and states. I would require school-by-school report cards, published on the Internet so that parents can hold schools and districts accountable for results. The Administration claims to want the same thing. Yet unlike them, I will insist on regular tests – selected by the states – so that we can measure results, and demand accountability.

I believe faith-based programs should play a greater part in the after-school activities the federal government supports for at-risk children. While the Administration would place strict limits on these kinds of programs, I will open the door wide and let private and religious charities compete for every contract they can.

Here's a third example of how my approach differs from the Administration. I believe seniors on Medicare should have more choices among private health care plans, including prescription drugs, just as every federal worker has. The failure to provide such choice is another example of government overlooking the needs of millions of Americans it is supposed to serve.

In size and scale, modern government will never resemble what the Framers envisioned. In spirit, however, it should always be citizen-centered, always listening and answering directly to the people.

That is why I will reduce the number of mid- and senior-level managers in the federal government. More than 80,000 federal employees in managerial positions are scheduled to retire over the next eight years. I propose that half of them not be replaced.

The idea here is to clear away the layers between the citizen and the decision-maker – between the person with the problem and the person with the answer. Every extra layer of management makes it harder to get things decided. There's always another form to be filled out in a layered bureaucracy, another sign-off from the next level up. Quality of service becomes an afterthought, and it's never clear who's really accountable.

Credit must go to this Administration for applying Internet technology to government departments and agencies. But even on this front, they lag far behind their counterparts in the private sector and at the state and local level.

I will expand the use of the Internet to empower citizens, allowing them to request customized information from Washington when they need it, not just when Washington wants to give it to them. True reform involves not just giving people information, but giving citizens the freedom to act on it.

Second, government should be results-oriented – guided not by process but guided by performance.

There comes a time when every program must be judged either a success or a failure. Where we find success, we should repeat it, share it, and make it the standard. And where we find failure, we must call it by its name. Government action that fails in its purpose must be reformed or be ended.

In government, sometimes just observing the process – going through the motions – becomes more important than actual results. Here's an example. Under a law signed by President Clinton, every federal department and agency faces an annual audit to improve accountability. Yet many of its departments and agencies have failed all three audits since the law took effect in 1997. And what happened as a result? Nothing.

Without accountability, how can we ever expect results? Under my Administration, we will bring this cycle of failure to an abrupt end. As President, I will hold all affected agencies accountable for passing their audits by no later than 2002. I will say to those I put in place, get your audits right.

I will also enforce the Government Performance and Results Act. This is a powerful tool that asks agencies to report what they are actually accomplishing. This law has not been taken seriously enough. For example, as the Department of Commerce has defined it, a goal is "substantially met" if performance is at just two-thirds of the target level. It's not right. We must set the highest of high standards.

In my Administration, standards will be higher, and results will matter.

In private contracting, government often treats contractors as if they were another government agency. That is, contracts are awarded based on compliance with bureaucratic rules. Results are secondary.

Under my proposal, over the next five years, a majority of the service contracts offered throughout the federal government will be performance-based. In other words, rather than micromanaging the details of how contractors operate, the government must set the standards, set the results and give the contractor the freedom to achieve it in the best way.

We must have a government that thinks differently, so we need to recruit talented and imaginative people to public service. We can do this by reforming the civil service with a few simple measures. We'll establish a meaningful system to measure performance. Create awards for employees who surpass expectations. Tie pay increases to results. With a system of rewards and accountability, we can promote a culture of achievement throughout the federal government.

In keeping with the principle of results-oriented government, we will eliminate duplicative and overlapping programs and agencies. Consider the federal government's efforts to help at-risk youth. We can all agree on this worthy objective. But with 117 federal programs – divided among 15 federal agencies – all aimed at this goal, who can tell whether or not we're succeeding at all?

The State of Texas has addressed this problem. Under a law passed some years ago, we have a Sunset Advisory Commission to clear away government activities that have outlived their purpose. The Commission has closed or consolidated 43 programs. The Commission also recommends ways to support agencies that are performing well, and to reform those that are not.

As President, I will ask Congress to establish a Sunset Review Board at the federal level. It will have a specific charge: To review every agency and every program at least once every decade.

Finally, government should be market-based – we should not be afraid of competition, innovation, and choice.

I will open government to the discipline of competition. We've seen how the private sector can achieve significant savings by using the Internet for purchases, through online auctions and business-to-business, or "B2B" transactions. We should work to use the same methods in federal procurement.

In addition, we should no longer allow agencies to exempt themselves from competitive pressures. Today, there are hundreds of thousands of full-time federal employees that are performing tasks that could be done by companies in the private sector. I will put as many of these tasks as possible up for competitive bidding. If the private sector can do a better job, the private sector should get the contract.

Government likes to begin things – to declare grand new programs and causes. But good beginnings are not the measure of success, in government or in any other pursuit. What matters in the end is completion. Performance. Results. Not just making promises, but making good on promises.

In my Administration, that will be the standard from the farthest regional office of government to the highest office in the land. We will do our duty – day in and day out – never forgetting why we are there, and whom we must serve. Only in this way is public confidence restored. Only in this way do we earn the right to lead.

Position Paper
Government Modernization:
Getting Results From Government

June 9, 2000

"Government likes to begin things – to declare grand new programs and causes. But good beginnings are not the measure of success. What matters in the end is completion. Performance. Results. Not just making promises, but making good on promises. In my Administration, that will be the standard from the farthest regional office of government to the highest office in the land."

Governor George W. Bush

EXECUTIVE SUMMARY

Governor Bush believes that the federal government has failed to adapt to the demands of the New Economy and a new century. Unlike American businesses and many state and local governments, the federal government is still based on an out-dated, centralized, "one-size-fits-all" hierarchical model. The Clinton-Gore Administration's "Reinventing Government" initiative has too often focused on oiling this old machinery, rather than transforming it.

In contrast, Governor Bush has called for a "limited, but active" federal government: one that empowers states, cities, and citizens to make decisions, ensures results through accountability, and promotes innovation through competition. As President, he will reform and modernize government on the basis of three key objectives.

To Make Government "Citizen-Centered," Governor Bush will:

- Flatten the federal hierarchy, bringing government closer to citizens by not replacing 40,000 senior and middle managers who will retire over the next eight years, and eliminating the new layers of management created by the current Administration.

- Accelerate e-government by appointing a government-wide Chief Information Officer, and creating a $100 million fund to support interagency e-government initiatives, especially ones enabling individuals to drill directly into the bureaucracy.

To Make Government "Results-Oriented," Governor Bush will:

- Ensure financial accountability by requiring agencies to pass their annual audit.

- Enforce the Government Performance and Results Act (GPRA) so that funds flow to programs that work. Agency Inspectors General will certify the accuracy of GPRA reports, and OMB will factor the results into its budget recommendations.

- Support legislation establishing a bipartisan "Sunset Review Board" to recommend elimination of duplicative and ineffective programs.

- Convert federal service contracts to performance-based contracts wherever possible.

- Reform the civil service by establishing performance-based incentives to reward achievement and recruit skilled private sector talent.

To Make Government "Market-Based," Governor Bush will:

- Establish the goal of moving all significant government procurement to the Internet.

- Open federal positions involving commercial activities to competition from the private sector wherever possible.

By transforming government, these basic reforms should save approximately $88 billion over five years, representing one percent of spending.

Objectives of Government Reform

The systems of the federal government were in large part developed over 50 years ago. These systems were designed so that solutions would flow from Washington along carefully established bureaucratic hierarchies. The result is a federal government today that is both insensitive and expensive.

Governor Bush believes that true government reform must be based on a reexamination of the role of the federal government itself. He has called for "limited, but active" government: government that empowers states, cities and citizens to make decisions, ensures results through accountability, and promotes innovation through competition.

Governor Bush believes that if reform is to help the federal government adapt to a rapidly changing world, its primary objectives must be to make government citizen-centered, results-oriented, and, wherever possible, market-based.

Proposals to Make Government "Citizen-Centered"

Governor Bush believes that the first priority of government reform should be to minimize the distance between citizens and decision-makers.

Flattening the Federal Hierarchy

In an effort to get closer to the customer, American businesses have increasingly replaced old, hierarchical organizations with flatter, more entrepreneurial ones. Under the Clinton-Gore Administration, the shape of the federal government has also changed – but instead of becoming flatter, it has actually become both thicker and taller.

One of the key successes claimed by the Administration's National Partnership for Reinventing Government is the reduction in the federal workforce, which is now roughly at the same level that it was in 1961: approximately 1,820,000 employees.

However, the bulk of the personnel cuts came from reductions in the Defense Department, and are better attributable to a natural downsizing in response to the end of the Cold War. The remaining cuts fell primarily on lower level, "line" employees. As a result, for the first time in modern history, senior-level and middle-level employees outnumber lower-level employees.

The Administration has also added new layers at the upper reaches of government. An examination of the top four executive levels of government (from

Secretary to Assistant Secretary and their associated positions) reveals that between 1993 and 1998, the Administration added 14 new layers in various agencies – the same number as were added over the prior three decades combined:

- The 44 different titles in the upper echelon of government, which include "Deputy Associate Deputy Secretary," "Principal Deputy to the Deputy Assistant Secretary" and "Associate Principal Deputy Assistant Secretary," are illustrative of the current excess of bureaucracy.

According to Paul Light, founding director of the Center for Public Service at the Brookings Institution, "Never has a president had so many layers of senior executives … juxtaposed between him and the front lines of government." The increase in layers of government has been accompanied by a corresponding decrease in accountability: "Every year, fewer front-line employees are reporting upward through what appears to be an ever-lengthening chain of command."

Fortunately, the next president will have an opportunity to flatten the federal hierarchy. As many as 80,000 managers will retire over the next eight years. Although government must be careful not to weaken its management capacity, this wave of retirements provides a rare opportunity to sharply reduce the number of layers between the top and the bottom of government.

Thus, to shrink the distance between citizen and cabinet member, as President, Governor Bush will:

Flatten the Federal Hierarchy: In aggregate, Governor Bush will not replace 40,000 of the 80,000 senior and middle-level managers retiring from the federal government over the next eight years. In addition, he will redistribute 10,000 positions from higher-level designations to front-line, service delivery functions that interact with citizens. These actions should make the federal government more nimble and responsive, while saving an estimated $9 billion over 5 years.

Reduce the Number of Layers in the Upper Echelon of Government: In order to make government more responsive to the needs of citizens, Governor Bush will, at a minimum, eliminate the new layers of management created under the Clinton-Gore Administration.

Using the Internet to Create a "Citizen-Centered" Government

The Internet promises to shift power from a handful of leaders in Washington to individual citizens. State and local governments are already using the Internet to become more "citizen-centric:"

- In Virginia, *VIPNET* provides services ranging from online auto registration to instantaneous access to official public meeting announcements.

- In Pennsylvania, Governor Ridge will shortly launch *PA PowerPort*, an online portal that will provide individuals with access to a database of government resources, help businesses to establish e-commerce "storefronts," and enable schools to promote greater parental involvement.

- In Texas, a bilingual, e-government portal and electronic payment system was launched this summer to provide individuals and businesses with a one-stop, Internet portal for conducting transactions with state and local government.

Governor Bush believes that these are just the first steps in e-government. In order to make government truly "citizen-centered," individuals should be allowed to create their own personalized interface with government.

This will require integration of government systems, the establishment of adequate security and privacy protections, and the use of "push" technologies to send individuals information tailored to their needs: the latest environmental regulations to an environmental activist, information on Education Savings Accounts to a new parent, or data on export markets to an entrepreneur.

Implementation of e-government will require leadership. The 1996 Clinger-Cohen Act mandated the appointment of 54 departmental and agency Chief Information Officers (CIOs) and established a government-wide CIO Council. But there is no one person responsible for coordinating e-government activities. According to Deputy Secretary of Commerce Robert Mallet, "There are many efforts ongoing… but they are not well-connected." Moreover, since most e-government appropriations are agency-specific, there is a lack of funding for e-government projects that cut across agencies.

Thus, to accelerate the implementation of "citizen-centered" e-government, Governor Bush will:

Appoint a Chief Information Officer for the Federal Government: Governor Bush will issue an Executive Order designating the current Deputy Director for Management of the Office of Management and Budget as the federal CIO. The federal CIO will be responsible for providing the leadership and coordination needed to realize the vision of a truly digital and citizen-centric government. The CIO will head agency cross-functional councils on information technology (IT), facilitate collaboration with state CIOs, and lead development of standards, protocols and privacy protections, among other things.

Create a $100 Million Fund to Support Interagency e-Government Initiatives: The federal CIO will control the allocation of this fund, which will support interagency IT projects, initiatives to promote customization of services, and systems integration.

Proposals to Make Government "Results-Oriented"

Governor Bush believes that government reform must establish accountability systems so citizens can judge the quality of government performance.

Ensuring Financial Accountability

The 1994 Government Management Reform Act specified 24 agencies that must be audited annually by the General Accounting Office. The government has failed all three audits since the law took effect in 1997:

- Eleven of the 24 agencies covered by the Act failed to pass their 1999 audits on time, including the Departments of Agriculture, Defense, Education, Justice, State, and Housing and Urban Development.

- The GAO identified $19.1 billion in erroneous payments made by agencies last year, and noted that the problem of erroneous payments could be considerably larger.

Therefore, to enforce a basic level of financial accountability, as President, Governor Bush will:

Ensure that All Relevant Agencies Pass Their Audits: As President, Governor Bush will hold the heads of all 24 agencies subject to the 1994 Management Reform Act accountable for passing their audits by no later than the 2002 audit cycle. In addition, he will conduct a high-level review of government accounting practices. These steps, along with expanded use of recovery auditing, could save $33 billion over five years through the reduction of erroneous payments alone.

Enforcing the Government Performance and Results Act

The 1993 Government Performance and Results Act (GPRA) was designed to determine whether agencies were accomplishing their stated missions. Under the law, agencies are required to set performance goals and measure their actual results. But implementation of the Results Act has been flawed. OMB has yet to effectively use the performance information for budget decisions. Moreover, since agencies grade themselves, there is little assurance that the data is reliable.

The failure to adequately use and enforce the Results Act can lead to a startling lack of accountability. For example, as the Department of Commerce has defined it, a goal is "substantially met" if performance is at just two-thirds of the target level.

In light of these failings, Virginia Thomas, Senior Fellow in Government Studies at the Heritage Foundation, recently testified that the Results Act is "useless" without "credible, accurate, objective information from federal agencies on performance – either through assistance from offices of Inspectors General" or other external auditors.

To enforce the Results Act and ensure accountability, Governor Bush will:

Require Agency Inspectors General to Certify Agency Performance Reports: As President, Governor Bush will issue an Executive Order requiring each agency's IG to certify the accuracy of performance reports under the Results Act.

Require OMB to Justify Budget Recommendations with Accurate Performance Measures and Data: To ensure accountability, Governor Bush will require OMB to link budget recommendations to performance.

Eliminating Duplicative and Ineffective Programs

Government spends billions of dollars on programs that are obsolete, demonstrably ineffective, or better performed by the private sector. In addition, there are many overlapping or duplicative programs and agencies. For example, there are 342 different economic development programs managed by 13 agencies, over 57 federal agencies with responsibility for drug control efforts, and 788 federal education programs managed by 20 different agencies.

While GAO and OMB periodically review agencies and programs, no entity conducts a regularly scheduled review of whether a program should continue to exist at all. In contrast, 24 states, including Texas, have established a process for regularly assessing and "sunsetting" programs. For example, the Texas bipartisan Sunset Advisory Commission has abolished 43 agencies and consolidated another 10 agencies, saving the state over $630 million since 1982.

As President, to eliminate duplicative and ineffective programs, Governor Bush will:

Support Legislation Establishing a Bipartisan "Sunset Review Board:" The bipartisan Sunset Review Board will review agencies and programs at least once every 10 years and make recommendations to Congress on whether they should be reauthorized, consolidated, devolved to state and local governments, privatized, or abolished. The activities of the Sunset Review Board will dovetail with another reform Governor Bush has called for – biennial budgeting. The Review Board will evaluate programs in the non-budget years, providing recommendations that could be acted upon in the budget years.

Expanding the Use of Performance-Based Contracting

Federal agencies are relying increasingly on outside contractors. The federal government spends roughly $110 billion a year in service contracts. Governor Bush believes more of these contracts should be performance-based.

Performance-based contracting focuses on the result to be achieved, rather than how the work gets done. For example, an EPA hotline administrator cut her department's costs by over 20 percent simply by contracting for a result – a minimum level of correct responses – rather than mandating specific training and testing procedures.

A 1998 OMB study of 15 agencies found that performance-based contracting resulted in an average 15 percent reduction in contract price and an 18 percent improvement in satisfaction. OMB also found that 15 of the 26 contracts studied were awarded to non-incumbent companies, suggesting that performance-based contracting stimulated competition. Unfortunately, OMB reported that, despite the "compelling logic" of performance-based contracting, government implementation was not being fully pursued.

Therefore, to make government contracts more results-oriented, Governor Bush will:

Convert Federal Service Contracts to a Performance Basis Wherever Possible: Governor Bush will issue an Executive Order encouraging agencies to convert federal service contracts to performance-based contracts wherever possible. If even half of the $110 billion in annual federal service contracts were converted to a performance basis, the federal government should save $14 billion over five years.

Reforming the Civil Service

The current civil service system has perverse incentives that reward under-achievement and discourage excellence. It also limits the ability of agency heads to compete against private business for highly-skilled senior talent. For example, the federal government:

- Makes no meaningful distinction between levels of performance, relying on inflated evaluations or assessing employees on a "pass-fail" basis.

- Awards pay raises simply on the basis of the number of years an employee spends in government.

- Lacks the flexibility to provide financial incentives to attract highly-skilled, non-career senior executives and managers.

In 1993, Vice President Gore's National Performance Review called for reforming civil service laws. Seven years later, little progress has been made in overhauling the cumbersome personnel laws. Today, only 29 percent of federal employees believe that creativity and innovation are rewarded.

Governor Bush believes it is time to extend results-oriented reforms to the federal workforce. Thus, to reform the civil service by using performance-based incentives, Governor Bush will seek legislation to:

Give Agency Heads Flexibility to Establish Performance-Based Incentive Systems: To reward achievement and reduce poor performance, Governor Bush will ensure that pay is based on performance, as measured by at least three distinct levels of achievement, and automatic pay increases no longer go to underperforming employees.

Give Agency Heads the Ability to Offer Incentives to Recruit Highly-Skilled, Non-Career Senior Managers: Governor Bush will allow bonuses of up to 40 percent of salary to be given to selected, non-career senior managers serving under performance contracts. These bonuses will help attract highly-skilled senior-level managers from the private sector to perform some of the government's most complex management tasks.

Expand Rewards for Employees who Generate Cost Savings: Governor Bush will expand rewards for employees who generate specific cost savings. In addition, he will allow Department Secretaries to award bonuses of up to $25,000 without having to obtain the approval of the Office of Personnel Management.

Proposals to Make Government "Market-Based"

Making e-Procurement the Government-Wide Standard

Businesses are experiencing significant cost savings by shifting their procurement to the Internet. Savings are derived from reduced transaction-processing costs, more efficient inventory management, and greater competition from vendors producing lower prices.

A Goldman Sachs study estimates that industries will reap cost savings from business-to-business e-commerce strategies, ranging from two percent in the coal industry to 40 percent in the electronics industry. Unfortunately, only a fraction of the federal government's procurement effort is now conducted in a paperless fashion via the Internet. Thus, to lower costs and utilize market-based solutions wherever possible, Governor Bush will:

Establish the Goal of Moving All Significant Government Procurement Online Within Three Years: Governor Bush will make paperless, e-procurement the government-wide standard by setting the target of shifting all significant government procurement to the Internet within three years. Adopting this market-based solution should generate procurement savings of $19 billion over five years.

Opening Government Activities to Competition

The 1998 Federal Activities Inventory Reform (FAIR) Act requires federal agencies to submit an annual inventory of activities performed that are commercial in nature. For those activities, agencies are directed to use an open, competitive process (considering both public and private bidders) to choose the provider.

Agencies have found that when competitive bidding is employed, they experience average savings of 30 percent when a private contractor wins, and 20 percent when the public sector wins.

Recently, 98 agencies identified over 900,000 employees as performing commercial activities. However, the FAIR Act gives agencies the right to exempt commercial activities from competition. As a result, many agencies have significantly limited competitive opportunities. For example, the EPA exempted 93 percent of its employees performing commercial activities from competition.

Governor Bush is committed to injecting competition into the government's commercial activities and, as President, he will:

Establish the Goal of Subjecting a Majority of the Federal Government's Commercial Positions to Competition: Governor Bush will issue an Executive Order establishing the goal of opening to competitive bid a majority of the 900,000 positions already identified as potentially commercial in nature. Opening government functions to competition to the fullest extent possible is the best way to ensure market-based pricing and encourage innovation, while saving the taxpayers an estimated $14 billion over five years.

Position Paper
Campaign Finance Reform

February 15, 2000

"In all instances, it should be individuals, not corporate directors or union bosses, who control the political process, because individuals are the backbone of democracy."

Governor George W. Bush

EXECUTIVE SUMMARY

Governor Bush has advocated campaign finance reform since the beginning of his campaign. He believes democracy is first and foremost about individuals. That is why his reforms address the abuses of the system, while at the same time respecting the First Amendment rights of individuals:

To Prevent Corporate Boards and Union Bosses from Diminishing the Influence of Individuals, Governor Bush will:

- Ban unions and corporations from giving "soft" money to political parties.

To Ensure Americans are Not Forced to Fund Candidates They Don't Support, Governor Bush will:

- Enact "Paycheck Protection," preventing union bosses from directly spending roughly $300 million in union dues annually – without members' permission – to support candidates of the bosses' choosing.

To Protect the Right of Individuals to Express Themselves, Governor Bush will:

- Preserve the right of individuals and groups – from the Christian Coalition to the Sierra Club – to run issue ads.

- Raise the limit on individual contributions to candidates by adjusting it for inflation.

To End "Double Dipping" and Respect Donors' Choices, Governor Bush will:

- Eliminate the "roll-over" loophole and prevent incumbents from transferring excess funds from a prior federal campaign to a subsequent campaign for a different federal office.

To Ensure Full and Timely Disclosure of Campaign Contributions, Governor Bush will:

- Require near real-time disclosure of contributions on the Internet, as he alone among the presidential candidates is already doing.

To Ensure that Lawmakers Serve the Public Interest, Governor Bush will:

- Prohibit federally registered lobbyists from contributing to Members of Congress, while Congress is in session.

The Current Federal Election Law

The Federal Election Campaign Act (FECA) is the principal law governing federal elections. As originally enacted, FECA imposed restrictions on both political contributions and expenditures. In 1976, in *Buckley v. Valeo*, the Supreme Court ruled that FECA's limits on contributions were constitutional, but struck down as unconstitutional FECA's limits on expenditures by:

- Candidates with their own money;

- Individuals and groups engaging in independent expenditures, or so-called "express advocacy" – advocating the election or defeat of a particular federal candidate (e.g., "Vote for Mr. Smith to go to Washington"); and

- Groups engaging in "issue advocacy" – advocacy not of a particular candidate, but of an issue (e.g., "Fight crime").

Under current law, contributions are divided into two categories. "Hard" money is money raised directly to elect candidates to federal office, and is governed by Federal Election Commission (FEC) regulations. Contributions are limited to $1,000 per election from individuals, and $5,000 from Political Action Committees (PACs are organizations – generally established by corporations, labor unions, ideological organizations, and trade associations – that get their money from their individual members or employees in increments of $5,000 or less.) Corporations and unions are totally barred from contributing hard money.

"Soft" money is money raised by national parties and other groups for everything other than advocating the election or defeat of a particular federal candidate. It is considered soft because it is exempt from FEC limits, although party soft money is reported to the FEC and regulated by states. Activities that are largely financed by party soft money include:

- "Party building," which includes funding a party's overhead costs and "get-out-the-vote" efforts, such as voter registration drives, direct mail, and phone banks.

- Issue advocacy – e.g., TV and radio ads supporting an issue, but not expressly advocating the election or defeat of a particular candidate.

- Direct contributions to state and local candidates and to state parties.

The Increasing Cost of Campaigns

The aggregate costs of political campaigns have increased dramatically in recent years. According to economist Robert Samuelson, total expenditures for all federal, state, and local campaigns have increased from $300 million in 1968 to over $3 billion in 1992.

The principal factors driving up campaign costs have been the increasing importance of television and radio in campaigns and rapidly escalating media costs. For example, the cost for federal candidates to advertise on television has increased from $24.5 million in 1972 to more than $400 million in 1996.

At the same time that campaign costs have been increasing, the value of individual contributions has been decreasing. Since the $1,000 cap on individual contributions has not been adjusted for inflation, it is now worth less than one-third of its value when it was established in 1974.

The direct consequence of these two factors – the increasing cost of campaigns and the declining value of individual contributions – is that candidates are forced to spend more and more time raising more and more money.

"Soft" Money and Third Party Money

One consequence of the imbalance between rising election costs and the eroding value of individual contributions is the increasing importance of soft money spent by the national parties, and money spent by third parties.

Soft money spent by the national political parties has increased from $83 million in the 1991-1992 election cycle to $262 million in 1995-1996. These funds are spent on state and local candidates, state party organizations, generic party-building activities, and issue advocacy, among other things. Soft money is contributed to national political parties by corporations, unions, and individuals.

Independent spending by third parties can be divided into two categories: spending by issue advocacy groups, and spending by labor unions. The Annenberg Public Policy Center estimated that in the 1995-1996 election cycle, between $135 million and $150 million was spent on issue advocacy advertising by at least 31 different groups, including the National Abortion and Reproductive Rights Action League (NARAL), the Sierra Club, and the U.S. Chamber of Commerce. Individual citizens voluntarily give money to support these groups, and the groups then use the money to run ads promoting their causes.

In contrast to third-party issue advocacy groups, whose members voluntarily give money to support specified causes, labor unions take an estimated $6 billion annually from their members' paychecks in mandatory dues. Although originally intended to support collective bargaining, that money is now used for many other purposes, including politics. Some of the money is contributed as soft money to national parties, while an even larger percentage of the money taken from members' paychecks is spent directly by the union bosses themselves – without their members' permission – to support candidates of the bosses' choosing.

Indeed, according to 1996 testimony before the House Oversight Committee by Professor Leo Troy of Rutgers University, union bosses spend an estimated $300 million to $500 million each year in direct spending to elect candidates they support.

The Goal of Campaign Finance Reform

Governor Bush has argued for campaign finance reform since the beginning of his campaign. He believes democracy is first and foremost about individuals, and that the key flaw in the current system is the ability of corporations and union bosses to spend unlimited amounts of money that is not theirs. That is why Governor Bush's reform proposals correct the abuses in the campaign finance system, but at the same time respect the First Amendment rights of individual voters.

Proposal 1: Ban All Corporate and Union "Soft" Money

In 1996, corporations contributed $204 million to national political parties, and labor unions contributed $9.5 million to the national parties. Current federal campaign finance laws not only permit these contributions, but also leave them completely unrestricted.

Thus, under the current law, big business and big labor can give unlimited sums to national political parties. Governor Bush believes that these huge flows of funds undermine confidence in our political system and diminish the influence of individuals. Therefore, as President, Governor Bush will:

Ban All Corporate and Union Contributions to Political Parties: Governor Bush will support legislation imposing a total, categorical ban on all corporate and union "soft" money contributions to national political parties.

Proposal 2: Ensure that Citizens Are Not Forced to Fund Causes and Candidates They Don't Support

Governor Bush believes that any ban on soft money must address the $300 million or more of union dues that union bosses spend each year directly to elect the politicians they support.

Governor Bush believes it is wrong to take money from the country's 18 million union members through mandatory dues and spend it on politics without their permission. Accordingly, as President, to ensure that no American is forced to fund causes and candidates he or she does not support, Governor Bush will:

Enact "Paycheck Protection" Legislation: Governor Bush will seek legislation that will require union bosses to get the permission of individual union members before their mandatory dues can be spent directly by the union on political activities.

Proposal 3: Protect the Rights of Individuals to Participate in Democracy

Governor Bush believes that individual citizens are the backbone of democracy. That is why he is committed to defending each citizen's First Amendment right to speak in the political process.

For example, Governor Bush has been attacked on TV by advocacy groups such as NARAL. He disagrees with their ads, and he would prefer that they not run them. But his response is not to muzzle them. Rather, because he believes in the First Amendment, he will:

<u>Preserve the Right of Individuals and Groups to Run Issue Ads</u>: Governor Bush will preserve the existing, constitutional right of individuals and advocacy groups to run issue ads without government restriction.

<u>Increase the Limit on Individual Contributions to Candidates</u>: Governor Bush will increase the limit on individual contributions of "hard" money to federal candidates. If the 1974 limit were indexed for inflation, it would increase from $1,000 to roughly $3,400 per election. This will reduce the amount of time candidates must spend raising money, and reduce the pressure to raise soft money.

<u>Maintain the Right of Individuals to Contribute to Political Parties</u>: Governor Bush would protect individuals' current rights to contribute to national political parties.

Proposal 4: Eliminate "Double Dipping" and Preserve Donors' Choice

Current law permits a federal candidate to transfer or "roll over" excess campaign funds from a prior federal campaign to a subsequent federal campaign. There is no limit on how much excess money may be transferred from the earlier campaign to the later campaign.

The consequences of the "roll-over" loophole are twofold. First, donors' money may be spent in ways they never intended. Just because a donor supported a candidate in one election, does not necessarily mean that the donor would support the candidate in a different election.

Second, the roll-over loophole allows a candidate to "double dip" and evade existing campaign laws. For example, even if an individual donor or PAC had already given the maximum allowed in a prior campaign ($1,000 and $5,000, respectively), the roll-over loophole allows the candidate to use that money, if left over, for the new campaign and still solicit another contribution from the same donor.

Governor Bush believes it is important to put an end to "double dipping" and will seek to amend the federal election laws to:

Eliminate the "Roll-Over" Loophole: Governor Bush will prohibit federal candidates from transferring excess funds from a prior federal campaign to a subsequent campaign for a different federal office.

Proposal 5: Ensure Full and Timely Disclosure of Campaign Contributions

Under current law, presidential candidates are required to report campaign contributions and spending to the FEC on a quarterly basis during the year preceding the election and on a monthly basis during the election year. As a result, there can be more than a three-month lag between when an individual or PAC donates to a presidential campaign and when that information is widely available to the public.

Governor Bush believes that an informed electorate is an effective electorate. In his view, every American has a right to know how candidates are funding their campaigns. Voters should not have to wait until months after the fact to glean contribution information from the fine print of an FEC report. Thus, as President, to ensure an informed electorate, Governor Bush will:

Require Near Real-Time Disclosure of Contributions on the Internet: Governor Bush will seek to amend federal law to require Internet disclosure of all campaign contributions within one week of receipt. Leading by example, Governor Bush is already voluntarily implementing this reform. Each week, Governor Bush posts the name of every single contributor to his campaign on the Internet in a fully searchable format. To date, none of the other presidential contenders has chosen to do the same.

Proposal 6: Ensure that Lawmakers Serve the Public Interest

Federal officials must avoid both improper conduct and conduct that creates an appearance of impropriety. One activity particularly likely to generate possible improprieties is federal officials' interaction with lobbyists – individuals whose very livelihood depends on buying and selling influence – at the same time they are acting on matters of great concern to those lobbyists.

In 1992, the Senate adopted ethics Rule 43. That rule prohibits Members from basing decisions on whether or not to assist a petitioner before federal agencies on whether that petitioner has contributed to the Member's campaign.

Governor Bush believes this somewhat general rule is an insufficient safeguard; it is too easy to create lawyerly distinctions to circumvent it. Accordingly, to ensure that lawmakers serve the public interest, as President, Governor Bush will:

Prohibit Members of Congress from Soliciting Contributions from Lobbyists While Congress is in Session: Under Governor Bush's proposed rule, Members of Congress will be prohibited from soliciting or accepting campaign contributions from federally-registered lobbyists, while Congress is in session (and not in recess). States such as Colorado have already enacted similar common-sense restrictions, and, in fact, the State of Texas currently prohibits campaign contributions during the legislative session.

Position Paper
Civil Justice Reform

February 9, 2000

"From people across America, I am hearing that our legal system needs reform. That our courts aren't serving the people, they are serving the lawyers. That frivolous lawsuits are hurting good people. Some think this special interest group is too powerful to take on. That money determines everything. This is not an argument; it is an excuse. This cause is not hopeless. But it requires leadership to get results."

Governor George W. Bush

EXECUTIVE SUMMARY

A litigation explosion is clogging America's civil courts, costing U.S. high-tech companies, small businesses, and consumers more than $150 billion a year. Over 50 cents of every dollar paid out in the average tort case goes not to the injured parties, but to paying lawyers' fees and transaction costs.

The Clinton-Gore Administration and the trial lawyers' lobby have opposed reform efforts in Congress. Despite opposition from these same special interests in Texas, Governor Bush fought for – and won – passage of seven major tort reform bills in his first legislative session, saving Texans an estimated $2.9 billion. As President, Governor Bush will fight to reform the federal civil justice system. His objective is not lower awards for victims, but higher standards for lawyers.

To Protect the Innocent Against Frivolous Federal Suits, Governor Bush will:

- Strengthen Federal Rule 11 to require stiffer penalties for frivolous suits, and impose a "Three Strikes, You're Out" rule on attorneys who repeatedly file frivolous claims.

- Limit "fishing expeditions" by amending federal discovery rules, and curb the use of "junk science" by raising the federal standard for admission of scientific testimony.

- Eliminate the much-abused private cause of action under the RICO statute.

- Enact the "Teacher Protection Act" to shield teachers from meritless lawsuits.

To Encourage Reasonable Settlements, Governor Bush will:

- Enact a "Fair Settlement Rule," requiring parties who reject a pre-trial settlement offer, and who ultimately lose their case or receive substantially less at trial, to pay the other party's costs, including legal fees.

To Curb Forum Shopping and Improve Access to Federal Courts, Governor Bush will:

- Allow large cases to be removed from state to federal court where only "minimal diversity" exists – i.e., where any plaintiff is from a different state than any defendant.

- Raise the amount in controversy for removal where there is complete diversity.

- Expand class-action removal rules so that national cases are heard in a federal forum.

To Protect Clients Against Unscrupulous Lawyers, Governor Bush will:

- Enact a "Client's Bill of Rights" to allow federal courts to hear challenges to attorneys' fees, and require attorneys to disclose their ethical obligation to charge reasonable fees.

To Ensure That Private Lawyers Do Not Profit Unreasonably at Public Expense, Governor Bush will:

- Require private lawyers who contract to represent states or municipalities to return any excessive fees to their governmental clients.

- Issue an Executive Order prohibiting federal agencies from paying contingency fees.

The Need for Legal Reform

America was founded upon the rule of law. Many of the defining moments of U.S. history have been legal victories: protecting free speech, ending segregation, ensuring the right to vote, safeguarding private property.

Today, however, a combination of frivolous lawsuits, trial attorneys who abuse the system for profit, and the lure of windfall recoveries is transforming America from a lawful society to a litigious one. As a result, the number of civil lawsuits has tripled since 1960, and America's civil courts are clogged by a litigation explosion.

As the number of lawsuits has increased, so too has the size of the awards. The top ten jury verdicts in 1999 totaled almost $9 billion – three times the 1998 total. However, more than 50 cents on the dollar paid out in the average tort case goes to lawyers, experts, and other costs – not the injured parties.

The litigation explosion imposes a variety of costs – economic and otherwise. In the first instance, clogged courts have led to significant delays in justice. On average, state civil actions that go to trial take more than two years from filing to verdict.

The economic costs imposed by the litigation explosion have escalated. Between 1930 and 1994, tort costs grew four times faster than the U.S. economy. The costs imposed by runaway civil litigation fall especially heavily on high-tech businesses and small businesses:

- High technology companies are almost twice as likely to be the subject of a class action securities suit as companies in other industries.

- One in four small-business owners have either been sued or threatened with a suit.

- The cost of a business owner's defense in the average civil suit is estimated at $100,000 – twice the average small business owner's salary.

The tort costs imposed by the litigation explosion are, in turn, passed on to individual consumers in the form of a hidden "lawsuit tax:"

- The costs attributable to litigation constitute an estimated $8 of an $11.50 DPT vaccine, $191 of a $578 tonsillectomy, $170 of a $1,000 motorized wheelchair, and $3,000 of an $18,000 heart pacemaker.

- The "lawsuit tax" – the cost of lawsuits in higher prices and insurance premiums – has been estimated at $466 per person in South Carolina, $547 per person in Michigan, $574 per person in California, and over $1,000 per person in Washington, D.C.

Finally, the litigation explosion undermines confidence in the civil courts. Surveys indicate a majority of Americans agree with Senator Spencer Abraham (R – MI), who has observed, "Our legal system is broken. The United States has been transformed from a nation of friends and neighbors into a nation of actual and potential litigants."

The Goals of Civil Justice Reform

Governor Bush has shown that in the fight for civil justice reform, leadership can prevail over special interests. The trial lawyers' lobby opposed his reform efforts in Texas, providing 25 percent of his opponent's campaign contributions in his first race for Governor, and nearly 40 percent of his opponent's contributions in his reelection campaign.

Despite this opposition, Governor Bush fought for – and won – passage of ten major pieces of tort reform legislation, over three legislative sessions, that have limited joint-and-several liability, curbed forum shopping, and punished frivolous suits. As a result, since 1996, Texans and Texas businesses have received an estimated $2.9 billion in savings through insurance rate reductions.

Governor Bush believes that reform of the federal civil justice system must be a presidential concern. Unfortunately, the Clinton-Gore Administration, together with the trial lawyers' lobby, has opposed key reform measures, including the Securities Litigation Reform Act, which was passed over President Clinton's veto, and the Products Liability Reform Act.

In contrast, Governor Bush will make it a priority as President to implement comprehensive legal reform. His plan respects federalism and the Constitution, allocating authority to the states over substantive state tort law and to the federal government over procedures in the federal courts. Its objective is not to lower awards for victims, but to raise standards of conduct for trial attorneys. To accomplish this, Governor Bush has set five goals for civil justice reform.

Goal 1: Protect the Innocent by Deterring Frivolous Litigation

Governor Bush believes that litigation must never be used as a weapon against the innocent. And when it is used as such, there must be consequences. That is why the first goal of his reform plan is to protect the innocent by deterring frivolous and junk lawsuits. These lawsuits have proliferated due to the weakening of key rules of federal court procedure, as well as the abuse of certain rights of action.

Rule 11

Attorneys and clients currently face little penalty for filing frivolous cases. The principal deterrent, Federal Rule of Civil Procedure 11, which requires attorneys to certify that legal filings have a basis in law and in fact, was weakened by amendment in 1993. Specifically, (1) sanctions were made discretionary; (2) attorney's fees of the opposing party were eliminated as the preferred punishment; (3) the Rule was made inapplicable to discovery abuses; and (4) a "safe harbor" was established, providing attorneys who file frivolous actions with 21 days to amend their claims with impunity.

According to Supreme Court Justice Antonin Scalia, these changes rendered Rule 11 "toothless." For example:

- Last year a man who attended an Elton John concert sued the City of San Diego and a beer vendor because, after drinking beer, he allegedly suffered "emotional distress" when he found women using the men's room. His case was dismissed, and the judge warned the plaintiff's attorney – under penalty of Rule 11 – not to try again. But Rule 11 proved such a minor deterrent that he refiled anyway. The result for having twice filed a frivolous claim and imposing significant costs on the defendants: a mere $4,000 fine.

As President, Governor Bush will establish a meaningful deterrent to frivolous suits in the federal courts by proposing legislation to:

Strengthen Rule 11 to Deter Frivolous Lawsuits: Rule 11 will be amended to make sanctions mandatory; to reinstate attorneys' fees and expenses as the preferred sanction; to require Rule 11 certification for discovery; and to eliminate the safe harbor for those who file frivolous suits and seek to withdraw them.

Authorize Double or Treble Damages for Egregiously Frivolous Claims: Governor Bush will propose legislation amending Rule 11 to expressly authorize federal judges to award defendants double or triple damages in cases involving egregiously frivolous claims.

Adopt a "Three Strikes, You're Out" Rule for Attorneys Who Repeatedly File Frivolous Federal Suits: If an attorney files three egregiously frivolous suits, that attorney will be barred from practicing in federal court for three years – one year for each suit.

Discovery

The abuse of discovery is another factor contributing to the surge in frivolous suits. Federal Rule of Civil Procedure 26(b)(1) permits discovery with respect to any issue relevant to the "subject matter involved in the pending action." This expansive rule allows litigants to engage in wide-ranging "fishing expeditions" in the hope of uncovering something incriminating.

The federal Civil Rules Advisory Committee has proposed limiting discovery to matters specifically "relevant to the claim or defense of any party." This proposal is currently pending Supreme Court and congressional review.

To limit costly and wide-ranging "fishing expeditions," as President, Governor Bush will propose legislation to:

Amend the Discovery Rules to Allow Inquiry Only into Issues Actually in Dispute: In order to limit unnecessary time and expense in civil litigation and to prevent "fishing expeditions," Governor Bush will adopt the proposed new rules limiting discoverable information to matters specifically "relevant to a claim or defense of any party."

Junk Science

The exploitation of "junk science" has contributed to the amount of high-profile, frivolous litigation. This is due to the weakening of the legal standard for the use of expert and scientific evidence.

The 1923 case of *Frye v. United States* held that, in order to be admissible, novel scientific evidence not only had to be relevant to the case, but had to be "generally accepted" as reliable by the relevant scientific community.

However, in 1975, Federal Rule of Evidence 702 displaced the "generally accepted" standard with a much broader and much less demanding standard, permitting any scientific testimony so long as it will "assist the trier of fact."

In order to limit suits based on junk science, as President, Governor Bush will:

<u>Raise the Standard for Admission of Scientific Testimony</u>: In order to limit the ability of experts to testify about questionable theories lacking in good scientific basis, Governor Bush will:

- Propose legislation codifying the original *Frye* test, requiring that expert testimony be "generally accepted" in the scientific community.

- Issue an Executive Order providing that federal litigators will rely only on evidence generally accepted as reliable in the relevant scientific community.

- Amend the Rules of Civil Procedure to encourage federal judges to convene expert Scientific Advisory Panels to resolve scientific disputes.

RICO

A fourth reason for the proliferation of frivolous suits is the abuse by plaintiffs' lawyers of the Racketeer Influenced and Corrupt Organizations Act ("RICO"). RICO was enacted in 1970 as a weapon against "organized crime," and explicitly permits triple damages.

Under RICO, government prosecutors can bring criminal or civil actions, and private parties can invoke RICO's civil penalties in private causes of action. However, as the Supreme Court has noted, civil RICO has been increasingly abused to extract lucrative settlements in ordinary business-related lawsuits. For example:

- Lawyers recently invoked RICO in a federal class-action lawsuit against Nintendo, complaining that the company is engaged in "racketeering activity" by selling the popular "Pokémon" trading cards. These lawyers claim that by placing rare cards in selected packages, Nintendo is turning children into gamblers. At least nine similar cases have already been filed against sports-card manufacturers.

To end the civil abuse of the RICO statute, Governor Bush will:

Eliminate the Private Cause of Action Under RICO: To limit the coercive – and unintended – use of RICO in ordinary civil litigation, Governor Bush will propose legislation to repeal the private cause of action under RICO. However, the legislation will leave untouched the full range of state tort remedies available to litigants, as well as the full scope of government criminal and civil RICO prosecutions.

School Discipline

Frivolous litigation is particularly destructive in the nation's schools. Sixty-five percent of public school teachers charge that discipline is a "serious" problem in their schools, and 88 percent think that academic achievement would improve "substantially," if persistent troublemakers were removed from class.

Unfortunately, the threat of litigation has made it more difficult to enforce discipline in the classroom. Indeed, 99 percent of principals say their policy on reporting bad behavior has been modified because of liability costs and concerns.

To ensure that litigation is not used as a weapon against the innocent, and to empower teachers and principals to maintain discipline in the classroom, Governor Bush will:

Enact the "Teacher Protection Act:" The Teacher Protection Act will shield teachers, principals, and school board members acting in their official capacity from federal liability arising out of their efforts to maintain discipline in the classroom, so long as they do not engage in reckless or criminal misconduct. In addition, plaintiffs who bring meritless claims in federal court challenging teacher and principal disciplinary actions will be liable for the legal expenses, including attorneys' fees, incurred in the defense of the teachers and principals.

Goal 2: Encourage Timely, Good-Faith Settlements

Governor Bush believes lawsuits should be viewed as a last resort. That is why the second goal of his federal legal reform is to encourage cases to be ended when a fair settlement is at hand. And when that offer is unreasonably refused, there must be consequences.

A mechanism already exists to facilitate settlements. Under Rule 68 of the Federal Rules of Civil Procedure, if a plaintiff rejects an "offer of judgment" (i.e., a settlement offer) before trial, the plaintiff is liable for the defendant's costs incurred thereafter, if the plaintiff fails to obtain a judgment at trial as favorable as the proposed settlement.

Unfortunately, courts have gutted Rule 68 by interpreting "costs" to exclude the defendant's legal bills. However, in the opinion of the Federal Judicial Center, if "costs" were defined to include reasonable attorneys' fees, and if the Rule were applied to "offers of judgment" by both plaintiffs and defendants, the rule "could contribute significantly" to swifter and less expensive justice.

Therefore, to increase the incentives for good-faith settlements, as President, Governor Bush will:

Enact a "Fair Settlement Rule" to Promote Settlements and Discourage Prolonged Litigation: Legislation will be proposed amending Federal Rule of Civil Procedure 68 to put "teeth" into the Rule's "offer of judgment" regime. The legislation will clarify, among other things, that if either party – defendant or plaintiff – rejects a timely, reasonable, and good-faith settlement offer, and ultimately loses the case or receives a judgment substantially less than the amount offered, that party must pay the other party's litigation costs – including legal fees – that were incurred after the settlement was rejected.

Goal 3: Curb "Forum Shopping" by Improving Access to Federal Courts

Some trial lawyers employ a wide array of technical rules in what is called "forum shopping," to manipulate the courts for tactical advantage. Thus, the third goal of Governor Bush's reform plan is to restore the design of the Framers of the Constitution by improving access to impartial federal courts.

Diversity Litigation

Article III of the Constitution extends the judicial power of the United States to "controversies . . . between citizens of different States." When Congress created the lower federal courts, it provided that these courts could hear such "diversity" cases to prevent local biases against out-of-state enterprises.

The Constitution itself requires only "minimal" diversity – i.e., a federal court has the power to hear a case so long as at least one plaintiff is a citizen of a different state than at least one defendant. However, in 1806 in *Strawbridge v. Curtiss*, the Supreme Court interpreted the diversity statutes to require "complete" diversity. Under this standard, every plaintiff must be from a different state than every defendant. This is the standard that controls under today's diversity statute, which, in addition, requires the amount in controversy to exceed $75,000.

The judicially created "complete diversity" requirement makes it harder for many out-of-state litigants to access the impartial forum of a federal court. Enterprising plaintiffs' lawyers routinely "defeat diversity" in interstate disputes simply by ensuring that at least one plaintiff and one defendant – even in a case involving thousands – are from the same state.

Therefore, to limit forum shopping and improve litigants' access to an impartial federal forum, Governor Bush will introduce legislation to:

Allow Removal of Large Cases From State to Federal Court Where Only "Minimal Diversity" Exists: Governor Bush will amend the diversity jurisdiction statute to allow removal of claims from state to federal court where there is only "minimal diversity" – i.e., where any defendant is from a different state than any plaintiff – so long as the amount in controversy exceeds $500,000.

Raise the Amount in Controversy for Removal Where There is "Complete Diversity": In order to avoid unduly increasing the caseload in federal courts, and because federal diversity jurisdiction is designed for larger interstate disputes, Governor Bush will raise the amount in controversy for complete diversity jurisdiction from $75,000 to $100,000.

State Class Action Lawsuits

Many interstate class actions assert claims that are marginal, at best. But because the cases are brought on behalf of thousands (and sometimes millions) of claimants, the potential exposure is enormous. Clever attorneys carefully draft their cases so that removal to federal court, which under current law requires complete diversity in class actions, is impossible, and they seek out the friendliest state court judge they can find.

Some state courts have proved extremely willing to certify a large class early on in litigation. As a result, many defendants facing state court class actions choose to settle early, even if the case is without merit. These coercive settlements frequently result in huge fees to the attorneys, but minimal benefits (such as largely worthless coupons) to the class members. For example:

- In a class action against a record company to recover the price paid for an album by the rock group Milli Vanilli (that contained the voices of other performers), the court awarded the lawyers $675,000, while the class members received $1 to $3 each.

- In a class action suit against a cereal maker for using oats sprayed with trace amounts of a pesticide, liability was uncontested – but the lawyers were paid nearly $1.75 million for less than six months of work, while class members who happened to save their cereal boxes ended up with coupons to buy more cereal.

In response to the abuse of state class actions, the House passed the Interstate Class Action Jurisdiction Act in September 1999. This Act, which is pending in the Senate, would give federal courts jurisdiction in class action cases involving even minimal diversity – where any member of the proposed class is a citizen of a different state from any defendant.

To curb state class action abuses, as President, Governor Bush will:

Expand Class-Action Removal Rules: Governor Bush will sign the Interstate Class Action Jurisdiction Act, changing the law to give federal courts jurisdiction in class action cases involving even minimal diversity.

Goal 4: Protect Clients Against Unscrupulous Attorneys

Governor Bush's fourth goal of civil justice reform comes directly from the lawyers' code of ethics: a client should not be charged excessive or unreasonable fees. Nevertheless, some unscrupulous attorneys take advantage of unsuspecting and unsophisticated clients and make enormous amounts of money for very little work:

- In a series of related cases involving a fatal school bus accident, the lawyers for the victims' families received an estimated $50 million out of an aggregate settlement of $156 million intended for the families – even though liability was uncontested.

- In a medical malpractice case in which liability was also uncontested, the plaintiff's contingency fee lawyer did nothing but write three letters – and received 40 percent of the injured girl's $400,000 settlement.

Under current law, a client who has been mistreated by his lawyer has very little recourse. He or she can file a complaint with the lawyer's respective state bar, but such complaints rarely result in action. Alternatively, the client can file a separate breach of contract suit in state court against the unethical attorney. This, too, is rarely effective.

Therefore, to ensure that attorneys' fees in federal court are reasonable, and that clients always have recourse when dealing with an unethical lawyer in federal court, Governor Bush will propose legislation to:

<u>Enact a "Client's Bill of Rights:"</u> The "Client's Bill of Rights" will amend the Federal Rules of Civil Procedure to:

- Give federal trial courts express authority to hear challenges to the reasonableness of attorneys' fees from the parties in any case before them.

- Allow the federal trial court to maintain authority to hear fee challenges for up to one year after final judgment.

- Require all attorneys practicing in federal court to give a series of truthful disclosures to their clients, informing them of their ethical obligation to charge reasonable fees, the court's authority to review those fees, and the potential range of those fees.

Goal 5: Require Lawyers Representing Governmental Agencies to be Compensated at a Level Commensurate with Public Service

All lawyers have an ethical responsibility to charge a "reasonable" fee. But Governor Bush believes that when a lawyer contracts with the government to represent the public, that lawyer has, and should have, an even higher obligation to act ethically and be reasonably compensated. In recent years, however, there have been numerous instances of attorneys working for the public and charging grossly excessive fees.

For example, in the recent litigation against the tobacco companies, many lawyers received unprecedented amounts of money for what was, in effect, a public service:

- In Florida, the lawyers will receive $3.43 billion, or 26 percent of the state's $13.2 billion recovery; this translates into an estimated fee of roughly $23,000 an hour.

- In Mississippi, the lawyers will receive $1.43 billion, or 35 percent of the state's $4.1 billion recovery; this represents an estimated fee of about $7,500 an hour.

- In Texas, the lawyers will receive fees totaling $3.3 billion, or 19 percent of the state's $17.4 billion recovery; this translates into an estimated fee of well over $100,000 an hour.

In Texas, no law existed to prevent private lawyers from profiting at the public's expense. Therefore, Governor Bush sought and signed legislation sharply restricting the power of the state Attorney General and state agencies to hire contingency fee lawyers in the future.

At the federal level, mechanisms already exist for ensuring that individuals in a fiduciary capacity abide by a higher ethical standard. For example, Section 4958 of the Tax Code currently penalizes executives of nonprofit organizations who abuse their fiduciary duty by profiting from "excess benefit transactions" – i.e., by paying themselves excessive fees. If they do so, the law imposes a 200 percent penalty on the excess, unless the individual returns it to the nonprofit organization. This penalty is never intended to be collected, but rather to force individuals who abuse positions of trust to disgorge excessive fees.

The reason for the "excess benefit" provision is that, because nonprofits have no profit motive, there is no stockholder check on those payments; nonprofit donors give their money expecting that employees will respect their fiduciary duties. The same principle should apply to individuals working for the government. States and municipalities also have no profit motive to reign in excessive payments, and taxpayers likewise expect public servants to fulfill their fiduciary duties to the people.

As President, to ensure that private lawyers do not profit unreasonably at public expense, Governor Bush will propose legislation to:

<u>Require Private Lawyers Contracting with States and Municipalities to Return Excessive Fees to Their Governmental Clients</u>: The legislation will extend the "excess benefit" provisions of the tax code to private lawyers who contract with states and municipalities. As a result, any compensation collected in excess of a reasonable fee will have to be returned to the state or city that hired the private lawyers. The reasonableness of the fees will be assessed using the standard judicial "lodestar" method of multiplying the hours worked by a reasonable hourly rate and any appropriate risk factor.

<u>Prohibit the Federal Government from Hiring Contingency Fee Lawyers</u>: As President, Governor Bush will issue an Executive Order prohibiting the federal government from hiring private lawyers on anything other than an hourly basis.

WHAT OTHERS SAY

"Bush Proposes a Much Leaner Government"

Maria L. La Ganga, <u>Los Angeles Times</u>, 6/10/00

"If Bush is elected President, he… will… push for change and achieve success by building coalitions across party lines…"

Norman Ornstein, <u>USA Today</u>, 6/8/00

"There is a good reason why Governor Bush is forging ahead in this race: He is becoming the candidate of fresh ideas."

David Gergen, <u>U.S. News and World Report</u>, 6/5/00

"Bush made...concrete proposals [to reform government]..."
Robert Zausner, <u>Philadelphia Inquirer</u>, 6/9/00

"...Paul Light, vice president of the centrist Brookings Institution in Washington and a frequent commentator on government reform, applauded many of Bush's proposals."
Maria L. La Ganga, <u>Los Angeles Times</u>, 6/09/00

"Bush...called for more cooperation between the White House and Congress in preparing the federal budget, approving presidential appointees and eliminating pork barrel spending."
Marsha Mercer, <u>The Tampa Tribune</u>, 6/10/00

"Bush...advocates a limited but active role for government..."
John C. Henry, <u>The Houston Chronicle</u>, 6/10/00

"...Governor George W. Bush proposed a wide-ranging overhaul of the federal budget process today in an effort to avoid the bitter annual standoff between Congress and the president over taxes and spending."
Allison Mitchell, <u>The New York Times</u>, 6/9/00

"'There is something different, going on here with George W.,' said Brian Lunde, former Democratic National Committee executive director. 'He is a powerful, new consensus-building leader...'"
Ralph Z. Hallow, <u>The Washington Times</u>, 6/9/00

"Mr. Bush is dominating the policy debate...[Bush] has seized on the opportunities to appear both bipartisan and statesmanlike..."
<u>The Economist</u>, 6/3/00

PART VI
National Strength and Purpose

The current President inherited a military ready for the dangers and challenges facing our country. The next President will inherit a military in serious decline.

At the Citadel almost a year ago, I set forth my vision of a modern military force – well-trained, well-supplied, and well-served by its Commander-in-Chief. But that is only the beginning. As I argued in subsequent speeches, we must return clarity, credibility, and purpose to American foreign policy.

We must also repair long-neglected alliances, supporting our friends in times of calm, so that we can rely on them in times of trouble.

We must use the power of our market to extend trade across the world, and with it democracy, pursuing what Ronald Reagan called a forward strategy for freedom.

We must keep faith with the veterans who gave honorable service to our country.

We must also move beyond the strategic assumptions that served us well during the Cold War but are no longer relevant. To defend our country against the new threats of the 21st century, we must build effective missile defenses; and, at the same time, seize the opportunity to reduce significantly our nuclear stockpiles.

These steps, taken together, will lead us toward a stronger, more secure, and more confident America.

Defense:
A Period of Consequences

The Citadel
Charleston, South Carolina

September 23, 1999

It is good to be with you. The Citadel is a place of pride and
tradition. A place where standards are high and discipline is strong
and leaders are born. The men, and now women, of this institution
represent a spirit of honor and accomplishment. And I am proud
to be with you.

This is a special place to talk about the future of our military,
because many of you will shape it. These are times of change and
challenge. But you will always return to the values you learned
here.

Three months ago, in Providence, Rhode Island, a man rose to
take the oath of American citizenship. He was one of many – but
his case was different. His name is Sergei Khruschev, a former
weapons scientist – and son of the Soviet leader. Sometimes history's great epochs are summed up in small events. The threat of the
Cold War was captured in Nikita Khruschev's vow to America, "We
will bury you." The story closes, in this final footnote to that age,
with America saying to his own son, "We welcome you."

It is a reminder of what this country and its allies have accomplished in a century of struggle. Young Americans in uniform –
today's veterans – wrote history with the bold strokes of their
courage. Their character was tested in death marches and jungle
firefights and desert battles. They left long rows of crosses and

Stars of David, fighting for people they did not know, and a future they would not see. And, in the end, they won an epic struggle to save liberty itself.

Those who want to lead America accept two obligations. One is to use our military power wisely, remembering the costs of war. The other is to honor our commitments to veterans who have paid those costs.

Our world, shaped by American courage, power and wisdom, now echoes with American ideals. We won a victory, not just for a nation, but for a vision. A vision of freedom and individual dignity – defended by democracy, nurtured by free markets, spread by information technology, carried to the world by free trade. The advance of freedom – from Asia to Latin America to East and Central Europe – is creating the conditions for peace.

For America, this is a time of unrivaled military power, economic promise, and cultural influence. It is, in Franklin Roosevelt's phrase, "the peace of overwhelming victory."

Now a new generation of American leaders will determine how that power and influence are used – a generation after the hard but clear struggle against an evil empire. Our challenge is not as obvious, but just as noble: To turn these years of influence into decades of peace.

But peace is not ordained, it is earned. It is not a harbor where we rest, it is a voyage we must chart. Even in this time of hope and confidence, we can see the signs of uncertainty.

We see the contagious spread of missile technology and weapons of mass destruction. We know that this era of American preeminence is also an era of car bombers and plutonium merchants and cyber terrorists and drug cartels and unbalanced dictators – all the unconventional and invisible threats of new technologies and old hatreds. These challenges can be overcome, but they can not be ignored.

Building a durable peace will require strong alliances, expanding trade and confident diplomacy. It will require tough realism in our dealings with China and Russia. It will require firmness with regimes like North Korea and Iraq – regimes that hate our values and resent our success. I will address all these priorities in the future. But I want to begin with the foundation of our peace – a strong, capable and modern military.

The American armed forces have an irreplaceable role in the world. They give confidence to our allies; deter the aggression of our enemies; and allow our nation to shape a stable peace. The common defense is the sworn duty and chief responsibility of a president. And, if elected, I will set three goals: I will renew the bond of trust between the American president and the American military. I will defend the American people against missiles and terror. And I will begin creating the military of the next century.

Our military is without peer, but it is not without problems.

The men and women of our armed forces stand in the best tradition of the citizen soldier, who for two centuries has kept our country safe and free. All are volunteers – active, Reserve and Guard – who willingly accept the burdens and dangers of service.

Volunteers who demonstrate the highest form of citizenship.

I have great faith in those who serve our nation – in the temper of their will and the quality of their spirit. These are men and women who love their country more than their comfort. Men and women who have never failed us, wherever there is honor to be earned, or interests defended. But even the highest morale is eventually undermined by back-to-back deployments, poor pay, shortages of spare parts and equipment, and rapidly declining readiness.

Not since the years before Pearl Harbor has our investment in national defense been so low as a percentage of GNP. Yet rarely has our military been so freely used – an average of one deployment every nine weeks in the last few years. Since the end of the Cold War, our ground forces have been deployed more frequently, while our defense budget has fallen by nearly 40 percent.

Something has to give, and it's giving. Resources are over-stretched. Frustration is up, as families are separated and strained. Morale is down. Recruitment is more difficult. And many of our best people in the military are headed for civilian life. In 1998, the Air Force missed its reenlistment goals for the first time since 1981. Army recruiting is at a 20 year low.

Consider a few facts: Thousands of members of the armed forces are on food stamps. Last year, more than $21 million worth of WIC vouchers – the Women, Infants and Children program – were redeemed at military commissaries. Many others in uniform get Army Emergency Relief or depend on their parents.

This is not the way that a great nation should reward courage and idealism. It is ungrateful, it is unwise and it is unacceptable.

This Administration wants things both ways: To command great forces, without supporting them. To launch today's new causes, with little thought of tomorrow's consequences.

A volunteer military has only two paths. It can lower its standards to fill its ranks. Or it can inspire the best and brightest to join and stay.

This starts with better pay, better treatment and better training. Recently, after years of neglect, a significant pay raise was finally passed. My first budget will go further – adding a billion dollars in salary increases. We also will provide targeted bonuses for those with special skills. Two-thirds of military family housing units are now substandard, and they must be renovated. And we must improve the quality of training at our bases and national training centers. Shortfalls on the proving ground become disasters on the battlefield.

But our military requires more than good treatment. It needs the rallying point of a defining mission. And that mission is to deter wars – and win wars when deterrence fails. Sending our military on vague, aimless and endless deployments is the swift solvent of morale.

As President, I will order an immediate review of our overseas deployments – in dozens of countries. The longstanding commitments we have made to our allies are the strong foundation of our current peace. I will keep these pledges to defend friends from aggression. The problem comes with open-ended deployments and unclear military missions. In these cases we will ask, "What is our goal, can it be met, and when do we leave?" As I've said before, I will work hard to find political solutions that allow an orderly and timely withdrawal from places like Kosovo and Bosnia. We will encourage our allies to take a broader role. We will not be hasty. But we will not be permanent peacekeepers, dividing warring parties. This is not our strength or our calling.

America will not retreat from the world. On the contrary, I will replace diffuse commitments with focused ones. I will replace uncertain missions with well-defined objectives. This will preserve the resources of American power and public will. The presence of American forces overseas is one of the most profound symbols of our commitment to allies and friends. And our allies know that if America is committed everywhere, our commitments are everywhere suspect. We must be selective in the use of our military, precisely because America has other great responsibilities that cannot be slighted or compromised. And this review of our deployments will also reduce the tension on an overstretched military. Nothing would be better for morale than clarity and focus from the commander-in-chief.

My second goal is to build America's defenses on the troubled frontiers of technology and terror. The protection of America itself will assume a high priority in a new century. Once a strategic afterthought, homeland defense has become an urgent duty.

For most of our history, America felt safe behind two great oceans. But with the spread of technology, distance no longer means security. North Korea is proving that even a poor and backward country, in the hands of a tyrant, can reach across oceans to threaten us. It has developed missiles capable of hitting Hawaii and Alaska. Iran has made rapid strides in its missile program, and Iraq persists in a race to do the same. In 1996, after some tension over Taiwan, a Chinese general reminded America that China possesses the means to incinerate Los Angeles with nuclear missiles.

Add to this the threat of biological, chemical and nuclear terrorism – barbarism emboldened by technology. These weapons can be delivered, not just by ballistic missiles, but by everything from airplanes to cruise missiles, from shipping containers to suitcases. And consider the prospect of information warfare, in which hacker terrorists may try to disrupt finance, communication, transportation and public health.

Let me be clear. Our first line of defense is a simple message: Every group or nation must know, if they sponsor such attacks, our response will be devastating.

But we must do more. At the earliest possible date, my Administration will deploy anti-ballistic missile systems, both theater and national, to guard against attack and blackmail. To make this possible, we will offer Russia the necessary amendments to the anti-ballistic missile treaty – an artifact of Cold War confrontation. Both sides know that we live in a different world from 1972, when that treaty was signed. If Russia refuses the changes we propose, we will give prompt notice, under the provisions of the treaty, that we can no longer be a party to it. I will have a solemn obligation to protect the American people and our allies, not to protect arms control agreements signed almost 30 years ago.

We will defend the American homeland by strengthening our intelligence community – focusing on human intelligence and the early detection of terrorist operations both here and abroad. And when direct threats to America are discovered, I know that the best defense can be a strong and swift offense – including the use of Special Operations Forces and long-range strike capabilities.

And there is more to be done preparing here at home. I will

put a high priority on detecting and responding to terrorism on our soil. The federal government must take this threat seriously – working closely with researchers and industry to increase surveillance and develop treatments for chemical and biological agents.

But defending our nation is just the beginning of our challenge. My third goal is to take advantage of a tremendous opportunity – given few nations in history – to extend the current peace into the far realm of the future. A chance to project America's peaceful influence, not just across the world, but across the years.

This opportunity is created by a revolution in the technology of war. Power is increasingly defined, not by mass or size, but by mobility and swiftness. Influence is measured in information, safety is gained in stealth, and force is projected on the long arc of precision-guided weapons. This revolution perfectly matches the strengths of our country – the skill of our people and the superiority of our technology. The best way to keep the peace is to redefine war on our terms.

Yet today our military is still organized more for Cold War threats than for the challenges of a new century – for industrial age operations, rather than for information age battles. There is almost no relationship between our budget priorities and a strategic vision. The last seven years have been wasted in inertia and idle talk. Now we must shape the future with new concepts, new strategies, new resolve.

In the late 1930s, as Britain refused to adapt to the new realities of war, Winston Churchill observed, "The era of procrastination, of half-measures, of soothing and baffling expedients, of delays, is coming to a close. In its place we are entering a period of consequences."

Our military and our nation are entering another period of consequences – a time of rapid change and momentous choices.

As President, I will begin an immediate, comprehensive review of our military – the structure of its forces, the state of its strategy, the priorities of its procurement – conducted by a leadership team under the Secretary of Defense. I will give the Secretary a broad mandate – to challenge the status quo and envision a new architecture of American defense for decades to come. We will modernize some existing weapons and equipment, necessary for current tasks. But our relative peace allows us to do this selectively. The real goal is to move beyond marginal improvements – to replace existing programs with new technologies and strategies. To use this window of opportunity to skip a generation of technology. This will require spending more – and spending more wisely.

We know that power, in the future, will be projected in different ways.

The Gulf War was a stunning victory. But it took six months of planning and transport to summon our fleets and divisions and position them for battle.

In the future, we are unlikely to have that kind of time. Enemy ballistic and cruise missiles and weapons of mass destruction may make such operations difficult. Satellite technology, commercially available, may reveal to potential enemies the location of our ships and troops. We may not have months to transport massive divisions to waiting bases, or to build new infrastructure on site.

Our forces in the next century must be agile, lethal, readily deployable, and require a minimum of logistical support. We must be able to project our power over long distances, in days or weeks rather than months. Our military must be able to identify targets by a variety of means – from a Marine patrol to a satellite. Then be able to destroy those targets almost instantly, with an array of weapons, from a submarine-launched cruise missile, to mobile long-range artillery.

On land, our heavy forces must be lighter. Our light forces must be more lethal. All must be easier to deploy. And these forces must be organized in smaller, more agile formations, rather than cumbersome divisions.

On the seas, we need to pursue promising ideas like the arsenal ship – a stealthy ship packed with long-range missiles to destroy targets from great distances.

In the air, we must be able to strike from across the world with pinpoint accuracy – with long-range aircraft and perhaps with unmanned systems.

In space, we must be able to protect our network of satellites, essential to the flow of our commerce and the defense of our country.

All this will require a new spirit of innovation. Many officers have expressed their impatience with a widespread, bureaucratic mindset that frustrates creativity. I will encourage a culture of command where change is welcomed and rewarded, not dreaded. I will ensure that visionary leaders who take risks are recognized and promoted.

When our comprehensive review is complete, I will expect the military's budget priorities to match our strategic vision – not the particular visions of the services, but a joint vision for change. I will earmark at least 20 percent of the procurement budget for acquisition programs that propel America generations ahead in military technology. And I will direct the Secretary of Defense to allocate these funds to the services that prove most effective in developing new programs that do so. I intend to force new thinking and hard choices.

The transformation of our military will require a new and greater emphasis on research and development. So I will also commit an additional $20 billion to defense R&D between the time I take office and 2006.

Even if I am elected, I will not command the new military we create. That will be left to a president who comes after me. The results of our effort will not be seen for many years. The outcome of great battles is often determined by decisions on funding and technology made decades before, in the quiet days of peace. But these choices on spending and strategy either support the young men and women who must fight the future's wars – or betray their lives and squander their valor.

I am under no illusions. I know that transforming our military is a massive undertaking. When President Lincoln was attempting to organize his army, he compared the job to bailing out the Potomac River with a teaspoon. What I propose will be impossible without allies – both in the military and in the Congress.

To the military I say: We intend to change your structure, but we will respect your culture. Our military culture was formed by generations of trial and tradition – codes and loyalties born of two centuries' worth of experience.

For the changes I seek, I will count on these codes and loyalties. I will count on a culture that prizes duty, welcomes clear orders, accepts sacrifice, and is devoted above all to the defense of the United States.

I will count on these values, because I will challenge our military to reform itself in fundamental ways.

To the Congress I say: Join me in creating a new strategic vision for our military – a set of goals that will take precedence over the narrow interests of states and regions. I will reach out to reform-minded members of Congress, particularly to overturn laws and regulations that discourage outsourcing and undermine efficiency. Our military must embrace the productivity revolution that has transformed American business. And once a new strategy is clear, I will confront the Congress when it uses the defense budget as a source of pork or patronage.

Moments of national opportunity are either seized or lost, and the consequences reach across decades. Our opportunity is here – to show that a new generation can renew America's purpose.

I know this is a world of hard choices and new tasks. A world of terror and missiles and madmen. A world requiring, not just might, but wisdom.

But my generation is fortunate. In the world of our fathers, we have seen how America should conduct itself. We have seen leaders who fought a world war and organized the peace. We have seen power exercised without swagger and influence displayed without bluster. We have seen the modesty of true strength, the humility of real greatness. We have seen American power tempered by American character. And I have seen all of this personally and closely and clearly.

Now comes our time of testing. Our measure is taken, not only by what we have and use, but what we build and leave behind. And nothing this generation could ever build will matter more than the means to defend our nation and extend our peace.

Position Paper
Defense: A Period of Consequences
September 23, 1999

"Today our military is still organized more for Cold War threats than for the challenges of a new century... There is almost no relationship between our budget priorities and a strategic vision. The last seven years have been wasted in inertia and idle talk. Now we must shape the future with new concepts, new strategies, new resolve...We are entering 'a period of consequences.'"

Governor George W. Bush

EXECUTIVE SUMMARY

Governor Bush believes that a strong, capable and modern military is essential to defend our nation, advance U.S. interests, and extend our peace. As President, he will set three goals for our nation's defense.

To Renew the Bond of Trust Between the President and the Military, Governor Bush will:

- Respect the military's tradition and culture, while changing its structure.

- Increase by $1 billion the currently planned military pay raise to encourage the best and brightest to enlist – and reenlist – in the armed forces.

- Renovate substandard military housing and improve military training.

- Maintain longstanding U.S. commitments, but order an immediate review of overseas deployments in dozens of countries, with the aim of replacing uncertain missions with well-defined objectives.

To Defend the American Homeland, Governor Bush will:

- Deter terrorist attacks by ensuring every group or nation understands if they sponsor attacks, the U.S. response will be devastating.

- Deploy both national and theater anti-ballistic missile defenses, as soon as possible.

- Amend the ABM Treaty, or, if Russia fails to agree, withdraw from it.

- Strengthen our intelligence community's ability to detect terrorist threats, and develop long-range strike capabilities to eliminate such threats before they arise.

- Promote cooperation with our allies, who should share the burden of defense.

To Begin to Create the Military of the Future, Governor Bush will:

- Order a comprehensive military review to develop a new architecture for American defense designed to meet the challenges of the next century.

- Seize the opportunity to skip a generation of weapons, not merely improving existing systems, but replacing them with a new generation of technology: land forces that are lighter but more lethal, air power – manned or unmanned – that can accurately strike across long distances, and naval power that packs a bigger punch in smaller platforms.

- Encourage a spirit of innovation and experimentation within the military.

- Earmark at least 20 percent of the procurement budget for acquisition programs that propel America generations ahead in military technology.

- Increase defense R&D spending by at least $20 billion from FY2002 to FY2006.

The State of Our Armed Forces: Overextended and Unprepared for the Future

Governor Bush believes a strong, capable, modern military is the foundation of the peace we enjoy today and hope to extend for future generations. Unfortunately, the Clinton-Gore Administration has presided over a debilitating mix of increased troop deployments and decreased defense spending:

- Since the end of the Cold War, overseas deployments of U.S. troops have increased dramatically. During the Clinton-Gore Administration, our military has undertaken an average of one new deployment every nine weeks.

- In the same period, U.S. defense spending has declined by nearly 40 percent. It is now at its lowest level as a percentage of GNP than at any time since 1940. This has led to what the Administration's own Under Secretary of Defense has called a budgetary "death spiral" – pouring more and more money into older and older equipment, draining funds from modernization.

Thus, U.S. forces are overused and underfunded precisely when they are confronted by a host of new threats and challenges: the spread of weapons of mass destruction, the rise of cyberterrorism, the proliferation of missile technology. The result is damaged morale, and a military force unprepared to deal with the threats of a new century.

Governor Bush believes that America's military is faced with a moment of opportunity – an opportunity to transform itself, and thus ensure peace for generations. Seizing this opportunity will require more spending, but equally as important, spending more wisely. The right choices must be made to repair morale, protect America, and create a military capable of meeting the challenges of the 21st Century. Thus, as President, Governor Bush will:

- Renew the bond of trust between the President and the military by increasing pay, improving housing, and insisting that deployments have well-defined objectives;

- Defend the American people against missiles and terrorists; and

- Begin to create the military of the future – lethal, agile, easier to deploy – by capitalizing on new technologies.

In implementing these goals, Governor Bush will challenge the military to transform itself. He will respect the military's tradition and culture, while changing its structure and encouraging a spirit of innovation.

Goal 1. Renew the Bond of Trust Between the President and the Military

The current Administration's combination of frequent but unfocused deployments and insufficient resources has led to lower morale and declining enlistment. Indeed, no aspect of the current neglect of the nation's armed forces is more worrisome than the effect on the men and women in uniform – and their families – who are forced to accept low pay and inadequate housing:

- The overall gap between civilian and military pay stands at more than 13 percent.

- According to the most recent survey, almost 12,000 members of the armed forces have been forced to rely on food stamps; others receive Women, Infants and Children funding or Army Emergency Relief – or depend on their parents.

- One-third of military families are housed in approximately 320,000 units, 66 percent of which are substandard, according to the Chairman of the Joint Chiefs of Staff.

In addition to dealing with low pay and poor housing, the men and women of the military are frequently subjected to deployments that are too often open-ended and lacking in clear objectives. This has produced serious morale problems that have triggered a growing crisis in retention and a shortage of skilled personnel.

As President, Governor Bush will renew the bond of trust between the Oval Office and America's men and women in uniform. Much as Ronald Reagan restored the attraction of military life for individuals and families.

Governor Bush will focus on making the military a magnet for the best and brightest in America and, as President, he will:

Increase by $1 Billion the Planned Military Pay Raise: In a Bush Administration, military pay will be increased by $1 billion – or an average of about $750 per active duty service member – over and above the pay increase recently passed by Congress. These additional funds will help narrow the overall difference in compensation between the armed forces and the civilian sector. Governor Bush will also increase targeted reenlistment bonuses and special pay for critical specialties. This will further reduce the pay gap for individuals with skills in high demand, such as pilots, computer programmers, and engineers.

Improve Military Housing: As President, Governor Bush will work with Congress to ensure that service members and their families no longer have to tolerate substandard housing. In some cases, this will involve renovation or construction of barracks or family housing units. In other cases, it will mean increasing basic housing allowances, especially in high cost areas.

Improve Military Training: Despite recent increases, unfunded requirements remain in training center facilities, equipment and operations. As President, Governor Bush will work with Congress to ensure that such shortfalls are addressed and the decline in the quality and level of training of our men and women in uniform is reversed.

Order an Immediate Review of Overseas Deployments: As President, Governor Bush will pledge to maintain longstanding commitments, but will order a review of other overseas deployments. To improve morale and preserve resources for important interests, diffuse commitments will be replaced with focused ones. National security planners will scrutinize open-ended deployments, reassess U.S. goals, and ascertain whether they can be met. For example, as he has previously stated, he will work hard as President for political solutions that allow an orderly and timely withdrawal from places like Kosovo and Bosnia.

Goal 2. Defend the American Homeland

The second pillar of Governor Bush's plan for America's defense is to protect America itself from attack. Today, over two dozen countries have ballistic missiles. A number of them – including North Korea, Iran, and Iraq – are developing missiles that may ultimately reach intercontinental range. Given this new reality, the U.S. government can no longer afford to drag its feet on building and deploying a missile defense system; nor can it continue to allow Cold War arms control agreements to restrict America's ability to defend itself and its allies.

Governor Bush also understands that the defense of our homeland involves much more than protection against missiles. A Congressionally appointed blue-ribbon commission recently concluded that the United States is unprepared to counter the rampant proliferation of nuclear, chemical, and biological weapons around the world. More important, the United States remains vulnerable to a state or terrorist group using those weapons.

To improve the nation's security against missile attack and bolster America's homeland defense, Governor Bush will:

Deter Attacks Against the United States: As President, Governor Bush will deter terrorist attacks by ensuring that every group or nation understands that if they sponsor such attacks, America's response will be devastating.

Deploy Ballistic Missile Defenses: Governor Bush will accelerate research on, and deployment of, both national and theater missile defenses, as soon as possible.

Amend the ABM Treaty, or Withdraw From It: The United States should offer Russia necessary amendments to the Cold War-era Anti-Ballistic Missile (ABM) Treaty to permit deployment of effective national and theater missile defenses. If Russia refuses those changes, the United States should give prompt notice, under the treaty, that we will withdraw from it.

Strengthen U.S. Intelligence Capabilities: As President, Governor Bush will make it a priority to strengthen U.S. intelligence resources, focusing on human intelligence and the early detection of threats to the homeland. Once such threats are detected, the best defense will be a good offense, including the use of Special Operations Forces and long-range strike capabilities.

Improve Cooperation with U.S. Allies: To counter emerging threats, the United States will need improved cooperation with its allies. They face many of the same threats as the United States, and should share in the burden of defense.

Goal 3. Begin Creating the Military of the Future

The third part of Governor Bush's plan for the nation's defense is to use the present window of relative peace to skip a generation of weapons systems and strategies. Today our military is still organized more for Cold War threats than for the challenges of a new century. What is needed is a new architecture for American defense – an architecture that will permit the U.S. to project power swiftly under new conditions. As in the past, the United States will need modern and well-trained forces, sufficient in size to project power rapidly to key regions of the world. Yet, the need to project power will require very different kinds of forces from those in the past:

- First, in the future, adversaries with access to ballistic and cruise missiles, weapons of mass destruction, and other technologies will attempt to deny the United States the enormous advantages of its forward bases and logistics capabilities.

- Second, enemy tactics against American forces will likely be directed at the weakest links in our extension of power. Airfields and ports critical to the flow of American forces and materiel will be targeted.

409

- Third, the enemy might choose environments in which to fight where American forces that depend on large amounts of logistical support will be at a disadvantage.

To meet such future challenges, Governor Bush believes that our military must develop the capability for very different sorts of forces for power projection. Therefore, as President, Governor Bush will:

Order a Review of U.S. Military Force Structure, Strategy, and Procurement: The review will be conducted by a leadership team under the Secretary of Defense that Governor Bush will charge with creating the military of the future – lethal, agile, easier to deploy. While some existing weapons will need to be modernized, the larger goal will be to skip a generation of technology, replacing existing systems with new technologies and strategies:

- Land Forces: On land, U.S. heavy armored forces must be lighter, and light forces must be made more lethal; all must be easier to deploy.

- Naval Forces: On the seas, U.S. carriers must be complemented by capable smaller platforms. That is why Governor Bush will pursue promising ideas such as the arsenal ship – a stealthy ship loaded with long-range missiles able to destroy targets accurately from great distances.

- Air Power: In the air, a larger portion of the force of the future must be able to strike from across the world with pinpoint accuracy using long-range aircraft – both manned and unmanned. Thus, as President, Governor Bush will order a review of the entire U.S. aircraft program, encompassing not only ongoing shorter-range fighter programs, but also bomber and support aircraft needs.

- Space and Information Systems: The military of tomorrow must also be as adept at operating in space and the information environment as it has been on land, sea, and in the air. Space-based assets will aid in projecting power and protecting the homeland. In addition, America must be prepared not only to defend its vulnerable infrastructure against cyber attacks, but also to develop offensive information warfare capabilities.

Once the comprehensive review is complete, Governor Bush will move aggressively to create the military of the future. Specifically, he will:

<u>Earmark at Least 20 Percent of the Procurement Budget to Address Future Challenges</u>: The military's budget priorities must match the new strategic vision. As President, Governor Bush will direct the Secretary of Defense to earmark at least 20 percent of the total procurement budget for acquisition programs that propel America generations ahead in military technology. To promote needed inter-service cooperation and reduce costly redundancy, the Secretary of Defense, not individual services, will set the spending priorities.

<u>Encourage a Spirit of Innovation</u>: Developing and leading the military of the future will require a new spirit of innovation. Thus, as President, Governor Bush will encourage a culture of command, and ensure that visionary leaders are recognized and promoted.

<u>Increase Defense R&D Spending by at Least $20 Billion</u>: Transforming the military and realizing the promise of new technology, will require a substantially greater emphasis on research and development. Thus, R&D spending will be increased by at least $20 billion from FY2002 to FY2006. Furthermore, to promote a culture of innovation, the military will be strongly encouraged to "wildcat" – to try various methods and technologies to solve operational problems. Military commanders and service chiefs will be judged on how well they experiment to meet the new operational challenges envisioned in the future.

<u>Ask Congress to Join in Creating a New Strategic Vision</u>: As President, Governor Bush will reach out to reform-minded members of Congress. He will also confront Congress when it uses the defense budget as a source of pork or patronage.

Foreign Policy:
A Distinctly American Internationalism

The Ronald Reagan Presidential Library
Simi Valley, California

November 19, 1999

It is an honor to be with you at the Reagan Library. Thank you Secretary Shultz for your decades of service to America – and for your kindness and counsel over the last several months. And thank you Mrs. Reagan for this invitation – and for your example of loyalty and love and courage.

My wife Laura says that behind every great man there is a surprised woman. But, Mrs. Reagan, you were never surprised by the greatness of your husband. You believed it from the start. And now the rest of the world sees him as you always have – as a hero in the American story. A story in which a single individual can shape history. A story in which evil is real, but courage and decency triumph.

We live in the nation President Reagan restored, and the world he helped to save. A world of nations reunited and tyrants humbled. A world of prisoners released and exiles come home. And today there is a prayer shared by free people everywhere: God bless you, Ronald Reagan.

Two months ago, at the Citadel in South Carolina, I talked about American defense. This must be the first focus of a president, because it is his first duty to the Constitution. Even in this time of pride and promise, America has determined enemies, who hate our values and resent our success – terrorists and crime syndicates and drug cartels and unbalanced dictators. The Empire has passed, but evil remains.

We must protect our homeland and our allies against missiles and terror and blackmail.

We must restore the morale of our military – squandered by shrinking resources and multiplying missions – with better training, better treatment and better pay.

And we must master the new technology of war – to extend our peaceful influence, not just across the world, but across the years.

In the defense of our nation, a president must be a clear-eyed realist. There are limits to the smiles and scowls of diplomacy. Armies and missiles are not stopped by stiff notes of condemnation. They are held in check by strength and purpose and the promise of swift punishment.

But there is more to say, because military power is not the final measure of might. Our realism must make a place for the human spirit.

This spirit, in our time, has caused dictators to fear and empires to fall. And it has left an honor roll of courage and idealism: Sharansky, Havel, Walesa, Mandela. The most powerful force in the world is not a weapon or a nation but a truth: that we are spiritual beings, and that freedom is "the soul's right to breathe."

In the dark days of 1941 – the low point of our modern epic – there were about a dozen democracies left on the planet. Entering a new century, there are nearly 120. There is a direction in events, a current in our times. "Depend on it," said Edmund Burke. "The lovers of freedom will be free."

America cherishes that freedom, but we do not own it. We value the elegant structures of our own democracy – but realize that, in other societies, the architecture will vary. We propose our principles, we must not impose our culture.

Yet the basic principles of human freedom and dignity are universal. People should be able to say what they think. Worship as they wish. Elect those who govern them. These ideals have proven their power on every continent. In former colonies – and the nations that ruled them. Among the allies of World War II – and the countries they vanquished. And these ideals are equally valid north of the 38th parallel. They are just as true in the Pearl River Delta. They remain true 90 miles from our shores, on an island prison, ruled by a revolutionary relic.

Some have tried to pose a choice between American ideals and American interests – between who we are and how we act. But the choice is false. America, by decision and destiny, promotes political freedom – and gains the most when democracy advances. America believes in free markets and free trade – and benefits most when markets are opened. America is a peaceful power – and gains the greatest dividend from democratic stability. Precisely because we have no territorial objectives, our gains are not measured in the losses of others. They are counted in the conflicts we avert, the prosperity we share and the peace we extend.

Sometimes this balance takes time to achieve – and requires us to deal with nations that do not share our values. Sometimes the defenders of freedom must show patience as well as resolution. But that patience comes of confidence, not compromise. We believe, with George Washington, that "Liberty, when it begins to take root, is a plant of rapid growth." And we firmly believe our nation is on the right side of history – the side of man's dignity and God's justice.

Few nations have been given the advantages and opportunities of our own. Few have been more powerful as a country, or more successful as a cause. But there are risks, even for the powerful. "I have many reasons to be optimistic," said Pericles in the golden age of Athens. "Indeed, I am more afraid of our own blunders than of the enemy's devices."

America's first temptation is withdrawal – to build a proud tower of protectionism and isolation.

In a world that depends on America to reconcile old rivals and balance ancient ambitions, this is the shortcut to chaos. It is an approach that abandons our allies, and our ideals. The vacuum left by America's retreat would invite challenges to our power. And the result, in the long run, would be a stagnant America and a savage world.

American foreign policy cannot be founded on fear. Fear that American workers can't compete. Fear that America will corrupt the world – or be corrupted by it. This fear has no place in the party of Reagan, or in the party of Truman. In times of peril, our nation did not shrink from leadership. At this moment of opportunity, I have no intention of betraying American interests, American obligations and American honor.

America's second temptation is drift – for our nation to move from crisis to crisis like a cork in a current.

Unless a president sets his own priorities, his priorities will be set by others – by adversaries, or the crisis of the moment, live on CNN. American policy can become random and reactive – untethered to the interests of our country.

America must be involved in the world. But that does not mean our military is the answer to every difficult foreign policy situation – a substitute for strategy. American internationalism should not mean action without vision, activity without priority, and missions without end – an approach that squanders American will and drains American energy.

American foreign policy must be more than the management of crisis. It must have a great and guiding goal: to turn this time of American influence into generations of democratic peace.

This is accomplished by concentrating on enduring national interests. And these are my priorities. An American president should work with our strong democratic allies in Europe and Asia to extend the peace. He should promote a fully democratic Western Hemisphere, bound together by free trade. He should defend

415

America's interests in the Persian Gulf and advance peace in the Middle East, based upon a secure Israel. He must check the contagious spread of weapons of mass destruction, and the means to deliver them. He must lead toward a world that trades in freedom. And he must pursue all these goals with focus, patience and strength.

I will address these responsibilities as this campaign continues. To each, I bring the same approach: A distinctly American internationalism. Idealism, without illusions. Confidence, without conceit. Realism, in the service of American ideals.

Today I want to talk about Europe and Asia...the world's strategic heartland...our greatest priority. Home of long-time allies, and looming rivals. Behind the United States, Eurasia has the next six largest economies. The next six largest military budgets.

The Eurasian landmass, in our century, has seen the indignities of colonialism and the excesses of nationalism. Its people have been sacrificed to brutal wars and totalitarian ambitions. America has discovered, again and again, that our history is inseparable from their tragedy. And we are rediscovering that our interests are served by their success.

In this immense region, we are guided, not by an ambition, but by a vision. A vision in which no great power, or coalition of great powers, dominates or endangers our friends. In which America encourages stability from a position of strength. A vision in which people and capital and information can move freely, creating bonds of progress, ties of culture and momentum toward democracy.

This is different from the trumpet call of the Cold War. We are no longer fighting a great enemy, we are asserting a great principle: that the talents and dreams of average people – their warm human hopes and loves – should be rewarded by freedom and protected by peace. We are defending the nobility of normal lives, lived in obedience to God and conscience, not to government.

The challenge comes because two of Eurasia's greatest powers

416

– China and Russia – are powers in transition. And it is difficult to know their intentions when they do not know their own futures. If they become America's friends, that friendship will steady the world. But if not, the peace we seek may not be found.

China, in particular, has taken different shapes in different eyes at different times. An empire to be divided. A door to be opened. A model of collective conformity. A diplomatic card to be played. One year, it is said to be run by "the butchers of Beijing." A few years later, the same administration pronounces it a "strategic partner."

We must see China clearly – not through the filters of posturing and partisanship. China is rising, and that is inevitable. Here, our interests are plain: We welcome a free and prosperous China. We predict no conflict. We intend no threat. And there are areas where we must try to cooperate: preventing the spread of weapons of mass destruction...attaining peace on the Korean peninsula.

Yet the conduct of China's government can be alarming abroad, and appalling at home. Beijing has been investing its growing wealth in strategic nuclear weapons...new ballistic missiles...a blue-water navy and a long-range airforce. It is an espionage threat to our country. Meanwhile, the State Department has reported that "all public dissent against the party and government [has been] effectively silenced" – a tragic achievement in a nation of 1.2 billion people. China's government is an enemy of religious freedom and a sponsor of forced abortion – policies without reason and without mercy.

All of these facts must be squarely faced. China is a competitor, not a strategic partner. We must deal with China without ill-will – but without illusions.

By the same token, that regime must have no illusions about American power and purpose. As Dean Rusk observed during the Cold War, "It is not healthy for a regime...to incur, by their lawlessness and aggressive conduct, the implacable opposition of the

417

American people."

We must show American power and purpose in strong support for our Asian friends and allies – for democratic South Korea across the Yellow Sea...for democratic Japan and the Philippines across the China seas...for democratic Australia and Thailand. This means keeping our pledge to deter aggression against the Republic of Korea, and strengthening security ties with Japan. This means expanding theater missile defenses among our allies.

And this means honoring our promises to the people of Taiwan. We do not deny there is one China. But we deny the right of Beijing to impose its rule on a free people. As I've said before, we will help Taiwan to defend itself.

The greatest threats to peace come when democratic forces are weak and disunited. Right now, America has many important bilateral alliances in Asia. We should work toward a day when the fellowship of free Pacific nations is as strong and united as our Atlantic Partnership. If I am President, China will find itself respected as a great power, but in a region of strong democratic alliances. It will be unthreatened, but not unchecked.

China will find in America a confident and willing trade partner. And with trade comes our standing invitation into the world of economic freedom. China's entry into the World Trade Organization is welcome, and this should open the door for Taiwan as well. But given China's poor record in honoring agreements, it will take a strong administration to hold them to their word.

If I am President, China will know that America's values are always part of America's agenda. Our advocacy of human freedom is not a formality of diplomacy, it is a fundamental commitment of our country. It is the source of our confidence that communism, in every form, has seen its day.

And I view free trade as an important ally in what Ronald Reagan called "a forward strategy for freedom." The case for trade is not just monetary, but moral. Economic freedom creates habits

418

of liberty. And habits of liberty create expectations of democracy. There are no guarantees, but there are good examples, from Chile to Taiwan. Trade freely with China, and time is on our side.

Russia stands as another reminder that a world increasingly at peace is also a world in transition. Here, too, patience is needed – patience, consistency, and a principled reliance on democratic forces.

In the breadth of its land, the talent and courage of its people, the wealth of its resources, and the reach of its weapons, Russia is a great power, and must always be treated as such. Few people have suffered more in this century. And though we trust the worst is behind them, their troubles are not over. This past decade, for Russia, has been an epic of deliverance and disappointment.

Our first order of business is the national security of our nation – and here both Russia and the United States face a changed world. Instead of confronting each other, we confront the legacy of a dead ideological rivalry – thousands of nuclear weapons, which, in the case of Russia, may not be secure. And together we also face an emerging threat – from rogue nations, nuclear theft and accidental launch. All this requires nothing short of a new strategic relation-ship to protect the peace of the world.

We can hope that the new Russian Duma will ratify START II, as we have done. But this is not our most pressing challenge. The greater problem was first addressed in 1991 by Senator Lugar and Senator Nunn. In an act of foresight and statesmanship, they real-ized that existing Russian nuclear facilities were in danger of being compromised. Under the Nunn-Lugar program, security at many Russian nuclear facilities has been improved and warheads have been destroyed.

Even so, the Energy Department warns us that our estimates of Russian nuclear stockpiles could be off by as much as 30 percent. In other words, a great deal of Russian nuclear material cannot be accounted for. The next president must press for an accurate inventory of all this material. And we must do more. I'll ask the Congress to increase substantially our assistance to dismantle as many of Russia's weapons as possible, as quickly as possible.

We will still, however, need missile defense systems – both theater and national. If I am commander-in-chief, we will develop and deploy them.

Under the mutual threat of rogue nations, there is a real possibility the Russians could join with us and our friends and allies to cooperate on missile defense systems. But there is a condition. Russia must break its dangerous habit of proliferation.

In the hard work of halting proliferation, the Comprehensive Test Ban Treaty is not the answer. I've said that our nation should continue its moratorium on testing. Yet far more important is to constrict the supply of nuclear materials and the means to deliver them – by making this a priority with Russia and China. Our nation must cut off the demand for nuclear weapons – by addressing the security concerns of those who renounce these weapons. And our nation must diminish the evil attraction of these weapons for rogue states – by rendering them useless with missile defense. The Comprehensive Test Ban Treaty does nothing to gain these goals. It does not stop proliferation, especially to renegade regimes. It is not verifiable. It is not enforceable. And it would stop us from ensuring the safety and reliability of our nation's deterrent, should the need arise. On these crucial matters, it offers only words and false hopes and high intentions – with no guarantees whatever. We can fight the spread of nuclear weapons, but we cannot wish them away with unwise treaties.

Dealing with Russia on essential issues will be far easier if we are dealing with a democratic and free Russia. Our goal is to promote, not only the appearance of democracy in Russia, but the structures, spirit, and reality of democracy. This is clearly not done by focusing our aid and attention on a corrupt and favored elite. Real change in Russia – as in China – will come not from above, but from below. From a rising class of entrepreneurs and business people. From new leaders in Russia's regions who will build a new Russian state, where power is shared, not controlled. Our assistance, investments and loans should go directly to the Russian people, not to enrich the bank accounts of corrupt officials.

America should reach out to a new generation of Russians through educational exchanges and programs to support the rule of law and a civil society. And the Russian people, next month, must be given a free and fair choice in their election. We cannot buy reform for Russia, but we can be Russia's ally in self-reform.

Even as we support Russian reform, we cannot excuse Russian brutality. When the Russian government attacks civilians – killing women and children, leaving orphans and refugees – it can no longer expect aid from international lending institutions. The Russian government will discover that it cannot build a stable and unified nation on the ruins of human rights. That it cannot learn the lessons of democracy from the textbook of tyranny. We want to cooperate with Russia on its concern with terrorism, but that is impossible unless Moscow operates with civilized self-restraint.

Just as we do not want Russia to descend into cruelty, we do not want it to return to imperialism. Russia does have interests with its newly independent neighbors. But those interests must be expressed in commerce and diplomacy – not coercion and domination. A return to Russian imperialism would endanger both Russian democracy and the states on Russia's borders. The United States should actively support the nations of the Baltics, the Caucasus and Central Asia, along with Ukraine, by promoting regional peace and economic development, and opening links to the wider world.

Often overlooked in our strategic calculations is that great land that rests at the south of Eurasia. This coming century will see democratic India's arrival as a force in the world. A vast population, before long the world's most populous nation. A changing economy, in which 3 of its 5 wealthiest citizens are software entrepreneurs.

India is now debating its future and its strategic path, and the United States must pay it more attention. We should establish more trade and investment with India as it opens to the world. And we should work with the Indian government, ensuring it is a force for stability and security in Asia. This should not undermine our long-standing relationship with Pakistan, which remains crucial to the peace of the region.

All our goals in Eurasia will depend on America strengthening the alliances that sustain our influence – in Europe and East Asia and the Middle East.

Alliances are not just for crises – summoned into action when the fire bell sounds. They are sustained by contact and trust. The Gulf War coalition, for example, was raised on the foundation of a president's vision and effort and integrity. Never again should an American president spend nine days in China, and not even bother to stop in Tokyo or Seoul or Manila. Never again should an American president fall silent when China criticizes our security ties with Japan.

For NATO to be strong, cohesive and active, the President must give it consistent direction: on the alliance's purpose; on Europe's need to invest more in defense capabilities; and, when necessary, in military conflict.

To be relied upon when they are needed, our allies must be respected when they are not.

We have partners, not satellites. Our goal is a fellowship of strong, not weak, nations. And this requires both more American consultation and more American leadership. The United States needs its European allies, as well as friends in other regions, to help us with security challenges as they arise. For our allies, sharing the enormous opportunities of Eurasia also means sharing the burdens and risks of sustaining the peace. The support of friends allows America to reserve its power and will for the vital interests we share.

Likewise, international organizations can serve the cause of peace. I will never place U.S. troops under U.N. command – but the U.N. can help in weapons inspections, peacekeeping and humanitarian efforts. If I am president, America will pay its dues – but only if the U.N.'s bureaucracy is reformed, and our disproportionate share of its costs is reduced.

There must also be reform of international financial institutions – the World Bank and the IMF. They can be a source of stability in economic crisis. But they should not impose austerity, bailing out bankers while impoverishing a middle class. They should not prop up failed and corrupt financial systems. These organizations should encourage the basics of economic growth and free markets. Spreading the rule of law and wise budget practices. Promoting sound banking laws and accounting rules. Most of all, these institutions themselves must be more transparent and accountable.

All the aims I've described today are important. But they are not imperial. America has never been an empire. We may be the only great power in history that had the chance, and refused – preferring greatness to power and justice to glory.

We are a nation that helped defeat Germany in 1945 – which had launched a war costing 55 million lives. Less than five years later we launched an airlift to save the people of Berlin from starvation and tyranny. And a generation of Germans remember the "raisin bombers" that dropped candy and raisins for children.

We are a nation that defeated Japan – then distributed food, wrote a constitution, encouraged labor unions and gave women the right to vote. Japanese who expected retribution received mercy instead. Over the entrance of one American army camp, there was a banner that read, "Be neat. Be soldierly. Be proud. Behave. Be American."

No one questioned what those words meant: "Be American."

They meant we were humble in victory. That we were liberators, not conquerors. And when American soldiers hugged the survivors of death camps, and shared their tears, and welcomed them back from a nightmare world, our country was confirmed in its calling.

The duties of our day are different. But the values of our nation do not change. Let us reject the blinders of isolationism, just as we refuse the crown of empire. Let us not dominate others with our power – or betray them with our indifference. And let us have an American foreign policy that reflects American character. The modesty of true strength. The humility of real greatness.

This is the strong heart of America. And this will be the spirit of my Administration.

I believe this kind of foreign policy will inspire our people and restore the bipartisanship so necessary to our peace and security.

Many years ago, Alexander Solzhenitsyn challenged American politicians. "Perhaps," he said, "some of you still feel yourselves just as representatives of your state or party. We do not perceive these differences. We do not look on you as Democrats or Republicans, not as representatives of the East or West Coast or the Midwest....Upon [you] depends whether the course of world history will tend to tragedy or salvation."

That is still our challenge. And that is still our choice.

Statement of Principles
Foreign Policy: A Distinctly American Internationalism

November 19, 1999

The Goal of U.S. Foreign Policy

American foreign policy must be more than the management of crisis. It must have a great and guiding goal: to turn this time of American influence into generations of democratic peace. This is accomplished by concentrating on enduring national interests and by resisting the temptation to withdraw from the world: withdrawal would abandon our allies and our ideals.

Governor Bush's Foreign Policy Priorities

An American president must set priorities and stick to them to avoid drift in foreign policy. Thus, as President, Governor Bush will:

- Work with our strong democratic allies in Europe and Asia to extend the peace and deal with the challenges of China and Russia – two great powers in transition.

- Promote a fully democratic Western Hemisphere, bound together by free trade.

- Defend America's interests in the Persian Gulf and advance peace in the Middle East, based upon a secure Israel.

- Check the contagious spread of weapons of mass destruction, and the means to deliver them.

- Lead toward a world that trades in freedom.

New Leadership on National Security

National Press Club
Washington, D.C.

May 23, 2000

Today, I am here with some of our nation's leading statesmen and defense experts. And there is broad agreement that our nation needs a new approach to nuclear security that matches a new era.

When it comes to nuclear weapons, the world has changed faster than U.S. policy. The emerging security threats to the United States, its friends and allies, and even to Russia, now come from rogue states, terrorist groups and other adversaries seeking weapons of mass destruction, and the means to deliver them. Threats also come from insecure nuclear stockpiles and the proliferation of dangerous technologies. Russia itself is no longer our enemy. The Cold War logic that led to the creation of massive stockpiles on both sides is now outdated. Our mutual security need no longer depend on a nuclear balance of terror.

While deterrence remains the first line of defense against nuclear attack, the standoff of the Cold War was born of a different time. That was a time when our arsenal also served to check the conventional superiority of the Warsaw Pact. Then, the Soviet Union's power reached deep into the heart of Europe – to Berlin, Warsaw, Budapest, Prague. Today, these are the capitals of NATO countries. Yet almost a decade after the end of the Cold War, our nuclear policy still resides in that already distant past. The Clinton-Gore administration has had over seven years to bring the

U.S. force posture into the post-Cold War world. Instead, they remain locked in a Cold War mentality.

It is time to leave the Cold War behind, and defend against the new threats of the 21st century.

America must build effective missile defenses, based on the best available options, at the earliest possible date. Our missile defense must be designed to protect all 50 states – and our friends and allies and deployed forces overseas – from missile attacks by rogue nations, or accidental launches.

The Clinton Administration at first denied the need for a national missile defense system. Then it delayed. Now the approach it proposes is flawed – a system initially based on a single site, when experts say that more is needed. A missile defense system should not only defend our country, it should defend our allies, with whom I will consult as we develop our plans. And any change in the ABM treaty must allow the technologies and experiments required to deploy adequate missile defenses. The Administration is driving toward a hasty decision, on a political timetable. No decision would be better than a flawed agreement that ties the hands of the next President and prevents America from defending itself.

Yet there are positive, practical ways to demonstrate to Russia that we are no longer enemies. Russia, our allies and the world need to understand our intentions. America's development of missile defenses is a search for security, not a search for advantage.

America should rethink the requirements for nuclear deterrence in a new security environment. The premises of Cold War nuclear targeting should no longer dictate the size of our arsenal. As President, I will ask the Secretary of Defense to conduct an assessment of our nuclear force posture and determine how best to meet our security needs. While the exact number of weapons can come only from such an assessment, I will pursue the lowest possible number consistent with our national security. It should be possible to reduce the number of American nuclear weapons significantly further than what has already been agreed to under START II, without compromising our security in any way. We should not keep weapons that our military planners do not need. These unneeded weapons are the expensive relics of dead conflicts. And they do nothing to make us more secure.

In addition, the United States should remove as many weapons as possible from high-alert, hair-trigger status – another unnecessary vestige of Cold War confrontation. Preparation for quick launch – within minutes after warning of an attack – was the rule during the era of superpower rivalry. But today, for two nations at peace, keeping so many weapons on high alert may create unacceptable risks of accidental or unauthorized launch. So, as President, I will ask for an assessment of what we can safely do to lower the alert status of our forces.

These changes to our forces should not require years and years of detailed arms control negotiations. There is a precedent that proves the power of leadership. In 1991, the United States invited the Soviet Union to join it in removing tactical nuclear weapons from the arsenal. Huge reductions were achieved in a matter of months, making the world much safer, more quickly.

Similarly, in the area of strategic nuclear weapons, we should invite the Russian government to accept the new vision I have outlined, and act on it. But the United States should be prepared to lead by example, because it is in our best interest and the best interest of the world. This would be an act of principled leadership – a chance to seize the moment and begin a new era of nuclear security. A new era of cooperation on proliferation and nuclear safety.

The Cold War era is history. Our nation must recognize new threats, not fixate on old ones. On the issue of nuclear weapons, the United States has an opportunity to lead to a safer world – both to defend against nuclear threats and reduce nuclear tensions. It is possible to build a missile defense, and defuse confrontation with Russia. America should do both.

Honoring Our Commitment To Veterans

Pickens County Courthouse
Pickens County, South Carolina

November 11, 1999

Thank you. I always look forward to visiting South Carolina, but this is a particular honor.

On Thursday, many of you will gather here again to dedicate this new monument to the sons and daughters of South Carolina lost in war. You have much to be proud of here in Pickens County, and many losses to remember.

Every town and county in America has its heroes and heritage, but few can match the story inscribed on this Wall of Valor.

There was Furman Smith, one of this county's four Congressional Medal of Honor recipients. His company withdrawing under intense fire, Private Smith stayed behind – alone – to defend his wounded comrades, dying with them. There was William McWhorter, who, as the citation reads, "picked up [a] ... grenade and held it close to his body, bending over and turning away from his companion." There was Charles Barker, who fell in Korea defending his comrades. And then there was James Howe, who also threw himself on a grenade to save his fellows.

Perhaps some of you here today knew those men. If so, you were privileged. Whatever it was about Pickens County that produced men like them – whatever it was about America – that thing is sacred. We must never lose it. In our own lives, we must always honor it.

Americans this week rededicate ourselves to the duty of memory. Behind each name we remember is a hero's story. They are stories of daring attacks, impossible rescues and last ditch stands. They are stories of hopeless odds and stubborn spirit and terrible injuries. From across the world and across the years, the courage in these stories still flashes; the honor still glows. Each action was beyond the call of duty, leaving a debt beyond our ability to repay. As your own Charles Barker's citation expresses it, he lives in "lasting glory." So do they all.

True courage, it's said, is the most generous of the virtues. It elevates ideals over self and duty over comfort. It leads young men and women to risk everything they have, everything they value, for a future they may not see. And it points to the greatest truth we can know: That love without cost, without sacrifice, is meaningless. It is the message of this new monument.

And it is also the lesson of Veteran's Day, when we pause, in busy lives, to remember the price of liberty, measured in young lives that ended so suddenly, so tragically, so very far from home. That grief has touched every city, every town, nearly every family in this country.

It is written on countless other monuments, some green with age, some covered today with flowers and tears, like that long, black wall in Washington.

Those of us who benefit from this sacrifice face a question: What do we owe the brave?

It is our first duty to remember what they have done. And that should not be hard, because it is one of the greatest stories of human history. Americans won world wars and a cold war. Kids fresh from farms and tenements humbled history's worst tyrants. They opened death camps and emptied Gulags. Their character was tested in death marches and jungle stalemates. And, in the end, they won an epic struggle – the struggle of a century – to save liberty itself.

We carve our thanks into stone. We stamp it into medals. We

carefully tend to vast fields of white crosses and Stars of David. But it is even more important to pass stories of American courage and character to the next generation. To capture their imaginations. To raise a monument in their hearts. It is the way our democracy renews its promise, by celebrating American heroes and American values, without hesitation and without apology. Let us resolve to teach America's story to America's children.

First we remember. But second, we must renew a commitment, in our generation, with our challenges, to the pride and power and purpose of America. We must act worthy of our history – worthy of these men and their sacrifice – by writing new chapters of American greatness in a new century that is our charge.

New threats are replacing old enemies. Unstable dictators seek weapons of mass destruction. Regional power grabs become global crises. We navigate through mines in the mist. But it is still America that preserves the peace. Our nation still determines the future of freedom. America is still a bright signal in a dark night.

Those who man the lighthouse of freedom ask little of our nation in return. But what they ask our nation must provide: a coherent vision of America's duties, a clear military mission in time of crisis, and, when sent in harm's way, the best support and equipment our nation can supply. With these things, they never fail us. Without these things, we have failed them.

Let us resolve never to multiply our missions while cutting our capabilities. Let us resolve to restore a belief in American interests, American character and American destiny. And let us resolve to keep faith with our past by being vigilant in our time.

Our laws, too, must reflect gratitude. But to many veterans, it seems like they are remembered in Washington only on Veteran's Day. Speeches are all well and good, but daily advocacy is needed too in such issues as health care and compensation claims.

Health care for veterans is an often complicated and bureaucratic process, involving too many delays and uncertainties in coverage. Disability compensation claims can be an even longer ordeal, taking on average 165 days to complete. So chaotic is the process that there is now a backlog of nearly half a million claims, a fourth of them involving lengthy appeals. And when the claims have been adjudicated and a decision finally made, a third of the decisions contain errors.

This is no way to treat any citizen, much less any veteran of the American armed forces. It is no way for government to discharge one of its most sacred commitments. Men once ordered by their government to stand in the line of fire should not now be ordered to stand in line at the nearest federal bureaucracy, waiting with hat in hand while VA officials take their time.

The veterans health care system and the claims process need an overhauling from top to bottom. It needs to be modernized, so that claims are handled in a fair and timely fashion. Veterans need advocates in the Veterans Administration, people sympathetic to their interests instead of suspicious. If I am elected, that is the only kind of veterans official I intend to appoint.

This applies to veterans of the Gulf War, too. They should not have to go to elaborate lengths to prove that they are ill, just because their malady has yet to be fully explained. A 1994 law was passed to grant them the presumption of disability. Yet even now they are met with skeptical looks and a paper-shuffling excuses for withholding coverage.

If I have anything to say about it, all that is going to end. In the military, when you are called to account for a mistake, you are expected to give one simple answer: "No excuse, sir." And that should be the attitude of any government official who fails to make good on our public responsibilities to veterans. There is no excuse for it.

America's veterans today ask only that government honor its commitments as they honored theirs. They ask that their interests be protected, as they protected their country's interests in foreign lands. In all matters of concern to veterans – from health care to program funding – you have my pledge that those commitments will be kept.

These are the ways to help repay our debt of honor to veterans.

There is an inscription on the Scottish National War Memorial which reads, "The whole earth is the tomb of heroes, and their story is not graven in stone over their clay, but abides everywhere, without visible symbol, woven into the stuff of other men's lives."

In dedicating this monument this week, you will be honoring the bravest of the brave. You pledge to preserve their memory in our time, for all time. Yet the greatest monument to the courage of Americans is the world they saved and shaped. And their story is not written in stone, it is woven into the lives of everyone who loves freedom.

And so we remember – as Americans will remember through our history – the heroes who saved a century.

Position Paper
Honoring Our Commitment to Veterans

November 11, 1999

> *"America's veterans today ask only that government honor its commitments as they honored theirs. They ask that their interests be protected, as they protected their country's interests in foreign lands. In all matters of concern to veterans – from health care to program funding – you have my pledge that those commitments will be kept."*
>
> Governor George W. Bush

Governor Bush's Record of Accomplishment for Veterans

Governor George W. Bush believes the nation's 25 million veterans deserve a President and a Department of Veterans Affairs that honors the commitments made to the men and women who have served in defense of freedom and democracy. This should be a year-round commitment and not one that is remembered only once a year.

As Governor, George W. Bush has a proven record as an advocate for veterans. During his term in office, he compiled a historic record on veterans' issues. Specifically, Governor Bush:

- More than doubled the state's property tax exemption for disabled veterans.

- Supported and signed legislation creating the first state-operated "Veterans Homes" system in Texas for veterans who need long-term care services.

- Increased Veterans Home Loans from $45,000 to $203,000.

- Increased funding for the State Veterans Commission by almost 20 percent.

Governor Bush's Commitment to Veterans

Governor Bush recognizes the unique mission of the Department of Veterans Affairs and as President will demand:

- <u>Leadership</u>: Governor Bush has a proven pro-veterans record in Texas. As President, he will continue to be an advocate for veterans and will appoint men and women who will also be advocates for the needs of the veteran's community.

- <u>Accountability</u>: The current system of long delays and the bureaucratic snafus make veterans wait an average of 165 days for claims to be processed. As President, Governor Bush will require that the Department of Veterans Affairs not only set new goals for claims processing, but meet them.

- <u>Modernization</u>: Governor Bush knows that the promise of access to quality health care is an integral part of our commitment to veterans. However, some veterans must wait 200 days for an appointment at a VA facility.

As President, Governor Bush will call for a top-to-bottom review of the VA Health Care system and work with the Veteran Service Organizations to target and modernize areas that hinder a veteran's access to the top-notch health care they deserve.

China:
A Forward Strategy For Freedom

The Boeing Company
Everett, Washington

May 17, 2000

Thank you. It's a pleasure to be here – and a little overwhelming. This is the first time I've ever been in a building with its own area code.

So... this is where you made Air Force One. Of all your works, I've always admired that one in particular. And I promise to take good care of it.

You are one of America's great companies in one of our greatest industries. This company is a source of pride not just to everyone here today, but to people everywhere who admire skill, ingenuity, and pride of workmanship. I congratulate you, and I thank you.

From the start of this campaign, I have defined some sharp disagreements with the Clinton-Gore Administration. But today I want to address an important area of agreement. A pressing question now confronts the Congress, and it will not wait until the next president takes office.

The issue is whether to extend normal trade relations to China on a permanent basis. This vote is one step in the process of drawing China into the world trading system. China is on the verge of joining the 136 members of the World Trade Organization. Congress must now decide whether the U.S. will gain the benefits of China's more open economy.

The stakes are high, on all sides. For businesses, workers and farmers across our country, it will mean much lower trade barriers and enormous opportunities for U.S. exports. For the people of East Asia, it will affect their relations with the region's major power. For the people of China, it holds out the hope of more open contact with the world of freedom.

In short, this will be among the most serious decisions our government will make this year.

Last year, when I laid out my vision of a distinctly American internationalism, I said that we must see China clearly, not through the filters of posturing and partisanship. And today I am acting on that principle. I am here to urge all members of Congress, both Republicans and Democrats, to join together in making China a normal trading partner of the United States.

I differ with the President and Vice President on many issues regarding China and trade. They place their confidence in the Chinese regime as a "strategic partner" of the United States. I know they are a competitor. They have been inconsistent on Taiwan. I will be clear. They failed to obtain "fast track" trade negotiating authority. I will fight for it. They mishandled the global trade negotiations right here in Seattle. I will make expanding trade a consistent priority of my Administration.

Today, however, all of us who believe in a more open China – in advancing the rule of law and trade – must work together. This is not a Republican or Democratic concern. It is an American concern. This trade agreement is the work of 13 years and three administrations. We cannot let that work be undone.

Let me explain why. There are three compelling reasons to support this agreement – freedom, security and economics.

First, trade with China will promote freedom. Freedom is not easily contained. Once a measure of economic freedom is permitted, a measure of political freedom will follow.

China today is not a free society. At home, toward its own people, it can be ruthless. Abroad, toward its neighbors, it can be reckless.

When I am President, China will know that America's values are always part of America's agenda. Our advocacy of human freedom is not a formality of diplomacy, it is a fundamental commitment of our country. It is the source of our confidence that communism, in every form, has seen its day.

I view free trade as an important ally in what Ronald Reagan called "a forward strategy for freedom." The case for trade is not just monetary, but moral – not just a matter of commerce, but a matter of conviction. Economic freedom creates habits of liberty. And habits of liberty create expectations of democracy. There are no guarantees, but there are good examples, from Chile to Taiwan. Trade freely with China, and time is on our side.

This is happening already. As one Chinese dissident recently wrote in *The Los Angeles Times*: "I believe that permanent normal trade status, with its implications of openness and fairness, is among the most powerful means of promoting freedom in China." She added, "Starting in 1978, the open-door policy completely changed the way China responded to the world." And she concluded that making normal trade relations permanent "is a powerful means to keep China's doors as open as possible."

Simply put: China is most free where it is most in contact with the world economy.

Second, trade with China serves our own national interest, as well as the security interests of China's neighbors.

China is not our "strategic partner." But neither is it our enemy. As I've said before, China is a competitor, to be faced without ill will and without illusions. When I am President, China will have no doubts about our power and purpose in the region – about our strong commitment to democratic allies throughout Asia.

But this is accomplished by confident diplomacy, strong alliances, and the military might to back them up. It is not accomplished by hindering free trade or seeking to isolate China.

Our friends in the region share this conviction – leaders who know the stakes firsthand. Taiwan's outgoing president has made this same point. "The model of [Taiwan's] quiet revolution," predicts Lee Teng-hui, "will eventually take hold in China."

His successor, President-Elect Chen Shui-bian, also supports the agreement to bring China into the WTO, provided that Taiwan is admitted to the WTO right afterward. And I strongly agree with him. When both China and Taiwan are members of the WTO, both will need to apply global rules to their trade, including trade with one another, and the prospects for cross-straits relations should improve.

Third, trade with China serves the economic interests of America.

Under this accord, China must cut its average industrial tariff from almost 25 percent to nine percent by 2005, and even down to about seven percent on U.S. priority products. Most quotas are phased out by the end of 2000, and the rest by 2005.

China today – even before these concessions – is the world's fourth largest market for our agricultural products. Under this agreement, the amount of wheat that China will allow into the country will increase immediately from two million metric tons to 7.3 million. The amount of corn that China allows will rise from 250 thousand metric tons to 4.5 million. China will cut tariffs by more than half on U.S. priority agricultural products. And China will eliminate export subsidies, leveling the playing field in important third-country markets for America's farmers.

The doors will open to providers of U.S. services – the import-export trade, banking, insurance, telecommunications, accounting, computers, motion pictures and more.

China will also adhere to WTO rules on intellectual property rights and investments. And if Europe negotiates a better deal in these or any other areas, by the terms of the agreement, we will get the same treatment.

This deal will not only benefit large exporters, such as Boeing, which expects China to be its largest foreign market for commercial aircraft over the next 20 years. It will also benefit America's many smaller exporters. China is the third-fastest growing market for small and medium-sized U.S. businesses, 7,600 of which already sell in China.

For all these gains, we will not have to change a single sentence of our existing trade rules. America will reserve the right to act against harmful trade policies. As President, I will safeguard American markets against unfair practices like dumping. And I will also ensure that the rules we negotiate are enforced.

Agreements are only as good as compliance, and we must hold China to the pledges it makes. We must encourage China to build the strong structures of the rule of law.

It is worth making one more point, a very practical one: Defeat of this bill won't even keep China out of the WTO, since President Clinton has already agreed to its entry. A "no" vote would only prevent the U.S. from enjoying the benefits of China's market opening – even as foreign rivals to American firms do enjoy those benefits.

After last year's confusion in Seattle, a leader in the protectionist camp confidently declared that by excluding China from the WTO the opponents hoped – as he put it – "to deliver the last blow" against our system of free trade. Neither the United States nor the world can afford such a setback.

The steady opening of international trade around the globe is the product of sixty years of American leadership from presidents and Congresses of both parties. This process is among the main reasons for the seventeen years of economic growth that we know today... for the trend toward peace and freedom we know today... for the confidence in the future we know today.

I believe that trade serves the deepest interests of our country and advances the hopes of the Chinese people for a freer society.

Our greatest export is not food or movies or even airplanes. Our greatest export is freedom. The people of China stand ready to receive it. The demand has never been greater.

Establishing normal trade relations is the right thing for China. It is the right thing for Taiwan and our allies. It is the right thing for the United States. And with the support of both parties this year, it will be a milestone in the advance of freedom.

Address to AIPAC

American Israel Public Affairs Committee
Annual Policy Conference
Washington, D.C.

May 22, 2000

Thank you, Bubba [Mitchell], for that generous introduction. Thank you for all you've done for the cause of U.S.-Israeli relations. Just a few days ago, my wife visited with you and Arlene at your home in Mobile, and felt your warmth and welcome. She brought home the *mezuzah* you gave as a gift. That evening you said: "In presenting this *mezuzah* fashioned in the Holy Land to you, Arlene and I do so with the blessing that God be with you to guide you and guard you, as the Bible states, 'When thou art in thy home and thou goest on thy way, when thou liest down and when thou risest up.'"

I need that blessing, especially at this time.

It's a pleasure visiting with you today to discuss one of the most important and abiding relationships our great country shares with another.

America and Israel have a special friendship. In fact, it's more than a friendship. America and Israel are brothers and sisters in the family of democracy – natural allies in the cause of peace.

The family of democracy transcends borders and oceans. What unites us is a powerful conviction – perhaps the greatest of all convictions: "We hold these truths to be self-evident, that all men are created equal, that they are endowed by their Creator with certain unalienable rights, that among these are life, liberty and the pursuit of happiness."

These truths were self-evident to America's Founding Fathers. They learned them not only from the great thinkers of the Enlightenment, but also from the example of Moses. The Ten Commandments, after all, are the core principles of democracy – the charter of human dignity and equality.

Our two nations share so much – not only core convictions, but also a vision for the future. Americans and Israelis alike understand that the family of democracy must be an educated family – a family that knows and understands its traditions, and passes them to the young.

Howard tells me that there are 700 college students with us here today. I can't think of a better symbol of AIPAC's commitment to education than bringing young people here to Washington and providing them with both an education in American government and a passion for promoting our nation's alliance with Israel.

Our American democracy needs to bring this kind of passion and devotion to the education of our children. A self-governing people must also be a literate people. We owe all American children – of every background – the pride and promise of learning.

America and Israel both know that the future is a high-tech future, and so we must work to teach our people the complex skills they will need to prosper. Just as this country has been enriched by the work done in places like Silicon Valley, Israeli computer companies are making large strides in providing the world with the next generation in software and hardware. If you go to any high-tech conference, you will see Israeli engineers and American software designers exchanging ideas. This economic and entrepreneurial cooperation is helping to redefine and strengthen the American – Israeli relationship.

Our high-tech cooperation is also taking shape in my own state of Texas. As many of you may know, the crew for flight 107 of the space shuttle Columbia is in training at the Johnson Space Center in Houston for a launch sometime next spring. One of those crew members is a 45 year-old colonel in the Israeli Air Force named Ilan Ramon, a child of Holocaust survivors.

One of the experiments Ilan will perform in space was designed by 35 eighth-graders from a school near Haifa. The space experiment will explore why some plants on earth defy the pull of gravity to grow upwards; an interesting experiment – and a fitting tribute to the nation that made the desert bloom.

The ties between America and Israel are of course deeper than a joint venture in space. They are more enduring than handshakes on the White House lawn and free-trade agreements, vital though such things may be. The things that bind us are as deep as our commitments to human dignity.

No nation can fulfill the God-given right of its people to life, liberty and the pursuit of happiness if it must live in a state of perpetual war. Israel wants peace. And like all Americans of good will, I want peace for Israel and peace in the Middle East. I recognize the importance of the peace process and the key role that the United States can play.

But my support for Israel is not conditional on the outcome of the peace process. America's special relationship with Israel precedes the peace process. And Israel's adversaries should know that in my Administration, the special relationship will continue even if they cannot bring themselves to make true peace with the Jewish state.

Let me say how sorry I am that I will not be meeting with Prime Minister Barak tomorrow as we had planned. I first met with him in Israel when he was opposition leader – a good reminder of the healthy democracy that thrives in Israel.

I am deeply disturbed by the violence that continues in the West Bank and in South Lebanon. And especially by reports of Palestinian police opening fire on Israeli soldiers last week. This is no way to make peace a reality.

We have seen Israel's desire for peace – and what can be

accomplished when moderate Arab states respond in kind. We saw how the Camp David accords ended the state of war with Egypt – with Israel sacrificing land and oil for peace, and Egypt taking great risks as well. We have seen the benefits to both Jordan and Israel when courageous leaders look beyond ancient rivalries – progress America must encourage with other Arab states. We have seen Israel's turn toward the Palestinians – sacrificing land in hopes of a better future for both peoples.

The United States is proud and respectful of the sacrifices Israel is making. Sacrifices that few nations are called upon to make.

In recent times, Washington has tried to make Israel conform to its own plans and timetables. But this is not the path to peace.

A clear and bad example was the Administration's attempt to take sides in the most recent Israeli election. America should not interfere in Israel's democratic process, and America will not interfere in Israeli elections when I'm President.

But something will happen when I'm President: as soon as I take office I will begin the process of moving the U.S. ambassador to the city Israel has chosen as its capital.

Too often, it is easy to forget that not every democracy is blessed in the way America is – by our size, our wealth, our geography. Too often, we forget what it means to be a small nation in an often hostile neighborhood. A few years ago, on a trip to Israel, General Sharon took me on a helicopter flight over the Golan Heights. And what struck me – as all of you know better than I do – is the tiny distance between enemy lines and Israel's population centers. I was told that before the Six Day War, Israel was only 9 miles wide at its narrowest point.

In Texas some driveways are longer than that.

It's sobering to think that while the distance between Dallas and Galveston is 270 miles, the distance between Israel and Saddam Hussein's Iraq is only 250 miles. And the world learned to its horror back in 1991 that those 250 miles can be crossed in a matter of

12 minutes by a Scud missile.

The Gulf War showed the world the danger posed to the family of democracy by rogue states armed with missiles. Who can forget the sight of millions of Israelis wearing gas masks to protect themselves in case those Scuds were carrying chemical weapons? Who can forget the Israeli children who had to be sealed away from their mothers and fathers in plastic tents during those air raids?

Saddam's attacks were the act of a tyrant without decency. And we are seeing similar hostility again today as 13 Jews are unjustly imprisoned in Iran on charges of espionage. Even in this new century, the ancient wrong of anti-Semitism remains. While the 13 remain imprisoned, their human rights must be respected. The leaders of Iran should know that America will judge them by their conduct and treatment of those 13.

Continuing acts of anti-Semitism in Iran and elsewhere in the world make clear the need for Israel to defend its people and its homeland. And Israel is leading the way in showing the world that nations can protect themselves from missile attacks.

We all saw how the relatively simple Patriot system worked to defend against Scud missiles during the Gulf war. And in the years since, Israel's successful deployment of the more sophisticated Arrow has offered its people greater protection from a growing threat.

This is something else the family of democracy has in common. The danger of totalitarianism is waning, but the threat from rogue states is rising. The danger crosses borders and oceans, and it means not only Israel but also the United States must be able to protect our citizens and our homeland with ballistic missile defense.

North Korea has developed missiles capable of hitting Hawaii and Alaska. That nation may be an ideological relic, but its tyrants are doing everything they can to be a 21st Century menace. Nations like Iran and Iraq are developing capabilities of their own. And four years ago, a Chinese general warned America that his country possesses the means to incinerate Los Angeles with nuclear missiles.

Israel offers an important reminder to Americans – a reminder that freedom is precious and that freedom's enemies remain a threat. We must cherish our freedom and we must protect it. That is why my Administration will build and deploy missile defenses to protect America's homeland, and our allies. That is why my Administration will restore America's military. I hope you will support my efforts, for as Ronald Reagan said, "an America that loses faith in the idea of a strong defense is an America that will lose faith in a nation at arms like Israel."

I appreciate all you've done for America and for Israel. The work you do is a vital part of our democratic process. You speak out boldly, and that's good for America, good for Israel, and good for the cause of peace and justice in the world. You make sure that politicians hear what voters have to say not only on election day, but every day of the year.

I am sure that in the course of my Administration, as in every administration, there will be times when we disagree. But I respect the role you play. Keep speaking. Keep working. Keep fighting for your principles. This nation, the land of Israel, the Middle East and the world are better for it.

World Trade Bridge Dedication

Dedication of World Trade Bridge
Nuevo Laredo, Mexico

April 25, 2000

Thank you all very much. It's good to be here in *"Los Dos Laredos." Siempre me da mucho gusto ver a mis amigos de México.*

My friend President Zedillo, my thanks to you especially for all you have done to join our countries in common purpose.

These bridge dedications are becoming quite a tradition. It was only seven months ago that we met for our last one, at Eagle Pass. In the past, there have been walls and divides between Mexico and the United States. How much better it is to raise up the bridges of trade and friendship and freedom.

The results of our friendship are strong. We trade over $200 billion dollars worth of goods every year. Half of all U.S. exports to Mexico pass through Texas – across this twelve-hundred mile border of ours.

This partnership may seem inevitable, but it wasn't always so. For a long while we heard just the opposite – that we were destined for distrust and division. It was said that our two nations would always be distant neighbors, divided by history and culture and the fortunes of economics.

Today, we are extensive trading partners and friends because we have chosen to change history. We formed NAFTA because we now understand that our two nations share more than a border.

We have common interests. And we have much to gain from one another, not only in commerce but in culture, not only in goods but in good will.

In all great partnerships, need and benefit run both ways. And respect must run both ways. That, really, is what we are celebrating today: Not just a bridge of concrete and steel, but a lasting alliance of common hopes and friendship.

And now we must build on the success of NAFTA. We must look to your southern border – to all the nations of Latin America, and to the possibilities of still broader trade and cooperation. What is true between Mexico and the U.S. is true among all the nations in our hemisphere. The more we trade among one another, the better we know and understand and respect one another.

Our last five presidents have contributed to achieving the goals of NAFTA. And I am proud to say that it was our forty-first president who negotiated and signed the agreement.

If I am elected President, I will work to create an entire hemisphere of free trade: A system of shared principles and obligations offering prosperity and democracy to all. To all who are willing, I will work to extend the benefits of NAFTA – free trade and open markets throughout the Americas, from northernmost Alaska to the tip of Cape Horn. And I will call upon Congress to grant me fast-track negotiating authority to aggressively pursue new trade agreements.

As President, I will look south, not as an afterthought, but as a fundamental commitment of my presidency. Just as we ended the great divide between East and West by winning the Cold War, so today we can overcome the world's North-South divide by transforming this hemisphere into connected continents of freedom and prosperity.

Today, one more barrier has fallen away. One more divide has been bridged. We have much to be proud of, and much to be grateful for as we look to the future of the Americas. A future we will share, and write, together as friends. *Comenzamos bien, ahora sigamos adelante. Muchas gracias.*

Position Paper
Southwest Border Initiative

June 7, 2000

"The federal government has a critical responsibility to enforce our nation's drug laws and to stop international drug traffickers. In our battle against the international drug trade, the Southwest border is the front line. Much of the burden from this national battle falls on border counties, whose limited resources are already stretched thin. The federal government must step up and do its part."

Governor George W. Bush

The Challenge of Prosecuting Federal Referrals

The Southwest border is a major corridor for the importation of marijuana, cocaine, and heroin into the United States. The five federal court districts that serve that border region now handle one-fourth of all federal court criminal filings, and criminal cases filed in federal courts in the region have jumped dramatically in recent years.

Federal drug arrests, however, far exceed federal cases filed. Each year, federal prosecutors "refer" thousands of cases – arrests made by federal officers on the border – to local prosecutors rather than prosecute them in federal court. Under agreements with local prosecutors, these referrals are designed to be for smaller quantities of drug possession, but reported thresholds for referral have ranged from 50 pounds to up to 200 pounds of marijuana (and there is at least one reported case of a 1,400 pound marijuana referral). Such large cases are the direct result of federal arrests on the Southwest border and indisputably have a broad national impact.

Border counties bear the burden of prosecuting these federal referrals, but almost none of these counties are reimbursed for the prosecution and pre-conviction incarceration of these criminals. The aggregate costs imposed on border counties from federal drug referrals have been roughly estimated by the National Institute of Justice at between $48.5 million and $148.6 million per year, with a mean of $94.6 million. These counties are some of the poorest counties in our nation; as a result, two have already refused to prosecute any more federal drug referrals, and five more are threatening to stop prosecuting these cases. To date, the Department of Justice has been unable to resolve the situation.

Governor Bush's Southwest Border Initiative

Because the federal government bears the responsibility to enforce our nation's borders and to combat international drug traffic, and because border counties are ill equipped to shoulder such a large share of the burden, as President, Governor Bush will:

- Provide $50 million in annual federal funds to reimburse border counties for prosecuting federal drug referrals.

- Direct U.S. Attorneys on the Southwest border to prosecute large drug cases in federal court: While it may be a reasonable allocation of resources to allow local jurisdictions to prosecute smaller cases, current referral standards of up to 200 pounds of marijuana are clearly too high. Prosecution of large international drug traffickers is a federal responsibility.

- Appoint a Southwest Border Coordinator to lead a joint federal-state partnership and coordinate drug enforcement and prosecution efforts along the Southwest border: The Coordinator would be responsible for working with federal and local agencies and prosecutors to implement a strategic plan to address illegal drug traffic.

WHAT OTHERS SAY

"The role of the U.S. Army is so essential to national security that it deserves to be debated by the presidential candidates. So far, only one – George W. Bush – has said anything significant…"
John Barry and Evan Thomas, <u>Newsweek</u>, 11/22/99

"With recent statements on trade with China, arms-control policy, and the urgent need for an effective missile defense…Bush has shown that he embraces the internationalist tradition of the Republican Party and intends to be a forceful advocate for American interests and values abroad."

Senator John McCain, <u>Wall Street Journal</u>, 5/30/00

"George W. Bush…proposed an ambitious rebuilding of the military to safe-guard American interests in a world still full of risks."

Boston Globe, 9/24/99

"There were shades of former President Ronald Reagan's thinking and oratory in the way Bush summoned the specter of foreign evils – 'a world of terror and missiles and madmen,' he said – and emphasized American technological prowess as the amulet against them."

Frank Bruni, The New York Times, 9/24/99

"George W. Bush's…speech at the Reagan Library represents the strongest and clearest articulation of a policy of American global leadership by a major political figure since the collapse of the Soviet Empire. In his call for renewed American strength, confidence, and leadership, Bush stakes a claim to the legacy of Ronald Reagan."

William Kristol and Robert Kagan, The Weekly Standard, 11/29/99

"George W. Bush has seized the upper hand in the race for president by laying out a broad issues agenda that has driven the campaign debate…the Governor has seemed the very model of statesmanship and sure-footedness. [In a recent foreign policy speech] he called for a new arms control policy that would include deep cuts in nuclear weapons, as a clutch of foreign policy Brahmins - Henry A. Kissinger, Gen. Colin L. Powell and George P. Shultz among them - looked on approvingly."

Los Angeles Times, 5/27/00

Biography of
Governor George W. Bush

George W. Bush is the 46th Governor of the State of Texas. Now in his second term, Governor Bush has earned a reputation as a compassionate conservative who shapes policy based on the principles of limited government, personal responsibility, strong families, and local control.

During three Texas legislative sessions, Governor Bush has worked in a spirit of bipartisan cooperation with state leaders and members of the Texas Legislature to enact historic reforms to improve public schools, put welfare recipients to work, curb frivolous lawsuits and strengthen criminal justice laws. In his five years in office, Governor Bush has delivered the two largest tax cuts in state history – nearly $3 billion dollars – to Texas taxpayers.

Governor Bush's first priority is the education of children. He has worked with the Legislature to increase the State's share of funding for schools, restore local control, strengthen the State's accountability system, give parents and students greater choice of schools, end social promotion, and foster competition and creativity through charter schools and an expanded menu of educational opportunity. His most profound goal for Texas is that every child will learn to read by third grade and will continue to read at grade level or better throughout public school.

George W. Bush was born July 6, 1946, and grew up in Midland and Houston, Texas. He received a bachelor's degree from Yale University and an MBA from Harvard Business School. He served as an F-102 pilot for the Texas Air National Guard. He began his career in the oil and gas business in Midland in 1975 and worked in the energy industry until 1986. After working on his father's 1988, presidential campaign, he assembled the group of partners that purchased the Texas Rangers baseball franchise in 1989 and later built the Rangers' new home, the Ballpark at Arlington.

He served as managing general partner of the Texas Rangers until he was elected Governor on November 8, 1994, with 53.5 percent of the vote. In a historic re-election victory, he became the first Texas Governor to be elected to consecutive four-year terms on November 3, 1998 winning 68.6 percent of the vote.

Governor Bush won 49 percent of the Hispanic vote, 27 percent of the African-American vote, 27 percent of Democrats and 65 percent of women. He won more Texas counties – 240 out of 254 – than any Republican other than Richard Nixon in 1972 and is the first Republican gubernatorial candidate to win the heavily Hispanic and Democratic border counties of El Paso, Cameron and Hidalgo.

Republicans won all 17 statewide races on the ballot in 1998 because of Governor Bush's coattails. Republicans, including eight women, two Hispanics, and an African American, now hold all 27 statewide constitutional and judicial offices.

Governor Bush and his wife, Laura, a former teacher and librarian who grew up in Midland, reside in the historic Governor's mansion in Austin with their 18-year-old twin daughters, Barbara and Jenna, their dog, Spot, and their two cats, India and Ernie.

Governor Bush is a Methodist and has served on the boards of various charitable, business, and civic organizations.

NOTES

NOTES

NOTES

NOTES

NOTES